Praise for *GUIL...*

'In connecting the architecture of De Qu...
physical surroundings, Wilson provides a...
and isolation*****'

'Brilliantly possessed'   Andrew Motion, *Observer*

'A richly intelligent and well-informed study, which will surely become the
favoured one of our time'   *Financial Times*

'Tremendous . . . A seamless, stirring, sublime biography, which takes you to the
heart, or rather the head, of the opium-eater'   *Evening Standard*

'*Guilty Thing* brings triumphantly into focus a life racked by opium's insidious
effects . . . Beautifully crafted, Frances Wilson's narrative sets up patterns, mirrors
and doublings that make multiple intersections between De Quincey's inner and
outer worlds'   *Literary Review*

'It is, like its subject's own best work, written with studied panache, respectful
irreverence and relish of the macabre'   *Glasgow Herald*

'Exhilarating . . . What distinguishes its achievement is Wilson's ability to mirror
the mercurial texture of De Quincey's own selective and thrillingly digressive way
of telling a story . . . Her remarkable book engenders in its readers those modes of
thinking necessary to follow De Quincey as he shifts unpredictably into and out
of every imaginable shape'   *Times Literary Supplement*

'Wilson's quirky, urgent biography . . . is an essential guide to this remarkable drug
addict'   *The Times*

'An ingeniously structured biography of a brilliant, ridiculously self-destructive
man, and a beautifully written cultural history full of arresting insights into
celebrity and hero-worship and the public's prurient fascination with violence'
Lucy Hughes-Hallett, *Observer*

'Excellent . . . A riveting glimpse into the opium-marinated Victorian age and its
tormented Romantic geniuses. De Quincey's story is stranger and more confound-
ing than most fiction'   *The Lady*

'A book that captures in both form and focus something of its subject's disorient-
ing, brilliant unpredictability . . . A great, complicated book, in which a host of
competing ideas and images jostle for supremacy'   *Observer*

'A riveting multi-tonal portrait . . . She beautifully binds and catches us in the web
of his imagination . . . In ... ... decisive ... ... his most
elusive characte... ...   *Spectator*

'Artful and nua... ... ... "... ... ... ast of the
Romantics" hir... ...   *Prospect*

GUILTY THING

A Life of Thomas De Quincey

Frances Wilson

BLOOMSBURY

LONDON · OXFORD · NEW YORK · NEW DELHI · SYDNEY

Bloomsbury Paperbacks
An imprint of Bloomsbury Publishing Plc

50 Bedford Square   1385 Broadway
London   New York
WC1B 3DP   NY 10018
UK   USA

www.bloomsbury.com

First published in Great Britain 2016
This paperback edition first published in 2017

Maps by Liane Payne

British Library Cataloguing-in-Publication Data
A catalogue record for this book is available from the British Library.

ISBN: HB: 978–1–4088–3977–5
       PB: 978–1–4088–4013–9
       ePub: 978–1–4088–3976–8

2 4 6 8 10 9 7 5 3 1

Typeset by Newgen Knowledge Works (P) Ltd., Chennai, India
Printed and bound in Great Britain by CPI Group (UK) Ltd, Croydon CR0 4YY

To find out more about our authors and books visit www.bloomsbury.com.
Here you will find extracts, author interviews, details of forthcoming
events and the option to sign up for our newsletters.

For Quincy W

. . . it started like a guilty thing
Upon a fearful summons.

Shakespeare, *Hamlet*, Act 1, Scene 1

Blank misgivings of a Creature
Moving about in worlds not realised,
High instincts before which our mortal Nature
Did tremble like a guilty thing surprised. . .

Wordsworth, 'Intimations of Immortality'

Contents

DE QUINCEY'S WANDERINGS

Glasgow
Edinburgh

COUNTY
MAYO

Grasmere

Liverpool Manchester

Dublin Bangor
Chester
Shrewsbury

Bristol Oxford
Bath London

0   50   100   150 miles

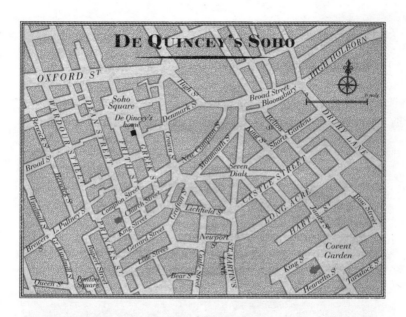

DE QUINCEY'S SOHO

OXFORD ST

Soho Square

De Quincey's home

Broad Street Bloomsbury

HIGH HOLBORN

DRURY LANE

WARDOUR STREET

DEAN STREET

FRITH ST

GREEK ST

High S.

Denmark S.

New Compton S.

Crown S.

Monmouth S.

Betton S.

King S.

Shorts Gardens

Seven Dials

CASTLE STREET

LONG ACRE

HART S.

James S.

Bow Street

Berwick S.

Broad S.

Francis S.

Compton Street

Church Street

King Street

PRINCES S.

Gerrard Street

Lisle Street

Grafton S.

Lichfield S.

Newport S.

S.t MARTIN'S LANE

King S.

Covent Garden

Windmill S.

L.t Pulteney

Brewers S.

S.t Ann's S.

Rupert Street

Castle Street

Bear S.

Henrietta S.

Tavistock S.

Queen S.

Penton Square

½ mile

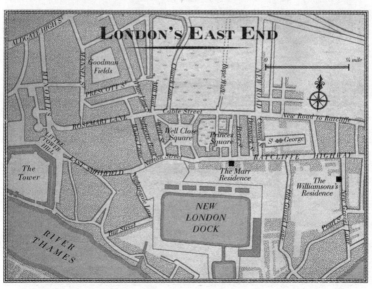

LONDON'S EAST END

ALDGATE HIGH S.

MINORIES

Goodman Fields

PRESCOTT S.

Rope Walk

NEW ROAD

¼ mile

New Road to Ratcliffe

LITTLE TOWER HILL

EAST SMITHFIELD

ROSEMARY LANE

Cable Street

Well Close Square

Sutton Street

Princes Square

Denmark S.

Cannon S.

Betts S.

S.t George

RATCLIFFE HIGHWAY

The Tower

Nightingale Lane

Old Gravel Lane

New Gravel Lane

The Marr Residence

The Williamson's Residence

Pearl S.

NEW LONDON DOCK

RIVER THAMES

Burr Street

The Residence of the late
M.ʳ MARR,
RATCLIFFE HIGHWAY.
where he was dreadfully murdered with his Wife, Infant Child,
& Apprentice, on the 7ᵗʰ Day of December 1811.

24 Ratcliffe Highway, 'a most chaotic quarter of eastern or
nautical London'.

The Prelude

Who knows the individual hour in which
His habits were first sown, even as a seed?
Who that shall point as with a wand and say
'This portion of the river of my mind
Came from yon fountain?'

Wordsworth, *The Prelude*, Book Second

A few minutes to midnight, 7 December 1811

Save for the quick light tap of Margaret Jewell's footsteps on the cobbles, the Ratcliffe Highway had fallen silent. The publicans of Shadwell had poured their last pitchers, the sailors and stevedores had turned in to their boarding houses, the pawnbrokers, block-builders and rope-makers had bolted their doors. Black water sloshed against the steps of the Wapping wharves and behind the wall of the London Docks the rigging of the ships creaked and swung. Margaret Jewell had been sent by her master, Timothy Marr of 'Marr's Silk, Lace, Pelisse, Mantle and Furr Warehouse' on 29 Ratcliffe Highway, to buy a dozen oysters for his family supper and to pay the baker's bill. Trading continued late on Saturday nights, and Marr's drapery was only now closing.

It was the last day of the working week and the end of the year in which a comet had been seen falling through the sky. Napoleon's Comet, as it was known in Europe, was held to portend unnatural times and in William Blake's miniature vision, *The Ghost of a Flea*, it hurls through the night between embroidered stage curtains while a monstrous creature with the face of a murderer and the legs of a man whips his tongue into a bowl of blood. Beneath the comet's luminous tail, America would be rocked by earthquakes and the Mississippi flow backwards; in England, those for whom comets were omens observed that the war with France had dragged into its twentieth year, the old, despised and dying King George had been once more declared insane by his doctors, and textile workers in Nottingham were smashing with hammers a thousand stocking machines. Samuel Taylor Coleridge, living through the worst days of his life, recorded in his notebooks a nightmarish version of the comet's trajectory: 'Suppose the Earth gradually to approach nearer the Sun or to be scorched by a close Comet – & still rolling on – with Cities menless – Channels riverless – 5 miles deep.'

Margaret Jewell made her way first to the oyster shop, but finding it already shut she turned around and headed back down the road towards the baker's. Marr had not yet put up the shutters on his freshly painted bay window – his establishment had recently undergone a refurbishment – and so she could see him as she passed by, standing at the counter on the ground floor with his young apprentice James Gowen, clearing away the rolls of cloth. Her route down Ratcliffe Highway took her past St George in the East, the most phantasmagoric and sinister of Hawksmoor's six London churches, its 160-foot tower rising pale above the rooftops like a schooner riding a storm. Ian Nairn later called St George 'the hardest building to describe in London'. It has the hypnotic pull of a pyramid, but resembles 'an entity like a hand or foot, total shape and total atmosphere'. With its four pepper-pot turrets, each marking the position of a spiral staircase, St George takes us to 'a stage beyond fantasy' and into 'the more than real world of the drug-addict's dream'.

Immediately south of Margaret Jewell's path lay the country's largest landing stage. Every year 13,000 ships laden with goods arrived at the London Docks from India, Greenland, China and Australia. Before the docks were completed in 1806, the river had been log-jammed with 2,000 vessels at a time packing into a mooring space that could hold 500, their precious cargoes exposed to pirates. Not even the river police could control the rackets of thieves and receivers, and so a fortress-like wall, thirty feet high and defended by guards, was girdled around the ships. The architect, Daniel Asher Alexander, Surveyor to the London Dock Company, also built the Dartmoor and Maidstone prisons and his design for the docks was inspired by Piranesi's semi-hallucinatory images of the *Carceri d'invenzione*, or 'Imaginary Prisons', etched in Rome in the late 1740s. The dock wall enclosed a citadel of merchandise, and the Ratcliffe Highway looked like a dwarf city on the other side. Vaults extending for acres beneath the streets stored Himalayan mounds of cocoa, tobacco, calico, indigo, muslin, wine, spices and coffee; as well as ostrich feathers, elephants' tusks, rugs, ambergris, monkey skins and cages of exotic beasts. Once a Bengal tiger imported for display in an emporium on the highway escaped from its box in the warehouse and took off with a boy between its jaws.

Margaret Jewell walked that night through a theatre of immensity: giant ramparts, narrow passageways, fortresses, dungeons and flights of steps – like Wapping Old Stairs, which led to the river that flowed out to the sea. The ocean was part of the lives of the shopkeepers, brothel-owners, landladies, publicans and laundresses who relied on the wages of the mariners who moored between berths. You could buy the largest oysters in England here, and shellfish scraped from the bottom of ships; even the vegetables had a scaly look.

The bakery had closed for the night and so Margaret Jewell returned home, having completed neither of her tasks. She had been out for no more than twenty minutes, she later said, but found the house 'closely shut up, and no light to be seen. I rang the bell, and no one answered. I rang repeatedly; whilst I was at the door, the watchman went by on the other side of the way.' She rang again, more insistently, and this time heard through the keyhole the sound of footsteps on the stairs which she took to be those of her master, followed by the low cry of the Marrs' baby.

The local watchman called the hour of one o'clock, and told her to move on. 'I said I belonged to the house,' she later explained, 'and thought it very strange that I should be locked out; he then observed that they had not fastened the pin of the window.' The watchman himself now started hammering and John Murray, who ran the pawnbroker's next door, rose from his bed to discover the cause of the disturbance. Finding the girl locked out, Murray suggested that he might try the back entrance.

He climbed over the wall dividing the back yards of their two homes, and called out for Marr. The house remained silent but the door being open, Murray went inside. A candle burned on the first-floor landing;

he went upstairs and, standing respectfully outside the bedroom door, called: 'Marr, Marr, your window shutters are not fastened.' No sound came from the room and so Murray went downstairs; on opening the door which led to the shop he pushed against the body of James Gowen, whose face and head had been shattered by blows so severe that his brains had splattered across the counter and up the walls; Murray could see them hanging from the ceiling like limpets. Staggering backwards, he fell against Mrs Marr, her cranium fractured and throat cut, blood draining from her wounds. Murray stumbled to the front door which he opened, shrieking 'Murder! Murder! Come and see what murder is here!' The watchman, Margaret Jewell and the neighbours, who had now joined them on the doorstep, crowded into the house. They found Timothy Marr lying face down behind the counter where, an hour before, Margaret Jewell had seen him standing. 'The child, where's the child?' somebody cried; there was a rush to the basement, where the baby lay floating in a cradle of blood, his head battered and his neck slashed.

Four throats had been cut in a matter of moments: there had been no evident struggle and no time to scream. The scene the murderer had left behind him was as foul as the final act of a revenge tragedy, save that there was no obvious motive for revenge, or apparent reason for wanting the Marr household dead. Nothing had been stolen – £40 remained in the drawer in his bedroom – and Marr, who had only recently set up in business, having formerly worked for the East India service, had no apparent enemies.

———

Having your throat slashed on the open road was never as interesting to Thomas De Quincey as having it slashed in the room of a house and, 300 miles north of London, in a slow and introspective valley in the Lake District, De Quincey eagerly followed the newspaper reports of the events on the Ratcliffe Highway. Murder was an infrequent enough occurrence: only nine of the sixty-seven convicts executed in 1810 had been murderers; more common by far was theft and fraud.

The column next to the story of 'The Murder of Mrs Marr and Family' in the *Morning Chronicle* on Monday 9 December ran an announcement of the Shakespeare lecture to be given that night by 'Mr Coleridge'. Coleridge's Shakespeare lectures at the Philosophical Society in Scott's Corporation Hall on Fetter Lane, behind Fleet Street and upriver from the Ratcliffe Highway, were 'quite the rage', as Byron put it. At his grandiloquent best, Coleridge was a mesmerising lecturer but his performances were nerve-racking experiences for the audience. Because he delivered his thoughts extempore he was liable to expound on more or less anything, and Londoners – including Byron himself and the philosopher William Godwin, who brought along his daughter Mary Wollstonecraft Godwin – braved the cold to watch the bloated, despairing, opium-exhausted poet swerve violently off course. The theme of his lecture on 9 December was *Romeo and Juliet*, but rather than discuss the star-crossed lovers Coleridge considered the nature of friendship, particularly between 'men of genius'. 'What is true of friendship is true of love,' Coleridge stated with mournful conviction. Men of genius are 'conscious of their own weakness, and are ready to believe others stronger than themselves, when, in truth, they are weaker: they have formed an ideal in their own minds, and they want to see it realised. . . in, perhaps, the first man they meet, they only see what is good; they have no sense of his deficiencies, and their friendship becomes so strong, that they almost fall down and worship one in every respect greatly their inferior.'

Sitting amongst the audience, Charles Lamb remarked to Henry Crabb Robinson that 'Coleridge said in his advertisement that he would speak about the nurse in *Romeo and Juliet*; and so he is delivering the lecture in the character of the nurse'. De Quincey understood that he was describing his relationship with Wordsworth, who said Coleridge was 'the only man to whom *at all times* and *in all modes of excellence* I feel myself inferior'.

De Quincey – Romantic acolyte, professional doppelgänger, transcendental hack – had replaced Coleridge as Wordsworth's inferior friend. He had also replaced Wordsworth as tenant of Dove Cottage, which he turned into literature's most famous opium den. It was here, in a house that became a 'scene of struggle the most tempestuous and bitter within my own mind', that he followed the reports of the Shakespeare lectures at the same time as absorbing the details of the

Ratcliffe Highway murders. Buildings, for De Quincey, were always crime scenes. 'Few writers,' says Peter Ackroyd, 'had so keen and horrified a sense of place' as Thomas De Quincey, who nurtured his horrified sense of place while living in the house that Wordsworth called 'the loveliest spot that man hath ever found'.

The Marrs were buried on Sunday 15 December, in a single grave in the churchyard of St George in the East. The investigation into the identity of their killer had drawn a blank; everyone, it seemed, especially the Portuguese, French and Irish, was a potential suspect. The magistrates were in despair and the residents of the highway in a state of suspense. Was the monster living and breathing amongst them? Would he strike again? Were they safer in their homes or on the streets? Coleridge later observed to De Quincey that 'the practice of putting the chain upon the door before it was opened. . . served as a record of the deep impression left' by the Ratcliffe Highway murders – but he himself had not been afraid. On the contrary, Coleridge confessed, the murders had inspired in him a 'profound reverie' on the power available to a man once he had 'rid himself of fear'. De Quincey, who gorged on scenes of violence, was also, so his daughter Florence said, 'quite incapable of fear', and unable to understand it in his children: 'When he was chilling our marrow with awesome stories of ghosts, murders, and mysteries he only thought he was producing a luxurious excitement.'

It was De Quincey who legitimised the luxurious excitement of murder, just as he legitimised, in his most famous work, *Confessions of an English Opium-Eater*, the pleasure of opiates. What took place in London in the winter of 1811 ignited his genius and became the subject of a series of essays he returned to and expanded for the rest of his life; 'On the Knocking at the Gate in *Macbeth*', 'On Murder Considered as One of the Fine Arts', 'Second Paper on Murder as One of the Fine Arts' and 'Postscript [To "Murder as One of the Fine Arts"]' are now embedded in our culture: all subsequent literary murders have conformed to De Quincey's taste. He had no interest in the fate of the victims or the skill of the police: De Quincey's concern was with the *mind of the murderer*. 'There must be raging some great storm of passion, jealousy, ambition, vengeance, hatred,' De Quincey wrote, 'which will create a hell within him. And into this hell we are to look.'

———

There have been several fine biographies of De Quincey, but so far no De Quinceyan biography. A fearless biographer himself – his scandalous portraits of Wordsworth and Coleridge tell a tale of pursuit and revenge – De Quincey had trenchant views about the genre. It was not necessary, he believed, to love your subject, but a biography based on hatred alone made for a bad book. The best biographies, such as Samuel Johnson's *Life of Savage*, were written '*con amore*' and also '*con odio*'. 'Some of our contemporaries,' De Quincey observed, 'we hate particularly and for that very reason we will not write their lives. . . for it is too odious a spectacle to imprison a fellow in a book, lock a stag in a cart, and turn him out to be hunted through all his doubles for a day's amusement.' It is a striking description of the biographer's peculiar transgression – to hunt a fellow through all his doubles – but this is precisely what is required of De Quincey, who always believed himself hunted and was inordinately preoccupied with the idea of multiplicity. 'We should not assert for De Quincey a double personality,' cautioned his friend and editor, James Hogg; he was 'no Dr Jekyll and Mr Hyde', but he was certainly composed of multiple tendencies. At the same time as proclaiming his exemplary singularity, De Quincey modelled his character on Coleridge and his writing on Wordsworth. So while there was no one quite like Thomas De Quincey, Thomas De Quincey was quite like everyone; it was this trick of camouflage that made him such an effective autobiographer.

He wrote during what a fellow journalist called 'the triumphant reign of the first person singular', but there is no ego in De Quincey's writing; the self he describes in his *Confessions* and other autobiographical essays is a fleeting form on the cusp of disappearing – into a city crowd, into the chasm of a dream, or into some other body entirely. De Quincey was excessively preoccupied with his own interiority, which he mapped as though it were a building: his mind was a hall of many rooms; his dreaming self was 'housed within himself, occupying, as it were, a separate chamber of the brain'; his waking thoughts were 'a lock that might open a door somewhere or somehow'. He was a houser of memories but also a reader of houses. In the following pages I have pursued him through the buildings he inhabited and those that inhabited him.

De Quincey was twenty-one when he met Coleridge, twenty-two when he met Wordsworth, and twenty-six when the Ratcliffe Highway murders took place. He waited until he was thirty-six before he began to write, after which he wrote unceasingly for the next forty years, producing 250 essays which now fill twenty-one volumes of his collected works. Writing in the glory days of the literary-political magazine – *The Edinburgh Review*, *Blackwood's Edinburgh Magazine*, *Tait's Edinburgh Magazine*, *The London Magazine* – De Quincey helped shape a new kind of professional critic and a new literary genre, called by Walter Bagehot the 'review-like essay and the essay-like review'. The magazines were a quintessentially Romantic form; the authority that the eighteenth century had afforded to books was replaced in the nineteenth century by these slippery, multi-authored, self-reflexive, fragmented, bold, pugnacious, parodic, combative, opinionated objects which were like books, but not quite. 'By and by,' imagined Thomas Carlyle, 'it will be found that all Literature has become one boundless self-devouring Review.' The image would have horrified De Quincey, but it was in these boundless, self-devouring reviews that he grew his voice.

De Quincey, whose writing was itself anarchic, thrived in the anarchic culture of contemporary journalism, where the flexibility of his editors allowed him to invent a new style: he contributed to the great age of rough house in the language of reverie. He was not an essayist in the polished manner of William Hazlitt; De Quincey did not create finished objects. The virtue of the essay is that it reflects a thought in the process of discovering itself, and De Quincey dramatised this process. He wrote in diversions, he recycled other people's words, he produced experiments in inwardness, works in progress; instead of moving in a horizontal direction he either plunged downward or rose, as Leslie Stephen said, like 'a bat. . . on the wings of prose to the borders of the true poetic region'. Reading De Quincey's individual essays can be a vertiginous experience; reading his collected works is like falling into Pandemonium. His subjects included the Greeks, the Caesars, the Westmorland dialect, contemporary politics, ocean navigation, velocity, philosophy, political economy, astronomy, opium-eating, China and the Opium Wars, literary style, the experiences of his childhood, the dream life and the structure of memory. A literary critic of outstanding originality, he also wrote a Gothic novel called *Klosterheim*, two novellas, 'The Household Wreck', and 'The Avenger', published translations from numerous German texts and, for one hectic year, he edited the local newspaper, *The Westmorland Gazette*, during which time he fed the Lakeland farmers a diet of Kantian metaphysics, Wordsworthian poetry and tales of the unexpected. The only literary form De Quincey did not employ was the one he most admired – poetry. Instead he made his name as a spokesman of poets, and was the first critic to separate decisively what T. S. Eliot called 'the man who suffers' from 'the mind which creates'. That the poet and his poetry had distinct identities was to prove De Quincey's greatest insight and bitterest disappointment.

Thomas De Quincey was an obsessive: he was obsessed with the Ratcliffe Highway murders and he was obsessed with William Wordsworth. *Guilty Thing* is an attempt to follow the growth of these twin obsessions from seed to full flowering and to trace the way in which they intertwined. Positioning his preoccupation with murderers and poets at the forefront of what follows, I have placed De Quincey's numerous other interests in the background, and sought permission for this biographical privilege in his own example. Revising his autobiographical writings for the collected edition of his works, De Quincey dismissed as 'wearisome and useless' the 'hackneyed roll-call' of a man's life, 'chronologically arranged'; it was surely better, he suggested, to 'detach' a 'single' scene that would record 'some of the deep impressions under which my childish sensibility expanded'. De Quincey never put childish things away, and the deep impressions under which his sensibility expanded tended to be scenes of terror, deluge and sudden death. These are the scenes on which I too have focused, believing that in his return to the Ratcliffe Highway murders we can find, dispersed in anagram, the story of De Quincey's life.

Like Shakespeare, De Quincey enjoyed the idea of a play within a play and he compared the 'The Murder of Gonzago', the tragedy performed under Hamlet's direction by the strolling players at Elsinore, to a room on whose wall is a picture of the room on whose wall is a picture of that room. 'We might,' De Quincey wrote, 'imagine this descent into a life below a life going on *ad infinitum*,' and we might see his folding of the Ratcliffe Highway murders into his possession by Wordsworth as achieving a similar effect: a story within a story within a story, a room within a room within a room, going on *ad infinitum*.

He was intensely aware of the spaces he occupied, the heights and widths surrounding him, the positions of windows, the number of steps on a staircase, but what were De Quincey's own dimensions? The amount of room taken up by a biographical subject is not always relevant but in De Quincey's case it cannot be underestimated. His opium trances describe descents into what Coleridge, in 'Kubla Khan', called 'caverns measureless to man' and his impacted writing impersonates endless growth, but De Quincey's body itself barely grew. Like Hogarth, Pope and Charles Lamb, he was one of those called by the tiny antiquary, George Vertue, 'the five foot men or less'. At four foot eleven inches, De Quincey was not small so much as Lilliputian – wiry, barely there. He was 'unfortunately diminutive', said Dorothy Wordsworth, who was the same height, 'but there is a sweetness in his looks, especially about the eyes, which soon overcomes the oddness of your first feeling at the sight of so very little a man'. Wordsworth's sister-in-law, Joanna Hutchinson, said that De Quincey looked 'helpless' and 'dissipid', and Robert Southey referred to him as 'Little Mr Quincey'. 'I wish,' Southey complained, 'he was not so little, and I wish he would not leave his greatcoat always behind him on the road.' Thomas Carlyle, who compared him to a pair of sugar tongs, left this description of De Quincey aged forty-two: 'When he sate, you would have taken him, by candlelight, for the beautifullest little child; blue-eyed, sparkling face, had there not been a something, too, which said, "*Eccovi* – this child has been in hell."'

It is into this hell we are to look.

Greenhay, De Quincey's childhood home, in which he learned that there
was nothing 'but a mighty darkness and a sorrow without a voice'.

Books

In memory of all books which lay
Their sure foundations in the heart of man

Wordsworth, *The Prelude*, Book Fifth

The first chapter of Thomas De Quincey's life, according to the account he gave in his *Autobiographic Sketches*, came 'suddenly' to a 'violent termination' at noon on a midsummer's day in 1792. It is typical of De Quincey's sense of time that he marked his beginning by an event he described as an ending. The date was 3 June and he was six years old; his nine-year-old sister Elizabeth had died the day before, after drinking tea 'in the house of a labouring man' and walking back through a meadow 'reeking with exhalations'. In De Quincey's mind the tea and reeking exhalations resulted in hydrocephalus, or water on the brain, which explained what he saw as the swelling of her forehead. Hydrocephalus was thought to stimulate the intellect, but De Quincey would always believe that it was the other way around, that Elizabeth's 'intellectual grandeur' brought on the hydrocephalus. His elder sister, he understood, died from excessive intelligence, a condition from which he also suffered.

De Quincey's childhood home was a country mansion with a porticoed front door and three tall chimneys. It was built by Mr Quincey – the 'De' was not prefixed to the family name until 1797 – according to Mrs Quincey's design, and was of a grandeur, De Quincey later noted, more suited to the fortune his father 'was rapidly approaching than the one he actually possessed'. His mother was a 'lady architect', and Greenhay, as the house was called, was her *coup d'essai*. The De Quincey children grew up around stonemasons, carpenters, painters, plasterers and bell-hangers; while other women of her class busied themselves with gentler pursuits, Elizabeth Quincey demolished walls and improved views, expanded floors and widened windows. Thomas De Quincey was raised in a world of interiors.

Greenhay was the shell in which he nurtured his mind. He would never forget the layout of the house: there were two staircases; a grand flight at the front for the family, and a narrow set at the back for their servants. On the day in question, young Thomas waited until the maids were taking their lunch in the kitchen before creeping up the back stairs and down the corridor to the bedroom in which the body of his sister now lay. The room was locked but the key was in place; he turned it and entered, closing 'the door so softly that, although it opened upon a hall which ascended through all the storeys, no echo ran along the silent walls'. Elizabeth's bed, which had been moved from its usual position, now faced an open window through which 'the sun of midsummer at mid-day was showering down in torrents of splendour' onto her 'frozen eyelids'. While Thomas stood gazing at the stiffening body, 'a solemn wind began to blow – the saddest that ear ever heard. It was a wind that might have swept the fields of mortality for a thousand centuries.' He fell into a reverie in which, 'A vault seemed to open in the zenith of the far blue sky, a shaft which ran up for ever. I, in spirit, rose as if on billows that also ran up the shaft for ever; and the billows seemed to pursue the throne of God; but *that* also ran before us and fled away continually. The flight and the pursuit seemed to go on for ever and ever. Frost gathering frost, some Sarsar wind of death, seemed to repel me. . .'

Hearing 'a foot on the stairs' the pulses of life began to beat again; Thomas kissed, for the last time, his sister's marble lips and, lest he be discovered, 'slunk, like a guilty thing, with stealthy steps from the room'. It was now that he lost his innocence: in Elizabeth's bedroom De Quincey learned that 'all men come into this world *alone*; all leave it *alone*' – a hard lesson for a boy whose heart was 'deeper than the Danube'. From this day forward he lived inside his sense of loss; there was 'nothing on the stage but a solitary infant, and its solitary combat with grief – a mighty darkness and a sorrow without a voice'. Many times since, De Quincey recalled, 'on a summer day, when the sun is about the hottest, I have remarked on the same wind arising and uttering the same hollow, solemn, Memnonian but saintly swell: it is in this world the one *audible* symbol of eternity. And three times in my life I have happened to hear the same sound in the same circumstances, viz, when standing between an open window and a dead body on a summer day.'

Few autobiographers have given us a more remarkable, or convoluted, childhood scene – part-memory, part-midsummer daydream, part-opium reverie – or one that propels us more swiftly into the furnishings of their imagination. It is an example of what De Quincey called his 'impassioned prose', which takes flight mid-sentence, and what Baudelaire called De Quincey's 'naturally spiral' way of thinking, his escalating up and down and circling around a line of associated ideas. What De Quincey describes is terror recollected in tranquillity; he always invested in the things that he feared, such as endless time and boundless space.

His vision occurred on the outskirts of Manchester, a prosaic setting for Aeolian intonations and Sarsar winds of death, but no more so than the 'tree filled with angels. . . bespangling every bough like stars' seen by the ten-year-old William Blake on Peckham Rye. The Manchester in which De Quincey was born was on the cusp of the industrial revolution; not yet the great Cottonopolis it would become in his lifetime, he knew it as a 'gloomy' town framed by 'mud below' and 'smoke above', whose only virtue lay in the philosophical interests of its inhabitants. Two such figures, Thomas Percival and Charles White – Manchester's most respected physicians – attended De Quincey's sick sister and then returned, the day after her death, to perform the post-mortem. This operation added a new dimension to De Quincey's trauma. The men, with their cases of equipment, entered his sister's room where they sawed through her skull and inspected the liquid deposits around the brain. Elizabeth's angelic head had been violently attacked; the room in which De Quincey had glimpsed the vaults of heaven was now a chamber of horrors. Was he on one side of the door listening, while on the other side the doctors coolly performed their task? He would recall the paradisical period of childhood as the time in which we trod 'without fear *every* chamber in [our] father's house', when 'no door was closed'.

An hour after Percival and White had departed, he returned to the bedroom but found it locked and the key removed. De Quincey was 'shut out forever'. This is his version of a paraclausithyron, meaning, from the Greek, 'lament by a shut door'; the motif, employed in Greek and Augustan love elegies, was parodied in *A Midsummer Night's Dream* where Pyramus and Thisbe communicate through a crack in the wall.

During Elizabeth's funeral, the small boy 'sank back' into his 'own solitary darkness' and heard nothing except 'some fugitive strains from the sublime chapter of St Paul': 'But now is Christ risen from the dead, and become the first fruits of them that slept.' He watched his sister's coffin, with its record of her name, age and date of death, 'dropped into darkness as messages addressed to worms'. Then came the work of the sacristan, with his shovel of earth and stones, and 'immediately the dread rattle ascend[ed] from the lid'. Earth to earth, ashes to ashes, dust to dust, 'and the grave, the coffin, the face are sealed up for ever and ever'. De Quincey's solitude and grief aligned with religious intimations, and throughout July and August he sought out sequestered nooks in the house and grounds where he could absorb the 'awful stillness' of 'summer noons' with their windless 'desert air'. Gazing into the skies for a sign of Elizabeth's face he took to 'shaping images in the distance out of slight elements'. On Sundays, the family attended a church 'on the old and natural model of England, having aisles, galleries, organ, all things ancient and venerable, and the proportions majestic'. Here, unwatched, he wept in silence at the passage on children and the sick and when the organ 'threw its vast columns of sound over the voices of the choir' he raised his 'streaming eyes to the upper windows of the galleries'. Through the storied glass, when the sun was shining, he saw clouds shaped as beds in 'chambers of the air' on which children lay 'tossing in anguish, and weeping clamorously for death'. De Quincey was always drawn to what he called cloud architecture, and later claimed Wordsworth as the poet of the sky's grand pageants.

He also had a lifelong love of majestic churches. In his dreams he returned to the aisles and galleries of this ancient building, to the swelling anthems of the funeral, 'the burst of the Hallelujah chorus, the storm, the trampling movement of the choral passion, the agitation of my own trembling sympathy, the tumult of the choir, the wrath of the organ', followed by 'the priest in his white surplice waiting with a book by the side of an open grave', and the sacristan waiting with his shovel.

Doctors Percival and White, both notable figures in the rich cultural, scientific and intellectual life of the town, were friends of De Quincey's father. Percival was co-president of the renowned Manchester Literary and Philosophical Society; White was vice-president, and Quincey senior was a founding member. The 'Lit & Phil' was composed of prominent Mancunian industrialists, engineers, doctors and intellectuals who would gather to discuss matters of natural philosophy, law, literature, education and advances in chemistry and science.

Dr P, as De Quincey referred to Thomas Percival, was 'a man, of elegant tastes and philosophic habits' who exchanged ideas with Voltaire. He was instinctively distrusted by De Quincey's practical and evangelical mother, who associated philosophers with infidels, and her dislike was fuelled by Percival's habit of reading aloud extracts from his erudite correspondence. She was bored by the society of Northern philosophers, but Thomas was captivated by Dr P, who had written a collection of improving fables for children called *A Father's Instructions*, a copy of which he had given to Thomas and Elizabeth. De Quincey had never before met the author of a book he admired.

His life imitated art in the fullest sense, and De Quincey's need to read was, as he put it, 'absolutely endless and inexorable as the grave'. He read voraciously, ravenously, for seventy years, creating layer upon layer of fictitious memory. In *The Prelude*, which De Quincey first read in manuscript form, Wordsworth celebrated 'all books which lay/ Their sure foundation in the heart of man', and the foundations of De Quincey's most significant moments can be found in novels, poems, plays, travelogues and works of philosophy. His reading provided a guide through the maelstrom of consciousness; it gave a shape to shapeless events, and a meaning to those things – such as death – that he found terrifying in their random cruelty. Because he used the inside of a book to make sense of the outside world his experiences might be seen as only half-true, but the relationship between fact and fiction was, for De Quincey, complicated. Again and again we find, in the books he loved, accounts of the events which formed him. For example in *Titan*, written by his second favourite novelist, the German Romantic Jean Paul Richter, is a description of the death of a girl which is identical in atmosphere to De Quincey's description of the death of his sister Elizabeth. *Titan*'s heroine, Liana, dies by an open window through which 'the golden sun gushed through the clouds', and 'suddenly the folding doors of an inspired concert-hall flew open, and outswelling harmonies floated by'. For De Quincey, reading was less an escape from reality than a perilous journey to the truth, as potentially devastating as opium itself. Before he discovered drugs, it was through books that De Quincey sought to find a route back to his original self, to the person he was before Elizabeth's death.

Accordingly, he was possessed by the power of writers and the first writer to lodge himself in De Quincey's psyche was Thomas Percival. The impression made on him by *A Father's Instructions* 'was deep and memorable: my sister wept over it and wept over the remembrance of it, and later carried its sweet aroma off with her to heaven'. Percival's tales, set in a contemporary Manchester which contained elements of ancient Greece, were principally about animals, the force of maternal affection, the importance of filial gratitude, and the racial superiority of Europeans. In one story, a country boy knowing nothing of life beyond his family home goes to Manchester to see an exhibition of wild beasts and is mesmerised by a Blakean tiger of sublime 'symmetry'; another is set on a heavenly June day when the 'clouds were dispersed, the sun shone with unusual brightness' and 'verdure of the meadows. . . regaled every sense'. Once absorbed into his imagination where they marinated for decades, these tales stalked De Quincey's own writings.

In addition to being the family doctor, Charles White was an enthusiastic craniologist who passed on to De Quincey – whose own skull, in contrast to his tiny body, was enormous – his belief that the shape and size of the head was an indication of intellect. Elizabeth's head, White pronounced, was 'the finest. . . in its development of any he had ever seen' and her brain 'the "most beautiful"', which confirmed – or formed – De Quincey's view of her as a superior being. 'For its superb developments,' De Quincey proudly recorded, his sister's skull 'was the astonishment of science'. Lord over life and death, Charles White was fascinating to De Quincey, who compared him to 'some mighty caliph, or lamp-bearing Aladdin'. Of all his childhood books, *Arabian Nights* was De Quincey's touchstone; his Manchester was less like ancient Greece than an Arab city. White had turned a room of his own house into a museum of medical curiosities consisting of body parts which he used to illustrate his lectures, and when De Quincey came here as a child it was he who was Aladdin, entering the magic cave.

'Memories are killing', said Samuel Beckett, and De Quincey, for whom there was no such thing as forgetting, believed himself cursed by memory; his mind was a palimpsest on which 'every chaos' was 'stamped' and 'arrayed in endless files incapable of obliteration'. Jorge Luis Borges based his story 'Funes the Memorious' on De Quincey's ghastly condition. Following a fall on his head, Funes can remember everything he ever saw and everything that ever happened to him. He remembers the shape and movement of every cloud, and the crevice and moulding of every house. Aged nineteen, Funes's face is 'more ancient than Egypt'.

De Quincey saw, standing in a clock case in Charles White's museum, the embalmed and mummified body of a woman called Hannah Beswick, alongside which hung the skeleton of the highwayman, Thomas Higgins. There is a peculiar horror to the sight of a dead body standing upright, and De Quincey would later find his appalled reaction to this sight caught in the fifth book of Wordsworth's *Prelude*, which is entitled 'Books'. The poet recalls how, roaming the margins of Lake Esthwaite as a child, he saw a boat of men 'with grappling-irons and long poles' sounding the water. 'At length' from the depths 'bolt upright rose' a dead man. His face was 'ghastly', a 'spectre shape' of 'terror'. Wordsworth claims to have felt 'no vulgar fear' because his 'inner eye' had 'seen such sights before among the shining streams of fairyland', but he is at his least convincing when he talks about fairyland. The tension with which he controls the scene suggests that in his terror Wordsworth became himself as rigid as the corpse.

De Quincey always remembered the stories attached to bolt-upright bodies. Hannah Beswick, born in 1688, developed a fear of being buried alive after her brother, pronounced dead, had opened his eyes when his coffin lid was being nailed down. The doctor who attended the unfortunate man – who then lived on for many years – was Charles White, and Hannah Beswick paid White £25,000 to ensure that, once her own body appeared to have expired, he keep it above ground and check it daily for signs of life. White was true to his word, and after her death, aged seventy, Hannah Beswick's unburied corpse became known as the Manchester Mummy. Fascinated by the resurrection (he knew by heart 'the great chapter of St Paul', which was read at his sister's funeral), De Quincey was doubtless also fascinated by the idea of Elizabeth herself being still alive on the other side of the bedroom door, while Percival and White cut open her head and then bandaged it up like a mummy.

'Highwayman' Higgins, as he was known around Manchester, had been in life a night-rider of gallantry and elegance. He was also, according to De Quincey, a 'noonday murderer' who was believed to have slaughtered a wealthy widow and her servant in their Bristol home. His guilt was never proved but in a typical flight of fancy De Quincey later imagined, in 'On Murder Considered as One of the Fine Arts', Highwayman Higgins pulling woollen stockings over the hoofs of his horses to muffle their clatter when he returned from his two-day journey from Bristol to Manchester, his pockets filled with the dead woman's gold. Higgins was hanged, but, Thomas learned, his body was cut down prematurely and when it arrived at the surgeon's table to be dissected, he too had not yet quite expired. A medical student was required to finish the job by plunging a knife into the still-beating heart.

Locked doors, open windows, footsteps on the stairs and guilty figures slipping away; midsummer days, Arabian Nights, echoing churches, damaged skulls and writers wielding knives: the death of Elizabeth stood at the centre of a vast web of associations for De Quincey. The summer of 1792 was the fair seed-time of his childhood, and he described his character as taking root in this strange soil.

———

Beyond the walls of the house, the country was responding to events in France. Three years earlier, the fall of the Bastille had been welcomed as the overthrow of absolutism and slavery. 'How much the greatest event it is that ever happened in the World! & how much the best!' cried Charles James Fox, leader of the opposition. 'With freedom, order and good government,' cautioned William Pitt, leader of the government, 'France would stand forward as one of the most brilliant Powers in Europe; she would enjoy just that kind of liberty which I venerate.' But order quickly broke down. In 1791 Louis XVI and Marie Antoinette had fled Versailles and were placed under guard in a Paris prison. The French National Assembly was dissolved and a legislative assembly established. Three months before the death of little Elizabeth Quincey, France had declared war on Austria and Prussia and it was now widely feared that Britain would be drawn into the hostilities. France was declared a republic, and Louis XVI was put on trial. English newspapers were filled with French horror stories from across the Channel – mob rule, mountains of carcasses, massacres in the Tuileries, massacres in the prisons. In late January 1793 the king was executed: regicide was open season. The Revolution had become the Terror. Dehumanised in France, the British turned Louis into a hero facing death with fortitude: his last night on earth was reconstructed by the British press as a tender domestic moment in which the noble king instructed his fainting wife and weeping children in the will of God. The following October, Marie Antoinette was also guillotined: in the French royal family, De Quincey found his first example of a household wreck. On 1 February 1793, France declared war on England.

———

Thomas De Quincey was the fourth of eight children. The eldest, William, was probably born in 1782; Elizabeth was born in 1783 and died, as we know, aged nine; Mary was born in 1784, a year before Thomas himself, who was born on 15 August 1785 and was therefore a Leo. (Lions would play a rich part in his imaginative life, and one of De Quincey's earliest dreams was of lying down before one.) Jane, who arrived in 1786, died aged three; Richard, known as 'Pink', appeared in 1789, to be followed by a second girl called Jane, and finally, in 1793, a boy eight years younger than Thomas, called Henry. The death of the first Jane, two years before Elizabeth, was 'scarcely intelligible' to Thomas – 'summer and winter came again. . . Why not little Jane?' – and in his *Autobiographic Sketches* he described her as his older and not his younger sister; De Quincey evidently believed himself to be his mother's fifth and not her fourth child. More disturbing to Thomas, then aged four, than the mystery of his position in the family, or of Jane's current whereabouts, was the rumour that went around the house that she had been treated cruelly by the servant who was nursing her. The effect on him of this suggestion was 'terrific. . . the feeling which fell upon me was a shuddering horror, as upon a first glimpse of the truth that I was in a world of evil and strife'.

For Thomas, birthdays, anniversaries and the dates of deaths would always be of great significance. His future editor, David Masson, who was introduced to him in the 1840s, remembered De Quincey's animated response to hearing that it was the birthday of another of the guests in the room: '"O," he exclaimed, "that is the anniversary of the battle of So-and-So"; and he seemed ready to catch as many birthdays as might be thrown him on the spot, and almanac them all round in a similar manner from his memory.' Also born on 15 August, sixteen years before Thomas himself, was Napoleon Bonaparte. Sharing a birthday can be both a bonding and a threatening experience, implying that we are in some ways twinned with that other person, destined to progress along parallel lines. Sharing his birthday with a man simultaneously regarded as a murderer, a genius, a usurper and a hero could only increase De Quincey's sense of destiny, and Bonaparte's presence as a nemesis would shadow his life.

'What is to be thought of sudden death?' De Quincey asked in his most famous essay, 'The English Mail-Coach'. Suddenness fascinated him: 'Wonderful it is to see the effect of sudden misery, sudden grief, or sudden fear. . . in sharpening the intellectual perceptions,' he wrote, and sudden death was a subject about which he had thought a great deal. The French king and queen had died suddenly, and at the hands of the lower classes. Did Thomas think that Jane had been killed by her violent nurse? He certainly associated Elizabeth's death with the visit, also in the care of a servant, to the house of the servant's father; and another of his earliest memories involved saving 'fugitive' spiders from the angry broom of a bloodthirsty housemaid, who stopped his campaign of salvation by telling him 'of the many murders that the spider had committed and next (which was worse) *would* commit if reprieved'. Servants would always play an important role in his internal dramas, but however De Quincey understood Jane's death, his grief had remained hidden like stars in the daylight until he found himself standing by Elizabeth's bedside.

His parents, also called Thomas and Elizabeth, had married in 1780 in Queen Square, London, at the heart of Bloomsbury. His mother's people, the Pensons, were a cut above his father's: she came from a military family and both her brothers served with the East India Company in Bengal. Elizabeth Penson was a snob; the 'De' in 'De Quincey' was an affectation she added as a widow in order to keep up appearances; her husband would have disapproved of such a flourish. De Quincey's father, known as Thomas Quincey, was another upright figure – a friend described him as being 'the most upright man I ever met with in my life'. Quincey started his working life as a draper in London's Cheapside before moving in 1780 to the burgeoning industrial centre of Manchester where, on a steep, half-timbered road called Market-Street Lane (under where the Arndale shopping centre now stands), he opened a shop selling 'printed Linens, Musslins, Furnitures, and other Cottons'. It was in a room above the shop that Thomas came into this world. He was keen to pin down for his readers the precise 'tier in the social scaffolding' occupied by his family: the Quinceys belonged to the urban middle-classes. By the time Thomas was born, his father had made the decision to exchange retail for importing Irish linen and West Indian cotton, and he was therefore a merchant and no longer a draper. While his children may have grown up in 'circumstances of luxury', with servants and underservants who were maintained, because his father was a moral man, in even more 'luxury', the family were not, De Quincey stressed, 'emphatically *rich*'. They might have become so had Thomas Quincey not been, unusually for a trader in the West Indies, a 'conscientious protester' against slavery, and had he not died aged forty from tuberculosis.

Soon after De Quincey's birth the family moved from Market-Street Lane to a larger house on the outskirts of the city. It was called The Farm, and described by De Quincey in Wordsworthian terms as 'a pretty rustic dwelling'. It was then fashionable for the homes of the elite to include a greenhouse, later known as an orangery or conservatory, and Mr Quincey's 'daily pleasure' lay in his books, his garden and his greenhouse. A sickly child, Thomas was lovingly nursed; he was always drawn to the nurturing qualities of women and, a lifelong hypochondriac, he never tired of describing, in baroque detail, the malfunctions of his body. Of the memories which date back to this time, the most powerful was his father's illumination of the house in 1789, when King George III recovered from his first attack of madness.

When Thomas was six the Quinceys moved to 'Greenhay', whose substantial greenhouse formed '*the* principal room' for family life. By then he had seen so little of his father that he doubted whether he 'would have been able to challenge me as a relative; nor I *him*, had we happened to meet on the public roads'. Mr Quincey's work, together with the weakness of his lungs, meant that his days were increasingly spent in warmer climes: 'he lived for months in Portugal, at Lisbon, and at Cintra, next in Madeira, then in the West Indies; sometimes in Jamaica, sometimes in St Kitts', wrote De Quincey, who would never travel further than Ireland. Thomas Quincey senior's membership of the Literary and Scientific Society, which he joined in the year that he moved to Manchester, suggests that he was held in high esteem by men of learning. He kept a small collection of Italian Renaissance paintings and a growing library; his favourite authors were Cowper and Dr Johnson. His reverence for them was such, De Quincey said, that had these great men visited Greenhay, his father 'might have been tempted to express his homage through the Pagan fashion of raising altars and burning incense'. Thomas would share his father's veneration for writers. Two aspects of the household library later struck him

as significant: the first was that his father's books were all in English,
and the second was that he had nothing from the 'Black Letter', or
Gothic script, period, which spanned the twelfth to the seventeenth
century. It was a book collection, De Quincey concluded, for the purposes of 'instant amusement' as opposed to prolonged study.

Aged twenty-three, Quincey senior had written a book of his own,
a topographical study called *A Short Tour in the Midland Counties of
England, Performed in the Summer of 1772*, which had previously been
published in five parts in the *Gentleman's Magazine*. It was by reading his father's accounts of the state of draining, mining, farming and
manufacturing in the Midlands that De Quincey later came to know
something of the man, and his own first book, *Confessions of an English
Opium-Eater*, which similarly began its life as magazine instalments,
would also describe a short English tour.

De Quincey's chief memory of his father was of learning, aged seven,
that he was coming home from the West Indies to die. The invalid was
expected on a summer evening of 'unusual solemnity' and the children
and servants had assembled on the front lawn to greet his carriage. The
experience was recorded by De Quincey as a 'chorus of restless images':
sunset came and night fell; still they stood listening for the sound of
the wheels which, because the house was isolated and the roads empty,
would be heard from a distance. As midnight approached, the silent
party walked up the lane where, out of the gloomy stillness, horses'
heads slowly appeared; the carriage was moving at such a hearse-like
pace that the wheels made no sound at all. Inside, against a 'mass of
white pillows' lay 'the dying patient'. Were it not for 'the midsummer
night's dream which glorified his return', De Quincey would not have
remembered his father at all.

Mr Quincey's life exhaled in July 1793, a year and one month after the
death of little Elizabeth and six months after the beheading of the French
king. From now on De Quincey would always associate the sting of death
with 'the endless days of summer'. Summer deaths, he suggested, were
more affecting than winter deaths because the heavens were more distant,
'more infinite', and the clouds seemed grander and 'more towering'.

Mrs Quincey inherited the house – which her husband advised her
not to sell until prices had risen – plus half the income that would
come from the sale of his businesses, a share in the New Linen Hall in

Chester, and a share in a ship called the *Isabella Brigantine of Drogheda*. The total income at her disposal was £1,600 a year. It was a fair sum; not Mr Darcy's ten thousand but enough to ensure the family's comfort. When the boys reached twenty-one they would receive a patrimony of their own, and until then their moral and financial welfare was left in the care of four unbending guardians: a clergyman, a magistrate, a merchant and a banker, named, respectively, Samuel Hall, James Entwhistle, Thomas Belcher and Henry Gee.

Like a stage direction, his father's exit was followed by the arrival back from school of De Quincey's 'horrid pugilistic' eleven-year-old brother, William, whom he also barely knew. William is given more space by far in the *Autobiographic Sketches* than the adored Elizabeth, who features only as a corpse. All we know of Elizabeth in life is that she read books, drank tea and fell ill, while William – a rider of 'whirlwinds' and director of 'storms' – is endowed with many dimensions in page after page of vividly recalled, rolling anecdote. The role played by his older brother was of profound significance to Thomas, who always 'had a sort of feeling, or omen of anticipation, that possibly there was some being in the world who was fated to do him. . . a great and irreparable injury'. The identity of this being would shift with the years, but in the nursery it was William. Not yet at school, Thomas had no knowledge of children other than his own siblings, and William was the only boy he knew who had seen the world beyond Greenhay. An excessively energetic child, family lore put William Quincey down as a disrupter of the peace and Mrs Quincey sent him away at the first opportunity. School only nurtured his love of conflict, and by the time William returned home he 'would have fastened a quarrel upon his own shadow for presuming to run before him'.

William despised Thomas, and Thomas had 'a perfect craze for being despised. I doted on it, and considered contempt a sort of luxury that I was in continual fear of losing.' This pertinent observation goes to the heart of De Quincey's nature. He also had a craze for being afraid, which was fed by William on a nightly basis. Between the ages of seven and twelve, De Quincey was dominated by his brother. He pictured himself, under William's tyrannical rule, as an 'Irish hodman' running up and down a 'vast Jacob's ladder towering upwards to the clouds, mile after mile, league after league', trying to reach the 'top of any Babel' his

assailant might 'choose to build'. Whether he was seeking the face of
his dead sister or keeping up with the demands of his living brother, De
Quincey saw himself as a figure on a perpetual staircase.

William, he said, was a 'tiger'. He was everything that Thomas was
not: William was masculine while Thomas was, as he put it, 'effeminate';
William was wilful, athletic, bossy, noisy and boisterous while Thomas was
fragile and introverted. Unlike Thomas, William 'detested all books excepting only such as he happened to write himself', one such work being 'How
to raise a Ghost; and when you've got him down, how to keep him down'.
There was seemingly nothing that William could not do and he ruled over
the nursery like a sorcerer. Literally so: William practised necromancy,
'legerdemain' – or sleight of hand – and 'thaumatology', the study of mira-
cles. As well as magic and illusion, he fascinated his siblings with lectures
on natural philosophy and displays of pyrotechnics; to demonstrate the
laws of physics he strapped cats into parachutes and dropped them from
great heights. He boasted that he could walk on the ceiling like a fly and
blamed his failure to do so on the friction from the plaster of Paris; if the
ceiling were coated with ice, he insisted, it would be different. He then
constructed an apparatus for getting himself launched like a humming-
top in the hope that he could 'spin upon his own axis, and sleep upon his
own axis – perhaps he might even dream upon it'. These performances
only ended after one of his sisters orchestrated a mutiny, at which point
William devoted himself to the writing and production of a bloody tragedy
in which his siblings were all massacred in the first act.

His next project was to form an army with Thomas as a foot soldier, and
to wage a two-year-long war with the boys who worked in the cotton factory
which lay between Greenhay and the city of Manchester. De Quincey had a
country childhood but one in which the city, a place of speed, mayhem and
blank anarchy, loomed large as an alternative, more dangerous, life form.
Twice a day, on either side of a road called Oxford Street (a name with great
significance in De Quincey's narrative), the opposing sides hailed stones
at one another. It was a re-enactment of events in France, with Oxford
Street as the cordon sanitaire dividing the gentrified De Quincey brothers
from the sans-culottes who were 'slovenly and forlorn in their dress, often
unwashed, with hair totally neglected, and always covered in flakes of cotton'. William and Thomas, dressed by their mother in hessian boots and
trousers – the latter garment being 'at that time unheard of except amongst

sailors' – were mocked as 'bucks', which Thomas thought preferable to being labelled either cowards, thieves or murderers. But William considered the term an insult. On one occasion when he was taken prisoner of war, De Quincey, not a natural warrior, fell into the hands of a group of factory girls by whom he was petted; he was subsequently placed 'under arrest' by his brother for not performing his regimental duties. On these occasions his bedroom became a prison. During one period of incarceration he pictured a visit from one of his guardians:

> *Guardian.* – What is this I hear, child? What are you fretting about?
> *I.* – Because I'm under arrest.
> *Guard.* – Arrest! Nonsense! Who could put *you* under arrest? A child like *you*? Who was it?

Peace did not return to De Quincey's life until William, who had shown evidence of a talent for drawing, was sent to London to be apprenticed – in return for a fee of 1,000 guineas – to one of Europe's most successful artists, Philippe de Loutherbourg, who had been shown some of the boy's sketches. It was an ideal pairing of master and pupil: Loutherbourg, who was also an illusionist, occultist, engineer, scientist and faith-healer, specialised in creating stage effects for London theatres and had designed scenery and lighting for David Garrick. He was also an artist at the forefront of the apocalyptic sublime, and his invention of the 'Eidophusikon', a mechanical theatre, six foot by eight, was one of the sights of London. A precursor of the cinema, the Eidophusikon's most famous production, in 1782, was a Gothic movie scene from *Paradise Lost* showing a bronze city apparently composed of incombustible flames, entitled *Satan arraying his troops on the banks of the Fiery Lake, and the rising of the Palace of Pandemonium.* Coloured lights, sound effects, three-dimensional models and clockwork automata produced a spatialising of sin terrifying to the audience who came to look at the fallen angel and the hell that was within him.

Before breakfast on the day that William left Greenhay, a 'most splendid' day in a 'splendid June', the children were once again gathered on the front lawn of the house. Running alongside the garden was a brook with a bridge and a gate; De Quincey, constrained, as ever, by his brother's exuberance, stood alone by the running water while his siblings span around their leader on the grass. The sound of their play was broken suddenly by the roar of a mob in the direction of Oxford Street, and a large dog 'suddenly wheeled into view'. Barred from the garden by the closed gate and the brook, the dog – foam oozing from his mouth, his eyes 'glazed, and as if in a dreamy state' – stopped in his tracks and looked directly at De Quincey, whose sympathy went out to the persecuted dreamer. The mob, wielding pitchforks, then appeared in view and the pariah took off; the pursuit continued for a further twenty-four miles, ending only when the 'deranged' creature was eventually run over by a cart. The threshold moments in De Quincey's life were often accompanied by an image of disaster hurtling in his direction; separation from William and narrowly avoiding being mauled to death by a rabid dog blended into a seamless story: 'freedom won and death escaped, almost in the same hour'.

Without William to stand in his way, Thomas's own greatness would now shine. Another chapter had closed on another midsummer day. It was now the start of what he called 'a new book'.

———

De Quincey's mother provided the first enigma for the boy whose world was composed of signs and symbols. Described by her son as a handsome but 'freezing' figure who 'delighted not in infancy, nor infancy in her', Elizabeth Quincey was a stickler for order and hierarchy. From a military family, she addressed her servants only through the intermediary of the housekeeper, and her presence was compared by a housemaid to that of a ghost. Distant, unyielding and holy as a nun, every day for six years Mrs Quincey had her children 'roll out' of their nursery 'as mail-coaches go down daily to London', in order that she might inspect their appearance, from back posture to skin pallor. 'Were the lamps of our equipage clean and bright? Were the linch-pins secured?' Before pronouncing them 'to be in proper trim' she performed 'two ceremonies that to us were mysterious and allegorical': she sprinkled the hair and faces of each with lavender water and milk of roses, and bestowed on their foreheads a single kiss. For the rest of his life De Quincey pondered the significance of these rituals.

There are many indications, however, of Elizabeth Quincey's softer side, not least the pet name of 'Pink' given to her son, Richard, as a tribute to his prettiness. She also had a weakness for fashion and her children were paraded in the latest styles. De Quincey did not share his mother's concern with appearances but he inherited other characteristics and interests, including her restlessness and enthusiasm for houses. She also implanted in him, in a tale about nearly drowning as a child, an image that would return in his opium dreams. As his mother came near to death, 'a mighty theatre expanded within her brain. In a moment, in the twinkling of an eye, every act – every design of her past life lived again – arraying themselves not as a succession, but as parts of a coexistence. . . her consciousness became omnipresent at one moment to every feature in the infinite review.'

Mrs Quincey's primary legacy to her children was a sense of guilt: 'Trial by jury, English laws of evidence, all were forgotten; and we were found guilty on the bare affidavit of the angry accuser.' De Quincey grew up believing himself to be a great criminal; not only must he be responsible in some way for the catalogue of ills which had befallen his family, he was also to blame for his precocity and for any praise his intelligence might receive. 'Usually mothers defend their own cubs right or wrong,' he remembered. 'Not so my mother.' Should a visitor or a tutor compliment one of her progeny, Mrs Quincey, rather than flushing with maternal pride, would protest 'so solemnly. . . that we children held it a point of filial duty to believe ourselves the very scamps and refuse of the universe.'

Soon after his sister Elizabeth's death, Thomas began to receive pocket money. It was a generous amount, too large, he thought, for a boy his age, and he spent it in the local bookshop. He could never have enough books. 'Had the Vatican, the Bodleian, and the Bibliothèque du Roi all been emptied into one collection for my private gratification, little progress would have been made in this particular craving.' A regular customer, he soon found himself owing the bookseller, evidently touched by the earnestness of the child, three guineas. The debt unleashed in Thomas a great panic; 'deep anxiety now began to oppress me as to the course in which this mysterious (and indeed guilty) current of debt would finally flow. For the present it was frozen up; but I had some reason for thinking that Christmas thawed all debts whatsoever, and set them in motion towards innumerable pockets. Now *my* debt would be thawed with all the rest; and in what direction would it flow? There was no river that would carry it off to sea. . .' He dragged his anxiety behind him like a ball and chain.

At the same time as he feared drowning in bottomless debt, Thomas ordered from the bookseller a multi-volume history of ocean navigation. This inspired a new fear: given 'what a huge thing the sea was' and the

number of men and ships 'eternally running up and down it', the parts
of such a work would surely themselves reach 'infinity'. In a fresh panic
about the size of his purchase, he took himself with pounding heart to
the bookshop to ask 'how many volumes did he think it would extend
to?' The answer he was given would determine for the seven-year-old
boy 'whether for the next two years I was to have an hour of peace'. But
instead of speaking to the kindly bookseller he knew, De Quincey was
served by an unknown assistant who mocked his anxiety. 'How many
volumes? Oh! Really I can't say. Maybe a matter of 15,000, be the same
more or less.' '*More*?' Thomas said in horror, imagining 'supplements
to supplements' in a series which 'might positively *never* end'. In addition to the three guineas he already owed, the payments for this never-
ending series would themselves never end – they would 'stretch to the
crack of doom'. De Quincey had a vision of being trapped in a lifetime
of rapidly accelerating debt and eventually hanging from the end of a
rope, like Highwayman Higgins.

As the fantasy took hold he imagined a knock 'at the front door' of
Greenhay, and a wagoner with 'a bland voice' on the step announcing a
delivery for him. 'Looking out, I should perceive a procession of carts and
wagons, all advancing in measured movements; each in turn would present
its rear, deliver its cargo of volumes, by shooting them, like a load of coals,
on the lawn, and wheel off to the rear, by way of clearing the road for its
successors. . . Men would not know of my guilt merely, *they would see it*.'
To his horror, De Quincey realised that he was reliving – 'literally. . . in
myself' – one of the tales he and Elizabeth had read together in *Arabian
Nights*. In the story, a young man with a bundle of ropes – one of which
Thomas doubtless imagined noosed about his neck – finds himself in the
house of a wicked magician who has imprisoned a beautiful girl. The man
pledges his love to the maiden and when he hears the magician returning
he slips away, leaving the ropes behind. The next morning the magician
knocks at his own front door, enquiring for the figure to whom the ropes
belong. Whenever De Quincey and his sister reached this point in the story,
Thomas would play the part of the guilty lover nervously approaching the
door and say, in a quivering voice, 'Oh Mr Magician, those ropes cannot be
mine! They are far too good; and one wouldn't like, you know, to rob some
other poor young man. If you please, Mr Magician, I never had money
enough to buy so beautiful a set of ropes.'

But Elizabeth was now dead, and De Quincey saw himself saying those same lines, in that same voice, to the wagoner who would soon be depositing on the front lawn the wagonloads of books.

Books and infinity were bound together for De Quincey, who 'fell', he said, 'into a downright midsummer madness' at the thought of there being 'one hundred thousand books' that he would never be able to read, or pictures that he would never see, or pieces of music that he would never hear. 'Every man and woman,' he told himself, 'was a most interesting book, if one knew how to read them. Here opened upon me a new world of misery; for, if books and works of art existed by millions, men existed by hundreds of millions. . . Nay, my madness took yet a higher flight. . .'

According to legend it is impossible to read *Arabian Nights* to the end. As vengeance against his faithless first wife, the king swears to take a new bride every few days and have her slaughtered: Scheherazade, his latest queen, diverts her husband's bloodlust with a ceaseless flow of tales. *Arabian Nights* is composed of stories within other stories which themselves contain further stories, all of which, with their attendant magicians, necromancers, illusionists, caliphs, genies and princes blend into one endless and ever-echoing palimpsest. Reading them through the filter of De Quincey's young mind there is clearly a resemblance between the fictional Baghdad of spires, alleyways and subterranean worlds and his later descriptions of East London. *Arabian Nights*, we also note, is a book without an author, which would have induced in the child endless wonder.

Jorge Luis Borges suggests that the Romantic movement began at the moment *Arabian Nights* was first read in France, in the translation by Antoine Galland between 1704 and 1717. It was through *Arabian Nights* that Coleridge had became 'habituated to the *vast*', and De Quincey's own preoccupation with the sublime may well have seeded itself with these nursery tales which he knew only in an annotated edition. His love for Gothic novels – the popular fiction of the day – was certainly born at this point. He would have preferred the French title, *Les Mille et Une Nuits*, because, as Borges puts it, 'To say "a thousand nights" is to say infinite nights, countless nights, endless nights. To say "a thousand and one nights" is to add to infinity. The title contains the suggestion of an infinite book.'

The story of Aladdin particularly fascinated De Quincey. 'The sublimity which it evoked was mysterious and unfathomable. . . made restless by the blind sense which I had of its grandeur, I could not for

a moment succeed in finding out *why* it should be grand.' Here was
an example, De Quincey said, of the power of 'involutes', a word he
took from conchology (an involute shell is intricately spiral or whorled)
but whose meaning is similar to the 'spots of time' described in Book
Eleventh of *The Prelude*. Wordsworth's spots of time are particular experiences (a drowned man rising bolt upright from the bottom of the
lake) or scenes of imaginative convergence (a rock, a naked pool, a beacon, a woman with a basket on her head, a single sheep, a blasted tree)
that penetrate the memory and allow us 'to mount,/ When high, more
high, and lift[. . .] us up when fallen.' De Quincey described as involutes those times, like the day he had crept into Elizabeth's bedroom,
where 'the materials of future thought or feeling' are 'carried impercep-
tibly into the mind as vegetable seeds are carried variously combined
through the atmosphere'. The experience is imbued with a complex
of heightened imaginative responses forming 'compound experiences
incapable of being disentangled'. De Quincey's autobiographical writing is saturated with such moments.

It was the beginning of 'Aladdin' which took on for him the power
of an involute. This is how he remembered it:

> At the opening of the tale a magician living in the central depths of Africa
> is introduced to us as one made aware by his secret art of an enchanted
> lamp. . . The lamp is imprisoned in subterraneous chambers, and from
> these it can be released only by the hands of an innocent child. But this is
> not enough: the child must have a special horoscope written in the stars,
> or else a peculiar destiny written in his constitution, entitling him to take
> possession of the lamp. Where shall such a child be found?. . . The magi-
> cian knows: he applies his ear to the earth; he listens to the innumerable
> sounds of footsteps that at the moment of his experiment are tormenting
> the surface of the globe; and amongst them all, at a distance of six thousand
> miles, playing in the streets of Bagdad, he distinguishes the peculiar steps
> of the child Aladdin.

So the magician 'fastens his murderous intention upon one insulated
tread', and in the 'flying footsteps' of the small boy he reads an 'alpha-
bet' of 'secret hieroglyphics'. The world, young Thomas understood as
he trembled before these pages, was composed of correspondences – 'so

many languages and ciphers that somewhere have their corresponding keys'.

But this image is nowhere to be found in 'Aladdin'. In the version of
Arabian Nights read in the De Quincey household the magician is guided
by the stars to the boy who is capable of exhuming the lamp; he does not
put his ear to the ground to catch his 'flying footsteps'. Like so many of
the formative memories layered in De Quincey's personal mythology, the
origins of the footsteps are vaporous. The image may have come from a
childhood dream, or from listening out for the sound of his father's carriage on the distant road; or perhaps it was the other way round and the
'memory' of his dying father's return home was the result of his 'memory' of the opening scene of 'Aladdin'. Like many of the experiences he
described as involutes, this one was not actual at all.

In the summer of 1797, after William departed for London, Elizabeth
Quincey put Greenhay on the market and moved the family 170 miles
south-west, to the watering-hole of Bath in Somerset. Now that the trading connection with Manchester was over, there was no reason to continue in the manufacturing North. On a stormy night in August, the
house she had built for £6,000 was sold to the only bidder for £2,500.
De Quincey had entered the world of rapidly disappearing money. Had
his mother waited a few years, he later believed, she would have received
six times that sum, but Elizabeth Quincey, like many a widow, wanted to
start a new chapter herself.

North Parade, Bath, where De Quincey first read Wordsworth, the 'greatest event in the unfolding of my own mind'.

Childhood and Schooltime

Genius of Burke!

Wordsworth, *The Prelude*, Book Seventh

Number 11, North Parade was a Georgian terrace fronted with beehive-yellow stone, a stroll away from the Abbey and the Grand Pump Room. In the other direction, it leads into Pulteney Street where in *Northanger Abbey* – written during the years that De Quincey lived in Bath – seventeen-year-old Catherine Morland took lodgings with Mr and Mrs Allen for the winter season. Catherine found Bath disappointingly jolly, containing none of the isolation and gloom of Ann Radcliffe's *The Mysteries of Udolpho*. The Assembly Rooms were over-hot and over-full, and the roads so cluttered they were impossible to cross.

The contrast between life at Greenhay and life on North Parade could not have been greater, and this was evidently Elizabeth Quincey's aim; she was expanding into her freedom. She now had a rented house rather than the burden of her own home, with windows that looked onto other windows rather than over lawns and across fields. She laid her carriage up in a coach house, and moved around the town by sedan chair.

Enclosed within a lush green valley, Bath is an assemblage of squares, circuses and crescents. Tobias Smollett, in *The Expedition of Humphry Clinker*, predicted that the city would soon also have a 'star', after which 'all the signs of the Zodiac' would be 'exhibited in the architecture at Bath'. The soft inland murmur of the River Avon could be heard from North Parade, and its presence felt in other ways too; Mrs Quincey battled with the damp and in 1799, when the river burst its banks, the damage she faced would have been immense. It was a small price to pay. Having lived amongst Northern philosophers for the sake of her husband, Elizabeth Quincey arrived here with the aim of launching her children, the youngest of whom was three, on the social ladder. No more mummified corpses in clock cases for Thomas; from now on her morbid and self-absorbed son would look outwards rather than inwards, and having formerly known only siblings, servants, family friends and private tutors, he would start to mix with the right sort. 'What a delightful place Bath is,' Jane Austen's Mrs Allen repeatedly says, 'and how pleasant it would be if we had any acquaintance here!' Mrs Quincey wasted no time in getting to know the neighbours.

———

Bath Abbey was built as the result of a dream. Bishop Oliver King had a vision of an olive tree from which ladders reached into the far blue sky. Looking up at the west front, De Quincey could see angels climbing up to the throne of God on their stone steps. At the eastern end is a vast window, extending the full height of the wall, through which the morning sun still shines in torrents of splendour, irradiating the vaulting, nave, aisles, bays and lanes. For a child used to the glass of his parish church in Manchester, the sublimity of such a scene was overwhelming; there could be no finer window through which to seek the face of Elizabeth formed by billowy clouds.

Along the walls are 700 memorials, one of which, on the south side, commemorates Richard Nash, Master of Ceremonies and self-crowned 'King' of Bath. 'Beau' Nash, as he was known, had died in 1761, but his influence had by no means been forgotten. Every street bore his mark. Bath was Nash's invention, and for fifty-seven years it had been his kingdom. Arriving in 1704, Nash had taken over the management of the sleepy town much as one might a private member's club. Under his eye, Bath became a stately pleasure dome; Nash was responsible for the Assembly Rooms with their ballroom, tea room, card room, and the Octagon, where nightly concerts were held. To accommodate the influx of tourists, he oversaw the construction of the rows of Palladian revival buildings which posed as palaces but were actually lodging houses. If London, as De Quincey would discover, was the city of disappearances,

Bath was the city of appearances. The classical façades of many of the finest buildings, such as North Parade itself, were designed by John Wood the elder; purchasers bought a length of John Wood frontage and then employed their own architect to construct the interior according to their own requirements. De Quincey's new home, built in 1741, was one of many Bath houses with a Queen Anne front and a Mary Anne back.

While maintaining its function as a health resort, Nash turned Bath into a centre of gossip, style and fashion. During De Quincey's childhood waistlines were growing higher, necklines were sinking lower; fabrics were light, skirts flowed and shoes had rounded heels. Bath was the only city in England designed entirely for diversion – as Monaco is today – and the first urban centre in which aristocrats and the newly rich merchant classes mingled on an equal footing. Evenings were filled with music, fireworks and the roaring of swells: 'Another stupid party last night,' wrote Jane Austen to her sister during one of her visits. Smollett described the city as 'the very centre of racket and dissipation', a place obsessed with matrimony or what he called 'mattermoney'. This was civilised living as spectacle, and still a work in progress. The year before the Quinceys arrived, the Pump Room had been little more than scaffolding and workmen whistling; Sydney Gardens, where Thomas went to read, was spanking new. Here he found a maze, a grotto, and the sort of sham ruined castle which would have thrilled Catherine Morland.

Until recently, Ann Radcliffe herself had been a resident of Bath and in 1801 Jane Austen and her family would move to a house in Sydney Place, overlooking Sydney Gardens. With the intersection of Ann Radcliffe and Jane Austen we see one of the contradictions of the age in which De Quincey was raised. The paranoid Gothic, with its inwardly recessive architecture, rested alongside what Horace Walpole called the 'cold reason' of Enlightenment rationality. Nailing his colours to the Gothic, De Quincey never moved on. His daughter Emily later explained that 'no one will make much out of my father who does not take in the extreme mixture of childish folly joined to a great intellect. The novels of his youth were of the Mrs Radcliffe order, full of mysteries, murders, highwaymen, mysterious people and dark corners. . . he never got beyond the Mrs Radcliffe stage and he was but a poor judge of a novel.'

He would remain as unaware of Jane Austen's novels as she would of Thomas De Quincey's essays. And while Bath stifled Austen, who fell into silence and depression when she lived here, the city had the opposite effect on De Quincey, who absorbed all it had to offer. It has been suggested that having previously enjoyed a country childhood, living in North Parade must have been 'purgatory' for De Quincey. But it was the making of him.

Twenty years earlier, 11 North Parade had been home to the Earl of Clare, patron of Oliver Goldsmith, and Goldsmith – another of De Quincey's favourite authors – had stayed in the house. But the most recent occupant was none other than Edmund Burke, politician, polemicist and author of the decade's most talked-about book, *Reflections on the Revolution in France*. Burke, whose wife was born in Bath and whose doctor was based here, occupied 11 North Parade for the first six months of 1797, moving out a month before the Quinceys moved in. He had been, as De Quincey put it, in 'decaying condition', and would die at home on his estate in July that year.

Thomas De Quincey's biographers pass over in a sentence the coincidence that he replaced Burke in North Parade, as though this experience made no impression on the boy who went on to become a house tourist. It was now that De Quincey's sense of entitlement set root; he was inhabiting the former rooms of the man who was the spirit of the age. Burke was also the spirit of the house; De Quincey was charging down stairs that Burke had ascended, slamming doors that Burke himself, just weeks earlier, had opened, and sitting at the desk where Burke had penned his last pamphlet, 'Letters on a Regicide Peace'. Not knowing that the great man had left town, the 'crowds of inquirers' who called to pay their respects were greeted by young Thomas at the door instead. Aged eleven, De Quincey found himself the representative of Edmund Burke.

If Elizabeth Quincey had not already purchased *Reflections on the Revolution in France* she would certainly have got hold of a copy now, when a French invasion was expected at any moment. The tension was palpable; seventy miles south, in the Quantock Hills, Wordsworth and Coleridge, planning their forthcoming *Lyrical Ballads* as they strode the coastline, were thought by the locals to be French spies.

'Reflections', published in 1790, was an antidote to the Francophilia popular amongst English intellectuals; selling 7,000 copies in the first two weeks, it triggered a debate about liberty which split Burke's own Whig party. His position on the French Revolution was the opposite of parliamentary colleagues such as Fox, and of fledgling poets like Wordsworth and Coleridge. Wordsworth, visiting France in 1790, saw 'a People risen up,/ Fresh as the Morning Star'. For Burke, the 'morning star' was Marie Antoinette herself, 'just above the horizon. . . glittering [with] life and splendour and joy'. Back on earth were what Burke described as the tyrannical 'swinish multitude', a phrase De Quincey loved to repeat when he referred to crowds. Thomas Paine, who remarked that Burke pitied the plumage but forgot the dying bird, responded to *Reflections* with the *Rights of Man*, published the following year. 'The very idea of hereditary legislation,' Paine wrote in his strong, plain prose, 'is as inconsistent as that of hereditary judges, or hereditary juries; and as absurd as an hereditary mathematician, or an hereditary wise man; and as ridiculous as an hereditary poet laureate.' The murder of the French king and queen and the subsequent Terror proved Burke right in his fears for France, but then, as Fox famously said: 'Burke is often right, only he was right too soon.'

His lament for a country in which 'the age of chivalry' had been replaced by 'sophisters, calculators and economists' was wholeheartedly shared by De Quincey, 'bred up' by his mother 'in a frenzied horror of Jacobinism' and 'French excesses'. Flinging a knife to the floor in a parliamentary debate, Burke had proclaimed it his 'object to keep the French infection from this country, their principles from our minds and their daggers from our hearts. . . When they smile, I see blood trickling down their faces.' De Quincey likewise feared the bloodthirsty French, incarnated in Bonaparte, the bogeyman of his childhood, and in the opening paragraph of *Confessions of an English Opium-Eater* he quoted Burke's description of the Jacobins 'rudely' tearing off 'the decent drapery of life'.

Burke's first book, *A Philosophical Enquiry into the Origin of our Ideas of the Sublime and Beautiful*, had been in the library at Greenhay. A beguiling treatise on the most fashionable subject of the age, the ideas expressed in the *Enquiry* were to influence De Quincey as much as those in 'Reflections'. If the Enlightenment venerated the beautiful, the Romantic age would aspire to the sublime. The difference between the sublime and the beautiful had become a national obsession and Burke, the first writer to attempt a categorisation of aesthetic responses, drew the distinction along psychological lines: the sublime is linked to

horror, gloom and infinity, while we find beautiful those things that
are calm, safe and small. The beautiful gives pleasure and relaxes the
body, while sublimity contains the destructive element. 'Suddenness'
is sublime while 'smoothness' is beautiful; a parish church is beautiful,
a cathedral sublime; a bull is sublime while a cow is beautiful; a king
is, of course, sublime – as is everything grand and powerful. Burke's
suggestion that all subjects can 'branch out to infinity' chimed with De
Quincey's own thinking, as did his belief that 'clear ideas are little ideas'
and the 'ruling principle of the sublime' is 'terror'.

———

To have taken over these hallowed rooms was also a feather in Elizabeth
Quincey's cap. De Quincey's mother was a celebrity hunter and around the
corner from North Parade, at 76 Great Pulteney Street, lived the celebrated
Hannah More. Like Burke, Hannah More was both a household name and
a moral icon. Burke had been one of Mrs More's close friends, and Mrs
More now became one of Mrs Quincey's close friends. So Mrs Quincey
balanced pleasure and prestige with a lesson in high-toned evangelicalism.

There were two acts to More's life, and her intimacy with Elizabeth
Quincey was formed at the point where she exchanged the first for
the second. In the 1770s, More, an aspiring poet and playwright, had
taken herself from Bristol to London to meet the actor-director David
Garrick. Under Garrick's patronage, she had enjoyed success on the
stage with her plays *The Inflexible Captive* and *Percy*. Brimful of confidence, Hannah More, said Hester Thrale, was 'the cleverest of all us
female wits', and her fame was sealed in 1779, when, posing in a Greek
toga alongside the artist Angelica Kauffman, the soprano Elizabeth
Linley Sheridan, and six other female luminaries, Hannah More was
included in Richard Samuel's painting *The Nine Living Muses*. After a
decade of gadding about in Covent Garden, she joined the Clapham
Sect, a group of religious social reformers with William Wilberforce,
a man much admired by De Quincey's father, at its prow. More then
returned to her native West Country to preach patience to the rural
poor and provide spiritual guidance during a time of political turbulence. The focus of her work when she met Elizabeth Quincey was
the moral education of the lower orders; as well as setting up schools

across Somerset, More had been immersed in the writing, production and nationwide distribution of 140 'Cheap Repository Tracts' whose purpose was to point out the pitfalls of drunkenness, sloth, gambling and debauchery, and show that salvation could be found in upward mobility. Despite widescale ridicule, More's 'Tracts' were remarkably successful; by 1797, when Elizabeth Quincey began to introduce them to her own children, two million copies had been sold.

De Quincey later participated in the national sport of Hannah More-baiting, but the impact on his childhood of 'Holy Hannah', as he referred to her, was formidable and he continued to visit her well into his twenties. He would describe several figures as his 'first literary acquaintance', but More claims the honour. Apart from his father, the only writer De Quincey had ever known was Dr Percival, the physician who had cut open his sister's head. Hannah More was a definite improvement. De Quincey was always quick to reveal that his mother was an intimate of Mrs More and to mock, as only an insider could, her society. In later letters to the Wordsworths, he derided her conversation as 'epigrammatic' and 'full of trite quotations', and in a waspish essay written on her death in 1833, he remembered with pride how, in her presence, he never 'travelled one hair's breadth beyond the line of frigid and distant politeness'. But it is hard to see the God-fearing boy being offensive to the woman who had God, and celebrity, on her side. De Quincey's exquisite manners were remarked upon throughout his life. His politeness was excessive and bewildering to those he met; he addressed servants, children, adults and friends in the same grave and elaborate formulations, using an English from a bygone age. The grand solemnity of his speech worked as a protective shield, his rhetorical flourishes creating a barrier between himself and the outside world.

In addition to her own celebrity, Mrs More knew, as De Quincey conceded, 'everybody of celebrity in the last age', including Dr Johnson, his father's favourite author, and Horace Walpole, godfather of the English Gothic, whose sham castle outside London, Strawberry Hill, was one of the most famous houses in England. Hannah More knew everyone of celebrity in the present age as well; De Quincey described meeting the actress Mrs Siddons in Mrs More's drawing room, which suggests that Holy Hannah had not forsaken the theatre as entirely frivolous. Her piety never got in the way of her appreciation of glamour; in this sense More was more morally flexible than Elizabeth Quincey, who considered the

theatre a den of iniquity. Compared to his mother, Mrs More was positively racy, and during his visits to her house De Quincey would draw
from her anecdotes of 'Edmund Burke – Garrick – Mrs Montague and
her society – Dr Johnson &c'. It was De Quincey's habit to scorn the people to whom he owed a debt, and he owed everything to Hannah More.

He also owed a good deal to the mother from whom he would later
distance himself. It was Elizabeth Quincey who taught Thomas to
attach his life to that of the writer he most admired, to position himself
as a planet orbiting a sun.

———

De Quincey, who had never been to school before, now started at Bath
grammar where he 'was honoured as never was man or boy since Mordecai
the Jew'. A classical scholar of note, 'at thirteen,' he boasted, 'I wrote
Greek with ease. . . owing to the practice of daily reading of the newspapers into the best Greek I could furnish extempore.' His brilliance won
him the admiration of his teachers and his arrogance provoked the taunts
of his peers; another schoolboy war ensued, only this time De Quincey,
who had grown boisterous and spirited, fought his side alone.

In January 1799 a teacher, aiming his cane at the shoulder of a
miscreant pupil, accidentally landed the blow on De Quincey's head
instead. Preternaturally anxious since his sister's death about damage to
the skull, De Quincey was thrown into a panic, and the physicians who
attended his injury were sufficiently alarmed by his expressions of pain
to suggest trepanning. Instead, the boy's hair was shaved and six suck-
ing leeches applied to the wound. For the next three weeks, as Thomas
wrote in a letter to his elder sister, Mary, currently at school in Bristol,
'I neither read, nor wrote, nor talked, nor eat [*sic*] meat, nor went out
of the back drawing-room, except when I went to bed. In the first week
I read for a quarter of an hour per day! and eat a little bit of meat; but
I did not write. I now do everything as I used to do, except dancing,
running, drinking wine. I am not to go to school till Easter.'

De Quincey was evidently in good humour. He makes a joke about his
'unhappy pate! worthy of a better fate', refers to 'Mademoiselle's ball, which
was put off (as I suppose) on my account', and to his smart new friend
'young Lord Westport', who will be coming soon to dine at North Parade;

he signs off as 'Tabitha Quincey', Tabitha being the name of the woman raised from the dead by St Peter – the undead being one of De Quincey's serious preoccupations, disguised here as a joke. The evidence suggests that before he was in his teens, Thomas was fond of dancing and drinking, and capable of manipulating a duo of doctors into being prepared to drill a hole through his skull. During his years in Bath, De Quincey was anything but the fragile melancholic he otherwise describes himself as having been.

He sufficiently exaggerated his frailty to earn a few months curled up in bed, being read to by his mother. The number of books they covered was 'past all counting', recalled De Quincey, and included Milton's *Paradise Lost*. This he described as 'not a book amongst books, not a poem amongst poems, but a central force amongst forces', and De Quincey would continually describe his own life as a fall from Paradise. There is always a gain to illness, and De Quincey found that maternal tenderness and a ceaseless supply of literature were the rewards of this one – his mother thawed when her son lay helpless between the sheets. The tenderness was not to last: when his headmaster, a brilliant and celebrated scholar himself, implored Mrs Quincey to return her son to school, she was appalled by the compliments lavished on the child's intelligence and to preserve Thomas's modesty she withdrew him immediately. De Quincey's education was now placed in the hands of an exiled French nobleman with romantic designs on his employer. The widow was evidently a catch, and De Quincey took on the role of driving his mother's suitors away. Accordingly, he and his two younger brothers behaved as badly as possible, spending the school hours making faces through the window at the old lady who lived opposite. When the exasperated neighbour complained, Thomas apologised with such formality and charm that she thought him quite the nicest boy she had ever met. Meanwhile, the tutor returned to his battered country without having won the hand of Mrs Quincey, who would never remarry.

At about this time, they heard that William, aged seventeen, had died from typhoid fever in London; this was presumably another reason for keeping Thomas at home. Three of his seven siblings, as well as his father, were now dead and De Quincey had become the male head of the family. The death of his father registered as wheels he was waiting to hear on a distant road; Jane's death made its impact only when Elizabeth died; Elizabeth's death took the form of the central tragedy of his life; and William's death was described as the answer to a prayer. De Quincey expressed no ambivalence

about this, and no guilt over his absence of grief. William '*had* controlled,'
he later wrote, 'and for years to come *would have* controlled, the free spontaneous movements of a contemplative dreamer like myself.' De Quincey
had, however, luxuriated in this control and abandoned himself to his
own slavish position; the sudden termination of the dynamic on which
his identity was constructed was like the removal of scaffolding around an
unfinished building. Nor was the high romance of William's status as the
family pariah lost on him. His brother was a warrior, a tiger, a destroyer of
domestic calm, whose adventure in London – a place that De Quincey had
only ever read about – had ended in tragedy.

   William's death did not mean, any more than Elizabeth's death, that
he disappeared from De Quincey's mind. The deaths of his siblings made
their power over him all the more potent. The direction of his own life
began to shadow that of his dead brother: just as William had been sent
away to school when he became unmanageable, Thomas was now enrolled
at a small boarding school in a nearby village called Winkfield, 'of which
the chief recommendation lay in the religious character of the master'. The
staff had nothing to teach him, and he did much of the Latin and Greek
teaching himself. There was, he told his mother, 'no emulation, no ambition, nothing to contend for – no honours to excite one'. Mrs Quincey
had not only failed to protect her son from vanity but in so doing, he
informed her, she had destroyed his education. Effortlessly at the top of
the class, De Quincey was worshipped more by the pupils at Winkfield
than he had been by the headmaster at Bath grammar. Bored, miserable,
and still fretting about his head injury, he divided his school fellows into
rival bands of Greeks and Trojans, and organised mock battles.

Ten miles west of genteel Bath lay her sister city: teeming, money-
grubbing, commercial Bristol, 'the greatest, the richest, the best port of
trade in Great Britain', as Daniel Defoe described it in 1725, 'London
only excepted'. A walled and gated citadel composed of narrow streets,
with quays high enough to accommodate forty-foot tides, Bristol had
a skyline of smoking glass kilns, which Alexander Pope compared to
pyramids. Bristol, said Pope, was like 'Wapping or Southwark [but] ten
times as big'. The trade was seaborne: ships returned here from Spain,

America, the Caribbean and the Barbary Coast, laden with soap, salt, leather, gunpowder, cheese, stockings, wine, wool and, of course, slaves. Bristol was England's premier slave port; twenty slaving voyages a year set out from the city's two quays. Edmund Burke had been MP for Bristol, and Hannah More was raised here; before the trade in human beings led her to become an abolitionist, the city's theatres had inspired her to become a playwright. More's sisters ran a respected School for Young Ladies in Trinity Street, near College Green, and De Quincey's own sister, Mary, was at school in Bristol.

There was a great deal of traffic between Bristol and Bath, and a great deal in Bristol to feed De Quincey's imagination. In College Green in 1764, Highwayman Higgins, whose skeleton he knew so well, had murdered the rich widow and her servant. Visiting the house in which the crime had taken place, De Quincey found it still unoccupied: 'forty years had not cicatrised the bloody remembrance; and, to this day, perhaps, it remains amongst the gloomy traditions of Bristol'. It was in Bristol that Richard Savage, the murderer and poet immortalised in Samuel Johnson's brief biography *The Life of Savage*, had died in a debtors' prison in 1743, cursing the city of 'upstarts and mushrooms' and 'proud relentless hearts'. Thomas Chatterton, born here ten years later, who identified with Savage ('Another Savage to be starv'd in me') also loathed Bristol, calling it a 'despicable place', a 'mercenary cell', a 'city of commerce and avarice' inhabited by 'little, mean, and contemptible men', no more than 'twenty' of whom could read.

Never had a city been more associated with a writer than Bristol was with the poet immortalised by Wordsworth in 'Resolution and Independence' as 'the marvellous boy. . . that perished in his prime'. Chatterton, the first of the Romantics, was raised in the school house on Pyle Street, Redcliffe Hill, in the shade of St Mary Redcliffe, still the grandest of all English parish churches. A Gothic masterpiece standing proud above the harbour where she towered over the masts of the ships, the church was the last thing mariners saw when they set sail and the first thing they saw as they returned home. Her medieval structure was substantially restored in the fifteenth century by Sir William Canynges, a local cloth and shipping merchant who, following the death of his wife, found his calling and joined the priesthood. Canynges is commemorated twice in the south transept of St Mary Redcliffe: in one effigy he lies, dressed in the finery of a merchant, alongside his spouse; in another he lies alone in the priestly garb of the Dean of Westbury. Thomas Chatterton would bestow on Canynges a third identity, as patron to the poet Thomas Rowley.

Chatterton's father, a sexton of the church, died when his son was still in the womb, and Chatterton would spend the best part of his brief life reinventing the world which existed before he was born. His family had been sextons of St Mary Redcliffe for generations, and as such he considered the church both his birthright and his playground. He whiled away the hours beneath its forest of flying buttresses, hexagonal vaults and polygonal arches. Drifting amongst the effigies and tombs he fantasised about the noble figures commemorated here, and the chivalric age gone by. Leaning with his book against the graveyard headstones he would occasionally look up to 'fix his eyes upon the church' in a state of 'trance' or 'ecstasy'.

The most magnificent part of St Mary Redcliffe is still the north porch, facing what would then have been the harbour. Inspired by the Moorish architecture of North Africa and Spain, its striking crisscross design would not be out of place in a tale of *Arabian Nights*. Through this oriental gateway is a spiral staircase, at the top of which can be found the muniment room whose chests contained, as Mrs Chatterton put it, 'a miscellaneous collection of odds and ends – bundles of shrivelled parchment covered with strange hieroglyphics'. Treated in a work-a-day fashion by Chatterton's father, these bundles found their way from the church to the school house where they were turned into dustjackets for books, splints to light fires, and knitting patterns for Mrs Chatterton; they also provided young Chatterton with his first experience of black-lettering. Until the age of seven he had shown no enthusiasm for reading and had been regarded by his teachers as a dunce; Chatterton now read everything he could get his hands on, so long as it was in Black Letter.

Aged sixteen he obtained the key for the muniment room from his uncle – then the church sexton – and began to explore the treasures himself. It was here that Thomas Rowley, blind monk and poet, began to take shape in his mind. Rowley was Chatterton's other self, his medieval double, a figure from another realm who existed only in an ornamental English of Chatterton's own construction. With the invention of Rowley came a poetry that bore no relation to the clipped etiquette of neoclassical couplets found in mid-eighteenth-century verse: Chatterton created a copy without an original. His minstrel was given an expansive, melodic voice in which he sang ballads of strange fragility and beauty; by embellishing spellings he changed the flavour of familiar words such as *wyllowe*, *waterre*, *wytches*, and *leathalle tyde*. Rowley's city returned to its former name of 'Bristowe', and Chatterton began to endow his birthplace with a noble past. Bristowe was everything that Bristol was not; a Camelot of culture, taste and sensibility presided over by Rowley's patron, the 'gloryous' Sir William Canynges.

Once Thomas Rowley was conceived, there was no stopping Thomas Chatterton. Rowley the monk was a lover of beauty who sang in praise of St Mary Redcliffe ('the pride of Bristowe and the Westerne lande. . . Greater than can by Rowlies pen be scande'), in praise of William Canynges ('Such is greate Conynge's mind when pared to God elate'), in praise of the splendid 'Kingdom of Lyghte' in which he was honoured to live. Rowley's works, smeared with yellow ochre and lamp charcoal to make them look old, were presented to the gullible citizens of Bristol as found documents. The muniment room of St Mary Redcliffe – or 'Radclift' as Rowley called it – was overflowing, so Chatterton explained, with manuscripts by the blind poet.

Chatterton had a precedent for his hoax: a similar trick had been played by Horace Walpole in a Gothic novel he published in 1764. The full title of Walpole's novel was *The Castle of Otranto: A Story. Translated by William Marshal, Gent. From the Original Italian of Onuphrio Muralto, Canon of the Church of St Nicholas at Otranto*. It purported to be a translation of an Italian manuscript, 'printed in the Black Letter in the year 1529', discovered in the library of 'an ancient Catholic family in the North of England', and brought to the attention of the reading public by William Marshal, the pseudonym of Walpole. In the second edition of the book Walpole dropped his mask and revealed his authorship; the public were entertained, and critics no more than mildly embarrassed. It was, said Sir Walter Scott, 'the first modern attempt to found a tale of amusing fiction upon the basis of the ancient romances of chivalry'. Chatterton assumed that if his cover was blown, it would be greeted in a similarly jocular fashion.

While the Rowley industry was churning away in the lumber room at the top of the house, Chatterton tested his powers of persuasion by practising a

fraud of a different kind. He convinced a lowborn pewterer named Burgum
that he had found, also in the muniment room, evidence that the Burgum
family were originally the De Berghams, whose pedigree could be traced
from the time of William the Conqueror. Burgum was descended from
one of the noblest families of the day: 'Simon de Leyncte Lyze, alias Senliz,
who married Matilda, daughter of Waltheof, Earl of Northumberland,
Northampton and Huntingdon' and so forth, the names spreading over
page after page. The baroque document, exquisitely penned by Chatterton
and presented to Burgum as evidence of the pewterer's impressive heritage, contained a complex roll call of fathers, sons, marriages and offspring,
including mention of a man called Redcliffe De Chatterton of Chatterton,
the heir general of many families. There was a bitterness to this con, played
on a susceptible man by an arrogant boy. Chatterton felt that Burgum, a
man on the make, got what he deserved, but while mocking the vulgarity
of Bristol's inhabitants, he indulged, to what might be called a pathological
degree, his own desire to hail from a more noble place. Chatterton was as
serious in his reinvention of Bristol as Beau Nash had been in his reinvention of Bath; and one senses that there was no more humour intended in
his conjuring of 'Redcliffe De Chatterton' than there was in the 'De' which
Elizabeth Quincey now added to her own family's name. The De Quinceys,
she explained to her children and her neighbours, could be traced back to
the time of William the Conqueror.

Chatterton left the works of Thomas Rowley behind in April 1770
and lit out for London, following in the footsteps of other ambitious
writers, such as Samuel Johnson and Oliver Goldsmith. 'Bristol's mercantile walls were never destined to hold me,' he announced on his
arrival. 'There, I was out of my element. Now I am in it – London! Good
God! How superior is London to that despicable place Bristol – here
is none of your little meannesses, none of your mercenary securities,
which disgrace that miserable hamlet.' He survived here for only four
months, but they were months of astonishing productivity. Presenting
himself to the city's newspaper and magazine editors, Chatterton was
commissioned by them all and penned, in his cramped attic bedroom
in Holborn, over fifty-six articles, many satirical. His journalism was
still appearing in print a year after his death.

During the height of the summer, Chatterton swallowed a lethal dose
of arsenic and opium. He was seventeen, and his body was found by the

landlady of his room on Brook Street, the appropriately named Mrs Angel. He was lying on the bed beneath the window, the sun streaming through. The door had been locked and on the floor around him, scattered like snow, were torn-up pieces of manuscript. Chatterton took the secret of Thomas Rowley's identity with him to the grave, but it is unclear where his grave actually was. His body may have been buried in London, it may have been removed to Bristol, or it may have been used for dissection by doctors.

Thomas Chatterton had died in obscurity, but Thomas Rowley became famous. Queues of tourists, including Samuel Johnson, made their way up the narrow staircase to inspect the now famous 'Muniment Room'. The first Rowley poem was published in 1772, and in 1777 Thomas Tyrwhitt brought out a scholarly edition of *Poems, Supposed to have been written at Bristol, by Thomas Rowley and Others*. In the same year Rowley was included in a major volume on the *History of English Poetry* edited by the future Poet Laureate, yet another Thomas – Thomas Warton. Before long, the doubts set in: had Rowley ever existed, or was he the invention of the boy Chatterton? If Rowley and Chatterton were the same person, was Chatterton an artist of rare skill or, as the red-faced Thomas Warton later put it, no more than an 'adventurer, a professed hireling in the trade of literature. . . artful, enterprising, unprincipled, indigent, and compelled to subsist by expedients'? By the time Thomas De Quincey was born, it was Chatterton-the-forger who was famous, while Rowley was forgotten.

The bulk of De Quincey's knowledge of Chatterton almost certainly came from Sir Herbert Croft's epistolary novel, *Love and Madness: A Story Too True*, published in 1780. This curious work, which is not about Chatterton at all, nonetheless contains a long biographical digression on the boy's life and death which is based on research undertaken by Croft himself, who reproduced private letters sent from Chatterton in London to his family in Bristol, purloined from the poet's grieving sister. In order to get a sense of his last days, Croft also interviewed Chatterton's Brook Street neighbours. The figure he presents in *Love and Madness* is a hack with a fatal pride and an active libido, who would sooner starve than admit defeat. De Quincey learned from these pages that Chatterton had 'presided over his playmates as their master and they his hired servants', and that he had tried to win the patronage of Horace Walpole. Knowing that Walpole was compiling a study of English art, Chatterton sent him some of Rowley's poetry and a document called 'The Ryse of Peyncteynge yn

Englade', which he suggested Walpole might find useful. Suspecting that
he was being made fun of, Walpole rebuffed Chatterton's advances; a cruel
rejection, it was later said, which killed poor Chatterton. Croft pointed his
finger at Walpole, but he also accused Bristol itself of driving Chatterton
away, and London of 'murdering' her newest young poet. Furthermore,
Croft raised the issue of Chatterton's lost corpse. 'Tell me, Bristol,' he asked:
'Where has thou hid the body of murdered Chatterton?'

Did Chatterton commit a crime? This was De Quincey's concern,
and in an essay he later wrote called 'Great Forgers: Chatterton, and
Walpole, and "Junius"' he proclaimed Chatterton's innocence. 'Whom
did he deceive? Nobody but those who well deserved to be deceived,
viz., shallow antiquaries, who pretended to a sort of knowledge which
they had not so much as tasted.' Walpole, on the other hand, *was*
guilty; he had committed 'a far more deliberate and audacious forgery'
in *The Castle of Otranto*. 'There, Laureate!' De Quincey imagined the
dead Chatterton triumphantly announcing to the scholars now quarrelling over Rowley's authenticity, 'there, Tyrwhitt, my man! Me you
have murdered amongst you. Now fight to death for the boy that living
you would not have hired as a shoeblack. My blood be upon you!'

Through Hannah More in Bath, De Quincey was near enough to
Chatterton's world to reach out and touch it. More, childhood friends
with Mrs Chatterton, had comforted her after the death of her son just
as she was comforting Mrs De Quincey – as we must now call her –
over the death of William. De Quincey of course identified with the
fatherless child who shared his first name, devoured books, lived inside
his own imaginings, and whose story was composed of locked doors,
staircases and forbidden rooms. But in his disruptive energy, Chatterton
recalls not so much Thomas as William Quincey, and while Thomas
claimed not to mourn for his brother, he became fixated by the figure
of Chatterton. De Quincey himself was more like a fledgling Thomas
Rowley. He too would spread the word about his magnificent patron
and, as the Victorian chronicler of the Romantic poets, he would also
celebrate the glories of a bygone age. And like Rowley, De Quincey was
destined to be a ghost crab inhabiting another's shell.

By the time he was sixteen, De Quincey had 'carried' himself, as he put
it, 'over the whole ground of the Rowley controversy; and that controversy,
by a necessary consequence, had so familiarised me with the "Black Letter",
that I had begun to find an unaffected pleasure in the ancient English

metrical romances'. Through Chatterton, De Quincey discovered Chaucer, and through Chaucer he developed his 'enthusiastic knowledge of the elder poets'. It was through Chatterton that he also found his way to the younger poets. De Quincey described his feelings for Chatterton as love, 'if it be possible to feel love for one who was in his unhonoured grave before I was born', but the story of the half-educated prodigy who escaped from the real world by inventing his own poetic tradition resonated with all the Romantics. Keats dedicated *Endymion* to 'the Most English of Poets Except Shakespeare: Thomas Chatterton'; Shelley and Byron offered their tributes to Chatterton; Chatterton was Coleridge's 'heart-sick wanderer', a poet out of place, both geographically and historically, and Wordsworth's lines, 'we poets in our youth begin in gladness;/ But thereof comes in the end despondency and madness' was written in Chatterton's memory. Southey had edited the first edition of Chatterton's collected works, donating the profits to the boy's impoverished mother and sister. 'Poor Chatterton!' Southey wrote, 'oft do I think upon him and sometimes indulge in the thought that had he been living he might have been my friend.'

The city was steeped in poetry. Wordsworth and Coleridge had first crossed paths in the late summer of 1795 at a political society in Bristol. Coleridge was living in rooms in College Street and making a name for himself as a radical lecturer; Wordsworth was a guest of John Pinney, the West Indian sugar merchant, in his newly built mansion on Great George Street. During his stay in Bristol, in the weeks before he and Dorothy set up home together in another of Pinney's houses in Racedown, Dorset, Wordsworth composed the first lines of *The Prelude*. That year, Coleridge had walked down the aisle of St Mary Redcliffe with a local girl called Sarah Fricker, while Southey married her sister Edith in the same church; the Fricker sisters were raised on Redcliffe Hill. Robert Southey had a point when he said, in response to Chatterton's derision, that the city 'deserves panegyric instead of satire. I know of no other mercantile place so literary.'

De Quincey could not have arrived in the West Country at a more auspicious moment. The Bristol that he encountered was not an uncultivated marketplace, but the cradle of English Romanticism.

During the summer of 1799, when he was home from Winkfield for the school holidays, De Quincey had a reading experience which was to prove what he called 'the greatest event in the unfolding of my own mind'. The manuscript of a poem called 'We Are Seven' was being 'handed about' in Bristol and Bath and found its way to him. It originated from the home of the book's Bristol-based publisher, Joseph Cottle, and came to De Quincey by way of Cottle's friend, Hannah More.

'We Are Seven' describes an exchange in a country graveyard in which a man asks an eight-year-old 'maid' how many there are in her family, and she answers 'seven': two are in Conwy, a town in Wales, two are at sea, and two are buried here, while she lives at home with her mother. The man protests that if two of her seven siblings are dead and buried, then she must surely be one of five. Ignoring his logic, the child persists:

'The first that died was sister Jane;
In bed she moaning lay,
Till God released her of her pain;
And then she went away.

So in the churchyard she was laid;
And, when the grass was dry,
Together round her grave we played,
My brother John and I.

And when the ground was white with snow
And I could run and slide,
My brother John was forced to go,
And he lies by her side.'

'How many are you, then,' said I,
'If they two are in heaven?'
Quick was the little maid's reply,
'O master! we are seven.'

'But they are dead; those two are dead!
Their spirits are in heaven!'
'Twas throwing words away; for still
The little maid would have her will,
And said, 'Nay, we are seven!'

This was to be De Quincey's first encounter with Wordsworth, although he did not then know the identity of the poet. Elemental and spare in comparison with the artifices of high eighteenth-century verse and the verbal curlicues of Thomas Rowley, the macabre exchange did not seem like poetry at all. Wordsworth's aim was to strip away ornament and expose a skeletal form which would take us straight to the centre of the subject. 'Nothing,' he later explained, 'was more difficult for me in childhood than to admit the notion of death as a state applicable to my own being.' The maid stands resolutely by the belief that her love for her deceased siblings makes them present, while the flat-footed adult stands resolutely by his belief that death means absence. It was a disturbing exchange for those, like Coleridge, with a belief in the afterlife. Most abhorrent to Coleridge was Wordsworth's 'frightful notion' of a boy 'lying awake in his grave' instead of being transported to heaven. The poem's whole meaning, Coleridge said in the *Biographia Literaria*, was 'reducible to the assertion that a *child*, who by the bye at six years would have been better instructed in most Christian families, has no other notion of death than of lying in a dark, cold place.' Wordsworth's friend, James Tobin, entreated him to 'cancel' the poem, 'for, if published, it will make you everlastingly ridiculous'.

To De Quincey, 'We Are Seven' was neither frightful nor ridiculous, but 'the height of the moral sublime': 'How deep must a man have gone below the thoughts of the generality, before he could have written such a ballad!' De Quincey's reaction to the death of his own first sister, also called Jane, was that 'summer and winter came again . . . Why not little Jane?' For the four-year-old boy, Jane, like Wordsworth's Lucy, was rolled around with rocks, and stones, and trees. When he reached the age of six, De Quincey imagined Elizabeth transported to heaven through vaults of light, but he had also seen her coffin 'dropped into darkness'. Were his sisters rolling around in the earth or singing in the sky? The stubborn refusal of resolution at the heart of 'We Are Seven' was, for De Quincey, part of its power. He found, as he later told Wordsworth, 'guidance' in the poem, and he found in the poet the tutor no school was able to provide. When Coleridge described admirers of Wordsworth as 'distinguished' by a '*religious* fervour', he was thinking principally of Thomas De Quincey.

The reading he had done so far in his life directed De Quincey towards the person he would later become, but 'We Are Seven' described an experience he had lived through already, and addressed the person he already was. The poem knew him; in its deceptive naivety it understood the loss of Jane and Elizabeth, but also of William, whose own sudden death coincided with De Quincey's chance discovery of the unknown poet's manuscript.

'William Wordsworth in the Lake District, at Cross-Purposes',
by Max Beerbohm, 1904.

'O Master! We are seven.'

Schooltime (continued)

> . . . the giddy top
> And Whispering Gallery of St Paul's; the Tombs
> Of Westminster; the Giants of Guildhall;
> Bedlam, and the two figures at its gates,
> Streets without end, and churches numberless. . .
>
> Wordsworth, *The Prelude*, Book Seventh

'We Are Seven', composed during the same summer as Coleridge's 'Rime of the Ancyent Marinere', appeared in the anonymously published 1798 edition of *Lyrical Ballads*. The volume opened with the mariner's tale: 'There was a ship – quoth he,' begins the old man, stopping an unsuspecting guest at a wedding. Setting sail from a harbour like the one beneath St Mary Redcliffe, 'Below the kirk, below the Hill', the ship blows along like chaff until the mariner does 'an hellish thing', and shoots the bird that brings the breeze. It is as though he had murdered a man, and the poem elides the difference. The mariner's expression as he reveals his crime is awful to behold. 'God save thee, ancient Mariner,' the horrified wedding guest exclaims, 'why looks't thou so?' The mariner, horrified by himself, can give no reason for his action. His punishment is severe; with his soul stripped bare he crosses into a world never entered before: 'We were the first that ever burst/ Into that silent sea.'

Like the wedding guest, De Quincey was held spellbound by this hypnotic confession, which set the tone for the rest of the volume. He found in these poems what he called the 'absolute revelation of untrodden worlds, teeming with power and beauty, as yet unsuspected amongst men'. Here was a landscape on the edge of society, peopled by figures reduced to the naked expression of suffering. Not all of the twenty-two verses are ballads, but many are expressly lyrical. While a traditional ballad rehearses an action, a 'lyrical' ballad investigates the telling of that action and each of these poems was an exercise in expression: 'the feeling therein developed,' Wordsworth later explained, 'gives importance to the action and situation and not the action and situation to the feeling'. 'The Ancient Mariner' contained a message that De Quincey understood: consciousness is a guilt-ridden voyage and wisdom comes at the cost of misery, solitude and sympathy with life in all its modes.

Lyrical Ballads was both a revolt against current definitions of literature and a vision of a deeper, wiser, better life. The initial plan, De Quincey later learned, had been for Wordsworth to write about the natural world and Coleridge to bring in the supernatural, but an air of mysticism pervades the whole. The language is stripped down, the plainness at times resulting in estranging literalism such as Wordsworth's description of the pond in 'The Thorn': 'I've measured it from side to side/ 'Tis three feet long and two feet wide'. The traditional heroes of grand narratives are replaced with idiot boys, convicts and vagrants. There are stark images of blasted trees, ruined cottages and devoted mothers. Children are brought forward as the spokes-men of truth and innocence; authority resides not in God or government but in the resilience of nature: 'One impulse from a vernal wood/ May teach you more of man,/ Of moral evil and of good,/ Than all the sages can,' De Quincey now read in 'The Tables Turned'. Here was the confirma-tion he needed that school was a waste of time.

In these pages De Quincey found a home for his subjectivity and his own yearning for an out-of-body experience. *Lyrical Ballads* was the book of his life, but the literary style he had yet to develop would be the opposite of the one employed here. Where Wordsworth was spartan, De Quincey would be lush; where Wordsworth was bare, De Quincey would be baroque.

'Lines Written a Few Miles Above Tintern Abbey', subtitled 'on Revisiting the Banks of the Wye during a Tour' and dated 'July 13, 1798', is the single rhapsodic poem in the volume and one of only four spoken in the poet's own voice. Wordsworth describes returning, after 'five summers, with the length/ Of five long winters', to the River Wye on the borders of Wales and England, where he reflects on the distance between 'what [he] was then' and who he is now. Time is measured according to emotional impact rather than sequential event, and the poet moves back and forth between the present, sitting 'under the dark sycamore' with his 'dear, dear sister', and the recent past, spent 'in lonely rooms, and mid the din/ Of towns and cities'. In his youthful enthusiasm for nature he was 'more like a man/ Flying from something that he dreads, than one/ Who sought the thing he loved.' Now, as a result of intense inner reflection, he is filled with:

> a sense sublime
> Of something far more deeply interfused,
> Whose dwelling is the light of setting suns,
> And the round ocean, and the living air,
> And the blue sky, and in the mind of man,
> A motion and a spirit, that impels
> All thinking things, all objects of all thought,
> And rolls through all things.

The diction rises like music, culminating in a crescendo in which the narrator wishes for his sister a future in which her mind, like his, 'Shall be a mansion for all lovely forms' and her 'memory be as a dwelling-place/ For all sweet sounds and harmonies.'

The title itself told De Quincey a story: Tintern Abbey is a Gothic ruin on the other side of the Bristol Channel, over the border to Wales. The poem had a local habitation and a name: De Quincey could visit the view above the former monastery and feel what the poet felt. Added to which, the poet also had a sister who reminded him of his former self, who also belonged to an earlier part of his existence.

The two poems framing the first edition of *Lyrical Ballads* were locked in dialogue. The book opened with a tale of homelessness and closed with the celebration of a building; it began with the cadences of a sea shanty and ended on an aria. Architecture not only stimulates the mind, but the mind can aspire to the magnificence of a mansion. Preceding 'The Ancient Mariner' was an 'Advertisement' explaining that the poems contained here were 'experiments' whose meaning would be lost on those looking for the perfume of eighteenth-century verse. Their purpose was to lean into the 'language of conversation in the middle and lower classes', and those readers used to 'the gaudiness and inane phraseology' of contemporary literature will 'struggle with feelings of strangeness and awkwardness'.

This was not an apologia but a manifesto: reading, done properly, is dangerous, and the reader of *Lyrical Ballads* should emerge from the strange and awkward encounter a different person. De Quincey followed these instructions to the letter, and immersed himself in the rhythm of the whole. Reading the *Lyrical Ballads*, his overriding preoccupation was that he had now grown up: there was nothing school could teach him, and nothing more to be learned from his mother. He was ready for a voyage of his own.

Writing to his eldest daughter towards the end of his life, De Quincey described the scene of his 'natal morning'. On one side of the bed was his good fairy, on the other side his bad fairy. The gift bestowed by his good fairy was that 'procrastination shall never dare to come near you', and the gift of the bad fairy was that while he would not procrastinate, he would 'reap the two grand penalties of procrastination. . . In the midst of *too-soonness* he shall suffer the killing anxieties of *too-lateness*.'

His too-lateness would indeed be the controlling feature of De Quincey's life. As a guest he would arrive not hours, but weeks, months and sometimes years after he was expected and as a writer for the journals he would consistently hold his long-suffering editors to ransom; but in his discovery of Wordsworth he prided himself on having been for once early, and by a 'full thirty years'. No other man 'in Europe' had encountered the *Lyrical Ballads* as he had, or foreseen, as he did, the effect they would have on poetic tradition. It was fundamental to De Quincey's self-mythology that he was the first to burst into this silent sea; his 'discovery' of *Lyrical Ballads* is repeatedly presented by him as a mark of his advanced sensibility. For fear of being laughed at, he was forced to keep his transgressive taste hidden from the world and thus he became, in honour of Wordsworth and Coleridge – although he did not then know the identity of the poets – a recluse. On one disastrous occasion he shared his passion with Lady Carbery, a family friend whose judgement he trusted. With 'a beating heart' he recited 'The Ancient Mariner', and she began to giggle. The sailor was, she said, 'an old quiz'; her reaction had De Quincey read her 'We Are Seven' would have been more wounding still. It was a lesson learned: Lady Carbery's response confirmed De Quincey's conviction that if the poet was a solitary genius, then so too was the sympathetic reader.

Wordsworth exaggerated the originality of the *Lyrical Ballads*, and De Quincey exaggerated its universal rejection. Until the middle of the nineteenth century, De Quincey insisted, 'The name of Wordsworth was trampled under foot' and 'the finger of scorn pointed at it'; the 'language' of critics 'was exhausted' by the effort of finding 'images and expressions vile enough, insolent enough, to convey [their] unutterable contempt'. Except that the primitive was in fashion; Blake's *Songs of Innocence* had appeared twenty years earlier and Wordsworth's experiments with 'native language' had been anticipated by Robert Burns in 1786, with his *Poems, Chiefly in the Scottish Dialect*. Individual poems in *Lyrical Ballads* such as 'The Idiot Boy', in which a mother's simple son goes missing, were mocked by readers, but the reviewers in general expressed interest in the experiment, and those writing for the *Analytical*, the *Monthly* and *The British Critic* largely praised the result. The *Anti-Jacobin* described *Lyrical Ballads* as showing 'genius, taste, elegance, wit and imagery of the most beautiful kind'. The only negative review, and the first to appear, was in the *Critical*, and this was by the poet's friend, Robert Southey. 'The Idiot Boy', Southey scoffed, 'resembles a Flemish picture in the worthlessness of its design and the excellence of its execution', while 'The Ancient Mariner' was a 'Dutch attempt at German sublimity'. Despite Southey's equivocation, sales were good enough for *Lyrical Ballads* to require reprinting in 1800 and again in 1802. As evidence of the popularity of their 'low' style, individual poems from the first edition appeared in twenty-three separate papers and journals, including *Lady's Magazine*, the *Star*, and the *Albion and Evening Advertiser*. In April 1799, 'We Are Seven' was reprinted in the *Derby Mercury*, the *Courier*, the *Morning Chronicle* and the *Whitehall Evening Post*. It is easy, however, to imagine De Quincey nursing his discovery, dreading the possibility that other, less sensitive, souls might intrude upon what, for him, had such potent significance.

Thomas was invited to spend the summer of 1800 in County Mayo on the west coast of Ireland, at the home of Howe Peter Browne, Viscount Westport. Lord Altamont, Westport's father, had been an associate of Mr Quincey, and Mrs De Quincey now brokered the friendship between the eleven-year-old Westport and her fourteen-year-old son. Thomas seems not to have minded the age gap; his role was to serve as mentor to the younger boy, who had adopted bad habits at Eton, and De Quincey, for the last time in his life, was thought to be a sobering influence. His self-esteem was riding high; his response to his mother's refusal to have his intellect praised was to encourage the adulation of everyone else. His translation of a Horace Ode had won third place in a schoolboy competition, and was published in the *Monthly Preceptor*; in drawing rooms outside his own, De Quincey found himself 'lionised'.

His display of intellectual superiority was an act of defiance but also compensation for his stature; while his peers were shooting up like weeds, bursting out of shirts and breeches, time stopped around De Quincey who remained locked in his childhood body. He felt himself, however, to be an adult and his summer excursion of 1800 was a rite of passage. From the moment he left Bath he was in pursuit of one thing only: sublimity. He was always invigorated by the risk and romance of travel; the 'finest men' of the eighteenth century, he said, were the highwaymen who 'cultivated their profession on the great leading roads' and lived 'in an element of danger and adventurous gallantry'. Intrepid and courteous, highwaymen belonged to the ancient chivalric order. He liked the sensation of speed and deepening distance; as a child standing at the window of his mother's carriage he had watched the view fly past, and as an adult he preferred to sit on the outside of mail-coaches. The improvement of roads, from 'mere beds of torrents and systems of ruts' to the 'appearance of gravel walks in private parks and shrubberies' pleased him, because smoother surfaces increased velocity. In this he resembled Dr Johnson, who would have happily spent his life, he said, 'driving briskly in a post-chaise with a pretty woman'.

Leaving Bath by coach on 14 July – the eleventh anniversary of the storming of the Bastille – De Quincey called at Eton College in Windsor to collect Westport and his tutor, Reverend Thomas Grace. Finding them both at a royal ball in nearby Frogmore, he was unexpectedly introduced to King George who inquired about his striking name. The 'De' sounded Gallic; were the De Quinceys of Huguenot origin? 'This was a tender point with me: of all things, I could not endure to be supposed of French descent.' 'Please your majesty,' Thomas replied with fervour, 'the family has been in England since the Conquest,' and explained that he had seen 'many notices of the family in books of heraldry', such as Robert of Gloucester's 'Metrical Chronicle', which dated from 'about 1280. . . the Black Letter period'.

With Grace as their charioteer the party trotted the twenty-five miles from Windsor to London by open carriage along the rural lanes, the hedgerows dotted with wild thyme and Queen Anne's lace. Avoiding the main arteries into the metropolis, Thomas later realised, he missed 'the sublimity' of the 'whirl and the uproar, the tumult and agitation' which thickened 'like a misgiving' as the city drew near. But on their quiet country route De Quincey, who had never seen London before, picked up 'the sublime expression' of approaching magnitude in other ways. It seemed as if the 'vast droves of cattle' were propelled towards the 'attracting body' by 'suction' along an immense radius, and he felt the pull of 'other radii still more vast, both by land and by sea' on which 'night and day, summer and winter', the same suction operated. De Quincey compared London to 'some vast, magnetic range of Alps'; he felt himself entering 'the stream of a Norwegian *maelstrom*'; the distant rumble was the 'roar of the Niagara'.

The nearer De Quincey came to the city – 'no! not the city, but the nation' – of London, the less visible he felt; he ceased to be noticeable, he ceased to notice himself; he became 'but one wave in a total Atlantic'. As they entered the fray, his first impression was of 'Babylonian confusion', a chaos of 'agitation' and 'trepidation'; no man 'left to himself for the first time' on these streets would fail to despair amongst the hordes with their 'masks of maniacs'. This was the 'mighty wilderness' that killed its inhabitants, the 'colossal emporium' in which both his brother and Chatterton had spent their last days. Locked in an 'icebound mass' of carriages, De Quincey's party crawled towards the interior, where the traffic melted away in a rapid thaw and they were propelled forwards in a great rush of motion. To either side, chariots flew up long-stretching vistas which reached into still longer-stretching perspectives, the termination of which was wrapped 'in gloom and uncertainty'.

Arriving mid-afternoon, the boys were given three hours in which to visit the sights before leaving to dine with Westport's grandmother. What were they to do in such an ocean? They headed to Christopher Wren's baroque masterpiece, St Paul's Cathedral: the sublime heart of the sublime city. Their 'first view' of the great white sepulchre 'overwhelmed us with awe'. Beneath their feet the crypt extended the full length of the cathedral; above, raised on a great drum pierced with windows separated by statues in niches, rose the dome, painted with scenes from the life of St Paul set in illusionistic perspective. Circling its base was the famous gallery, and De Quincey and Westport climbed the 259 stone steps to try out its acoustics. Westport, on one side, murmured a secret into the wall and the sound, 'running along', reached Thomas on the other side 'as a deafening menace in tempestuous uproars'. The lightest words were made to seem irrevocable; even those only half spoken had thunderous consequences. It was a symbol, De Quincey felt, of the impossibility of escape – from past error, from hidden thoughts – and an encounter with the 'dark sublime'.

The Whispering Gallery taught him that actions which were now behind him 'would magnify themselves at every stage of life, in proportion as they were viewed retrospectively from greater and greater distances'. St Paul's Cathedral was a stage-set of De Quincey's mind, and the gallery now took its place amongst the hieroglyphics of his dreams. Years later he wrote some lines of verse, Cyrus of Elam, suggestive of this afternoon excursion, his hexameters being indistinguishable from his prose:

> Depths behind depths were there labyrinthine apartments,
> Where golden galleries ran overhead through an endless tire
> Of staircases climbing; till sight grew dizzy with effort
> Of chasing the corridors up to their whispering gloomy recesses.

A great reader of travel books, De Quincey would compare the effect of the Whispering Gallery to the frozen words 'exploding like minute guns' in *The Travels of Sir John Mandeville*.

———

The route to Holyhead, where they were to pick up the Irish packet, took them through Warwickshire and Stratford-upon-Avon. Here De Quincey visited the house in which Shakespeare was born, and in north Wales they passed through the walled castle town of Conwy, where two of the siblings in 'We Are Seven' were said to dwell. De Quincey now found himself for the first time amongst mountains. He later compared the Welsh peaks to those in the Lakes, seeing them through Wordsworth's trained eyes (Welsh mountains, Wordsworth said, too often take 'the basin shape'; Westmorland mountains, on the other hand, present a flat area at the base of a hill, 'as the floor of a temple'.) In his letters to his mother, however, De Quincey was less critical of the landscape. Their road, he reported, looked 'down into an immensely deep valley surrounded by mountains and rocks which rise in rugged grandeur to the skies'. At sunset, 'the effect of the glowing light on the woods, the winding river, and the cattle below, and on the distant mountains, and gigantic rocks above, was far more beautiful in the former, and sublime in the latter, than I am able to describe'.

De Quincey had never boarded a ship before but he knew what a huge thing the ocean was. Here was the immensity he had dreamed about, but instead of depths below depths he discovered that the sea, like the Sahara, was monotonous. Dullness was the downside of sublimity. Added to which, his crossing contained all the easy chat of an afternoon in the Bath Pump Room. On the same packet, her travelling coach unhinged from its wheels and placed on the apron of the deck like a private apartment, was the luscious Lady Conyngham, future mistress of King George IV. Enchanted by De Quincey's manners, she invited him into her carriage where she kept him hostage for eight hours, afterwards suggesting that they continue their conversation on her Irish estates at Slane Castle. His time already accounted for, De Quincey declined the invitation.

He and Westport stayed for two weeks at Lord Altamont's townhouse in Dublin's Sackville Street. Father and son had not seen one another for three years and De Quincey feared that his presence at their reunion would be like that of a man who had 'been chased by a Bengal tiger into the very centre of the Eleusinian mysteries'. How could he not feel an intruder at such an occasion, or 'a criminal without a crime?' As it was, Altamont treated him like a second son. He introduced De Quincey to 'persons of historical names' such as Lord Clare, the Chancellor, Lord Castlereagh, then Irish Chancellor of the Exchequer, and Lord Cornwallis, the Lord Lieutenant.

On 1 August 1800 De Quincey climbed the steps to another gallery, where he watched the Irish parliament pass the Act of Union, according to which Britain and Ireland became a single state. It was typical of his Zelig-like qualities that he should arrive in the very week that the Union was ratified. No other 'public act, or celebration, or solemnity, in my time', he recalled, 'could so much engage my profoundest sympathies'. The Irish parliament was dissolved; the country would now be represented at Westminster by twenty-eight peers, of whom Altamont was one. As for those remaining, 'this morning they rose from their couches Peers of Parliament, individual pillars of the realm' and 'tomorrow they will be nobody'. Fascinated by the moment of historical transformation, De Quincey interviewed 'everybody who had personally participated in the commotions'. These 'nobodies' had turned into 'a pack of vagabonds. . . and interlopers, with actually no more right to be here than myself. I am an intruder, so are you.'

Altamont referred to his young companion as a 'zealous Englishman', which suggests that De Quincey voiced his horror of the revolutionaries.

But his politics were uncertain at this point. Not yet the solid Tory he would become, he swung, like Burke, between extremes, backing the cause he found the most romantic.

In early August, the party left the ceremonies, installations, dinners, masked balls, bonfires and celebratory fireworks of the newly colonial Dublin for Altamont's estate in County Mayo. They travelled to Tullamore by canal boat, where De Quincey talked poetry with a beautiful young Irish woman called Miss Blake, whose brother-in-law, Lord Errol, had recently taken his own life. De Quincey's sexuality was now awakened; he shone in the presence of the grieving girl and found himself, to his great delight, the 'lion' of the company. 'Never, until this hour, had I thought of women as objects of a possible interest, or of a reverential love,' he recalled. Such feelings, clearly excited by Miss Blake's proximity to a self-murderer, were 'a *revelation*' which 'fixed a great era of change in my life'. Giving his mother a muted version of his new friendship, he suggested that they call on Miss Blake's widowed sister, Lady Errol, in Bath.

Rattling along in the carriage, he helped Westport with his Greek while Westport regaled him with stories of Eton life. De Quincey was particularly struck by an account of a pack of boys beating an old porter half to death while the masters stood by and watched. The travellers dined and slept in the houses of 'old Irish nobility and gentry'. Built in the style of 'antique manorial chateaux' with 'long rambling galleries, and windows innumerable. . . old libraries, old butlers, old customs', no other experience 'throughout my whole life' had 'interested' De Quincey as much. He liked the privileges of being both a guest and the older boy: drinking wine, sitting with the gentlemen after dinner, and throwing out his 'vast command of words, as from a cornucopia'.

The day after De Quincey's fifteenth birthday they arrived at Westport House, one of Ireland's loveliest classical revival buildings, completed by James Wyatt just over a decade earlier in 1788. Set in 300 acres of park and built on the site of an ancient castle whose dungeons were still intact, the house bore the marks of the country's recent history. The French, briefly invading from the nearby shore, had taken possession of the rooms and pillaged the best books from the library, leaving behind, to De Quincey's irritation, only law reports and manuals on drainage. This was as close as he would come to the French Revolution. As for the stillborn Irish revolution, on one occasion he and Westport were pelted with stones by the locals, but the country otherwise felt safer than he had expected. 'In England, I remember,' he reported home, 'we heard such horrid accounts of murders, and battles, and robberies, and here everybody tells me the country *is* in as quiet a state as England, and *has* been so for some time past.' The English, he concluded, 'use the *amplifying,* and the Irish the *diminishing hyperbole*; the former view it with a *magnifying glass*, the latter with a *microscope*'. As the Irishman Dean Swift remarked: 'Elephants are always drawn smaller than life, but a flea always larger.'

De Quincey's time was spent 'Reading, Hunting, Riding, Shooting, bathing and Sea excursions', or so he told his mother. 'We generally ride sixteen or seventeen miles a day, by which means we get to see almost everything worth seeing in this most romantic country.' From the park he looked onto the 'cloud-capt' Croagh Patrick, Ireland's holy mountain, which he and Westport conquered. 'It is about two miles to the top,' Thomas reported home, 'from which may be seen a great part of Connaught. When I was at the summit, I thought of Shakespeare looking "abroad from some high cliff, and enjoying the elemental war".'

When he returned to England in late September, De Quincey considered himself a man of the world. He had been to London, crossed the sea, climbed a mountain, marched along in the progress of history, and had his first taste of romantic love. He had stretched into his liberty; the development of his 'whole mind was rushing in like a cataract, forcing channels for itself'. Describing, in *The Prelude*, his experience of France, Wordsworth put it thus: 'Bliss was it in that dawn to be alive,/ But to be young was very heaven!' So had it been for De Quincey in Ireland.

De Quincey and Westport parted at Holyhead, never to meet again. Their lives followed parallel lines, however, as both became satellites of Romantic poets; Westport, after inheriting the title of Lord Sligo, becoming the raffish companion of Lord Byron.

———

De Quincey took the coach to Birmingham where a letter from his mother, waiting at the post office, ordered him to Laxton Hall, the Northamptonshire home of her friend, Lady Carbery. He liked Lady Carbery a good deal and the next seven weeks were spent in vigorous theological debate with his hostess. Once again, De Quincey's learning was respected and he was treated as an adult. The only shadow to pass over his happiness was the question of what would happen next. His letters from Ireland had returned again and again to the vexed question of his education. Winkfield, Thomas repeated, was filled with block-heads and had nothing to offer a boy of his ambition; Eton, mooted as a possibility, was clearly too violent – he had already suffered one severe blow to the head. If he had to continue at school at all, he begged that it be Bath Grammar. Bewildered by her son's rebelliousness, Elizabeth De Quincey chose, as parents do, to rein him in. She decided that he should return to neither Winkfield nor Bath, but to the city of his birth. He was to be enrolled as a boarder at Manchester Grammar with the aim of starting at Oxford University when he was nineteen years old. Pupils who had been at the school for three years were eligible to receive, from Brasenose College, an annual allowance of £50. This, added to De Quincey's personal income of £150 a year, would make up the require-ment needed to support an undergraduate. The plan was sensible, but De Quincey was uninterested in the limits of his own economy and frustrated by the thought of yet another upheaval. He was to continue, he realised, in a state of protracted boredom until well into adulthood, a prospect which left him with a 'sickening oppression'.

Having been pushed forwards on a straight gravel road, De Quincey now found himself diverted down beds of torrents and systems of ruts. He compared his fate to that of 'some victim of evil destiny' in the Middle Ages, an 'inheritor of a false fleeting prosperity' who was then 'detected as a leper'. 'Misgivingly I went forwards,' he said of the way ahead, 'feeling forever that, through clouds of thick darkness, I was continually nearing a danger, or was myself perhaps wilfully provoking a trial, before which my constitutional despondency would cause me to lie down without a struggle.' On 9 November he was transferred 'from the glittering halls of the English nobility' to the 'cheerless. . . and rude benches of an antique school-room'.

His life was in fact moving backwards. His mother, dissatisfied with Bath, determined to build a new house and took herself on a tour of the country, assessing each town and village in terms of the quality of medical advice, the availability of aristocratic society, the pleasant-ness of the scenery, and the proximity to an evangelical clergyman. She also reverted to the plainer name of 'Quincey'. Her son, returning to Manchester, decided to retain the pseudonymous particle 'De'.

Four years after leaving it behind him, Thomas was back in Cottonopolis, city of dust and lucre, and the noisiest place in England. From now on he could not 'stir out of doors' without being 'nosed by a factory, a cotton-bag, cotton dealer, or something else allied to that most detestable commerce' – the commerce which had been the trade of his father. Manchester, he told his mother, dissipated 'the whole train of romantic visions I had conjured up'. De Quincey would never reinvent his hometown as Chatterton had reinvented Bristol, but it was here that his identification with the marvellous boy began in earnest.

Friedrich Engels, in the early 1840s, described the area which housed Manchester Grammar as 'an almost undisguised working men's quarter, for even the shops and beer houses hardly take the trouble to exhibit a trifling degree of cleanliness'. De Quincey's new home, on a cramped and hectic street which also served as the apple market, was 'a cave of despair' (the line is from Edmund Spenser). Arriving at nine o'clock on a rainy Sunday night, he was conducted to the headmaster's study through a 'series of unfurnished little rooms, having small windows but no doors'. The interior was as bald and blank as a poorhouse; the walls, which might have been embellished by friezes or medallions illustrating 'the most memorable glorifications of literature', were 'a dreary expanse' of whitewash. De Quincey boarded with the headmaster, Charles Lawson, a kindly, jaded figure with a tottering gait and diamond buckles on his shoes, who had taught at the school for half a century. His wig, from the back, looked like a cauliflower.

Lawson's house was built in the Roman style around a quadrangle which allowed, De Quincey imagined, the old man to fantasise that he was still at Oxford and that everything afterwards 'had been a dream'. De Quincey's room, 'a quiet study lifted by two storeys above the vapours of the earth', could be found 'up dilapidated staircases' and down 'old worm-eaten passages'. Sequestered in his Chattertonian attic, he read and worked through the nights, paper scattering around him, waiting for his sentence to be over. By now he was fluent in Greek, and writing Greek verse in lyric metre.

Manchester had its distractions and De Quincey returned to the museum of Charles White; the mummy in the clock case was no longer on view, but the handsome highwayman's skeleton was still there to greet him. Lady Carbery moved to the city and her company gave De Quincey some respite. Then, in January 1801, to jolt him back into consciousness, a new edition of *Lyrical Ballads* appeared. This time it was in two volumes, and

the title page contained the name of an author: 'W. Wordsworth'. Volume
one contained the same selection as the 1798 edition, with the inclusion of
'Love' and the omission of 'The Convict'. 'The Ancient Mariner' had been
placed ominously at the end, just before 'Tintern Abbey', a new arrangement that broke the conversational balance. The mariner's altered position
gave his voyage a different meaning; no longer heralding the journey that
lay in wait for the reader, he seemed more like a dotty relation ranting in a
back room at a family reunion.

Lyrical Ballads opened instead with 'Expostulation and Reply' which,
like 'We Are Seven', dramatises an exchange between a visionary and a logi-
cian. A man called William, sitting dreamily on a stone by Lake Esthwaite,
is goaded by his friend Matthew to do something more useful instead:

> 'Why William, on that old grey stone,
> Thus for the length of half a day,
> Why, William, sit you thus alone,
> And dream your time away?'

William replies that,

> 'The eye it cannot chuse but see,
> We cannot bid the ear be still;
> Our bodies feel, where'er they be,
> Against, or with our will.'

Wordsworth, De Quincey wrote, 'sees the same objects' as other
men, 'but he sees them engraved in lines far stronger and more deter-
minate'. His visual authority lay not in the novelty of what he saw, but
in his ability to awaken 'into illuminated consciousness ancient lineaments of truth long slumbering in the mind'.

'Expostulation and Reply' was followed by 'The Tables Turned', in
which the dreamy William now explains to the studious Matthew that
self-knowledge comes from nature and not books:

> Up! up! my friend, and quit your books,
> Or surely you'll grow double:
> Up! up! my friend, and clear your looks,
> Why all this toil and trouble?

We learn more about ourselves, explains William, from a 'vernal wood' than from the words of dead philosophers. Not only does scholarship detract from the truth but it destroys the life of things:

> Our meddling intellect
> Misshapes the beauteous form of things –
> We murder to dissect.

For the next thirty years, De Quincey later wrote, besides himself only one man in fifty 'knew what was meant by "that poet who had cautioned his friend against growing double". To all others it was a profound secret.'

In the second edition of *Lyrical Ballads*, De Quincey discovered the enigmatic 'Lucy' poems, in which Wordsworth returns again and again to the sudden death of a young girl, and 'Ruth', the poem of abandonment to which De Quincey would himself return throughout his relationship with Wordsworth. Ruth was 'not seven years old' when, 'left half desolate' by her father, she began 'wandering over hill and dale'. When she 'grew to woman's height' she was courted by an American soldier who promised her a life in the New World, but he deserted his bride. Mad with grief, Ruth was 'in a prison housed' and lived the rest of her days 'under the greenwood tree'. De Quincey was also struck by a poem called 'Nutting', in which Wordsworth recalled how, as a boy, he had savagely destroyed a scene of virgin beauty:

> Then up I rose
> And dragged to earth both branch and bough, with crash
> And merciless ravage; and the shady nook
> Of hazels, and the green and mossy bower,
> Deformed and sullied, patiently gave up
> Their quiet being. . .

The brief 'Advertisement' accompanying the first edition of *Lyrical Ballads* had been replaced by a hefty forty-page 'Preface' in which Wordsworth expounded the theory on which his poetry was based. 'All good poetry' was 'the spontaneous overflow of powerful feelings', a poet was a man of 'more than usual organic sensibility', the taste for 'frantic novels' and 'sickly and stupid German tragedies' was driving the works of great writers, like Shakespeare and Milton, 'into neglect'.

De Quincey, identifying himself as one of the readers shamed by Wordsworth, found here 'the most finished and masterly specimen of reasoning which has in any age or nation been called forth by any one of the fine arts'. He also discovered that the poet had a collaborator: a 'friend', whose opinions on the subject coincided entirely with Wordsworth's own, and who had written 'The Ancient Mariner', 'The Foster-Mother's Tale', 'The Nightingale', 'The Dungeon' and 'Love'. But nothing was said about why this friend's name did not appear on the title page of the present edition.

———

Elizabeth Quincey was still hunting for land on which to build her house, and so the school holidays in the summer of 1801 were spent in a rented cottage in Everton, now part of Liverpool but then a smart village on the hill above the great port. Gentrified for wealthy tradesmen, Everton looked onto the Welsh mountains and the Irish Sea. 'When you approach the cottage, you may reach the chimneys with your hat,' Elizabeth warned her son. Sending directions, she described herself as his 'steering chart'.

> You will leave Manchester on Saturday morning in the canal-boat, first of all informing yourselves whether there is a boat sailing upon a Saturday morning, of which I have great doubts; almost a certainty, indeed, that Saturday morning is the only one in the week it does not go. You will be landed about a mile from Warrington London Bridge, where you will meet coaches, into one of which you will get and go to Warrington to dinner; and you must secure your places in the Long Coach to Liverpool, which (with all the Manchester coaches) comes to the Angel Inn, Dale Street. Should my suspicion about the boat be right, you must come directly from Manchester in the Long Coach in the morning of Saturday; — lose no time as soon as you can on Thursday to know all this, and let your place be arranged.

It was a bossy letter which no doubt irritated him, but Mrs Quincey had once again placed her son in surprisingly congenial surroundings. 'You need bring no books,' she wrote, 'for Mr. Clarke, our neighbour, will lend you any Greek or Latin author. Of Italian, French, and English books he seems to have store also; and in the town there is really a noble library, to which Mr. Cragg will introduce you.' The address was 9 Middle Lane, and Mr Clarke, who was part of a literary coterie, lived in the large house across the street. Every day he and De Quincey would read Aeschylus together, and Clarke introduced the boy to his friends: William Shepherd, author of a life of the Florentine humanist Poggio Bracciolini; William Roscoe, who had written a popular biography of Lorenzo de' Medici; and James Currie, whose recent edition of Robert Burns included a study of the poet's life. The men were 'fraternisers with French Republicanism' at a time when, as De Quincey later put it, 'such politics were absolutely disreputable'. They were also versifiers of the kind Wordsworth despised; their poems displayed, to De Quincey's mind, 'the most timid and blind servility to the narrowest of conventional usages, conventional ways of viewing things, conventional forms of expression'. He quarrelled with them over literary matters, disagreeing in particular over Burns, who De Quincey was currently reading in Currie's own edition. These disreputable radicals, he felt, 'taxed Burns with ingratitude' towards his aristocratic patrons, while De Quincey, who presented himself as having been the most radical of them all, was alone in upholding the poetic spirit of independence.

It was as biographers rather than poets that the group impressed De Quincey, who had already absorbed Boswell's *Life of Johnson* and Johnson's *Lives of the Poets*, which included his *Life of Savage*. His web of connections grew wider; he learned that Roscoe was friends with the artist, Fuseli, and with the scientist, Joseph Priestley. He could bring to the table a few trophies of his own: his mother's intimacy with Hannah More and his proximity to Edmund Burke; More was intensely disliked by the group, and Roscoe had written a pamphlet against Burke. But De Quincey's most important discovery by far during this first Everton summer was that Mr Clarke, Mr Roscoe and Dr Currie were all intimate with *Lyrical Ballads*, and knew the name of the invisible 'friend' who had furnished the volumes with five of his own poems. It was Samuel Taylor Coleridge, well known in Bristol for his radical lectures and for editing *The Watchman*, a journal of the type to make Mrs Quincey quake.

There was more: Roscoe had been aware of Coleridge since his *Poems on Various Subjects* appeared in 1796, when he recognised the poet's 'genius' to be 'of the highest class'. He had even invited Coleridge,

after the failure of *The Watchman*, to recommence his political career in
Liverpool, as 'Bristol is not a place likely to reward his merits'. Coleridge
and De Quincey were tracing the same path across the country; leaving
Bristol, Coleridge was now living in the Cumbrian town of Keswick
in order to be near the 'giant Wordsworth'. En route to his new home
the previous summer, Coleridge had stayed in Liverpool for a week and
seen 'a great deal of Dr Currie and Roscoe'. Currie he described as 'a
genuine philosopher', and Roscoe as 'a republican with all the feelings
of prudence and all the manners of good sense'. He had liked them
enough to recommend their good company to Southey.

In De Quincey's later accounts of Roscoe and Currie he erased his discovery that *Lyrical Ballads* had more than one admirer. 'To me,' he imperiously
wrote, 'who in that year, 1801, already knew of a grand renovation of poetic
power – of a new birth of poetry, interesting not so much to England as
to the human mind – it was secretly amusing to contrast the little artificial
uses of their petty traditional knack with the natural forms of a divine art.'
He was '"indebted"' as he put it – in inverted commas – to Roscoe for the
information about Coleridge, but 'discharged that debt ill, for I quarrelled
with my informant for what I considered his profane way of dealing with a
subject so hallowed to my own thoughts'. Roscoe's profanity was to suggest
that Coleridge should concentrate on his political journalism at the expense
of his poetry. From now on De Quincey 'searched east and west, north and
south, for all known works or fragments of the same authors'.

Leaving Thomas and his siblings in Everton, Mrs Quincey set out that
August to find them all a home. But instead of buying the land on which
to build a new house, she was offered an excellent price (£500) for an old
house in the cathedral city of Chester, on the border with north Wales,
where she had been left shares in her husband's linen company. The
Priory, as it was called, was a curious building in a more curious setting.
Picturesque rather than sublime, De Quincey described it as 'a beautiful
place', 'a gem', and he must have been struck by his mother's unconscious
Wordsworthian affinities: she had bought a ruined cottage in the grounds
of a Tintern Abbey. Enclosed within high and rugged exterior walls, the
Priory had once been attached to the medieval church of St John; fol-
lowing the dissolution of the monasteries, the religious foundation had

fallen into decay and its remains were left scattered about like the stones of Carthage. In De Quincey's terminology, the Priory had 'dwindled by successive abridgements from a royal quarto into a pretty duodecimo'. When Elizabeth Quincey discovered the house, it was hidden amongst ivy-covered relics and arches. To the left of the front door was a desiccated statue of the Madonna and Child, and to the right a chubby saint at prayer. She bought it with a view to making alterations; Mrs Quincey's new home, Thomas explained, was to be a building she 'in part planned, and built, but chiefly repaired out of [the] ancient gothic monastery'.

Once again, De Quincey's interest was ignited by the former occupant: 200 years earlier, what was left of the Priory had been lived in by antiquarian and bibliomane Sir Robert Cotton. De Quincey was a book collector, and Cotton's library, still considered the most important collection of manuscripts ever assembled by a private individual, contained the Lindisfarne Gospels, two of the contemporary exemplifications of Magna Carta and the only surviving manuscript of 'Beowulf'. Here was a Black Letter heritage which exceeded even Chatterton's dreams. Cotton had been friends with the Jacobean poet, dramatist and critic, Ben Jonson, who was considered the equal of Shakespeare, and was said to have come here as a guest. A pattern had been established whereby De Quincey took over the homes of the country's literary giants.

There were ten rooms in the Priory, and Mrs Quincey, at the cost of £1,000, added ten more of her own (which subsequently fell down). Those from 'Sir Robert's day' were, for De Quincey, the treasures. Cotton had lived like a 'literary bachelor'; the monastic kitchen had a 'noble groined ceiling of stone' which 'indicated, by its disproportionate scale, the magnitude of the establishment to which once it had ministered'. On the upper storey were Sir Robert's private quarters – his former bedroom, a 'pretty old hall' with a 'mosaic painted window' in the door, and an 'elegant dining room'. Thomas also loved the 'miniature pleasure ground' whose ruined archways were 'so small that Drury Lane could easily have found room for them on its stage'. The Gothicisms were never-ending: in the church itself was a mysterious oak coffin, said to belong to a monk who murdered one of his brethren and was subsequently refused a Christian burial. Framed inside a white Corinthian niche, a full-length skeleton stood behind a shroud.

When he returned to school in the autumn, De Quincey continued to plague his mother with bids for freedom, and she replied with letters of fire and brimstone. 'Every human being is brought upon this stage for the greater purposes of glorifying God. . . and if any one temper of mind may singly be put to denote the whole anti-Christian character, it is self-glory.' Her message was clear: 'I know what your ideas are. . . and I plainly perceive that you have exalted one, and that the most dangerous faculty of mind, the imagination, over all the rest. . . you are now carried away, wholly blinded by the bewildering light of your fancy.' The school, Thomas claimed, had 'murdered' his 'health', his liver in particular, and he suggested he might study alone at the Priory. Elizabeth replied that 'a year spent at home in desultory reading, without an object, is an evil of such incalculable extent that I shall never consent to it'. The books he was currently consuming, she noted, were the work of 'infidels and Jacobins'. He argued that he was more idle at school than he would ever be at home; she, in despair, offered him £100 if he completed the year. Thomas, like her eldest son William, was slipping out of her control: 'Must you govern me or must I govern you?' Mrs Quincey asked.

In March 1802 a peace was agreed between England and France. Under the Treaty of Amiens, as it was called, the English recognised the French Republic. It was once more possible to cross the Channel, and as troops were coming home those civilians, together with art lovers and Grand Tourists, who had been trapped on British shores for the past nine years, poured into Paris. No longer a tyrannical monster, Napoleon had become the restorer of order. It was like, said Thomas Robinson, the brother of Henry Crabb, the 'transformation in a pantomime, where a devil is suddenly converted to an angel'.

Spring slipped into summer and then, 'like an army with banners', midsummer had arrived. It was the most dangerous time of year for De Quincey and on 2 July he decided his own future: he would run away from school and place himself outside the realm of established values. On his last evening as a schoolboy, the sky was high and the sun shimmered 'light and broad and gaudy'. He went through the rituals of terminating the day. Now that he knew he would never see his headmaster again, the old man did not seem such a villain; 'he had been uniformly kind to me, and had allowed me such indulgences as lay in his power'. During the final hours in his study, De Quincey fell into 'a sort of trance, a frost as of some death-like revelation'.

He remembered his midsummer visit two years before to the Whispering Gallery of St Paul's, and its terrible effect: 'a word once uttered is irrevocable'. On this, the most significant night of his life, 'a voice, too late for warning, seemed audibly to say, "Once leave this house, and a Rubicon is placed between thee and all possibility of return. . . Even now thy conscience speaks against it in sullen whispers; but at the other end of thy long life-gallery that same conscience will speak to thee in volleying thunders."' His reverie was broken by 'a sudden step upon the stairs'. Darkness fell, and after a brief sleep De Quincey rose at half past three in the morning. 'I dressed myself, took my hat and gloves, and lingered a little in the room. For nearly a year and a-half this room had been my "pensive citadel". . . I shed tears as I looked around on the chair, hearth, writing-table, and other familiar objects, knowing too certainly that I looked upon them for the last time.'

'Pensive citadel' comes from Wordsworth's 'Nuns Fret Not' ('And students with their pensive citadels'). Over the mantelpiece in his room hung a picture of the Duchess of Somerset, a seventeenth-century benefactress of Manchester grammar. De Quincey had gazed at the image a thousand times, and he now kissed her frozen lips before closing the door 'for ever'. His possessions, mainly books, were packed in a trunk which the groom, whose back was 'as spacious as Salisbury Plain', carried from the attic. Down the staircase they crept, De Quincey leading the way. 'The silence was more profound than that of midnight,' he recalled, adding that 'to me the silence of a summer morning is more touching than all other silence.' He stood at the foot of the last flight, listening to the 'slow and firm' tread of the groom as he reached the 'dangerous quarter' of the house, an area called the gallery. This was where the headmaster slept. With only a few steps to go, the groom slipped and the trunk fell, hitting 'each step of the descent' like a series of great chords. It leapt, when it reached the floor, 'with the noise of twenty devils, against the very bedroom door of the archididasculus', who lay within, sequestered in some deep recess. The groom began to laugh; the world of ordinary life was arrested as De Quincey waited, breathing hard, for what would happen next.

No one stirred. The groom retrieved the trunk and sent it to the carrier to be delivered to the Priory. *Lyrical Ballads* in his pocket, De Quincey stepped out of the school and onto the stinking street. Above him, the sky was 'beginning to crimson' with 'radiant lustre'. He launched himself into the dawn of the new day, drawn by the 'deep, deep magnet' of William Wordsworth.

Soho Square, De Quincey's 'stony-hearted stepmother'.

4

Residence in London

. . . and when the deed was done
I heard among the solitary hills
Low breathings coming after me, and sounds
Of undistinguishable motion, steps
Almost as silent as the turf they trod.

Wordsworth, *The Prelude*, Book First

His plan had been to head ninety miles north to the Lakes, but once he was on the road De Quincey changed his mind and bent his way south-west towards Chester. He wanted to see his sister, Mary, and reassure her that all was well.

There was a difference between running away to meet a revered poet and running home to see your sister, and De Quincey carried his sense of failure. He was running from, rather than to, Wordsworth; more like a man flying from something he dreaded than one who sought the thing he loved. Wordsworth had taken on such a 'hallowed character' that any journey in his direction was, De Quincey felt, like that of a 'devout Mahometan' to Mecca, or a 'Christian devotee' looking with 'rapt adoration to St Peter's at Rome'. He needed to approach his god with the solemnity of a pilgrim on a saintly mission, and not as a grammar school dropout in need of a loan and a good wash. This was the wrong time to make his introduction: the prospect of Wordsworth's first hearing his name 'associated with some case of pecuniary embarrassment' was intolerable to him.

There was another risk attached to meeting Wordsworth at this precise moment. The morning before leaving the school, De Quincey had received a letter addressed in the aristocratic script of a foreign hand to a 'Monsieur Monsieur De Quincy, Chester'. The envelope, postmarked 'Hamburg', contained a banknote for forty guineas. Deciphering the accompanying message – a 'Sphinx's riddle' – it became clear that the 'windfall' was meant for another De Quincey, a French émigré wanting, now that the Channel was open once again, to return home. 'Monsieur Monsieur De Quincy' not being known in Chester, the post office delivered the letter to the eldest son of their newest resident, the redoubtable Mrs Quincey. Receiving such a sum at the very moment he needed it was an astonishing coincidence which deepened De Quincey's resolution to abscond, and to waste no time in doing so. But equally astonishing was his growing realisation that there was someone else in Chester – a Frenchman, no less – carrying his name, and that this man was also living with 'friendlessness and exile'. Thomas felt a quickening sympathy for his other.

De Quincey had wanted a new identity, and this is what he got. 'By the touch of the pen' he had been 'translated. . . not only in a *Monsieur*, but even into a self-multiplied *Monsieur*'. But of the two De Quinceys, he was the dissembler. His excitement at receiving the banknote turned to guilt: he was in possession of another man's money; if he kept it he was a 'robber', if he cashed it he would 'be punished inexorably with death'. If he returned it to the post office he ran the risk of being arrested; had Monsieur Monsieur De Quincy been expecting the banknote, he may have already informed officials of its possible theft, in which case uniforms would be waiting for him. To enter the post office would be equivalent to a 'fawn' walking into a 'lion's den'. De Quincey was now not only a runaway but a fugitive; throughout his long walk home he could hear footsteps approaching: 'Two separate parties, I felt satisfied, must by this time be in chase of me; and the two chasers would be confluent at the post office.'

His fears were not ungrounded: the minute De Quincey's absence from Manchester Grammar was discovered a horse had been dispatched to the Priory, which had flown past him on the Chester Road. And an hour after Mrs Quincey was informed by the school that her son had absconded, she was visited by a post office official who explained the problem of the misdirected missive. The two incidents naturally segued into one: Thomas, reasoned his mother, had used the money to run to that Jacobin, William Wordsworth.

Had it not been for the 'accursed letter', De Quincey would have luxuriated in his liberty. To exchange the fug of Manchester for an open road beneath high summer skies was wildly exhilarating. This, he later wrote, is 'what Wordsworth, when describing the festal state of France during the happy morning-tide of her First Revolution. . . calls "*the senselessness of joy*": this it was, joy – headlong – frantic – irreflective – and (as Wordsworth truly calls it), for that very reason, *sublime* – which swallowed up all capacities of rankling care or heart-corroding doubt.' He was crippled, however, by rankling care and heart-corroding doubt, and would remain so until he had rid himself of the 'odious responsibility' of the money. Always convinced of his powers of destruction, De Quincey was made frantic by the thought that he was denying the Frenchman the freedom that he himself was currently enjoying. He had to return the banknote, but how?

By breakfast time he had reached Altringham, a small town he had last visited as a boy recovering from whooping cough. He remembered it clearly: at eight o'clock in the morning on another 'dazzling day in July', his nurse had held him up to an open window where he had looked onto a market square filled with fruit, flowers and bonny women wearing aprons and caps. The gaiety 'rose up like a fountain' to his casement. It was once again eight o'clock when De Quincey found himself returning to the same square where – to his delight – he saw the same fruit, the same flowers, the same caps and aprons. Perhaps, in the same house, the same window was opening onto the same scene. 'All places, it seems, are not Whispering Galleries,' he told himself with relief. He ate his fill and then walked throughout the day, sleeping that night at an inn. On 4 July 1802, the ninth anniversary of his father's death, he reached his new home town.

To prevent his capture he kept close to Chester's city walls, where his route to the Priory took him along the banks of the River Dee. Here, apart from a country woman walking up ahead, he was alone. Suddenly a 'tumultuous' sound came roaring towards him. 'What was it? Where was it? Whence was it? Earthquake was it?' It came from the river where, wheeling upstream 'at the rate of forty miles an hour' was a 'huge charging block of waters'. The river was flowing backwards: it was as though 'the Atlantic ocean had broke loose'. De Quincey and the country woman 'ran like hares' to the top of a hill as the wave passed 'with the ferocious uproar of a hurricane'. 'How,' De Quincey asked, approaching his companion, 'did she read the mystery' of the river's sudden 'hysterics'? It was a phenomenon called 'the Bore', the woman explained, caused by high sea tides from the Dee estuary. It was well known to the locals. Having shared one near-death experience, De Quincey confided in her the problem of the banknote and she agreed to return it to the post office on his behalf in exchange for half a crown. At which point, like the colossal tidal wave, De Quincey's own hysteria passed. Everyone was now free: he was 'suddenly released' from the burden of guilt, the 'poor emigrant' was released from exile, the post office was released from 'the scandal and embarrassment of a gross irregularity', and De Quincey's family were 'released from all anxieties. . . on the question of my fancied felony'. He could safely return to the Priory and talk to Mary, his 'soul auxiliary'.

But to prevent her son's arrest, Mrs Quincey had already made plans for his expatriation. She had put Mary in a coach to the Lakes with orders to scoop up the wretched boy and put him on the next boat to the continent. So when De Quincey arrived at the Priory to find Mary, she had gone north to find him.

It was dusk when Thomas appeared in the garden of ruins and stood beneath his sister's window. No light came from her room, so he scribbled a note asking her to meet him outside and gave it to a servant to deliver. He had waited for only a few moments when he 'heard a step' behind him. 'Blindly and mechanically' De Quincey turned around and 'stretched out' his arms to greet the young girl but found instead, gliding between the Lilliputian arches, the bronzed figure of his military Uncle Penson, back on leave from India: 'a Bengal tiger would not have more startled me'. De Quincey was in luck. Uncle Penson, who had been expecting him, heartily approved of the boy's spirit: far better to be al fresco than sweating over Greek grammar. Elizabeth Quincey of course disagreed; her son's behaviour represented 'total revolt' from her 'rule'. But she was close to her brother and respected his views, so after reminding Thomas of the many sacrifices she had made on his behalf, she gave in and allowed him his 'unnatural liberty'. She would not immediately return him to school; he could cross the border to Wales and walk amongst the mountains he had admired on his journey to Holyhead. Moreover, she would fund his trip to the tune of a guinea a week; any more than this and her younger sons would think there was a reward for disobedience.

De Quincey was horrified by his mother's suggestion that his 'head-strong act' might have 'evil consequences' for his brothers, and his awakened conscience 'rang like a solemn knell'. Her drubbing had given him a dreadful – and correct – foreboding that his 'error' would 'magnify' itself at every stage of his life; he was reminded once more of the Belshazzar thunderings upon the wall of the Whispering Gallery.

He had achieved his freedom. But when De Quincey wandered in Wales, a period he describes in his *Confessions* as one of great suffering and hardship, he was less a romantic 'pariah' than a student on his gap year. This was not running away; it was licensed misrule.

Setting out in late summer, his first stop was seven miles from home, in the vale of Gresford. Here, in a manicured cottage where 'even the brooks were trained to behave themselves', lived two ladies, friends of De Quincey's mother. Their pampering was not what Thomas had in mind, and so he packed his bag and headed a further fourteen miles, into Llangollen, where another two ladies resided. Miss Ponsonby and Lady Eleanor Butler, celebrated eccentrics, were a local tourist attraction. De Quincey knocked at the door. Courtesies followed, but neither party had much interest in the other. 'It was not ladies I was seeking in Wales,' he conceded, as he set out on the road once more.

He stopped in Bangor, whose cathedral cemetery was said to be the most beautiful in the country. To De Quincey it resembled a 'well-kept shrubbery'. Wherever he went, he felt eyes upon him: 'Was I not liable to the suspicion of pedestrianism?' he asked, knowing that a walking man was generally considered a vagrant. He took a small room in a house; here his paranoia reached its peak when his landlady idly reported the response of her former employer, the Bishop of Bangor, to the news that a young man was currently lodging with her. 'You must recollect, Betty,' the bishop had warned, 'that Bangor is in the High Road to the Head' – 'the Head' being Holyhead – 'so that multitudes of Irish swindlers, running away from their debts into England, and of English swindlers, running away from their debts to the Isle of Man, are likely to take this place in their route.' 'Oh my lord,' Betty had blithely replied, 'I really don't think that this young gentleman is a swindler.' She did not *think* he was a swindler? De Quincey erupted. 'For the future I shall spare you the trouble of thinking about it,' and he rose from the table, packed his bag, and took his leave.

While his landlady's apparent lack of certainty regarding his honesty sounded to De Quincey like suspicion, what sounded to her like pride was the anger he had been unable express to his mother, who had not doubted for a moment that her son was a swindler. It was also a rush of fear: De Quincey had returned the banknote, but the whispers were still pursuing him.

It was at this point that De Quincey, so aware of the domestic space he occupied, rid himself of it altogether. It was the tyranny of houses rather than of school from which he was now escaping, and he needed wilderness in which to disappear. Next stop was Caernarfon, 'two and a half hours smart walking', during which his head was filled with hatred, not for his mother or for his landlady, but for the bishop who had offended his honour. No longer trusting the hospitality of lodgings, he booked into solitary inns for single nights and absorbed himself in 'the eternal motion of winds and rivers'. He felt like 'the Wandering Jew liberated from. . . persecution', and could not imagine a 'happier life' than 'this vagrancy'. But vagrancy did not come cheap. De Quincey's guinea a week was barely sufficient; it was costing half a guinea a day to keep himself warm and fed. Money management was always beyond him and the Welsh experiment anticipated a lifetime of running away from debts, exactly as the bishop had warned. His only option, if De Quincey was to eat more than berries picked from the hedgerows, was to sleep amongst the ferns and furze of the hillside. He constructed a makeshift tent which covered him like an umbrella, but it was difficult to pitch and offered no protection against the weather. Added to which, if he slept exposed to the stars he worried that a cow might tread on his face.

The October nights drew in. De Quincey befriended other gentlemen walkers, one of whom introduced him to German literature, which became a lifelong passion. He found himself a guest in a household of kind-hearted siblings whose parents were away; here he stayed for three happy days as a Cyrano de Bergerac, writing love letters on behalf of the sisters. When the adults were due to return, De Quincey swiftly departed. Once considered the most charming of guests, he was now bundled out of back doors. Winter was coming; it would soon be too cold to sleep outside, and besides, he was growing weary of Wales. His tour was over, but rather than return to the rule of the Priory he decided to 'slip' his 'anchor' and 'launch' himself 'upon the boundless ocean of London'. It was as if 'some overmastering fiend, some instinct of migration' were driving him 'to fly where no man pursued'.

De Quincey's biographers have wondered at the impetuousness of this decision. Why, when he had finished his tour of north Wales, did he not return to Chester as agreed? And why go to London, when it was fresh air and the open road that he was craving? One answer is to be found in the pages of *London Labour and the London Poor* where, fifty years later, Henry Mayhew divided the world into wanderers and settlers: De Quincey's tribe was the former. Another answer is that he needed to run away for a second time in order to do it properly. De Quincey's rebellion had so far been a tame affair, added to which his suffering had not been sufficient. 'There is,' he believed, 'a mysterious sensibility connected with real suffering,' and it was this that he needed to experience. His voyage would be incomplete until he had known what it was to live *in extremis*, and London was the city that killed its inhabitants. Added to which, in London he had felt invisible. He was seventeen, the same age as his brother and Chatterton when they had both arrived in the city; he was following in their footsteps while also preparing himself to meet Wordsworth. De Quincey needed to prove his Romantic credentials, and to study the religion of solitude before worshipping at Wordsworth's altar.

It was late November 1802 when he crossed back into England, but the days seemed to him like 'the last brief resurrection of summer'. The departing season was 'awful' in its 'universal silence' and 'death-like stillness', the light over the woods and fields resembling 'lambent and fitful gleams from an expiring lamp'. Some kind lawyers De Quincey had met on the road gave him twelve guineas to keep him going, now that he would no longer be drawing on his mother's purse, and the final night of his walking tour was spent in the Lion Inn at Shrewsbury. Here he waited in an empty ballroom for the arrival of the Holyhead mail that would take him to Birmingham. Outside, the wind was rising and the 'whole atmosphere had become one vast laboratory of hostile movements'. Midnight came and the household retired; De Quincey, listening for the wheels of the carriage, was left alone to reflect. He was facing a 'precipice'; the next stage of his adventure filled him with 'terror', 'horror'. Three 'gorgeous chandeliers' illuminated the musicians' galleries, and he thought of the Whispering Gallery, 'for once again I was preparing to utter an irrevocable word'. The 'unusual dimensions' of the walls and ceiling mirrored those of the city lying in wait; he noticed, as a 'terrific feature' of the room's altitude, an 'echoing hollowness' and imagined the 'flying feet' that had crossed the floor when the air was

ringing with music and the room filled with dancers. Beyond the windows
the night was as dark 'as the inside of a wolf's throat'.

At two in the morning the carriage rolled up to the old inn door and
De Quincey took his seat. On the road to London eighteen months
earlier he had imagined the traffic being sucked in by the city, but he
now described London as hurtling towards him, like a hysterical River
Dee or a mad dog with a foaming mouth. With 'every step' of the
twenty-eight-hour journey the metropolis was 'coming nearer, and
beckoning. . . for purposes as dim, for issues as incalculable, as the path
of cannon-shots fired at random and in darkness'.

———

The idea was to borrow against the patrimony he was due to receive
when he reached twenty-one. Therefore, the first thing De Quincey did
when he was deposited in Lombard Street in the City of London was to
take himself to a money lender he had heard about called Mr Dell, and
arrange a loan of £200. Unaware of the complexity involved in such a
transaction, he expected to see his riches immediately and was dismayed
to find himself referred to an attorney. The attorney lived at 38 Greek
Street, one of the five roads leading off from Soho Square, immediately
south of Oxford Street. The significance of the names cannot have been
lost on De Quincey, a scholar of Greek who longed to go to Oxford.
Added to which, he had spent much of his childhood on another Oxford
Street – in battle with the boys from the Manchester cotton factory.

The exterior of 38 Greek Street had an 'unhappy countenance of
gloom and unsocial fretfulness'. De Quincey knocked. A face peered sus-
piciously through a narrow window by the side of the front door, which
then opened slowly. The attorney, a hulk of a man, led the boy through
a house of 'desolation' and 'deep silence'. In a room at the back which he
used as an office, he enquired into his young client's circumstances. De
Quincey, who never knew if the attorney's name was Brown or Brunell
but referred to him as Brunell, now learned that it would take a dreary
fortnight for the loan to be finalised. Dispirited, he found himself 'barely
decent' lodgings at half a guinea a week in which to wait. He does not
say where these lodgings were but they are unlikely to have been far from
Soho. From now on his London life was organised around daily visits to
Greek Street; paperwork was done, letters were paid for, promises were

made; nothing appeared. Meanwhile the money De Quincey handed over in order to 'process' his non-existent loan drained his purse.

For the remainder of each day, he walked. He may have returned to St Paul's, he may have taken himself to Westminster Abbey, which he had longed to see; he may have visited the house in Holborn where Chatterton took his own life, or followed the Thames down to Wapping to see the Hawksmoor church on the Ratcliffe Highway. De Quincey left no record of his movements, but he was young and restless and filled with curiosity. He may well have followed the river to Hammersmith Terrace to find the house in which William had died four years earlier, during his own brief stay in London. Loutherbourg still lived there with his wife, Lucy, once reputed to be the most beautiful woman in England: would De Quincey have gazed through the windows at the man who had killed his brother while he was in his care? The Loutherbourgs, former occultists, had turned their home into a famous public healing clinic; a contemporary described how the poor came here in their thousands to be healed by 'heavenly and divine influx coming from the Radix God'. When, in 1789, Loutherbourg was lampooned in *The Times* as 'Dr Lutherburgo Humbuggo' he renounced his role as public prophet and limited his healing powers to his inner circle. What did Loutherbourg do while his apprentice lay sweating with typhoid in one of his beds? William's letters home from his days in London have not survived, but he would have enjoyed telling his family about the shadow world of Philippe De Loutherbourg, illusionist, mystic and apocalyptic artist.

His twelve guineas soon ran out and by Christmas De Quincey could no longer afford his lodgings. He could have offered his services as 'a corrector of Greek proofs', but it never occurred to him to find work. In any case, to get a job he would need a recommendation and he knew no one in London except Brunell. Faced with sleeping on the streets, he now turned to the attorney to ask if he might bed down in a corner of his empty house. Brunell, who had money problems of his own and slept in a different quarter of London every night in order to avoid the bailiffs, assented and thus began De Quincey's experience of starving in Soho, recorded in loving detail in the opening section of *Confessions of an English Opium-Eater*. His suffering now reached its zenith: 'extremities such as these. . . cannot be contemplated. . . without a rueful pity that is painful to the natural goodness of the human heart'. De Quincey, who says nothing about the various other places in London where he would lay down his head, turns the house in which he squatted into the centre of his experience.

Number 38 was a standard four-storey Georgian terrace but to De Quincey it was a 'London mansion', with 'as large a choice of rooms, or even of apartments' as he could 'possibly desire'. Except for the 'Bluebeard room', as De Quincey called it, which Brunell used as his office and kept locked at all times, the house 'from the attics to the cellars' was 'at our service'. It was not quite empty; also living there was a 'plain' and 'hunger-bitten' girl who was glad to have the older boy's protection. The two small bodies slept where they fell, huddling together for warmth, bundles of law reports serving as pillows. They lived like children from a storybook, in a land where loving adults had simply dissolved. In the attics they found an old sofa cover and a piece of rug which they added to their nest. All night De Quincey listened to the rats scuttle up and down the bare stairs.

Who was this nameless child? 'She did not herself know,' De Quincey said, though he suspected she was Brunell's daughter. Dickens lifted her from the *Confessions* and reinstated her as the marchioness in *The Old Curiosity Shop*, but for De Quincey she was, like all the angels who appear and just as suddenly disappear in his writing, an incarnation of Elizabeth. Meanwhile, his own identity was evaporating. Dell now wanted proof that the ragged boy calling himself Thomas De Quincey was the same Thomas Quincey junior named as second son in the will of Thomas Quincey senior. 'It was strange to me to find my own self. . . suspected of counterfeiting my own self,' De Quincey recalled, as if he hadn't already, as Monsieur Monsieur De Quincy, been pursued by the post office for a similar impersonation. His identity was hard to prove since he had made himself a missing person; not wanting to be discovered by his mother or guardians, De Quincey could not ask for their verification. Should his location be discovered he would be returned, with the full weight of the law, to Manchester Grammar – 'a humiliation worse to me than death, and which would, indeed, have terminated in death'. He was, however, able to produce letters from Lord Altamont which satisfied Dell that his client had connections, and De Quincey continued his wait at Greek Street. Here he saw in the new year of 1803, looking forward to the day when he could again afford to eat.

————

London was, and still is, composed of self-contained districts with distinct identities, and De Quincey had washed up in the Bohemian quarter.

Bounded from north to south by Oxford Street and Leicester Fields, and from east to west by St Giles and Royal St James, the once aristocratic parish of St Anne's, Soho was now known for the turbulence of its inhabitants. De Quincey later spoke of Greek Street as an obscure enclave, but it had been, until recently, the literary heart of the city. On the other side of the street stood the Turk's Head tavern, where Dr Johnson's celebrated 'Literary Club' had met for twenty years, until 1783. Members included Edmund Burke, Joshua Reynolds, Oliver Goldsmith, David Garrick and the botanist Joseph Banks, who still lived with his sister in Soho Square. De Quincey may well have sat on their front doorstep and watched as Miss Banks left the house every day with her pockets full of books, followed by a six-foot servant with a cane as tall as himself. 'Miss Banks,' the locals noted, 'when she wanted to purchase a broadside in the streets, was more than once taken for a member of the ballad-singing confraternity.' Another local was the Royal Academician, George Dawe. Known by his friends as 'the grub', Dawe washed once a week and then, according to Charles Lamb, applied water only to the 'inner oval, or portrait, of his countenance, leaving the unwashed temples to form a natural black frame'. Soho's middling sort were indistinguishable from its paupers, and De Quincey was camouflaged by his rags.

Forty years earlier Casanova had lodged in great discomfort at 47 Greek Street before finding himself more salubrious accommodation in Pall Mall. He was visiting his former lover, the Venetian courtesan Teresa Cornelys, whose home, Carlisle House, on the corner of Soho Square and Sutton Street, was, during the time of the Literary Club, the city's centre of sexual intrigue. A double-fronted five-storey mansion, Carlisle House had been the scene of lavish masquerades to which thousands came. Mrs Cornelys trans-formed the building into a seemingly endless space; crowds flooded the Tea Room, the Gallery, the Bridge Room, the Star Room, the Stage Room, the Chinese Room and the Pavilion, which was 'ceiled with looking glasses' and decorated as a 'delightful garden' with 'the choicest Flowers and bordered with a thicket of the most curious shrubs'. In the supper rooms diners found 'an elegant walk, bordered with two regular green hedges', while the tables themselves were 'enriched with trees'. Soho Square had been an epicentre of deception and disguise. The balls at Carlisle House were occasions when high and low or, as Horace Walpole said, the 'righteous and the ungodly', hid behind their dominoes. Countesses dressed as courtesans, courtesans dressed as queens, and rich young men dressed as paupers.

Across the square stood the White House, a high-class brothel masquer-
ading as a house of horror. A set of lavishly themed rooms contained springs,
traps and various other contrivances; skeletons sprung forward from behind
curtains, coffins rose from the ground. Carlisle House had closed in 1788,
but the White House stayed open until the year De Quincey arrived here.
His Soho Square was a ghost town where Mrs Cornelys was a folk memory, and the White House a creepy reminder of Mr White's Manchester
museum. Since then the Duke of Portland, who owned the Square, had
sold the freeholds and the residents now managed the garden themselves.
Standing at its centre, the once handsome statue of Charles II had adopted
the local uniform of desiccation and abandonment.

The area was teeming with prostitutes, and as a 'peripatetic' De Quincey
'naturally fell in more frequently with those female peripatetics who are
called street walkers'. He romanticised 'the outcasts and pariahs of our
female population', not least because those he met pitied him and took his
part 'against watchmen who wished to drive me off the steps where I was
sitting'. He says nothing about the appearance of his defenders but the
radical tailor, Francis Place, described London's prostitutes as wretched
figures in 'ragged dirty shoes and stockings and some no stockings at all. . .
their gowns were low around the neck and open to the front, those who
wore handkerchiefs had them always open to the front to expose their
breasts. . . but numbers wore no handkerchiefs at all in warm weather and
the breasts of many hung down in the most disgusting manner, their hair
among the generality was straight and "hung in rat tails" over their eyes,
and was filled with lice, or at least was inhabited by considerable colonies
of insects. Drunkenness was common to them all.' One of these figures,
a fifteen-year-old girl called Ann, became De Quincey's friend. He never
knew her surname – De Quincey's London was a blur of anonymity – and
he tells us nothing about her save that she was kind, innocent and plain.
Stressing Ann's plainness was De Quincey's way of reassuring his readers
that he did not take advantage of her, but their relationship may well have
been sexual. De Quincey, longing to prove himself a man, had hinted
to his mother already that he knew 'women of the town' while he was
at Manchester Grammar. Enjoying Ann's undernourished body would
account for the crippling guilt he would always feel about her, and explain
his drawn-out insistence on her saintly virtue. A child of the outdoors,
Ann was like Wordsworth's 'Ruth', but De Quincey did not want to be
seen as the villain who abandoned her to madness.

De Quincey fantasised about saving Ann, but it was she who saved him. One night, having wandered the length of Oxford Street, they turned wearily into Soho Square. Here they sat, as they were wont to do, on the steps of one of the mansions; she with her persistent hacking cough and he weak with hunger. Lying in her arms, De Quincey collapsed and 'without some powerful and reviving stimulus' he would 'have died on the spot'. Ann ran into Oxford Street and returned with a glass of port wine and spices, which instantly restored him. She had purchased it with her earnings, and had no expectation of the money being repaid. It was an act of kindness that he would never forget, and whenever he found himself 'by dreamy lamplight' in the 'great Mediterranean' of Oxford Street and heard again 'those airs played on a common street organ', De Quincey 'shed tears' at Ann's memory.

———

De Quincey's stories lead back not to events but to other stories, and his account of roaming the labyrinthine city with Ann as his world-weary guide echoes the legend of young Samuel Johnson and Richard Savage.

Planning to live by his pen, Johnson had newly arrived in London when he befriended Savage, a poet and convicted killer. Too poor to afford food or lodging, the shambolic, bear-like Johnson and the battered, nimble Savage spent their nights walking the London squares, talking politics and exchanging life stories. Savage's history was barely credible, and De Quincey would later ridicule Johnson's belief in its veracity. Claiming to be the illegitimate son of high-born parents, Savage blamed his current poverty on the cruelty of his putative mother, Lady Macclesfield, who had disowned him at birth. Pining for her love and recognition, he haunted her house in the hope of seeing her glide past a window or climb into her coach and on one occasion, finding the front door open, Savage crept upstairs to her bedroom. Assuming that he had come to kill her, Lady Macclesfield raised the alarm. It was not an unreasonable fear; Savage had killed a man in a pub brawl and consequently been imprisoned. Since his release he had written an accusatory autobiographical poem called 'The Wanderer', and condemned his mother in another verse polemic called 'The Bastard'.

De Quincey, who picked quarrels with Dr Johnson at every turn, took him to task in his *Life of Savage* for treating the poetry seriously and being conned by Savage's obvious 'hoax'. Johnson saw Savage as a boy 'defrauded by his mother. . . of the fortune his father had allotted him', and De Quincey saw

Johnson as a man taken in by Savage's own 'fraud'. Johnson, who described Savage as the spokesman for pariahs everywhere, including those 'beauteous Wretches' who the 'nightly Streets annoy', celebrated his friend as a 'Man of exalted Sentiments, extensive Views and curious Observations'. Such a figure slept 'among the Riot and Filth of the meanest and most profligate of the Rabble; and sometimes, when he had no Money to support even the Expences of these Receptacles, walked about the Streets till he was weary, and lay down in the Summer upon a Bulk, or in the Winter with his Associates in Poverty, among the Ashes of a Glass-house'. Johnson's Savage was trapped in his own inner darkness; he had 'lulled his Imagination' with the 'ideal Opiates' of self-exoneration. Savage was a man who, by 'imputing none of his miseries to himself. . . proceeded throughout his life to tread the same steps on the same circle'. His friends – Johnson among them – suggested that he 'exile himself from London' and 'retire into Wales' to live the rest of his days on money they raised for him by subscription. Dragging his heels, Savage sloped off and stuck it out for a year, complaining throughout that his income was not sufficient. He then absconded to Bristol where, living off the generosity of further friends, he wrote a poem satirising the city and its inhabitants. Here he died, in a debtors' prison.

Dr Johnson's delicate, complex portrait of his strange friend became, as De Quincey put it, the young author's 'nest-egg'. The beauty of biography was that the author could couple himself to his subject: Dr Johnson found fame by linking his name to that of Savage, just as Boswell was spoken of in the same breath as Johnson. De Quincey, who would write his own lives of the poets, took note.

———

Oxford Street, the threshold between London's low and high life, was the centre of De Quincey's new world. From here he would 'on moonlight nights. . . gaze up every avenue in succession which pierces through the heart of Marylebone to the fields and the woods; for *that*, said I, travelling with my eyes up the long vistas which lay part in light and part in shade, *that* is the road to the North and therefore to [Wordsworth], and if I had the wings of a dove, *that* way would I fly to comfort'. He and Ann wandered the pavements, past the 'Stately Pantheon', as Wordsworth called the theatre, past watchmakers, fan stores, drapers, silversmiths, confectioners and fruiterers. The shops stayed open until eleven o'clock and the road and pavements teemed with life. Streetlights blazed and black, lacquered coaches clattered along, two abreast.

Fourteen years earlier, a German visitor, Sophie von La Roche, had described looking through the illuminated windows of Oxford Street to the living rooms of the shopkeepers, where 'many a charming family scene [was] enacted: some are still at work, others drinking tea, a third party is entertaining a friendly visitor, in a fourth parents are joking and playing with their children'. De Quincey, a seasoned watcher of windows, would have done the same. When, in later years, he returned to London he would revisit the house in Greek Street, which was 'now in the occupation of some family, apparently respectable'. Through the glass, 'no longer coated by paste composed of ancient soot and superannuated rain', he saw a chamber brightly lit with candles in which 'a domestic party' was 'assembled, perhaps, at tea, and apparently cheerful and gay'. They had inherited the rooms of the famous Thomas De Quincey, just as he had inherited those of Edmund Burke, Sir Robert Cotton and William Wordsworth.

His fortunes appeared to improve when, on Albemarle Street, De Quincey ran into a former friend of his father who furnished him with ten guineas and promised to say nothing of their encounter to Mrs Quincey. In addition, Dell now agreed to forward De Quincey £200 if Lord Westport could guarantee the loan. Buoyed up, De Quincey prepared to visit his friend in Eton. Two years ago Westport had looked up to him as a mentor and introduced him to the king; anticipating the young man's reaction to the arrival of this derelict version of his former self, De Quincey broke into his new funds to buy some clothes. He also gave Ann a guinea, and promised to divide the full sum of the loan with her when he returned. Together they walked to Piccadilly to wait for the Bristol mail which would drop De Quincey at Salt Hill, a few miles from Windsor. They agreed to meet again in five days' time, at the bottom of Great Titchfield Street. If De Quincey did not appear at six o'clock, Ann was to return the following evening.

He took an outside seat, and the coach clattered past the Mayfair palaces. After the toll gate at Hyde Park, London dissolved into pastures and the road turned to rubble. De Quincey fell into the first deep sleep he had known for months.

He awoke at midnight to find that he had missed his stop. They were now at Maidenhead, six miles west of Salt Hill; jumping down at the first opportunity he began the slow walk back to Eton. He was heading towards Hounslow Heath where, a few weeks earlier, a man called Steele had been murdered in a field of lavender; De Quincey imagined himself and the murderer approaching one another through the darkness. Overcome by the weariness, he fell asleep by the roadside and woke at dawn to find the ground covered with frost and the trees with rime. He washed the portrait of his face in a public house in Windsor, and slipped into the school where he enquired about Westport and discovered that the boy was now at Cambridge. This information must have stung even more than the realisation that his journey had been wasted. He fumbled for the names of other Etonians who might be hospitable to him in his current state. Remembering that Westport's cousin, Lord Dorset, was also a pupil, De Quincey invited himself to breakfast. Dorset's table groaned with food, but the starvation of the last few months had made De Quincey's stomach fragile and he was unable to eat. He thirsted, however, for wine and after several glasses found the courage to ask his host to guarantee the loan. The schoolboy reluctantly agreed, and after three further wine-filled days De Quincey returned to London where Dell did not approve Dorset's conditions, and Ann was nowhere to be found. She had, to use one of De Quincey's newly minted words, 'evanesced' into the city. He waited at Great Titchfield Street every evening, and searched the streets every day. He knew neither her full name nor her address. Her fate, he later said, had been his 'heaviest affliction': 'If she lived, doubtless we must have been sometimes in search of each other, at the very same moment, through the mighty labyrinths of London; perhaps, even within a few feet of each other . . . I may say that on my different visits to London, I have looked into many, many myriads of female faces, in the hope of meeting her.'

De Quincey's suffering was now complete, and when spring arrived he said goodbye to Oxford Street, his 'stony-hearted stepmother', and headed back to Chester to face the wrath of his stony-hearted mother. Having run away from Wales, he was now running away from London and with nowhere else to go, he ran back home. An 'opening' had apparently been made with his guardians, and while he does not reveal the terms of their agreement we can surmise that he returned to Chester in exchange for the guarantee that he would not also have to return to school. His challenge now was to persuade his guardians to allow him to enrol at Oxford, a move they were 'resolutely bent' on preventing, as De Quincey put it, until he made certain 'concessions'. The nature of these concessions is not given, but they related to control of his finances and his choice of future profession.

Life for De Quincey was either angels ascending on vaults of cloud or vagrants shivering on the city streets. It was being earthbound that he found hardest to describe. Despite the vivid account he gives of this period in *Confessions of an English Opium-Eater*, De Quincey's four months on the doorsteps of Soho mansions are the time when he is least visible to the reader. In his *Autobiographic Sketches,* where he variously presents himself as a dreamy child, a precocious schoolboy, a neurasthenic adolescent and a young man in a hurry, De Quincey ensures that he is distinguished from the other faces. But *Confessions*, written twenty years earlier, is about his disappearance into the swinish multitude rather than his shining singularity, and it is this that was picked up by Edgar Allan Poe in his short story, 'The Man of the Crowd', published in 1840. Poe's narrator sits in a coffee house in one of London's 'principal thoroughfares', watching the 'tumultuous sea of human heads'. His attention is arrested by the countenance of a 'decrepit old man' which contains 'ideas of vast mental power. . . of blood thirstiness. . . of excessive terror, of intense – of extreme – despair'. The man to whom it belongs is 'short in stature, very thin, and apparently very feeble', and the narrator stalks his frail form for a day and a night as the figure treads a meaningless circuit through the city's streets and squares. Tired almost to death of walking, the narrator eventually faces his victim and sees in his features 'the type and genius of deep crime. He refuses to be alone. *He is the man of the crowd.*' The form he has followed is described as being like a 'book that . . . does not permit itself to be read'.

At the time of *Confessions of an English Opium-Eater*, De Quincey regarded his experience in London as the central scene of his life. His sufferings smack of theatre but was he, in the winter of 1802/03, playing a part? Was his winter on the streets a work-in-progress, a rehearsal for a future dominated by homelessness? De Quincey's London was a book in which he turned the pages of Thomas Chatterton, Samuel Johnson and Richard Savage, and in which he imagined the story of William Quincey, but also written into his experiences were the poems he had carried in his pocket since he left school that summer. If he began his voyage on the high seas of the city with the innocence of 'The Ancient Mariner', he returned to the Priory having imbibed the introspective wisdom of 'Tintern Abbey'.

The Priory, Chester. Elizabeth Quincey had purchased a ruined cottage in the grounds of Tintern Abbey.

Summer Vacation

> I love a public road: few sights there are
> That please me more; such object hath had power
> O'er my imagination since the dawn
> Of childhood . . .
>
> Wordsworth, *The Prelude*, Book Twelfth

It was Elizabeth Quincey's habit, when her sons became too much for her, to put them into the hands of someone else and this is what she had in mind for Thomas, whose delinquency now exceeded that of his elder brother. No sooner had he found his way back to the Priory than he was dispatched to the cottage in Middle Lane, Everton, with orders to pull himself together. It was a sensible move; Thomas, badly in need of mothering, could not have been in better hands than those of his landlady, Mrs Best. Known in the village as 'a good and kind matron', Anabela Best was the local Samaritan. Her neighbours remembered how she 'attended and cherished, with care and tenderness, the sick, the infirm, the delicate of constitution; and the convalescent, and at all times administered to the comforts, wants, conveniences of those who occasionally lodged under her roof'.

Late March 1803 saw De Quincey once again in the cabin on the hilltop village. Stretched to one side of him lay Liverpool with its surrounding necklace of windmills, before him unrolled the Mersey estuary, the Wirral peninsula, the northern coast of Lancashire, and the round ocean. Liverpool was a pleasant walk away, and De Quincey came here every day to dine at the house of his mother's friend, Mr Cragg. He also went to the theatre, the newspaper rooms, the libraries, the coffee shops and, on Sundays, to church.

Liverpool, like Bristol, was a place of masts and sails. To a stranger, warned *The Liverpool Guide* in 1801, it might seem as though ships were 'afloat *in the heart of the town*, without discovering any communication with the *sea*'. A sailor could 'step into and out of his ship with as much ease as he passes the threshold of the door to his house'. The city was hemmed in with wet docks, dry docks, basins, twenty-five-foot-high floodgates, towers, giant warehouses, piers, buoys, ropes, and – to prevent the drunks from falling into the water – rows of chains. The nearby prison held French prisoners of war and around the corner of the tobacco warehouse, on a street called 'Wapping' (named after its twin in London), were clusters of roperies, anchor smiths, block-makers and sail-makers. Deep underground, the wet docks communicated by tunnels so that by opening and closing their sluices they could lick one another clean, like lionesses caring for their cubs. De Quincey spent afternoons lounging on the pier at the end of St George's Dock, watching the ships set sail or return from their voyages. The Peace of Amiens, fragile from the start, was over. In May, England declared war on France and the soldiers and sailors dusted down their uniforms. Soon afterwards, sitting on a stone and 'lost in thought', De Quincey 'heard the rushing of a crowd of people behind me. I started up. . . and found that the tumult was occasioned by the circumstance of a press-gang bringing down their booty to a boat.' The press-ganging of men around Liverpool was a common enough sight but 'never', De Quincey wrote, 'did I behold such exquisite sorrow contend with such manliness of appearance'. The man's expression recalled for him the ancient mariner's description of his dead shipmates: 'The look with which they look'd on me/ Had never passed away.'

In July the Levy en Masse Act was passed, which required lords lieutenant to make lists of all men aged between seventeen and fifty-five who were eligible to be called up. Under this law, should there be too few volunteers De Quincey would be yoked in to defend his country. As it was, the levy was never needed but De Quincey was now not only on the run from school but also from the prospect of being rounded up and marched into battle.

The next three months represented a crucial threshold in his life, and the survival of the diary he kept during this time makes it possible for us to see De Quincey as he currently saw himself rather than as he painted himself to his readers many years later. Like the *Confessions*, his diary tells a tale of exile. But because it was not written to be read by others, there is no romanticising of suffering, no narrative tension, no flirtation with the reader, and no sense of moving through time. A record of despondency and boredom, its purpose was to provide De Quincey with an occupation and allow him an outlet. It is also a story of loneliness; there is no man on earth except Wordsworth, De Quincey believes, with whom he can share his thoughts. Having nothing to do and no one to discipline him, he idled away his time in the harbour, walking along the pier, taking tea, coffee and wine with Mr Cragg and his friends, sexually experimenting with the local prostitutes, and bingeing on library books. He documents every face he meets – De Quincey was haunted by 'the tyranny of the human face' – details the precise quantities of alcohol consumed, the titles of everything he read, and the topics of every discussion that took place during the long, slow Liverpool evenings. He was measuring his life in coffee spoons. His copious reading was, as ever, both eclectic and contemporary. He kept abreast of the monthly magazines, read the most recent celebrity memoirs and popular novels, bought his poetry hot off the press, chewed over modern philosophy, wrestled with the latest literary theories, and imbibed the current vocabulary of 'pathos', 'sublime' and 'melancholy'. He kept notes on his inner weather, queried the meanings and spellings of words ('Ancient – ancient?'), and wondered about correct pronunciation. His diary also served as a notebook in which he drafted letters, such as those he sent to his mother which had to be carefully phrased if he was to win the argument over the 'Oxford scheme'. Buried like plovers' eggs are his thoughts on poets and other writers: 'Bacon's mind appears to me like a great abyss, on the brink of which imagination starts and shudders to look down'; 'in Stewart we may observe that he always gives us one strong and comprehensive word as the hinge on which the rest of the sentence hangs and turns'. The image of the mind as an abyss down which imagination fears to look, and of strong words as hinges on door-like sentences, formed the centre of De Quincey's critical theory.

Once again he was living opposite Mr Clarke but there is no mention in De Quincey's diary of his former friend or of the biographers,

Shepherd, Roscoe and Currie. He does not say why the literary coterie has been dropped, but it is presumably to do with the 'profane way' in which they had spoken of Coleridge (as a politician rather than a poet) two years earlier. It is always curious to see what information diaries contain and what they omit; in Grasmere, Dorothy Wordsworth had recently been keeping a journal which detailed the movements of the sky but made no mention of her brother's forthcoming marriage, an event whose impact on her life she was dreading. De Quincey recorded only those things he could say to no one other than himself. He writes nothing about the war with France because his thoughts on Napoleon, an 'idol of fear', were being well aired in his daily conversations: 'Of that gilded fly of Corsica – *Bonaparte* – I said just now (what I have applied to others too – using it as a general curse) "May he be thirsty to all eternity – and have nothing but cups of damnation to drink".'

For a man who preferred his own company, De Quincey was dependent on a host of people with whom he threw himself into talk: 'talk about the war – the immense wealth of England and the proportionate superiority of honour on her part to that of other nations in thus risking her wealth – talk of free will – origin of evil – association of ideas – the incompatibility of eternal punishment – talk about Rousseau, love etc.'. One night, to relieve his own apathy, he talked about 'the clouds which hang thick and heavy on my brain'. Did he talk to Everton society about his recent experiences as a down-and-out? There is no mention of London in these pages; poor Ann – if she ever existed – has been, for now, forgotten. As an autobiographer, De Quincey would write obsessively about his past and coat every experience with meaning, but as a diarist he is fixed in the present tense.

Mrs Best provided him with breakfast and tea, but De Quincey spent his evenings either with Mr Cragg – asked by Elizabeth Quincey to keep a close eye on the truant – or with Cragg's friend, James Wright, one half of the Liverpool printing house, Merritt and Wright. De Quincey referred to the two men as W and C, but they were not the W and C he wanted to spend his time with. While he suffered their ignorance in literary matters, they suffered a good deal in the company of their guest. Surly and arrogant, De Quincey enjoyed the combat of conversation and the sense of his own superiority. His companions, he noted with pride, assumed that he 'looked down' on them 'with contempt as inferior beings'. When not fighting his corner, he employed the frigid and distant politeness he claimed to have rehearsed in the company of Hannah More; otherwise he adopted a chilly silence which was broken only to deride his host's literary opinions. Like all adolescents, De Quincey was aware of the image he projected, and he recorded in his diary the occasions on which he felt that his rudeness had triumphed. One evening James Wright suggested that 'seeing a play well performed. . . [is] the greatest pleasure human nature is susceptible of'. '"Do you think so, Sir?" said I.' Silence followed. Another time, Mr Cragg asked if De Quincey liked *The Odyssey*, 'which he himself thought mightily entertaining'. '"No," said I coolly.' Silence again. Sometimes they were joined by ladies, who De Quincey amused by 'saying that there was some road down to hell by which I might descend for a short time'. The bright-eyed boy who had charmed the whole of Ireland was nowhere to be seen.

His identification with Chatterton was now sealed: 'Last night my Chattertonian melancholia. . . returned for the 1st time this two years,' De Quincey noted in April. He does not feel suicidal or depressed: he feels 'Chattertonian'. He later described a vision in which 'I see Chatterton in the exceeding pain of death! In exhausted slumber of agony I see his arm weak as a child's – languid and faint in ye extreme. . . stretched out and raised at midnight.' De Quincey's thoughts often formed themselves as pictures. A few days later, under the heading 'POETS', he listed the individuals he considered the most important, from the seventeenth century to the present day:

Edmund Spenser;
William Shakespeare;
John Milton;

James Thomson;
William Collins;

Thomas Chatterton;
James Beattie;
Robert Burns;

Robert Southey;
S. T. Coleridge;
William Wordsworth!!!

Q. Gray?
A. <u>NO</u>

The exclamation marks after Wordsworth denote wonder, but also warning.

He was concerned about his persona. 'What shall be my charac-ter?' De Quincey wondered, 'wild – impetuous – *splendidly* sublime? Dignified – melancholy – *gloomily* sublime? Or shrouded in mystery – supernatural – like the "ancient mariner" – *awfully* sublime?' When he thought of 'character', Coleridge increasingly came to mind.

But what were De Quincey's characteristics? He made a new head-ing, 'Notes on my own character': 'A few days ago. . . I became fully convinced that one leading trait in my mental character. . . is – *Facility of impression.* My hopes and fears are alternately raised and quelled by the minutest – the most trivial circumstances – by the slightest words. . . witness the strong effects which striking descriptions of a *new sort* have . . . To me these are always paintings. Thus is my under-standing triumphed over by my heart.' This is a sound account of his rapid responses, sensitivity to language, proximity to fear and power-ful visual imagination. On 28 April he made another list:

> The Sources of Happiness.
> 1. Poetry; –
> 2. Pathos; –
> 3. Glory; –
> 4. Love; –
> 5. Benevolence; –
> 6. Music.

The presence of poetry as the antidote to his current apathy is so resound-ing that he must have struggled to find the following five items. There are moments in the diary when we recognise the Opium-Eater of his later writings: 'I image myself looking through a glass. "What do you see?" I see a man in the dim and shadowy perspective and (as it were) in a dream. He passes along in silence, and the hues of sorrow appear on his countenance. Who is he? A man darkly wonderful above the beings of the world; but whether that shadow of him, which you saw, be ye shadow of a man long since passed away or of one yet hid in futurity, I may not tell you.'

Long before opium enhanced his visions, De Quincey recognised what he called his 'constitutional determination to reverie'. From an early age he would 'view' himself as preceded by a 'second identity projected from my own consciousness', akin to the shadowy perspective in the back of the glass. The German novelist, Jean Paul Richter (known as Jean Paul) put it differently: 'there are two forms of you present in the room at any one time'. It was Jean Paul who coined, in his 1796 novella *Siebenkäs*, the term 'doppelgänger'.

De Quincey's sense of being accompanied by a duplicate is one of the reasons why he was such an effective autobiographer. His *Confessions* and *Autobiographic Sketches* present two selves: the man of experience who holds the reader in the palm of his hand, and the child of innocence who is the subject of the story. The two figures move back and forth in the narrative, anticipating and reflecting on one another. What makes De Quincey's writing so unnerving is that he felt rivalrous with this other self; his mind was 'haunted' by jealousy of the 'ghostly being' who walked before him.

———

There is nothing in De Quincey's adolescent diary so far, however, that the reader would not expect to find. Apart from being pedantic, other-worldly, dramatic and self-absorbed, he is acutely self-aware. Noting his encounters with prostitutes there is none of the eulogising over angels and noble defenders that we find in the *Confessions*: he is mired in self-disgust. 'Seized with the delicious thought the [sic] of the girl give her two shillings'; 'enjoy a girl in the fields for 1s and 6d'; 'go home with a whore to Everton where I give all the change I have; is 2d'; 'go to the same fat whore's as I was at the last time; – give her 1s and a cambrick pocket handkerchief; – go home miserable'. The unexpected occurs in his encounter with a vagrant: 'walked into the lanes ; – met a fellow who counterfeited drunkenness or lunacy or idiocy; – I say *counterfeited*, because I am well convinced he was some vile outcast of society – a pest and disgrace to humanity. I was just on the point of hitting him a dab on his disgusting face when a gentleman (coming up) alarmed him and saved me trouble.'

Reading this passage, you think there must be some mistake. Is this the young Romantic so transformed by the social sympathies of the *Lyrical Ballads* that he too became a 'vile outcast'? When he wrote for publication, De Quincey presented himself as elevated by his identification with the marginalised and the dispossessed, as a figure who straddled boundaries, who conversed alike with lords and leech-gatherers, Etonians

and street-walkers. Here he gives us a Wordsworthian encounter – one
that Wordsworth himself would have turned to advantage – but instead
of seeing the vagrant as a visionary, De Quincey sees him as 'vile' and
wants to punch him.

His bourgeois reflexes appear to be as deeply rooted as his childhood
reading and his grief for his sister, but De Quincey's response has nothing
to do with class antagonism. What makes him angry is that the outcast
is 'counterfeiting' his 'drunkenness or lunacy'; he is a fake and therefore
perhaps too close for comfort. Currently concerned with what 'character'
he might adopt himself, De Quincey had also recently posed as a vagrant
while Chatterton, who he is going about impersonating, masterminded
the most notorious counterfeit identity of the previous century.

All the time, he was moving closer and closer to his goal. The eleventh of May was spent in preparation, visiting James Wright and drinking coffee, before going back to Mrs Best's to 'write a rough copy of [a]
letter to *Wordsworth*'.

'Sir,' De Quincey nervously began. 'I take this method of requesting–'
This was clouding into heavy weather and so he crossed the sentence out,
replacing it with, 'What I am going to say would seem strange to most men;
and to most men therefore I would *not* say it; but to you I will, because your
feelings do not follow the current of the world.' As an opening line it could
hardly be better; his letter to Wordsworth was De Quincey's first masterpiece.
The poet was described in his own terms as a singular figure, and the use of
the word 'strange', which Wordsworth himself employed in the preface to the
Lyrical Ballads, was a stroke of genius. De Quincey went hesitantly forward,
and after several more crossings-out he came up with the next paragraph:

> From the time when I first saw the *Lyrical Ballads* I made a resolution to
> obtain (if I could) the friendship of their author. In taking this resolution
> I was influenced (I believe) by my reverence for the astonishing genius
> displayed in those delightful poems, and in an inferior degree, for the
> dignity of moral character which I persuaded myself their author possessed.
> Since then I have sought every opportunity. . . and resolved many a scheme
> of gaining an introduction into your society. But all have failed; and I am
> compelled either to take this method of soliciting your friendship (which, I
> am afraid, you will think a liberty), or of giving up almost every chance for
> obtaining that without which what good can my life do one?

In 'painful circumstances' and amidst 'gnawing anxieties', he continued, thoughts of Wordsworth's friendship had provided his 'only solace'. Not that De Quincey would impose on his 'hallowed solitude' or detract his attention from the 'sweet retreats of poetry'. He was, De Quincey stressed, 'but a boy', and as such came accompanied by neither 'friends' nor worldly 'connections'. And nor was it only Wordsworth he held in high esteem; De Quincey revered 'each dear soul in that enchanting community of yours', all of whom 'to me . . . are dearer than the sun'. The line, from 'Ruth', describes a father's love for his children. Despite his hallowed solitude, Wordsworth was not a lone figure but part of an 'enchanting community', a 'fellowship' of genius, a magic circle a world away from the Everton coterie.

De Quincey then reached his climax: 'What allurements can my friendship, unknown and unhonoured as I am, hold out to you?' What indeed?

> This only thing can I say – that, though you may find minds more congenial with your own. . . and therefore more worthy of your regard than mine, you will never find one more zealously attached to you – more willing to sacrifice every low consideration of this earth to your happiness – one filled with more admiration of your genius and of reverential love for your virtues than the writer of this letter. And I will add that to no man upon earth except yourself and one other (a friend of yours). . . would my pride suffer one thus lowly to prostrate myself.

The 'friend of yours' was, of course, Coleridge.

De Quincey copied the draft into his diary, beneath the draft of a letter to his mother in which he remained steadfast about his plans to go to Oxford: 'I thought it had been understood between us that my views cannot change; however circumstances may hasten or retard (or, in any ways vary) the means of their accomplishment.'

The next day, 12 May, he read through the latest *Edinburgh Review*. The journal had launched in October the previous year, its debut carrying a critique by Francis Jeffrey of Southey's *Thalaba the Destroyer*. One of the four founding editors, Jeffrey described the role of the *Review* as going beyond the 'humble task of pronouncing on the mere literary merits of the works that came before it'. Its writers were instructed to extend the usual critical boundaries and 'take large and original views of all the important questions to which those works might relate'. This usually resulted in hatchet jobs, and the *Edinburgh* house style became known as 'slashing'. Sydney Smith joked that, given the solar system to assess, the *Edinburgh Review* would conclude that it showed 'bad light – planets too distant – pestered with comets – feeble contrivance – could make a better with great ease'. In his review of *Thalaba*, Jeffrey slashed the 'new *sect* of poets' associated with Southey, 'dissenters from the established systems in poetry and criticism' who 'constitute. . . the most formidable conspiracy against sound judgment in matters poetical'. The 'Lake poets', as Jeffrey later baptised them, were distinguished by 'a splenetic and idle discontent with the existing conditions of society', with Wordsworth's theory of poetry singled out as a betrayal of its ancient function: 'Poetry has this much, at least, in common with religion, that its standards were fixed long ago, by certain inspired writers, whose authority it is no longer lawful to call in question.'

In April 1803 a third edition of *Lyrical Ballads* had appeared. There were no new poems but the preface, which had already built on the initial advertisement, had been expanded by a further 3,000 words. De Quincey followed the growth of Wordsworth's thought. 'What is a poet?' Wordsworth now asked. This was the question that also preoccupied De Quincey, and he cellared the answer as he would a good wine: 'He is a man speaking to men: a man, it is true, endued with more lively sensibility, more enthusiasm and tenderness, who has a greater knowledge of human nature, and a more comprehensive soul, than are supposed to be common among mankind; a man pleased with his own passions and volitions, and who rejoices more than other men in the spirit of life that is in him.' Coleridge, addressing the same question in a letter to William Sotheby, answered more poetically: the poet is a man who, 'for all sounds & forms of human nature. . . must have the *ear* of a wild Arab listening in the silent desert – the *eye* of a North American Indian tracing the footsteps on an Enemy upon the Leaves that strew the Forest; the *Touch* of a Blind Man feeling the face of a darling Child'.

It was now that De Quincey began to think about the importance of criticism, and to consider the difference between the poet and the critic. What is a critic? So far he had belonged to a class of men, 'feeble, fluttering, ingenious, who make it their highest ambition not to lead, but, with a slave's adulation, to obey and follow all the caprices of the public mind'. But the *Edinburgh Review* had elevated the critic: today he was, like the poet, a legislator of opinion. The effect on the reading public was 'electrical. . . The old periodical opiates were extinguished at once. The learning of the new Journal, its talent, its spirit, its writing, its independence, were all new.'

In his diary, De Quincey expanded on the points made in Wordsworth's extended preface: 'A poet never investigates the principles of the sublimities which flow from him,' he wrote, 'that is the business of the critic. . . it is the business of [the poet's] accidental coolness or the critic's perpetual coldness to point out the springs and principles of those "thoughts that breathe and words that burn" which had spontaneously rushed into his mind.' To illustrate his argument, De Quincey explained that while the sublimities of Milton were spontaneous, it took Burke, in his *Enquiry*, to point out 'the *causes* of that sublime'. His path as a future voice on the *Edinburgh Review*'s rival journal was being forged.

De Quincey followed these thoughts by drafting a cold response to his mother's burning queries about his 'particular plan for life'. 'I was not,' he wrote, 'aware that *you* – as opposed to his guardians – 'considered any positive and final determination on this point as a necessary preliminary to my entering at college. But, allowing that (in my case) it *is* so, still it seems natural that the long uncertainty I have been in as to the chance of my ever going to college (with Mr Hall's consent) would have made it as right and natural for me to keep my thoughts on the subject as wavering hitherto as the certainty of my going there.' This letter to his mother he took to the post office, while the letter to Wordsworth remained unsent. The next day De Quincey lunched with Cragg where the talk was 'about the *Edinburgh Review*, about Coleridge – Wordsworth – Southey – Cottle', after which he returned home to read Burke. When he woke the following morning, so he recorded in Greek, he masturbated.

Awash with ideas, De Quincey listed the works he intended to write. These included dramas, essays on character and pathos, an ode 'in which two angels or spirits were to meet in the middle of the Atlantic', and 'many different travels and voyages'. He sketched the outline of a novel in which a heroine lay 'dying on an island of a lake, her windows (opening on a lawn) set wide open', noting that the setting was located in his childhood home at The Farm. The scene was used not in a novel however, but in his *Autobiographic Sketches* where it was transposed to Greenhay and the dying heroine became his sister. He planned an 'Essay on Poetry' and revealed that 'I have besides always intended of course that poems should form the cornerstone of my fame'. But instead of writing poems or posting his letter, De Quincey embarked on an extended reading of Southey, whose poetry he defended with his usual vigour, finding in his 1801 epic *Thalaba*, 'the most wonderful display' of Gothic sublimity.

Before Wordsworth appeared, Southey had been Coleridge's collaborator and the two had written a poetic drama called *The Fall of Robespierre* which circulated around Bath in 1795. Since then, Southey's reputation as a poet had grown to the point where Coleridge described himself as 'jealous' of his 'fame'. He would continue to overshadow his peers; Byron thought of Southey as 'the ballad-monger', and of Wordsworth as Southey's 'dull disciple'.

De Quincey would later discover how much he and Southey had in common. Southey was born in Bristol although much of his childhood was spent in Bath; he had lost two sisters, one from hydrocephalus, and his father, who died young, had been a draper. What sort of a poet was Southey? De Quincey noted that while strong poetry did not tend to be humorous, Southey, Burns and Shakespeare – '3 of our 12 poets' – 'possessed' the faculty of humour 'in a very great degree'. This thought led on to another: there were two kinds of nature. The first was beautiful, and found in the tamer aspects – 'hedge – lane – rose – hawthorn – violet – cuckoo' and 'milkmaid', while the second was sublime and found in 'boundless forest – mighty river – wild wild solitude'. Humour might accompany the beautiful but never the sublime – so how then explain the humour of Southey, whose poems were consistent with 'the great awful torrid zone'? De Quincey's answer is that Southey did not write what is strictly called '*Poetry*'; he fitted into a 'newly discovered state or sometimes perhaps to the medium Ratcliffian kind [De Quincey's spelling of 'Radcliffe' was always 'Ratcliff'] which. . . certainly admits of humour'. Southey wrote Gothic tales in verse rather than poems. De Quincey's opinion coincided with that of Coleridge, who confided to Cottle his fears that Southey 'will begin to rely too much on *story* and *event* in his poems, to the neglect of those *lofty imaginings*, that are peculiar to, and definitive of, the poet'. The distinction between the two kinds of nature – beautiful and sublime – and thus the two kinds of poetry, was central to De Quincey's thoughts this spring, and he repeatedly returned to it in his diary.

One evening he was comparing with John Merritt, the publishing partner of James Wright, the poetry of Southey and Matthew 'Monk'

Lewis. 'Southey,' opined Merritt, 'is an inferior man to Lewis.' '"Take care, take care," said Mr Wright pointing at me; – "he is a *Southeian.*" "Oh! Sir," said Mr Merritt, "Southey is greatly inferior."'

Lewis, asserted De Quincey – determined to disagree – was driven by feeling rather than imagination, and therefore produced not poetry but '*metrical pathos*'. A writer of mysteries, Monk Lewis erred by containing no mystery in himself; De Quincey could 'see' straight 'through him': he was the type of man one might look for 'in a ballroom'. Southey, on the other hand, De Quincey argued, addressed not the 'heart' but the 'imagination', and the distinction lay at the centre of his developing definition of poetry. 'The world has more *feeling* than *imagination*,' he patiently explained to Merritt and Wright, 'and therefore. . . *verses of feeling* were sure to be more popular than *poetry*.' While he contained his irritation at the 'confusion' shown by his friends, he refused to air in public his doubts about Southey's imaginative powers. De Quincey knew full well that the dramas in Southey's work were all external, while those in Wordsworth and Coleridge took place in the minds of the protagonists; that Southey's readers would look in vain for the numinous, for fresh worlds or encounters with the soul of another living being. Southey was more interested in the ghoulish side of death than the mysterious processes of life. His 'Ode to Horror', which De Quincey read on 27 May, contains lines such as these:

Black HORROR! speed we to the bed of Death,
Where he whose murderous power afar
Blasts with the myriad plagues of war
Struggles with his last breath,
Then to his wildly starting eyes
The phantoms of the murder'd rise . . .

Southey could never have contributed to the *Lyrical Ballads.* Instead he plundered them, producing his own airless impersonations. In 'The Idiot', a ghastly marriage of 'The Idiot Boy' with 'We are Seven', we are introduced to Ned, a child who digs up his mother's coffin, removes her corpse and warms it by the fire:

He plac'd his mother in her chair,
And in her wonted place,

And blew the kindling fire, that shone
Reflected on her face;

And pausing now, her hand would feel,
And now her face behold,
'Why, mother, do you look so pale,
'And why are you so cold?'

Southey was not a bad poet so much as a counterfeit poet. He could never be the real thing because he found no fear in the act of writing: while the business of wielding a pen made Wordsworth so ill that Dorothy was roped in as his amanuensis, Southey's quill flowed blithely over page after page. Southey, noted Wordsworth, 'seldom "feels his burthened breast/ Heaving beneath th'incumbent Deity" '. De Quincey later noted how his 'poetry was composed according to a predetermined rule; that so many lines should be produced, by contract, as it were, before breakfast; so many at such another definite interval'.

On the last day of May, rising three hours after Mrs Best had called him, De Quincey walked along the pier, sheltered under a hedge during a shower, and dined in silence with Cragg. When he returned home, he took a clean sheet of paper and started his letter to Wordsworth again. It took him six hours, but it was now, he hoped, perfect.

'Sir,' he began. 'I suppose that most men would think what I am going to say strange at least or rude: but I am bold enough to imagine that, as you are not yourself "in the roll of common men", you may be willing to excuse anything uncommon in the liberty I am now taking.' The line about 'common men' is from *Henry IV, Part I*, the scene set in the archdeacon's house in Bangor; six months earlier in another house in Bangor, De Quincey's honesty had been slighted by the bishop. Writing to Wordsworth, his moral beacon, De Quincey was protesting his authenticity to everyone who had ever dismissed him as 'in the roll of common men'. The object of his revised letter was to try more effectively to win the poet's friendship and explain that *Lyrical Ballads* had provided more than the 'whole aggregate of pleasure' he had received from the 'nine' other poets he had 'been able to find'. Added to which, De Quincey confessed that he too was a poet with 'a spark' of 'heavenly fire', and his own life had also been 'passed chiefly in the contemplation and altogether in the worship of nature'. Neither of these facts was strictly true, but he was able to say, hand on heart, that he had experienced suffering.

As he came to the end, De Quincey reconsidered the passage deleted in his draft, in which he paid tribute to Wordsworth's 'friend', expressed his 'reverential love', and offered to 'sacrifice even his life whenever it could have a chance of promoting your interest and happiness'. His 'oriental homage', as he later described it, went in unchanged. De Quincey addressed the letter to Wordsworth's publishers in London, delivered it to the post office, and then quarrelled over dinner with Cragg. Throughout that day two phrases had been stuck in his head: 'flashing brief splendour', and 'labouring *to get away.*' Both define his life, but the second one De Quincey found 'exquisitely touching'. All he could now do was to wait for the poet to reply.

The following evening, visiting friends in Liverpool, De Quincey picked up some vital information about his favourite subject from a fellow guest, who lived in Keswick:

> These particulars I gathered from Miss Bearcroft concerning the Poets! Coleridge is very absent – frequently walks half a mile (to her *uncles*, I think she said) without being sensible that he has no hat on; – has married the sister of *Southey's* wife, lives (I believe she said this of Coleridge) in a house where he has lodgings; – when she first saw him in church she took him for some great boy just come from school; – *Wordsworth* is rather handsome – has a beautiful little cottage; (NB, both he and C live near Keswick) – has a sister about 29 years old.

He also learned that 'Coleridge intends to astonish the world with a *Metaphysical* work. . . on which he intends to found his fame; – Mrs *Coleridge*. . . speaks in the high terms of it; – his conversation is even more wonderful. . . than his works; – he is so intellectual as to be quite oppressive'. Added to which, Miss Bearcroft 'has seen little Charles Lamb or Charles Lloyd or both' at the home of either Wordsworth or Coleridge. Charles Lloyd was a novelist and poet who had collaborated on a collection of verses with Lamb, and been published by Cottle in a volume together with Southey and Coleridge. The enchanting community was increasing in size, and so too was De Quincey's regard for Coleridge, another dreamer with literary ambitions beyond those of poetry.

De Quincey walked home that night in a daze, filled with thoughts 'of Coleridge; – am in transports of love and admiration for him. . . go to bed. . . still thinking of Coleridge who strikes me (as I believe he always did) with a resemblance to my mysterious character (a compound of ancient mariner and Bath concert room traveller with bushy hair) – I begin to think him the greatest man that has ever appeared and go to sleep.' The bushy-haired traveller was an eccentric known as Walking Stewart, whom De Quincey had seen in the Bath Assembly Rooms walking 'up and down, and dispersing his philosophic opinions to the right and the left, like a Grecian philosopher'.

The next morning he masturbated, an act he again recorded in Greek, before spending the day reading Southey, whom he now knew to be Coleridge's brother-in-law. He then discussed with Wright the revelations of the night before.

Midsummer had arrived with its army of banners. De Quincey killed the days by drinking, walking, disputing, filling his diary, working through copies of the *Edinburgh Review*, and playing with a child called William K. Williams, who was the son of neighbours. Elizabeth Quincey, hearing reports of her son's activities from Cragg, complained that he was 'idling his life away'. After two weeks of waiting for a reply to his letter, De Quincey described how, 'My imagination flies, like Noah's Dove, from the ark of my mind. . . and finds no place on which to rest the sole of her foot except Coleridge – Wordsworth and Southey.' It was Coleridge who now came first in the hierarchy, but each man would occupy a distinct place in De Quincey's imaginative life.

His final diary entry was made on the night of 24 June 1803: 'Last night, in walking out, I invented this metaphor. . . "he was obliged to run the gauntlet through all the *reviews*".' De Quincey followed this with another thought: 'I have frequently said to myself – "Englishmen wear daggers; – not *literally* but *figuratively*".' The world of reviewing was beginning to look like a bloodbath.

He was due to return to the Priory on 3 August. Having despaired of hearing from Wordsworth, he devised 'other plans for compassing my point', which included sending the poet some of his own verses. But on De Quincey's final evening in Everton, all his 'fears and schemes were put to flight' when a letter arrived from Grasmere.

Dove Cottage. In what Wordsworth called 'the loveliest spot that man ever found', De Quincey nurtured his horrified sense of place.

6

Residence at Oxford

I was the Dreamer, they the Dream.

Wordsworth, *The Prelude*, Book Third

There are many descriptions of the cottage where De Quincey's letter arrived after a six-week delay in London, but the one in *Confessions of an English Opium-Eater* is the finest. It comes from the passage where De Quincey defines his idea of happiness:

> Let there be a cottage, standing in a valley, 18 miles from a town – no spacious valley, but about two miles long, by three quarters of a mile in average width. . . Let the mountains be real mountains, between 3 and 4,000 feet high; and the cottage a real cottage. . . Let it be, in fact (for I must abide by the actual scene), a white cottage, embowered with flowering shrubs, so chosen as to unfold a succession of flowers upon the walls, and clustering round the windows, through all the months of spring, summer and autumn – beginning, in fact, with May roses, and ending with Jasmine.

The cottage was then known as the house at Town End, because it was the last dwelling on the road that led out of Grasmere and up towards the village of Ambleside, three miles away. The name Dove Cottage, bestowed in 1890 when the building was bought for the nation, harked back to the previous century when it had been a roadside inn called the Dove and Olive Bough. It amused Wordsworth that a 'simple water-drinking Bard' should inhabit a former tavern, and De Quincey would always associate the house with doves.

De Quincey's letter had created a flurry in the household; it was, Dorothy exclaimed, 'A remarkable instance of the power of my brother's poems over a lonely and contemplative mind, unwarped by any established laws of taste'. Less excitable than his sister, Wordsworth penned a polite reply on 29 July, saying that 'it would be out of nature were I not to have kind feelings towards one who expresses sentiments of such profound esteem and admiration of my writings as you have done'. He added that 'you are young and ingenuous, and I wrote with a hope of pleasing the young, the ingenuous and the unworldly above all others'.

Wordsworth was happy to accept his role as De Quincey's teacher, but in requesting friendship the boy had touched on one of the poet's sacred subjects. The man who described himself to Coleridge as 'naturally slow to love, and to cease loving', cautioned De Quincey that 'My friendship is not in my power to give. . . this is a gift which no man can make. . . a sound and healthy friendship is the growth of time and circumstance, it will spring up and thrive, like a wildflower when these favour, and when they do not, it is in vain to look for it'. A further caution warned De Quincey that a poet lived another life separate from that of his poetry, and he must not expect to find in Wordsworth an incarnation of his words: 'How many things are there in a man's character of which his writings however miscellaneous and voluminous will give no idea.' Admitting that he 'was the most lazy and impatient letter writer in the world', Wordsworth then explained that he was imminently 'going with my friend Coleridge and my sister upon a tour of Scotland for six weeks or two months', adding that if De Quincey replied 'immediately, I may have the pleasure of receiving your letter before our departure'. Beneath his signature he penned, probably at the request of Dorothy, a quick postscript apologising for any impression he may have given of 'coldness', and stressed that should De Quincey ever find himself in Grasmere, Wordsworth would be 'very happy' to see him.

The arrival of De Quincey's letter coincided with the beginnings of two important new friendships in Wordsworth's life. The first was with Sir George Beaumont, a landowner and amateur painter who was currently renting part of Greta Hall in Keswick, where Coleridge was also now living. Sir George and his wife had come in June, said Coleridge, 'half-mad to see Wordsworth'; not only were they admirers of *Lyrical Ballads* but Beaumont, as Walter Scott put it, 'understood Wordsworth's poetry, which is a rare thing'. Coleridge, whose politics the Beaumonts were not disposed to like, soon charmed the couple; 'as far as I can judge,' Sir George conceded, 'a more amiable man with a more affectionate & kind heart does not exist'. Lady Beaumont, so Coleridge told Wordsworth, could not 'keep the tears in her eye' when his poetry was read aloud, and when she 'was reading your Poem on Cape RASH JUDGEMENT ['A narrow girdle of rough stones and crags'] had you entered the room, she believes she should have fallen at your feet'.

In tribute to Wordsworth, Sir George presented him with the deeds to a plot of land at the head of Bassenthwaite, between Grasmere and Keswick: 'Plant it delve it', Beaumont told him, '– & build upon it or not, as it suits your convenience, but let me live & die with the idea of the sweet place with its rocks, its banks, & mountain streams in possession of such a mind as yours'. De Quincey's offer of a bended knee had been trumped. Wordsworth did not build a house on the land, but it was through the influence and example of gentle Sir George that the poet found himself, as Byron put it, 'a Tory at last'. 'There can be no valuable friendship,' Wordsworth wrote to Beaumont, 'where the parties are not mutually capable of instructing and delighting one another.'

The second valuable friendship to spring up like a wildflower was with Walter Scott himself, whom Wordsworth would meet on his tour of Scotland. So immediate was the sympathy between the two writers that Wordsworth signed himself, in a letter written to Scott on his return, 'Your sincere friend', stressing that he was 'slow to use a word of such solemn meaning to any one'.

De Quincey's timing was unfortunate. Had he written to Wordsworth a few months earlier he might have gained more attention; had he written a few years earlier, he would have caught the poet in his hot youth rather than his staid middle age. Nor was De Quincey's letter the first from an admirer to arrive at the cottage; the previous summer Wordsworth had begun a correspondence with John Wilson, a robust, hearty and back-slappingly confident student at Oxford University. 'The Beau', as Dorothy proudly called him, was 'a very amiable young man. . . a friend and *adorer* of William and his verses'. Under the pseudonym 'Christopher North', Wilson would become famous as a merciless reviewer for *Blackwood's*

Magazine, and he approached Wordsworth now as both critic and 'adorer'. 'In your poems,' Wilson wrote, 'I discovered such marks of delicate feeling, such benevolence of disposition, and such knowledge of human nature as made an impression on my mind that nothing will ever efface.' His tribute paid, Wilson then assumed the fact of Wordsworth's friendship – 'I may, perhaps, never have the happiness of seeing you, yet I will always consider you as a friend.' He addressed the poet as a man speaking to men, and as a man to whom it was possible to point out what Wilson felt were 'errors' in his work: 'no feeling, no state of mind ought, in my opinion', he wrote, 'to become the subject of poetry, that does not please. . . you have described feelings with which I cannot sympathise, and situations in which I take no interest'. The offensive poem was 'The Idiot Boy', and everyone he knew, John Wilson claimed, hated it as much as he did. De Quincey later described himself and John Wilson as the only 'two persons' 'intrepid' enough to 'attach themselves to a banner not yet raised and planted'.

———

Coleridge had discovered Greta Hall in May 1800, during a visit to Grasmere. A large bay-windowed, three-storey house on the outskirts of Keswick, it gleamed through the trees at the foot of monumental Skiddaw, one of the highest mountains in the country. The River Greta flowed behind, while Derwentwater lay in front. The mountains beyond the lake had the effect, said De Quincey, of cutting the county into 'great chambers'. By the end of June, Coleridge, his pregnant wife Sarah, his young son Hartley, and an endless trail of book chests, were settling in. Sarah, who had never before left Bristol, felt cautious about inhabiting this strange new landscape with the Wordsworths – who considered her shallow and vain – as her only friends. Coleridge, who had married Sarah to please Southey, rejected her to please William and Dorothy. Sarah was the elder sister of Southey's own wife, Edith, and Coleridge was now in love with Sara Hutchinson, the sister of Wordsworth's wife; his sister complex was one of the many things he would have in common with De Quincey. Increasingly in thrall to opium, Coleridge's next three years saw the disintegration of his marriage, his health, his relationship with Wordsworth, and his belief in his powers as a poet.

In August 1803, after their first child had died from hydrocephalus, Southey and Edith also made the journey from Bristol to Greta Hall.

'Nothing in England can be more beautiful than the site of this house,' Southey exclaimed, and having come for a visit they stayed for the rest of their lives. No sooner were the Southeys ensconced than Coleridge took off, first to Scotland with the Wordsworths, then to Malta by himself, and after that to London. Southey's punishment for pushing Coleridge into an unhappy marriage was to become *pater familias* to his young family. He was sanguine about his brother-in-law's revenge: no man, Southey conceded, was less suited to domestic life than Coleridge. And few men were more suited to its responsibilities and routines than Southey himself.

Also at Greta Hall that summer was the young William Hazlitt, who had met Wordsworth and Coleridge in 1798, when Coleridge was living in Nether Stowey, and Dorothy and William had moved to nearby Alfoxden. Like John Wilson, Hazlitt was to be always one step ahead of De Quincey. He had seen *Lyrical Ballads* in manuscript form on Wordsworth's kitchen table, and heard Coleridge recite both 'The Ancient Mariner' and 'Kubla Khan', the poem 'composed in a sort of reverie brought on by two grains of opium'. Now a twenty-five-year-old art student, Hazlitt accepted a commission from Beaumont to paint portraits of the poets in their respective homes. Wordsworth's features, Hazlitt noted, were 'as a book where men might read strange matters'; he had 'a convulsive inclination to laugh around the mouth, a good deal at variance with the solemn, stately expression of the rest of his face'. Neither likeness has survived; instead we have his pen portraits of the poets in *Spirit of the Age*. Hazlitt made a tempestuous guest that summer; Wordsworth dismissed him as an upstart, too quick to have his own opinions, but the vivid description left by Coleridge shows remarkable prescience. It also shows how, despite his verbosity and psychological abstraction, Coleridge was acutely attuned to those in his company:

William Hazlitt is a thinking, observant, original man, of great power as a Painter of Character Portraits. . . his manners are 99 in 100 singularly repulsive– : brow-hanging, shoe-contemplative, *strange* . . . he is jealous, gloomy, & of an irritable pride – & addicted to women, as objects of sexual indulgence. With all this, there is much good in him – he is disinterested, an enthusiastic Lover of the great men, who have been before us – he says things that are his own in a way of his own – & tho' from habitual Shyness & the Outside & bearskin at least of misanthropy, he is strangely confused & dark in his conversation, & delivers himself of almost all his conceptions

with a Forceps, yet he says more than any man, I ever knew. . . He sends
well-headed & well-feathered Thoughts straight forwards to the mark with
a Twang of the Bow-string.

Both Romantic essayists and satellites of the Wordsworth circle, De
Quincey and Hazlitt would write on the same subjects for the same editions of the same journals, but neither sought out the other's company.
While De Quincey acknowledged Hazlitt's genius, Hazlitt would act as
though De Quincey were invisible.

———

With Wordsworth's letter tucked safely in his pocket, De Quincey
returned as scheduled to the Priory on 3 August, where his mother, feeling
the force of her son's conviction and increasingly irritated by his company, at last caved in to the 'Oxford scheme'. His guardians also conceded:
De Quincey could go to the university provided that he live within his
school allowance of £100 a year; no further money from his father's legacy
would be released until he came of age. When, on 6 August, he penned
his reply to Wordsworth, De Quincey put the situation rather differently:
'Unfortunately. . . I am not yet my own master,' he explained, 'and (in
compliance with the wishes of my mother and my guardians) I am going,
in a month or two, to enter myself at Oxford.' By coincidence, De Quincey
added, he too had 'an intention of making a tour of the Highlands this
autumn; but now, just at the time when I find that I should have a chance
of meeting you there, my plans (I fear) will be traversed'.

De Quincey's second letter to Wordsworth began with an account of
the anxiety he had endured during the last two months. Fearing that
the poet might have found 'disgusting' his expression of 'languor and
despondency', De Quincey explained that he had 'given up almost every
hope' of receiving a reply; as for the specific request in his earlier letter: 'What foolish thing I said of friendship I cannot now recollect.'
He defended his former praise of *Lyrical Ballads*, claiming that nothing
'which the world has yet seen can so well claim the title of pure poetry',
that he could 'rest on no other poems with such permanent and increasing delight', and 'from the wreck of all earthly things which belong to
me, I should endeavour to save that work by an impulse second to none

but that of self-preservation'. Referring to Wordsworth's invitation to call on him, were he to ever visit Grasmere, De Quincey wrote that 'I scarcely know how to reply: it did indeed fill up the measure of my joy. . . Henceforward I shall look to that country as to the land of promise: I cannot say how many emotions the land of the lakes raises in my mind of itself: I have always felt a strange love for everything connected with it; and the magic of the *Lyrical Ballads* has completed and established the charm' (it was Ann Radcliffe, De Quincey wrote in his *Autobiographic Sketches*, who initially brought the mountains and ruins of the region into 'sunny splendour'). He would, De Quincey concluded, 'bend [his] course to the lakes' in the summer and have then 'the happiness of seeing those persons whom above all the world I honour and amidst those scenes too which, delightful as they are in themselves, are much more so on their account'. His final line contains an unmistakable echo of the final line of 'Tintern Abbey', in which the poet asks his 'dear sister' to not forget that 'these steep woods and lofty cliffs,/ And this green pastoral landscape, were to me/ More dear, both for themselves and for thy sake!'

Carried away and quite forgetting Wordsworth's sober warning about friendship, De Quincey added a postscript in which he tried to elbow his way further into the community: 'You mention Miss Wordsworth (I speak at a venture) and Mr Coleridge; and this emboldens me to use the privilege of a friend and take a liberty which I should not otherwise have done – when I beg you to convey my most sincere and respectful good wishes to them both.'

On 15 August 1803, De Quincey's eighteenth birthday, the triumvirate of Wordsworth, Dorothy and Coleridge departed for their Scottish tour. He 'had never yet', Coleridge told Southey, 'commenced a journey with such an inauspicious heaviness of heart before'. Meanwhile, 85,000 French soldiers were encamped at Boulogne, and England waited for Napoleon to invade.

Wordsworth, who had been in France during the early days of the Revolution and had an illegitimate French daughter, now grieved for the country he once loved, and on his return from Scotland enrolled in the Grasmere home defence volunteers. 'Surely there was never a more determined hater of the French,' Dorothy wrote proudly to her friend, Catherine Clarkson, 'nor one more willing to do his utmost if they really do come.'

The previous Christmas had been spent by De Quincey on the streets of London. Now, in late December and in the middle of a snowstorm, he arrived at last in Oxford. 'No longer absorbed into the general unity of a family, I felt myself, for the first time, burthened with the anxieties of a man, and a member of the world.' Important changes to the general unity of his family had taken place in the weeks before he left home: his younger brother, Richard, had run away from school to work as a cabin boy on a South Sea whaler, and his mother had sold the Priory and moved temporarily to Hinckley in Leicestershire before returning to Bristol. In the domestic upheavals, the finer details of De Quincey's enrolment at the university had been overlooked and he arrived in the city without arranging entry to a particular college. Had he stayed at Manchester Grammar he would have been eligible for a bursary at Brasenose, but De Quincey was now faced with a bewildering number of options. Wanting a college large enough in which to disappear, and preferably attached to a cathedral and choir, he knocked on the door of Christ Church. Here he was interviewed by the dean who informed him that immediate entry was impossible, there being not so much as a spare dog kennel in which to sleep. De Quincey was recommended the smaller and less distinguished Worcester College, which was 'Singularly barren of either virtue or talents or knowledge', and lacked its own chapel.

De Quincey, who did not consider himself among the usual run of roaring undergraduates, found the social life of the university infantile and the intellectual life non-existent. His fellow students – except John Wilson, who he had not then met – 'knew nothing at all of English Literature', let alone modern poetry. The reason De Quincey gave for the 'morbid excess' of his antisocial behaviour was that his 'eye had been couched in a secondary power of vision, by misery, by solitude, by sympathy with life in all its modes, by experience too early won, and by the sense of danger critically escaped'. He had, in other words, been through the journey prescribed for Dorothy in 'Tintern Abbey'. His small income was spent on acquiring the books which would form the basis of the vast and impressive library which would later be carted around the country; his increasingly threadbare appearance was excused on the grounds of his evident genius. De Quincey spoke not more than 'one hundred words' during his first two years, and his sole encounter with his personal tutor consisted of a chance meeting during which three sentences were exchanged, 'two of which fell to his share, one to mine'. Asked what he had been reading, De Quincey replied 'Paley', referring to the utilitarian clergyman philosopher and advocate of natural theology. (He had actually been reading Plato's *Parmenides* but imagined his tutor would not know 'so very unusual' a book.) 'Ah! An excellent author,' was the don's response to Paley. 'Excellent for his matter; only you must be on your guard as to his style; he is very vicious *there*.' De Quincey's own understanding, on the contrary, was that while Paley was a 'master' of style, as a philosopher he was 'the disgrace of the age'. His tutor had shown himself 'a stiff lover of the artificial and the pompous', and no further meetings took place. For the next five years, De Quincey simply continued with his programme of self-education. His later paean to the university – 'Oxford, ancient Mother! Hoary with ancestral honours . . . – I owe thee nothing!' – was not an exaggeration.

When spring came he moved out of his college rooms and took lodgings in the nearby village of Littlemore. By now De Quincey had 'entered the cave of Trophonius'; the image referred to the Greek architect who was swallowed up by the earth.

Thus it was that six months would pass before he wrote again to Wordsworth. 'When you gave me permission to write you must have wondered, (when you remembered me) that I made so little use of it,' De Quincey's next letter began. His silence was due to being absorbed in 'little, & then unknown cares' and only now that he had 'retired to this little village' could he 'marshall [his] thoughts afresh'. Afraid that Wordsworth might think his admiration for *Lyrical Ballads* had been exaggerated, he described his first 'acquaintance' with the poems. Like everything De Quincey said to Wordsworth, the story he now told was tailored to make their friendship seem as inevitable as a breaking wave.

'Some years ago spending my holidays at Bath I was shewn the poem of We are Seven which was handed about in manuscript. Between this period & that when I afterwards discovered the volume from which it was taken, a long time intervened.' During this long interval, De Quincey explained, he had become 'intoxicated' with the 'delirious and lawless pleasures' of literature as low as 'German drama'. He would have lost himself in a 'frenzy' of melodrama had it not been for the 'purer & more permanent pleasure' he had, from his 'infancy', found in the 'Love of Nature'. In his attempt to 'wean' himself from Gothic turbulence, he 'looked round for some guide who might assist to develop &

tutor to new feelings, & then it was that from a recollection of the deep impression made on me by the short poem I have mentioned I knew where to seek that guidance, & where I sought, I found it'.

De Quincey's way of paying homage was to claim complete identification with his idols. Wordsworth had no idea that his pupil was not quite the reflective mirror he presented himself as being, that he quite happily balanced a love of the Gothic alongside the 'purifying pleasures' of contemporary poetry. He was now, De Quincey explained to Wordsworth, awaiting the hour when he too could become his 'own Master' and 'live with those Brothers & Sisters who still remain to me, in solitary converse with Nature'. Of De Quincey's surviving siblings, Richard had run away to sea, Henry was still at school, and Jane and Mary had shown no interest in setting up house with their delinquent brother.

Only after posting the letter did De Quincey discover, to his frustration, that Wordsworth had written to him twice since August. The first of the letters had been forwarded from the Priory to Bristol, and then on to Oxford, and the second had been waiting for him at Worcester College. Amongst the information contained, Wordsworth told De Quincey that he was writing a poem 'on his own life', and that Coleridge had become separated from them during the Scottish tour due to illness. De Quincey, now dashing off a supplementary letter, expressed delight in the prospect of the anticipated poem and suggested that should Coleridge try the waters at Bath, he could find him lodgings in the city. He then replied in detail to Wordsworth's query about his moral virtue. Intemperance, De Quincey explained, was 'disgusting' to him; he was immune to the dissolute temptations of college life; he had 'not much to reproach [himself] with', and nothing in his conduct could make Wordsworth 'repent the notice you have taken of me'. His description of himself was, for the moment, true.

That summer, 1804, De Quincey celebrated his nineteenth birthday. On the same day, the newly crowned Napoleon spent his thirty-fifth birthday reviewing his troops stationed in Boulogne. His ancient throne was placed on the top of a hill, surrounded by 200 bullet-riddled and bloodstained banners brought from his victories at Lodi, Marengo and Areola, a piece of theatre reported in detail in the English papers.

In the autumn De Quincey returned to London for reasons unexplained, but which were almost certainly to do with borrowing money against his patrimony. As the interminable negotiations with Mr Dell once more creaked into action, he awoke with rheumatic pains in his face. These he attributed to his morning ritual of immersing his head in cold water. After twenty-one days of agony a fellow student recommended opium and soon afterwards, on a 'wet and cheerless' Sunday afternoon, De Quincey found himself back on Oxford Street and entering a druggist's shop. The druggist was a 'dull and stupid' man, but in De Quincey's mind he became a 'beautific vision . . . sent down to earth on a special mission to myself'. His first taste of 'eloquent opium' produced one of the most celebrated passages in his *Confessions*:

> In an hour, oh! Heavens! What a revulsion! What an upheaving, from its lowest depths, of the inner spirit! What an apocalypse of the world within me! That my pains vanished, was now a trifle in my eyes: – this negative effect was swallowed up in the immensity of those positive effects which had opened up before me – in the abyss of divine enjoyment thus suddenly revealed. Here was the panacea. . . for all human woes, here was the secret of happiness, about which philosophers had disputed for so many ages, at once discovered: happiness might now be bought for a penny, and carried in the waistcoat pocket: portable ecstasies might be had corked-up in a pint bottle: and peace of mind could be sent down in gallows to the mail-coach.

Opium was the making of De Quincey. Under the pseudonym of 'the Opium-Eater' he would find the 'character' he had been searching for in the pages of his diary, and in the drug itself he discovered the 'master key' to the 'diviner part of his nature'. With opium by his side, his 'moral affections [were] in a state of cloudless serenity; and over all [shone] the great light of the majestic intellect'. He could dissolve self-conflict, eliminate self-recrimination, divest himself of fear and anxiety. He found the peace which had eluded him since that midsummer day in 1792. He could 'run away' from his 'torments'; he was no longer pursued by whispers, footsteps, hysterical rivers, angry mobs or mad dogs. As George Gilfillan put it in his portrait of De Quincey, opium 'shut him up (like the Genie in the "Arabian Tales") in a phial filled with dusky fire'.

De Quincey tried to return to the experience of this rainy afternoon for the rest of his life; his future addiction was born of the hope that he might feel once again this initial euphoria. But like everything to do with Oxford Street, it simply evanesced. So too did the druggist himself: 'I sought him near the stately Pantheon and found him not: and thus to me, who knew not his name (if indeed he had one) he seemed rather to have vanished from Oxford-street than to have removed in any bodily fashion.'

We have always been in awe of opium. Fossilised poppy seeds found at the remains of a lake village in Zurich suggest that the drug was consumed in the late Stone Age; Egyptian scrolls reveal that Ra recommended it for headaches; Homer relates how Helen, pitying the dejection of Telemachus and his men after Troy, pours an ointment into their wine called 'no sorrow'; Sibyl sedates Cerberus, the three-headed guard dog at the gates of Hades, with an opiate, and Galen prescribed opium as an antidote for 'confusion' in the elderly. 'It is time, poppy, to give up your secrets,' said Diocles of Carystus in the fourth century AD, and for his next fifty-five years De Quincey remained convinced that the poppy allowed him access to the 'inner world of secret self-consciousness' in which 'each of us lives a second life apart and with himself alone'.

While crude opium, the juice of the seed heads, forms a sticky brown cake which can be chewed, smoked or injected, a tincture dissolved in wine or brandy produces laudanum, a bitter-tasting ruby-coloured liquid which, sweetened with nutmeg or another spice, can be served from a wine decanter. Like Coleridge and many of his contemporaries, De Quincey was a laudanum-drinker rather than an opium-eater, which raises a question about the sensational title he gave his *Confessions*. The effects of laudanum, De Quincey noted, were the opposite of drunkenness. While wine ignited a fast-burning fire, laudanum created a steady gemlike glow; wine aggravated what laudanum sedated; wine disordered the faculties that laudanum focused. What De Quincey discovered that day was that the doors of perception could be cleansed by experiences other than poetry, that opium also offered 'an absolute revelation of untrodden worlds, teeming with power and beauty, as yet unsuspected amongst men'.

At first he would plan his indulgences in advance, and take himself to London once every three weeks for a debauch of opium and opera. He felt his world now 'spiritualised and sublimed'; having swallowed the magic potion, he would purchase a cheap seat high up in the gallery of the King's Theatre and, shivering with pleasure, absorb the experience of the contralto, Giuseppina Grassini, singing Neapolitan revivals of Andreozzi's *La vergine del sole*, Nasolini's *La morte di Cleopatra* and Fioravanti's *Camilla*. Opium gave De Quincey a form of synaesthesia, allowing him to see in the 'elaborate harmony displayed before me, as in a piece of arras-work, the whole of my past life'.

He then walked, 'without much regarding the direction or the distance, to all the markets, and other parts of London, to which the poor resort on a Saturday night, for laying out their wages'. Laudanum London bore no relation to the cruel city he had known two years before. 'Like the bee, that extracts its materials indiscriminately from roses and from the soot of chimneys,' his tonic 'overruled' the differences between wealth and poverty. Imagining himself invisible, he walked amongst the crowds, taking in 'the motion of time' and the rhythm of talk. 'Whenever I saw occasion, or could do it without appearing to be intrusive, I joined their parties; and gave my opinion upon the matter in discussion.' His mother had once described herself as his steering map; now, when the city fell silent, De Quincey would 'steer' his own way 'homewards upon nautical principles, by fixing my eye on the pole-star, and seeking ambitiously for a north-west passage'. Since John Cabot was sent by Henry VII in 1497, Arctic voyages to discover a north-west passage to connect the Atlantic and Pacific Oceans had been plentiful. Navigating back to his lodgings through the labyrinthine streets, De Quincey identified himself with a whole host of ancient mariners feeling their way forwards through the emerald green ice. When the terrible isolation of addiction took hold, these walks amongst the multitude became a happy memory.

As an 'opium-eater', De Quincey found not only found a literary identity, but a subject suited to his style. He was never to be, like Dorothy Wordsworth, a miniaturist. He thought in terms of accumulation and he piled his sentences high; he observed distortion rather than detail, crowds rather than individuals. A face, for De Quincey, rarely had features. 'It was my disease,' he said, 'to meditate too much and to observe too little'; he 'suffered', said Virginia Woolf, 'from the gift of seeing everything a size too large, and of reproducing his vision in words which are also a size too large'. But his writing could always support the weight of his reveries, and opium gave voice to De Quincey's stylistic insatiability.

During his London visits, he introduced himself to Charles Lamb, another of London's night-walkers and a friend of the poets. A clerk at the East India House on Leadenhall Street, Lamb lived in the Temple with his sister, Mary, who in a fit of lunacy eight years earlier had fatally stabbed their mother at the supper table. The same height as De Quincey, Lamb was gentle and teasing, with a great deal of eclectic learning, a love of puns and a severe stammer. De Quincey professed to admire his writing and so Lamb invited him to supper, only realising when the conversation turned immediately to his knowledge of Coleridge, that he was being used. Irritated by De Quincey's duplicity and by the reverential manner in which he couched his enquiries, Lamb had fun at his guest's expense by ridiculing the authors of *Lyrical Ballads*, 'their books, their thoughts, their places, their persons'. 'The Ancient Mariner' – a poem Lamb pretended to dislike – also came into his line of fire, leaving De Quincey to gasp: 'But, Mr Lamb, good heavens! How is it possible you can allow yourself such opinions? What instance could you bring from the poem that would bear you out in these insinuations?' 'Instances!' said Lamb: 'oh, I'll instance you, if you come to that. Instance, indeed! Pray, what do you say to this –

The many men so beautiful
And they all dead did lie – ?

So *beautiful*, indeed! Beautiful! Just think of such a gang of Wapping vagabonds, all covered with pitch, and chewing tobacco; and the old gentleman himself, – what do you call him? – the bright-eyed fellow?'

De Quincey placed hands over his ears in 'horror'. When Lamb had finished, he assumed a 'sarcastic smile' and told his guest that had he known they were going to talk 'in this strain' they should 'have said grace before we began our conversation'.

It was probably Lamb who let him know that Coleridge was currently living in Malta. De Quincey later joked that when he heard this news he 'began to inquire about the best route' to the Mediterranean, 'but, as any route at that time promised an inside place in a French prison, I reconciled myself to waiting'. Introducing himself to Coleridge, however, was

never as important as introducing himself to Wordsworth and it was the
passage north which still preoccupied De Quincey. It had, inexplicably,
been a year since his last letter to the poet: how much longer was he going
to wait before taking up the offer to call on the household in Grasmere?

Eventually, in the spring of 1805, De Quincey screwed his courage to
the sticking place. His love for the hills and forest lawns of Westmorland
had long been determined, he suggested, by 'a sense of mysterious pre-
existence', which was De Quincey's version of Wordsworth's 'gleams
of past existence'. Not only had he haunted the lakes in the form of 'a
phantom-self', but as a Lancastrian he felt some 'fraction of denizen-
ship' with the 'mountainous labyrinths' and silent glens whose names –
Scafell Pike, Bowfell, Pillar, Great Gable, Fairfield, Grisdale, Seat Sandal,
Blencathra, Glaramara, Borrowdale, Buttermere, Derwent – had cast
their spell over him. The journey from London is 300 miles, and his
preferred mode of transport was the outside of the mail.

The English mail-coach was, to De Quincey, a 'spiritualised object' which
revealed for the first time 'the glory of motion'. The mail-coach owned the
road. Nothing could delay its progress; other vehicles scurried to the side at
the blast of its horn. Drawn by horses of great 'beauty and power', it covered vast distances at speeds of up to thirteen miles an hour. De Quincey
enjoyed the velocity, but also the sense of inviolability and escape. 'A bedroom in a quiet house' was vulnerable to robbers, rats and fire, but the box
of the mail was the safest place a man could be – 'nobody can touch you
there'. Some travellers called the top the 'attic' but to De Quincey the top
was 'the drawing-room' and 'the box was the chief ottoman or sofa in that
drawing-room'. The interior of the coach, generally considered the most
civilised place in which to sit, was the 'coal cellar in disguise'.

He was dropped eight miles south of Grasmere in the village of
Coniston, between the slender reach of Coniston Water and the vast
fell of Coniston Old Man. The thrill of the journey over, De Quincey
now faced the ordeal ahead. It had been too long, he feared as the mail
thundered away, to appear unannounced on Wordsworth's doorstep;
indeed the very image of Wordsworth, 'as I prefigured it to my own
planet-struck eye' crushed his 'faculties'. What happened next was what
De Quincey called 'foolish panic' and what we might today call a panic
attack; an orchestration of symptoms left him petrified. De Quincey
usually signals anxiety with an image of intense motion rushing towards

him and stopping him in his tracks; in 'The English Mail-Coach' he described the sensation as one in which, 'when the signal is flying for *action*', the 'guilty weight of dark unfathomed remembrances' hung upon and stalled his 'energies'. Here, in Coniston, the signal was flying for action and he found himself weighted to the spot. Consumed by self-loathing, he turned around and returned to Oxford.

A year later, in the spring of 1806, he set out once again, this time breaking his journey at Mrs Best's cabin in Everton. He had, in the intervening twelve months, still not written to Wordsworth. The Everton air always buoyed up his confidence, and so he now composed a letter to the poet apologising for his 'long silence', explaining that he was on a 'tour' of the Lakes, and asking whether 'it would be agreeable to you that I should call at your cottage'. Between this letter and his last he had suffered, De Quincey explained, a 'long interval of pain'. He had been 'struggling with an unconfirmed pulmonary consumption' – presumably the undiagnosed effects of opium – but the 'great affliction was the loss of my brother'. Richard had run away to sea at the same time as De Quincey had departed to Oxford, but 'in losing him I lost a future friend; for, besides what we had of alliance in our minds, we had passed so much of our childhood together (though latterly we had been separated) that we had between us common remembrances of early life'. His reference to Richard was another stab at identification; De Quincey, who followed Wordsworth's every move, had read in the newspapers the previous February that the poet's brother John Wordsworth, captain of the East Indiaman *The Abergavenny*, had drowned when his ship sank off Portland. 'These things,' De Quincey continued of Richard's whereabouts, 'have shed blight upon my mind and have made the last two years of my life so complete a blank in the account of happiness that I know not whether there be one hour in that whole time which I would willingly recall.'

Wordsworth sent a warm reply confirming that De Quincey was still welcome to visit, and suggesting that he come in late May. But by June, De Quincey had still not appeared. He wrote again to Wordsworth, providing another jumble of excuses for his change of plan, but he was still in Everton in 'daily expectation of hearing some final account of the

Cambridge, the ship in which my brother sailed'. The *Cambridge*, which he expected to dock in Liverpool, did not appear either. Giving up on the return of his brother, De Quincey told Wordsworth that it was 'almost certain' he would 'come into Westmorland before the end of this month'. Meanwhile, he spent the long summer nights in his cabin, drinking laudanum and gazing out of 'an open window'. The sea, a mile below, was 'brooded over by a dove-like calm' while the great spread of Liverpool seemed to him to be 'the earth, with its sorrows and its graves left behind'. His trances 'called into sunny light the faces of long-buried beauties' and all those 'blessed household countenances' which in the graveyard lay.

Memories, long buried, streamed to the surface. When he slept, 'dream form[ed] itself mysteriously within dream', and 'the nursery of my childhood expanded before me: my sister was moaning in bed. . . I was beginning to be restless with fears not intelligible to myself.' Continually he returned to the 'trance in my sister's chamber': vaults, shafts and billows transported him to the realm he had glimpsed through the window on that midsummer day. 'Again I am in the chamber with my sister's corpse, again the pomps of life rise up in silence, the glory of the summer, the Syrian sunlights, the frost of death.'

With this 'drowsy syrup', De Quincey said, combining imagery from *Othello* and *Macbeth*, a 'guilty man' could regain 'for one night. . . the hopes of his youth and hands washed pure from blood'. But opium became itself a source of guilt: 'In the one CRIME of OPIUM,' wrote Coleridge, 'what crime have I not made myself guilty of!'

———

De Quincey eventually left Everton and spent 15 August 1806, his twenty-first birthday, on the road to Grasmere. He was now the recipient of a modest fortune of £2,600, of which £600 was already accounted for in debts accumulated over the last three years, including the costs incurred by his sister, Mary, when she searched these same roads for her brother after he ran away from school. By 18 August he had, once again, reached Coniston. Here, at the Black Bull Inn, De Quincey gathered his thoughts as we do when we arrive at a turning point in our lives. What were his future goals? A new list was drawn up in his diary, titled 'The Constituents of Happiness'. The 'Sources of Happiness' he had listed three years before had begun with 'Poetry' and ended with 'Music'. De Quincey's requirements were now more specific:

1. A capacity of thinking – i.e., of abstraction and reverie
2. The cultivation of an interest in all that concerns human life and human nature
3. A fixed and not merely temporary residence in some spot of eminent beauty: – I say *not merely temporary* because frequent change of abode is unfavourable to the growth of local attachment which must of necessity exercise on any (but more especially on the contemplative mind) a most beneficial influence. . .
4. Such an interchange of solitude and interesting society as that each may give to each an intense glow of pleasure.
5. Books. . .
6. Some great intellectual project to which all intellectual pursuits may be made tributary. . .
7. Health and vigour
8. The consciousness of a supreme mastery over all unworldly passions (anger – contempt – and fear). . .
9. A vast predominance of contemplation varied with only so much of action as the feelings may prompt by way of relief. . .
10. . . . *emancipation from worldly cares* – anxieties – and connexions – and from all that is comprehended under the term *business*
11. The education of a child
12. . . . a personal appearance tolerably respectable. . .

Opium would help him in the achievement of numbers 1, 8, 9 and 10, but would work against 7 and 12. Regardless of any effort he made, De Quincey's clothing would always require improvement. Throughout his life, as Michael Neve puts it, he would continue to 'look dreadful while keeping up appearances'. Number 3 revealed his exasperation with his mother's domestic arrangements and his longing for stability; 5 and 6 were within his reach, and 11, a fashionable Romantic hobby, would be realised in the next few years. What is striking is not just the certainty with which De Quincey understood his own needs, but how little his requirements would change from now on. Also remarkable is how near he had already come, through sheer endeavour, to fulfilling the ambitions of a lifetime. Meanwhile his overruling desire, to meet Wordsworth, was within hours of completion.

Master of his own destiny, with money to spend and no one to answer to, De Quincey pushed forwards to the gorge of Hammerscar where he shuddered to look down into the vale of Grasmere. The 'loveliest of landscapes' broke 'upon the view in a style of almost theatrical surprise'. He took in the dimensions: here was the lake, 'with its solemn bend-like island of five acres in size, seemingly afloat on its surface', and 'just two bow-shots from the water' at the foot of 'a vast and seemingly never-ending series of ascents', gleamed the 'little white cottage' which he knew to belong to the poet. Standing a few miles above the building, he was positioned like Wordsworth in 'Tintern Abbey' – and De Quincey was also revisiting the view. Beneath him lay his future. Eight years earlier, in anticipation of such a moment, Coleridge had bounded the forty miles from his home at Nether Stowey to Wordsworth's home at Racedown, where he leapt over a gate and tore through an unmown field to embrace the man who would become the greatest friend of his life. But De Quincey once again turned around – and 'retreated like a guilty thing'.

The image he used to describe his second flight from Wordsworth was the same as the one he used to describe his departure from Elizabeth's bedroom in Greenhay, when he heard footsteps on the stairs. The phrase was from Wordsworth's 'Intimations of Immortality', where the poet 'Did tremble like a guilty thing surprised', and Wordsworth himself had taken it from Act 1 of *Hamlet*, where the murdered king's ghost is described by Horatio as disappearing with the dawn, 'like a guilty thing/ Upon a fearful summons'. It was Hamlet, indecisive, philosophising, obsessed by another world, whom De Quincey was starting to resemble.

Within days of De Quincey's second retreat from Grasmere, and his return to Oxford, Coleridge's ship was docking on the Medway. After two and a half years, the mariner had come home – except that he no longer knew where in the world such a place might be. His trunk of books got lost in Wapping and after a fruitless search of the warehouses along the Ratcliffe Highway, he took himself to London. Three months of procrastination followed before Coleridge returned to his family at Greta Hall. 'I have a smack of Hamlet myself, if I may say so,' he famously observed.

Gustave Doré, 'The Mariner gazes on the serpents in the ocean',
from the *The Rime of the Ancient Mariner* by Samuel Taylor Coleridge.

'In his loneliness and fixedness he yearneth toward the journeying
Moon, and the stars that still sojourn, yet still move forward.'

Retrospect: Love of Nature Leading to Love of Mankind

> . . . so wide appears
> The vacancy between me and those days
> Which yet have such self-presence in my mind,
> That, sometimes, when I think of them, I seem
> Two consciousnesses, conscious of myself
> And of some other Being.
>
> Wordsworth, *The Prelude*, Book Second

One reason behind what De Quincey called his 'mysterious delay' in meeting Wordsworth was his fear that the poet might prove a disappointment to him. Or – worse – that he, lionised by his school teachers and the self-proclaimed spokesman for *Lyrical Ballads* in Everton literary society, would prove a disappointment to Wordsworth. Unlike Coleridge, whose talk was famously circumambient, De Quincey was as shy as an ibex. In those days he moved cautiously in conversation as if through a tangled wood, and he found it hard to 'unravel' or 'even make perfectly conscious' to himself the 'subsidiary thoughts into which one leading thought often radiates'. This was an area in which De Quincey believed he resembled the young Wordsworth, who had laboured under a similar curse at the same age before finding his spoken voice in his late twenties. Despite luxuriating in the contempt of others, De Quincey drew a line at inviting Wordsworth's scorn: 'there was a limit. People there were in this world whose respect I could not dispense with.'

Coleridge, however, being like 'some great boy just come from school', inspired less fear than the parental Wordsworth. Added to which, De Quincey knew that they shared a love of German metaphysics which meant that they would never run out of things to say. And should De Quincey find himself tongue-tied, Coleridge, from what he had heard, would happily continue the conversation alone. De Quincey decided to rethink his tactics, and approach Wordsworth through the conduit of his friend and collaborator.

In the summer of 1807 Elizabeth Quincey was living in Downy Parade, Bristol, two bowshots from Wrington in Somerset, where Hannah More had her headquarters. De Quincey, who liked this corner of the country a great deal more than he liked Oxford, was a regular visitor to his mother's house. An added attraction was the presence in the city of Joseph Cottle, publisher of *Lyrical Ballads*, and it was Cottle who told De Quincey that Coleridge was back in England and staying with Thomas Poole, forty miles away in Nether Stowey. On 26 July, De Quincey mounted his steed and swerved south, arriving at Poole's house that evening.

A loyal friend of Coleridge, Poole was a 'stout, plain-looking farmer, leading a bachelor life'. De Quincey handed him a letter of introduction from Cottle, only to learn that Coleridge had temporarily left to pay a visit to Lord Egmont. Intrigued by Coleridge's admirer, Poole invited the young man to stay until his guest returned, which gave De Quincey time to explore the local sights and continue his research into the lives of the poets. First on his agenda was a visit to Wordsworth's former home at Alfoxden, 'a place of singular interest to myself'. It was here, he noted, surrounded by the 'ferny Quantock hills which are so beautifully sketched in the poem of "Ruth"', that Wordsworth and Dorothy lived before they returned to their native lakes.

That evening the two men talked over dinner. As his guest was a philosopher, Poole asked whether De Quincey had ever formed an opinion on why Pythagoras forbade his disciples from eating beans. Coleridge, Poole added darkly, had recently proposed an explanation which he suspected 'to have not been original'. This was the first hint that De Quincey received of there being an 'infirmity' in his hero's 'mind': at times Coleridge represented the thoughts of others as his own. De Quincey was able to tell his host that he had read in the pages of a certain 'German author' that beans in ancient Greece were used as tokens for voting, and so Pythagoras's prohibition was not against the eating of beans but against involvement in politics. 'By Jove,' spluttered Poole, 'that was the very explanation [Coleridge] gave us!'

Who knows if this conversation took place? It was described by De Quincey twenty-seven years later in a series of essays for *Tait's Edinburgh*

Magazine on 'Samuel Taylor Coleridge'. Having died some months before, Coleridge was unavailable for comment. 'Here was a trait of Coleridge's mind,' De Quincey trumpeted, 'to be first made known to me by his best friend, and first published to the world by me, the foremost of his admirers!' The whole premise of the anecdote about Pythagoras and the beans is unstable: devoted to Coleridge, Poole was unlikely to spread rumours which would destroy the reputation of his friend and discredit him in the eyes of a young admirer. Added to which, it is hard to imagine the genial Poole wrestling with the fear that something said over supper might not have been freshly coined. Coleridge had a porous intellect; it was assumed by those who enjoyed his company that his conversation was infused with deep reading.

The day after his dinner with Poole, Lord Egmont paid a visit to Nether Stowey to report that Coleridge had gone for the night to the market town of Bridgwater, eight miles away at the edge of the Somerset Levels. Egmont said this with a laugh at 'his own simplicity' in assuming the stability of any plan made by Coleridge. The ruling feature of Coleridge's daily life, De Quincey gathered, was his timekeeping. 'Nobody who. . . knew him ever thought of depending on any appointment he might make. . . those who asked him to dinner or any other party, as a matter of course, sent a carriage for him.' Rather than wait indefinitely for his return, De Quincey decided to ambush Coleridge in Bridgwater, where he arrived later that day. Leading his horse down the main street of the town he saw in front of him, standing beneath a gateway, a 'gazing' figure:

> In height he might be about five feet eight; (he was, in reality, about an inch and a half taller, but his figure was of an order which drowns the height); his person was broad and full, and tended even to corpulence. . . his eyes were large and soft in their expression; and it was from the peculiar appearance of haze or dreaminess, which mixed with their light, that I recognised my object. . . I examined him steadfastly for a minute or more; and it struck me that he saw neither myself nor any other object in the street. He was in a deep reverie.

De Quincey's writing always resounds like an echo chamber, and his description of Coleridge recalls that of the persecuted dog whose 'glazed' and 'dreamy' eyes had met his own on the last morning he saw his brother William alive. Startled back into the material world, Coleridge now 'repeated rapidly a number of words which had no relation to either of us' before greeting the young man 'with a kindness of manner so marked that it might be called gracious'. De Quincey handed him the gift of 'a scarce Latin pamphlet' written by the philosopher David Hartley, after whom Coleridge's eldest son was named. Coleridge pressed him to stay to dinner and then, for three uninterrupted hours, talked philosophy 'like some great river, the Orellana, or the St Lawrence, that had been checked and fretted by rocks or thwarting islands, and suddenly recovers its volume of waters, and its mighty music. . .' At one point a well-presented woman, whose prettiness was of a 'commonplace order', briefly entered the room: 'Mrs Coleridge', announced a frigid Coleridge. The 'Coleridges' marriage,' De Quincey noted, 'had not been a happy one.'

———

When he and Wordsworth had first met in 1797, it was Coleridge who was the contented family man while Wordsworth, with a pregnant mistress in revolutionary France, was the more fragile figure. And it was Coleridge with the growing reputation, while Wordsworth was unheard of. The tables had now turned: Wordsworth's name was gathering strength and Coleridge felt his own diminishing; Wordsworth was floating in deep domestic calm while Coleridge, swollen with laudanum and 'a wretched wrack' of his former self, was 'rolling, rudderless' into the roughest seas of his life. He had returned from Malta, thought Dorothy, 'utterly changed. . . that he is ill I am well assured, and must sink if he does not grow more happy'. Coleridge is often associated, and often associated himself, with water imagery. Wordsworth, he said, had been happy to let him 'flow' in his own 'main stream' but had discouraged 'every attempt of mine to roll forward into a distinct current of my own'.

Their friendship had taken a severe blow in the winter of 1806/07 when the Wordsworth party, bursting at the seams of Dove Cottage, had decamped to Sir George Beaumont's estate at Coleorton where Coleridge, still desperately in love with Sara Hutchinson, had joined them. Here Wordsworth read aloud the manuscript of the poem which would later be known as *The Prelude*. When he had finished, 'hanging still upon the sound' of the poet's deep voice, Coleridge 'rose' and found himself 'in prayer'. *The Prelude,* he knew, would ensure Wordsworth's place in 'the choir of ever-enduring men'. Coleridge described his friend as standing 'at the helm of a noble bark', sailing 'right onward' in 'open ocean and a steady breeze'. Himself a sinking mariner, Coleridge's own poetic silence contrasted sorely with the unstoppable stream of his friend, 'driven in surges now beneath the stars'. His agony of self-laceration was compounded by a hellish vision on the morning of Saturday 27 December, of Wordsworth and Sara together in a bedroom, her 'beautiful breasts uncovered'. Coleridge spent the rest of the day in the Queen's Head, drinking ale and frantically writing in his notebook.

Whatever took place in that dreadful 'phantasm' – and Coleridge himself seemed not to know if the scene was real or imagined – the result was catastrophic. All we have to go on is what he described in his notebooks ten months later – during the time that he was seeing De Quincey on a daily basis – when he described the 'agony' of 'the vision of that Saturday Morning – of the bed – O cruel!/ is he not beloved, adored by two [Sara and Mary] & two such Beings! and must I not be beloved *near* him except as a Satellite?' Coleridge followed this lament with a passage decrying Wordsworth's incapacity to love, and resenting his friend's 'greater, better, manlier' attractions. The entry ends with the plea: 'Love me, Sara! Sara! Love me!'

When De Quincey now approached him on the high street in Bridgwater, Coleridge had lost his compass. He remained convinced that separating from his wife was the answer to his troubles, that the 'perpetual struggle, and endless *heart-wasting*' of his domestic life lay 'at the bottom of all my irresolution, procrastination, languor, and former detestable habit of poison-taking'. The Wordsworths agreed that 'poor Coleridge', as they now referred to him, was being destroyed less by opium than by a superficial spouse and felt confident that they could wean their friend off both. For Southey, who shared a house with Sarah Coleridge, it was from 'idolatry of that family' that Coleridge's problems began; the Wordsworths 'have always humoured him in all his follies, listened to his complaints of his wife, and when he complained of his itch, helped him to scratch, instead of covering him with brimstone ointment, and shutting him up by himself'.

After dinner, De Quincey and Coleridge took a walk through the town and De Quincey mentioned that he had taken laudanum for a toothache. Coleridge then apparently 'revealed', with 'a deep expression of horror at the hideous bondage', that he was 'under the full dominion' of the drug. The biographical consensus is to doubt that Coleridge, who was appalled by his own addiction, would confide such information to a relative stranger, but neither man would have been acting out of character in having such an exchange. De Quincey, a wily operator, was exercising the 'gossiping taste', as he called it, of the future biographer while Coleridge's emotional incontinence, his most beguiling feature, was at its worst when the subject was his own wretched state. Added to which, Coleridge opened up around his acolytes and De Quincey, an earnest and talented Greek scholar with an extensive knowledge of metaphysics, was calculated to arouse his identification and concern.

If he had not heard from Cottle already about Coleridge's problems with opium, De Quincey would have recognised the effects of the drug in his host's dreamy and wandering talk. With the patient help of Poole, Coleridge was currently reducing his daily intake and we know from his notebooks the 'evil' effects of his current withdrawal: 'a cruel sweat on the brow, & on the chest – windy sickness at the Stomach. . . a reprobate Despair'. His physical suffering was only part of the battle; like all addicts he could only break his addiction by addressing it, and Coleridge was thrown into a maelstrom whenever he looked at himself: 'the habit of Brooding daily makes it harder to confess the Thing I am, to any one – least of all to those, whom I most love & who most love me'. Such a confession would be easier to make to someone he did not love, and extracting a confession was De Quincey's aim in raising the subject: confessions and opium were for him natural bedfellows.

De Quincey always liked to describe the journey home following a momentous encounter. His reflections during these times tend to be presented as prophetic, as though he were on the brink of something vast. Tonight he walked back to Bristol guided by the 'Northern constellations'. Coleridge was both more than and less than the man he had imagined him to be: he was, without doubt, an 'extraordinary person', but his character contained a fatal flaw, and his 'majestic powers' were 'already besieged by decay'. His golden days were behind him, but it was still more glorious to listen to a sinking Coleridge than to any rising orator. In his essay on 'Coleridge and Conversation', De Quincey wrote that 'To have heard Coleridge has now indeed become so great a distinction, that if it were transferable, and a man could sell it by auction, the biddings for it would run up as fast as for a genuine autograph of Shakespeare.'

But did Coleridge hear anything of De Quincey's voice? And what did he see when he looked into the eyes of his elfin visitor? An entry made in his notebook at the time he met De Quincey describes an impression of

'Two faces, each of a confused countenance: In the eyes of the one, mud-diness and lustre were blended; and the eyes of the other were the same, but in them there was a red fever that made them appear more fierce. And yet, methought, the former struck a greater trouble, a fear and distress of the mind; and sometimes all the face looked meek and mild, but the eye was ever the same.'

Of the two pairs of eyes the first, which belong to De Quincey, reveal nothing of their subject, they muddy the waters, while the second – Coleridge's eyes – are a window into a fierce and feverish soul. It is the first pair which unnerves him; gazing from an otherwise mild face they suggest trouble, 'a fear and distress of the mind'. Coleridge saw in De Quincey what the Wordsworths were never able to recognise: that his façade of meekness disguised turbulence and ferocity. De Quincey was a figure of fearful immensity.

In May 1807, five years after the publication of the third edition of *Lyrical Ballads*, Wordsworth's *Poems, in Two Volumes* appeared. Amongst the sonnets, lyrics and odes was Wordsworth's lament for Coleridge: 'There is a change – and I am poor.' The reviewers were unanimous in their weariness of what they considered tedious introspection. 'I reviewed Wordsworth's trash of the time,' Byron later recalled, while another critic exhorted the poet to stop 'drivelling' to the 'common pile-wort' and to spend less time in the company of the 'moods of his own mind'. Francis Jeffrey in the *Edinburgh Review* despaired at Wordsworth's determination 'to court literary martyrdom' by 'connecting his most lofty, tender, or impassioned conceptions, with objects and incidents, which the greater part of his readers will probably persist in thinking low, silly, or uninteresting'. For most readers, Jeffrey argued, 'the sight of a friend's garden-spade' is unlikely to engender 'powerful impressions and interesting reflections': 'All the world laughs at Elegiac stanzas to a sucking-pig – a Hymn on Washing-day – Sonnets to one's grandmother – or Pindarics on gooseberry-pye; and yet, we are afraid, it will not be quite easy to convince Mr. Wordsworth, that the same ridicule must infallibly attach to most of the pathetic pieces in these volumes.'

In his condemnation of *Poems, in Two Volumes*, Jeffrey at least con-ceded that *Lyrical Ballads* had been a success: 'If these volumes. . . turn out to be nearly as popular as the lyrical ballads – if they sell nearly to the

same extent – or are quoted and imitated among half as many individuals, we shall admit that Mr. Wordsworth has come much nearer the truth
in his judgment of what constitutes the charm of poetry, than we had
previously imagined.' Wordsworth considered himself above the criticism of those trapped by the conventions of taste. What, he asked Lady
Beaumont, did his poems have to do with the world of 'routs, dinners,
morning calls, hurry from door to door, from street to street, on foot or
in Carriage. . . what have they to do. . . with a life without love?' In a
mind where there is no 'imagination', he explained, 'the voice which is
the voice of my poetry' cannot be heard.

———

That September, Sarah Coleridge and her three children, Hartley, aged
eleven, Derwent, aged seven and a four-year-old daughter also called
Sara moved to College Street in Bristol, leaving Coleridge to prepare
a lecture series on the fine arts which he was due to deliver in London
later in the autumn. De Quincey divided his time between helping
Coleridge gather together his thoughts in Nether Stowey, and currying
favour with Sarah in Bristol. Always more relaxed with children, he
invited Hartley – the 'faery voyager' of Wordsworth's exquisite lyric,
'To H C, six years old' – to dinner and took him on a tour of the dells
of Leighwood.

His next move was to send Coleridge, via Cottle, a gift of £300 (the equivalent in today's money of £10,000) from an 'anonymous benefactor'. Cottle
assured Coleridge that the source was known to him, and that there was 'not
a man in the Kingdom of whom you could rather accept a favour'. Much
has been made of the generosity of the gift and little said about its inten-
tions; knowing that Coleridge – despite his annuity of £150 from Josiah and
Thomas Wedgwood – was in no position to refuse such a sum, De Quincey
found a way of purchasing the friendship and bestowing on him an obligation. Before he became a borrower, De Quincey was a lender: he experienced
from both sides the deep moral power of debt. The 'anonymity' of the gift –
which De Quincey later explained had been a loan – could not be taken
seriously; there was only one person in Coleridge's life determined to make
himself indispensible, and Cottle later said that the poet had '*no doubt* of the
source whence the money was derived'.

When Coleridge returned his family to Greta Hall, De Quincey seized the opportunity to propose himself as their escort. Sarah was glad of the company, the children were delighted to have a playfellow, and De Quincey had solved his problem. This was the third time he had tried to make his wish come true: now, when he appeared at the door of Dove Cottage, it would be not as a ragamuffin runaway or a pilgrim devotee but as the official representative of Samuel Taylor Coleridge.

Everyone was changing places. De Quincey had replaced Coleridge as protector of his wife and children, and Coleridge moved into the household of his friend, John Morgan, whose wife and sister-in-law quickly replaced Mary Wordsworth and Sara Hutchinson: 'I never knew two pairs of humans so alike,' Coleridge enthused to Dorothy, 'as Mrs Morgan & her sister. . . and Mary and Sara. I was reminded afresh of the resemblance every hour – & at times felt a self-reproach, that I could not love two such amiable, pure & affectionate Beings for their own sakes. But there is a time in Life, when the heart stops growing.'

The Grasmere party left Bristol at the end of October, and once again the children lost sight of their father. De Quincey kept spirits high on the journey by betrothing himself to little Sara, and they stopped for a week in Liverpool where the Coleridges stayed with friends while De Quincey paid a visit to Everton. From here it was ninety miles to their destination; they spent their last night in Lancaster before entering the land of mist and cloud through the gateway at Kendal.

When their chaise reached Rydal Water it crawled so slowly to the summit of White Moss that De Quincey leapt off and ran down the hill for the final mile, leaving the horses far behind and even losing 'the sound of the wheels at times'. Spreading out to his left was Lake Grasmere, its sylvan margin feathered with ferns and the surrounding copses burning with autumnal gold. Rearing into view at a turn in the road, he saw, with a 'sudden shock', the white cottage he had spied the year before from the gorge of Hammerscar. His panic returned; had the chaise not then rolled up behind him, De Quincey would have fled.

And so it was that at four o'clock on 4 November 1807, four and a half years after first writing to him, De Quincey was able to say that he bounded down the road to greet Wordsworth.

According to Coleridge, the man who finds himself facing an 'appari-tion' is sure to die. De Quincey, remembering this theory, felt as though his first 'face to face' encounter with Wordsworth was similarly fatal. 'Never before or since can I reproach myself with having trembled at the approaching presence of any creature,' he said of the long-anticipated moment. Pushing open the garden gate, De Quincey 'heard a step', and then 'a voice', after which, like 'a flash of lightning', he saw emerging from the house 'a tallish man, who held out his hand, and saluted me with the most cordial manner'. Coleridge had first appeared to De Quincey in a haze, but Wordsworth came as a flash. De Quincey would always associ-ate the Wordsworths with suddenness.

Mrs Coleridge, sitting in the coach, required handing down; it was Wordsworth who did the honours while De Quincey, 'stunned' at having 'survived' what had been 'so long anticipated and so long postponed', made his way mechanically through the front door of the cottage and into the parlour which, according to his measurements, 'was an oblong square, not above eight and a half feet high, sixteen feet long and twelve broad'. Here two ladies appeared. The first was tall, slender ('for my taste. . . rather too slender'), and 'very plain', with a squint in one eye which went 'much beyond' what might be considered 'an attractive foible'. Constitutionally silent, she wore 'the most win-ning expression of benignity' that De Quincey had ever beheld. This was Wordsworth's wife, Mary, the 'perfect woman, nobly planned', and celebrated in *Poems, in Two Volumes*. The second figure, her opposite in every way, was Dorothy. Mary had grace, and Dorothy 'was all fire': small, 'Egyptian brown', with the 'wild eyes' so finely noticed in the 'Tintern Abbey', Wordsworth's sister blazed with 'impassioned intel-lect'. A combination of the 'unsexual' and the 'fervent', Dorothy stam-mered when she talked ('as distressingly as Charles Lamb himself') and stooped when she walked. She was, De Quincey felt, liable to flare out at any moment, and he found her freedom of expression unfeminine.

The ladies ushered De Quincey up 'fourteen steps' to Wordsworth's study, which was 'seventeen feet by twelve, and not more than seven and a half feet high'. A single diamond-paned window looked down towards Grasmere Lake, and one of two shallow recesses in the wall contained the poet's books – only two or three hundred volumes, De Quincey noticed with surprise – unbound and uncared for. This served as Wordsworth's composing room, the children's playroom, the dining room, and the drawing room. When that dedicated Wordsworthian the Reverend Stopford Brooke, chaplain to Queen Victoria, secured the cottage for the nation at the end of the century, he imagined the poet in this same 'low, dark room, his life from boyhood pass[ing] before him, vision after vision' while 'the walls opened and showed him the universe'.

Few writers' homes have been as mythologised by their own inhabitants as the house occupied for eight years by William and Dorothy Wordsworth. They were not the owners of the cottage, which they rented for £8 a year from a neighbour called John Benson, and nor was it their only significant home. Racedown in Dorset, where Wordsworth lived in 1797 before moving briefly to Alfoxden, represented equally important moments in his biography. It was in Racedown that he and Dorothy, separated as children, first reclaimed their lost years; where Wordsworth had courted Mary, and formed his friendship with Coleridge. It was in Alfoxden, where the Wordsworths then moved in order to be close to Coleridge, that *Lyrical Ballads* was conceived and born. But it was the cottage in the county of his childhood that was understood by Wordsworth to be his shrine. He and Dorothy had taken possession of the house at six o'clock in the evening on 20 December 1799 – the date and time were sacred to them both – and in 'this sequestered nook', Wordsworth wrote his finest poems, many of which commemorated the 'embracing' vale itself.

After greeting Mrs Coleridge and her children, Wordsworth joined De Quincey and the ladies in his study. 'And *what-like*,' wrote De Quincey, using a Cumbrian expression, 'was Wordsworth?' He had been led to expect a handsome man but Wordsworth, who at thirty-eight looked 'rather over than under sixty', was 'not well-made': his legs were thick and, while not exactly 'deformed', proved too short for his torso. Considering the distance they had covered – around 180,000 miles, De Quincey calculated – they made up in service for what was lacking in ornament, but it was a shame that he did not have a second pair 'for evening dress parties'. On one occasion, walking several paces behind her brother, Dorothy exclaimed to De Quincey: 'Is it possible? – can that be William? How very mean he looks!' When seen from the back, Wordsworth carried 'a sense of absolute meanness', but he never looked worse than in motion, at which point he took on a 'twisted', insect-like appearance, manoeuvring himself at an angle and pushing his companions off the road. Equally unappealing was his narrow chest: hanging beneath drooping shoulders, the upper half of his body also contained an 'effect of meanness'. Meanness would be De Quincey's retrospective watchword for Wordsworth; he was the man least likely to help a lady with her reticule, and his marriage had astounded everyone, De Quincey learned, because he seemed incapable of romantic love. The poet's head, however, 'made amends for the. . . defects of figure'. The brow was heavy, the nose arched (like those 'amongst some of the lowest of the species') but the light from the eyes came from 'from depths below all depths'. When Thomas Carlyle met Wordsworth, he described his head as 'immense', with 'great jaws like a crocodile's'. De Quincey, who had a horror of crocodiles, likened Wordsworth's features to those he had seen in a portrait of Milton; but out on the hills the poet bore 'a natural resemblance to Mrs Ratcliffe's [sic] Schedoni and other assassins roaming through prose and verse'. (Father Schedoni is the murderer and confessor in Ann Radcliffe's *The Italian,* a book Wordsworth read 'but only to laugh at it'.)

And *what-like,* for the Wordsworths, was De Quincey? They noted his size of course – he looked, Dorothy said, 'insignificant' – as well as his keenness to please and his great shyness. Their guest, said Dorothy, was 'so very shy that. . . I wonder how he ever had the courage to address himself to my brother by letter'. De Quincey must have brought with him echoes of her other brother John, drowned at sea two years before. When William and Dorothy first moved to Dove Cottage, gentle John Wordsworth, known by his siblings as the 'silent poet', had been similarly anxious about calling at the house, and he too had retreated before finding the courage to knock on the door, eventually waiting for his siblings in the local inn. John played a marginal role in the group which comprised Wordsworth, Dorothy, Coleridge, and Mary and Sara Hutchinson; he lived at Dove Cottage for ten months in 1800, but Dorothy's daily journals record only the presence of herself and William. Letters from John to Mary on the announcement of her engagement suggest that he would have married her himself had William not got there first: 'whatever fate Befal me I shall love thee to the last and bear thy memory to the grave', he wrote in his final letter to his future sister-in-law. His death three years later left them all hollow with pain, but there was guilt in the grief. John was a shadow presence in the 'enchanting community'; his was the only role that was inessential. Any introspective and worshipful man could understudy John.

The conversation during high tea that afternoon was 'superior by much, in its tone and subject', to any De Quincey had heard before, apart from that of Coleridge. De Quincey himself said nothing. For the rest of the evening Wordsworth talked about Tasso and at eleven o'clock De Quincey was shown into a 'pretty bedroom, about fourteen feet by twelve'. He drifted into sleep, freed for the first time in years from the 'vexation and self-blame, almost self-contempt' which had dominated his life since writing to Wordsworth. He woke the next morning to the sounds of heavy rain and a tiny voice reciting the Creed: 'Suffered under Pontius Pilate; was crucified, dead, and buried. . .' The voice belonged to four-year-old Johnny Wordsworth, who had slept in a cot in the corner of the room. Sarah Coleridge and her children had also stayed the night, presumably sharing Dorothy's bedroom next door, while the Wordsworths' younger children, Dora, aged three, and eighteen-month Thomas, slept with their parents downstairs. The family were, as Dorothy put it, 'crammed into our little nest edge-full': it was impossible to see how Wordsworth could ever be alone. Dorothy made breakfast over the fire, after which she and William took their guest for a soggy walk around Grasmere Lake and Rydal Water. De Quincey could now observe how unsexual Dorothy looked out of doors, and the meanness of Wordsworth's figure when seen from behind.

He also took in their dynamic: William and Dorothy shared the intimacy that De Quincey had once known with his own sister. He had been six when he lost Elizabeth; Wordsworth was a year older when he and Dorothy were separated after the death of their mother, after which Dorothy was taken from the family home in Cockermouth to live with an aunt in Halifax. But, ten years later, the siblings were reunited, never to be parted again. Without Dorothy, De Quincey saw, there would be no Wordsworth. Wordsworth's 'ascetic harsh-sublimity' was 'humanised' by Dorothy's perfect sensibility; Dorothy's eye for beauty 'clothed the forest of his genius'. In order to be close to Wordsworth, De Quincey needed to win the trust of Dorothy, and Dorothy could never resist anyone who made her nephews and nieces happy. De Quincey was always good with children, and it was the Wordsworth children who opened the door to him: 'Mr De Quincey,' Johnny would say, 'is my friend.'

Much of the Wordsworths' talk was of 'intruders', as they called tourists, and the developers whose buildings destroyed the views. On the other side of Grasmere Lake a Liverpudlian businessman with the Dickensian name of Crump had recently built himself a mansion. Crump, Wordsworth said, was 'a wretched creature, wretched in name and nature' with a 'still more wretched wife', and in 1806 the poet had warned a friend that 'when you next enter the sweet paradise of Grasmere you will see staring you in the face, upon that beautiful ridge that elbows out into the vale (behind the church and towering far above its steeple), a temple of abomination, in which are to be enshrined Mr and Mrs Crump'. Houses like this, said Wordsworth in his *Guide through the District of the Lakes*, 'rising as they do from the summit of naked hills' were out of kilter with the 'snugness and privacy' of traditional Lakeland dwellings; these 'disgusting' and 'discordant objects' destroyed the prospect for everyone else. The name of the temple of abomination was Allan Bank, an eyesore even today. Wordsworth was known for his trenchant opinions on architecture; later in the century Canon Rawnsley (who, together with Octavia Hill, founded the National Trust to save the Lake District) described a conversation with a local builder who remembered the poet as having 'his say at t' maist o' t' houses i' these parts'. Houses should blend into their surroundings rather than compete with nature for attention; particularly frustrating to Wordsworth was the glare throughout the valley of the whitewash on the stone. He and Dorothy swathed their own cottage in flowering shrubs and roses, but the gleam of the walls could, as De Quincey testified, still be seen from a distance.

The next day, De Quincey joined the rest of the household on a trip to Ullswater, which was undertaken in the back of a farmer's cart driven by a local girl. His mother had been transported around Bath in a sedan chair but, De Quincey conceded as he clambered into the wagon, 'what was good enough for the Wordsworths was good enough for me'. They descended the Kirkstone Pass, as steep as a wall, at full gallop, and spent the night in a house by the shores of Ullswater. The following day De Quincey and Wordsworth walked alone to Penrith, where Wordsworth's grandparents had once lived above their draper's shop. De Quincey, who knew by heart every word Wordsworth had ever written, now heard from the poet's own mouth lines from his work in progress, 'The White Doe of Rylstone'. At Penrith the two men parted and De Quincey 'sauntered' the seventeen miles to Greta Hall to pay his respects to Mrs Coleridge. He arrived at seven o'clock and was greeted at the door by Southey, dark-haired and solidly handsome.

Southey was a good foot higher than De Quincey, but his guest was quick to cut him down to size. The poet's short jacket and breeches gave him the 'air of a Tyrolese mountaineer' and he lived among the mountains like a 'city tailor'. A more 'amiable' man than Wordsworth, Southey was less profound or original. He was one of those who Coleridge might have called a 'goody' person. Southey, De Quincey noted, gave himself nine hours sleep a night, produced his poetry 'by contract' before breakfast, and answered his letters on the day he received them. His manner was 'uniformly' polite, but 'a little too freezing' to those 'who were not among the *corps* of his ancient fireside friends'. Who were these friends? Wordsworth, who arrived the next day, was evidently not one of them. De Quincey believed that the *froideur* between the two was due to their differing views of poetry, but it was due more to their differing views of Coleridge. His brother-in-law, Southey believed, would be safer on board his own steady and reliable ship than floating rudderless in the Wordsworths' current. Wordsworth stayed the night, and the next morning De Quincey listened in horror while the two radicals, sitting in Southey's study, discussed the dissolution of the monarchy.

Back in Grasmere, De Quincey and Dorothy took an excursion to Esthwaite Water. Returning in blinding rain, Dorothy suggested that they stop at the house of Charles Lloyd in the tiny village of Clappersgate, on the River Brathay. A relation of sorts – Charles's sister, Priscilla, was married to William and Dorothy's brother, Christopher – Lloyd was known to De Quincey as a poet, novelist, and satellite of Wordsworth and Coleridge. Now aged twenty-seven, Lloyd had once been Coleridge's pupil and had lodged with his family in Bristol and Nether Stowey. In 1795, Cottle had published a volume of poems by Lloyd, Southey and Coleridge, and in 1797 he published Lloyd's novel, *Edmund Oliver*, which contained a caricature of Coleridge in the figure of the eponymous hero, a lovesick opium addict. Coleridge thereafter described Lloyd as 'unfit to be any man's friend'; the friendship 'fostered in the bosom of my confidence' had been treated with 'calumny and ingratitude'. The Wordsworths shared Coleridge's assessment of Lloyd's 'perilous' character. When Lloyd and his wife moved to Ambleside in 1800, Dorothy revealed to her friend, Jane Marshall, that 'we are by no means glad that they are to be our neighbours because Charles Lloyd is a man who is perpetually forming new friendships, quarrelling with his old ones, and upon the whole a dangerous acquaintance'.

But De Quincey immediately liked and sympathised with Lloyd, a fellow opium-eater who was then 'at the zenith of the brief happiness that was granted to him on earth'. A critic of 'gossamer subtlety' and 'exquisite sensibility', neither Wordsworth nor Coleridge, De Quincey later wrote, 'suspected the amount of power. . . latent' in this man, and Lloyd 'firmly believed that they despised him'. The same was of course true of De Quincey: Coleridge had his suspicions, but Wordsworth had no idea that this mild creature, so keen to please, would be capable of writing about them with such candour. Wordsworth, whose character, De Quincey noted, wore a 'masculine or Roman hardness', 'ridiculed' Lloyd for being 'effeminate', while Coleridge parodied Lloyd's writing. Psychologically fragile, Lloyd later lost his mind and his family fell apart; Dorothy had taken De Quincey to what he called a 'doomed household', and shown him, as through a dark glass, a version of his future self.

What about Dorothy? De Quincey was twenty-two when they met and Dorothy thirty-five, although he remembered her as twenty-eight. Their bond was immediate, and De Quincey, hammering home her absence of 'personal charms', protests too much about how unattractive he found her. He described Dorothy's unconventional appeal as 'impassioned', 'ardent', 'trembling' and 'inevitable'. 'Beyond any person I have known in this world,' De Quincey said, Dorothy was 'the creature of impulse', and the words De Quincey returns to like a mantra are 'wild' and 'fervent'. She was 'the very wildest (in the sense of the most natural) person I have ever known'; she was fervent in all she did. Dorothy was like one of the heroines later imagined by the Brontës, who owed a good deal to the depictions of the Wordsworths in De Quincey's 'Lake Reminiscences'. None of these rare qualities, however, are apparent in the chatty letters Dorothy wrote to De Quincey. Here we see only the warmth and kindness he craved.

Did Dorothy hope that her new friend, whose arrival in her life delighted her so much and whose company she enjoyed more than that of any other visitor, might marry her? De Quincey's sister, Jane, certainly teased him about the prospect of having Dorothy as a sister-in-law, anticipating, in her letters, visits to see the future 'Mrs De Quincey' in Grasmere. 'I would like to know Miss Wordsworth,' Jane wrote, 'and see what sort of a woman you admire.' To 'admire' was a term of sexual appreciation, and De Quincey 'admired' Dorothy. 'All of us loved her,' he recalled, and she had 'several offers, amongst them one from Hazlitt; all, without a moment's hesitation, she rejected decisively.' Aside from her independence of spirit, Dorothy was of course the creation of her brother and for this attribute alone she 'won the sympathy and respectful regard of every man worthy to approach her'. Dorothy, said De Quincey, was Wordsworth's 'gift from God': her 'mission' was to love, counsel and cheer her brother, to 'wait upon him as the tenderest and most faithful of domestics' and to 'ingraft, by her sexual sense of beauty, upon his masculine austerity that delicacy and those graces which else. . . it would not have had'.

It may be that De Quincey was rejected by Dorothy but it is more likely, given her future sensitivity, that she felt rejected by him. De Quincey was clearly eligible: he was a gentleman and he had money. A marriage between the two would seem natural, and harmless enough. Dorothy's life with her brother would continue much as before, while De Quincey's place in the community would be confirmed.

His visit to Grasmere lasted only one week; by mid-November he was back in Oxford for Michaelmas term. The acerbic tone De Quincey took in his 'Lake Reminiscences' does not reflect his initial experience of the Wordsworths, which was one of adulation. His excursion had exceeded all expectations, and he had achieved the near-impossible: he had won the trust of Coleridge, been welcomed into the home of Wordsworth, walked with the poet's immortal sister, endeared himself to his eldest son, and discussed his work in progress. Many people adopt an alternative family who they feel to be more suitable than their own, and De Quincey adopted the Wordsworths. The poet could see into his heart: De Quincey had known this since the day 'We are Seven' was first placed in his hands. *Lyrical Ballads* was his steering chart, and Grasmere was his journey's end.

At ten o'clock on 12 November, Wordsworth and Dorothy saw De Quincey onto the night coach at Ambleside. As he rolled away, listening to the 'half-flute, half-clarionet' whistling of the driver, he projected himself into the future. Perhaps one day this road, this vale, these people, would be his. 'What happy fortune were it here to live!' Wordsworth had written in 'Home at Grasmere', with 'One of thy lowly Dwellings [as] my Home'.

Imaginary Prisons by Giovanni Battista Piranesi, 1761.

De Quincey compared the endless growth and reproduction
of the architecture in his dreams to Piranesi's *Carceri*,
described to him by Coleridge.

Home at Grasmere

. . . to have a house
It was enough (what matter for a home?)
That owned me. . .

Wordsworth, *The Prelude*, Book Seventh

No sooner had he returned to Oxford in the late November of 1807 than De Quincey fell ill with 'a determination of blood to the head'. Always anxious about this part of his body, he consulted a London surgeon who advised him to stay off wine and avoid bending his neck. So for the next few months he transported himself like an automaton, his chin rigid, his shoulders stiff, his eyes, when not aimed straight ahead, flicking to the left and right. It was in this guise that he re-engaged with Coleridge, whose lecture series on 'Poetry and the Fine Arts' had now begun. De Quincey had promised Dorothy that he would attend and report back.

Coleridge was also ill. De Quincey found him living in the *Courier* offices in the Strand, a guest of the editor, Daniel Stuart, where he was 'enveloped in night caps' and 'surmounted by handkerchiefs endorsed upon handkerchiefs'. To quell the racket of the printing press outside his door and the roar of the street coming up through the window, he was taking 'more than ordinary doses of opium'. The first of his lectures – which De Quincey missed – had been on 'Taste' in poetry, and the next two were postponed due to his health. The second lecture took place on 5 February 1808 and De Quincey sat in the audience at the Royal Institution on Albemarle Street and watched Coleridge 'struggling with pain and overmastering illness'. The steep, semi-circular theatre had magnificent acoustics but Coleridge, whose habit was to propound without notes, 'seemed to labour under an almost paralytic inability to raise the upper jaw from the lower'. He fumbled and froze in a 'feverish heat', his lips were baked 'black'; he drank glass after glass of water but nothing could quench his thirst (De Quincey's imagery comes from 'The Ancient Mariner': 'Water, water, everywhere/ Nor any drop to drink,' and 'With throats unslaked, with black lips baked'). What Coleridge said lacked heart and when, to the relief of the audience, he read aloud from one of the books piled on the podium he chose, at random, passages of interminable duration. This was the effect not of opium, but of its withdrawal. The mariner's performance, De Quincey concluded, was 'a poor faint reflection of jewels once scattered in the highway by himself'.

Walking home that night, De Quincey repeated to himself lines from the soliloquy of Milton's blind Samson.

> O dark, dark, dark, amid the blaze of noon,
> Irrecoverably dark, total eclipse
> Without all hope of day!

All further lectures were cancelled until 30 March. It is a dismal description of Coleridge and impossible to miss De Quincey's relish, in his 'Lake Reminiscences', in the comic horror of it all, from the excess of handkerchiefs to the blackened lips. He does not mention that Coleridge recovered enough to give twenty of the twenty-five scheduled talks, or that he had taken meticulous notes beforehand and thought deeply about their content.

Hearing reports that his friend was dying, Wordsworth arrived at the *Courier* offices on 24 February. 'Wordsworth the great poet,' teased the mischievous Lamb, 'is coming to Town. He is to have apartments in the Mansion House. He says he does not see much difficulty in writing like Shakespeare, if he had a mind to try it. It is clear then nothing is wanting but the mind. Even Coleridge a little checked at this hardihood of assertion.' The diarist Henry Crabb Robinson, who now met Wordsworth for the first time, left a memorable portrait of him during this visit: the great poet was a 'sloven' whose 'manners though not arrogant yet indicate a sense of his own worth. He is not attentive to others and speaks with decision of his own opinion. He does not spare those he opposes.' On 3 March, Coleridge gave a tea party from his bed, inviting Wordsworth, Lamb, the radical philosopher William Godwin and De Quincey as his guests. De Quincey's first foray into London salon society was a stolid affair. Coleridge was muted and Wordsworth cold; the occasion was saved by the playfulness of Lamb, who now redeemed himself in De Quincey's eyes.

Two days later De Quincey was back in Oxford, preparing for his own great challenge. He had been persuaded to sit for the honours examination, where he could at last prove himself the superior of his tutors. His recent wanderings had set back his studies and in order to be prepared, he told Dorothy, he needed to read thirty-three Greek tragedies in one week. This he could do with the help of a book stand sent by his mother, which allowed him to turn the pages without bending his neck. Anxiety prevented him from sleeping; when he did he dreamed of 'finding the whole university on tiptoe for the approaching prize-fighting and myself in a state of palsy as to any power of exertion'. He was reminded of a recurring dream he had as a child, in which he was pursued by a lion and unable to move. He worried about the effect of all this study on his brain, fearing that it would bring on the dreaded hydrocephalus. He did not reveal to the Wordsworths how much of his pride and self-worth were invested in getting his degree. Instead, he told Dorothy that he was motivated by duty alone: 'having been treated with very great kindness by my college, I cannot endure to disappoint their expectations'.

De Quincey's first examination, on 14 May, went triumphantly. 'You have sent us today the cleverest man I ever met with,' one of the examiners told the Worcester College dons. 'If his *viva voce* examination tomorrow correspond with what he has done in writing, he will carry everything before him.' The viva was to be in Greek, and De Quincey had been looking forward to it. At the last minute, however, the rules were changed and he learned that while the questions would be asked in Greek, he was expected to answer in English. Oral examinations were public events where the examinees performed before an audience, and De Quincey had been speaking Greek since his schooldays: if he could not distinguish himself now, his honours degree would be 'without honour'. All the examination would prove was that he was able to do what any other undergraduate was able to do. He pronounced himself disgusted by his examiners, who were not worthy of his respect.

So the night before his viva De Quincey bolted. He leaves no account of the circumstances around his departure, but his thought processes must have been similar to those that accompanied his moonlight flit from Manchester Grammar. 'Leave this house,' he had then told himself, and 'a Rubicon is placed between thee and all possibility of return.' Now, once again, his conscience spoke in 'sullen whispers' against his 'irrevocable' action, and having left the city of Oxford, De Quincey never went back.

He took himself to London, home of runaways, where he joined the audience for Coleridge's final lecture on 8 June.

De Quincey told Dorothy that he had left Oxford because he was ill, but the most likely explanation for his departure lay in his growing relationship with laudanum. Hoping that the drug would calm his nerves and improve his thought, he may have dosed himself up with Coleridgean quantities and found himself unable to function. Coleridge's recent appearance served as a deterrent: were De Quincey to go ahead with the viva, his performance might resemble the chaos on the podium at the Royal Institution. Another of laudanum's effects is to open the mind to suggestion: why, De Quincey must have asked himself, suffer fools when he had found himself a superior university in Grasmere? The only praise worth having came from Wordsworth. But there was another possible reason for his flight: what if he did not distinguish himself in his viva? He had gone through his life promoting himself as singular: there was too much to lose in putting his superiority to the test.

He moved into the rooms of a former college friend at 5 Northumberland Street in the parish of St Marylebone, at the other end of Oxford Street. His windows looked onto a workhouse which was built to accommodate a thousand tramps and 'casual poor', including any foundling abandoned on the doorstep.

From here, De Quincey made himself indispensable to Coleridge, who was still living at the *Courier* offices. He visited the invalid every day, found him rare books, and discussed his work in progress. Coleridge's respect for De Quincey is apparent in the letters he dispatched across London: 'I do therefore ask you as proof of Friendship,' he implored, 'that you will so far get over your natural modesty and timidity as without reserve or withholding to tell me exactly what you think and feel on perusal of anything I may submit to you.' By February 1808, Coleridge was sufficiently dependent on De Quincey's visits to feel panic when he did not see him. 'I have suffered considerable alarm,' he wrote one Tuesday evening, 'at not having seen you for so many days. . .' It was probably now that the event took place which De Quincey described in his *Confessions*. The two men were leafing through Piranesi's *Antiquities of Rome*, when Coleridge told De Quincey about another a set of plates by Piranesi called 'Dreams' which recorded 'the scenery of his own visions during the delirium of a fever'.

> Some of them (I describe only from the memory of Mr Coleridge's account) represented vast Gothic halls: on the floor of which stood all sorts of engines and machinery, wheels, cables, pulleys, levers, catapults, &c. &c. expressive of enormous power to pull forth, and resistance overcome. Creeping along the sides of the walls, you perceived a staircase; and upon it, groping his way upwards, was Piranesi himself: follow the stairs a little further, and you perceive it come to a sudden abrupt termination, without any balustrade, and allowing no step onwards to him who had reached the extremity, except into the depths below. Whatever is to become of poor Piranesi, you suppose, at least, that his labours must in some way terminate here. But raise your eyes, and behold a second flight of stairs still higher: on which again Piranesi is perceived, but this time standing on the very brink of the abyss. Again elevate your eye, and a still more aerial flight of stairs is beheld: and again is poor Piranesi busy on his aspiring labours: and so on, until the unfinished stairs and Piranesi both are lost in the upper gloom of the hall.

Piranesi did not produce a series called 'Dreams', and De Quincey is almost certainly describing the *Carceri d'invenzione* ('Imaginary Prisons'). Never seen by him, the images came from the 'memory' of Coleridge. Perhaps Coleridge had not seen them either and only knew them from the memory of someone else, in which case De Quincey's description is of what he imagined Coleridge to have imagined Piranesi to have imagined; the memory of the Piranesi becomes a form of palimpsest in which De Quincey imposes an impression on the surface of Coleridge's impression, which is itself imposed on another impression.

The series of thirteen prints, published in 1750, depict a gargantuan dungeon without entrance or exit, floor or ceiling; the building is simply an infinite interior of stairs, chains, vaults, bridges, pulleys and chasms. De Quincey's purpose in describing the image in his *Confessions* is to compare Piranesi's 'dreams' with the 'endless growth and reproduction' of the architecture in his own opium dreams, but he saw architecture like this everywhere. His whole world was a stage-set designed by Piranesi: the most modest domestic interiors are given by him vertiginous climbs and perilous descents. While Wordsworth found poetry in nature, for De Quincey a building was a poem, and nature itself a Piranesi prison. Gowbarrow Park, at Ullswater, contains an 'aerial dungeon . . . frightful to look down'; retreat for the walker is 'impossible', the 'chasm' is the only escape from danger. In relation to Grasmere, Easedale is 'a chamber within a chamber, or rather a closet within a chamber – a chapel within a cathedral – a little private oratory within a chapel'.

More fascinating than the endlessly repeated staircase in the non-existent Piranesi engraving is the figure he imagines ascending them. While De Quincey describes the climber as Piranesi, it is himself he sees here pursuing his 'aspiring labours'. These are De Quincey's own thwarted journeys, the abysses only he looks down. This scene recurred in De Quincey's nightmares: he is trapped; every staircase he climbs ends with the same 'abrupt termination', but instead of falling into the depths below he simply reappears on another staircase, facing another abrupt termination, the brink of another abyss, and so on. Each of his experiences would be duplicated, not once but an infinite number of times.

The 'Imaginary Prisons' capture De Quincey's style as an autobiographer. The story of his life is one of labour and repetition: this is how much I mourned when my sister died; this is how hard I worked to get to Oxford; this is what I went through in order to meet Wordsworth. And on each occasion, when it seems he can go no further in his agony, when he depicts himself looking with terror over a literal or a metaphorical gorge of Hammerscar, he appears on another staircase making another dramatic ascent. In meeting Wordsworth, De Quincey was nearing the pinnacle of his ambition; and with no more stairs to climb, he had only the depths below.

It was Dorothy, of course, who invited him to return to Grasmere. The Wordsworths had left Dove Cottage and moved into Allan Bank, the abomination on the other side of the lake. They had little choice in the matter; if they were to stay in the vale they had to take what was available. Their household now consisted of Wordsworth, Mary, Dorothy, Sara Hutchinson, two servants and the three young children. Coleridge soon moved in as well (looking, said Southey, 'about half as big as the house') and Hartley and Derwent joined them all for weekend visits. Allan Bank had ten rooms rather than six, and more breathing space – just. But, Dorothy complained, the house was uninhabitable, having chimneys which wouldn't draw. The problem was severe and apparently insurmountable; smoke blackened the windows, soot covered the dishes, and to keep themselves warm the women and children were forced to their beds in the middle of the day.

Coleridge stayed in bed all day anyway. A famously difficult guest, he now excelled himself. Rising with the owls, he worked throughout the night on his latest project, a philosophical periodical to be called *The Friend*. Rejecting the Wordsworths' frugal fare, he put the maid to the trouble of preparing him a separate dinner of meat and roast potatoes, and was otherwise either mired in opium or withdrawing from its effects. In comparison, the porcelain-mannered De Quincey could do no wrong. 'Mr De Quincey,' Dorothy enthused in a letter to her friend, Mrs Clarkson, 'will stay with us, we hope, at least till the Spring. We feel often as if he were one of the Family – "he is loving, gentle and happy".' Sara Hutchinson was, as ever, drier in her praise: 'Mr de Quincey has been here 3 weeks & I daresay will make a long stay – he is a good tempered amiable creature & uncommonly clever & an excellent scholar – but he is very shy & so reverences Wm & C that he chats very little but is content to listen.' As always, his shyness disappeared around the children, who adored him for his willingness to play and tell stories. Johnny, with whom he shared a bed, was, Dorothy noted, 'passionately fond of him' but the child De Quincey loved most was baby Catherine, born in September 1808. Called by Wordsworth his 'little Chinese maiden', Catherine may have had Down's Syndrome. (The suggestion, made by Grevel Lindop, is convincing: Mary was thirty-eight when Catherine was born, and the child's health problems – convulsions, difficulty with swallowing – are consistent with the condition.) De Quincey bonded himself to Catherine, bouncing her on his knee,

sharing her mother's concerns about her sleep, and extracting a promise, Dorothy told Mrs Clarkson, that he was to be 'her sole tutor, so
that we shall not dare to show her a letter in a book. . . If, however, he
fails in inspiring her with a love of learning, I am sure that he cannot
fail in one thing. His gentle, sweet manners must lead her to sweetness
and gentle thoughts.'

When Wordsworth looked up from his desk he saw a creature cooing
at babies, drawing dragons for Johnny, and fussing with the womenfolk
over every little cough in the nursery. De Quincey was neither one
thing nor the other; no longer a child, he could not be described as an
adult, but nor was he fully masculine: as far as Wordsworth was concerned, his houseguest was effeminate, particularly in contrast with his
other young acolyte, John Wilson, who had also moved to the Lakes
and who De Quincey now met for the first time one evening at sunset,
when Coleridge was preparing for breakfast.

Wilson, whose fan letter to Wordsworth had preceded his own,
cut a striking figure. Twenty years later he was described as 'a sixteen
stoner. . . a cocker, a racer, a six bottler, a twenty-four tumbler – an
out-and-outer – a true, upright, knocking-down, poetical, prosaic,
moral, professorial, hard-drinking, fierce-eating, good-looking, honourable, and straight-forward Tory', and we must add to this picture
the energies of youth. A six-footer in a sailor suit with wild, yellow
hair, De Quincey's first impression of him was of a man 'in robust
health' with an expression of 'animated intelligence' and 'an intense
enjoyment of life'. Wilson, who won the Newdigate poetry prize at
Oxford and left the university at the same time as De Quincey, but with
a degree, lived off a sizeable inheritance with which he had bought, to
be close to Wordsworth, an estate called Elleray which looked down on
Windermere. Here he hunted, fished, rowed, wrestled with farmers and
wrote Wordsworthian verse. In his later journalism he would be equally
pugnacious. Wilson was, as Thomas Carlyle put it, one of those tropical
trees that exhales itself in 'balmy odours' instead of 'producing fruit'.

Wilson's appearance in his life was exactly what De Quincey most
dreaded. He had a horror of being rejected by Wordsworth for someone
'more brilliant. . . who might have the power (which I feared I should never
have) of talking to him on something like equal terms, as respected the laws
and principles of poetry'. But rather than set himself up as Wilson's rival, De

Quincey became his brother-in-arms. While Wilson has come down to us as a Rabelaisian extrovert and De Quincey as an introspective dreamer, the two men had a good deal in common. Born in the same year, Wilson also lost his father at an early age, also inherited money, also came to the Lakes to be near Wordsworth, and had been resident a full year before having the courage to call on his idol. Another Gothic novel-reading night-walker, Wilson had what De Quincey called a 'furious love for nonsense – head-long nonsense'. They were bonded by their humour. Wilson's reputation as a man of letters has not survived, but he was a journalist of high jinks and knock-about brilliance. (The pleasure of reading his 'Noctes Ambrosianae' in *Blackwood's Magazine* is hard to equal.) John Wilson excelled in the three areas considered during the Regency period to be the most important: per-sonality, physiognomy and parody. The parodies of his literary friends and rivals are priceless, and he even wrote parodies of himself. He was, as De Quincey memorably said, 'the very sublime of fun'.

De Quincey likened Wilson's fearlessness to that of Robin Hood, and his 'marvellous versatility' to the Athenian general, Alcibiades. But in his love of 'the stormiest pleasures of real life', Wilson resembled William, that 'horrid pugilistic brother' who had died nine years earlier, in 1799. The masochist in De Quincey responded readily to authority, and in part-nership with Wilson he retrieved his role in the nursery at Greenhay.

Wilson, meanwhile, was rebuilding his cottage at Elleray. The Wordsworths were unable to accuse him of destroying their view because Wilson planned a building with only one storey. 'I abhor stairs,' he explained, 'and there can be no peace in any mansion where heavy footsteps may be heard overhead.' De Quincey described the house as 'a silent commentary on its master's state of mind, and an exemplification of his character'. It was, Wilson described, to be approached 'by a fine serpentine avenue' after which you 'enter slap-bang through a wide glass door into a green-house, a conservatory of everything rich and rare in the world of flowers. Folding-doors are drawn noiselessly into the walls as if by magic, and lo! Drawing-room and dining-room stretching east and west in dim and distant perspective.' De Quincey, who delighted in Elleray, described it as the project of a man in 'the very heyday of a most tempestuous youth'.

Throughout the autumn of 1808, Coleridge was absorbed in writing, launching, and selling *The Friend*. De Quincey, to make himself useful, subscribed to no less than five copies and proposed, in a plan as dreamy as any of Coleridge's own, that the journal be printed, at his own expense, on a private press they would set up in Grasmere.

Wordsworth was preoccupied with events in the Peninsular War. On 30 August 1808 an agreement, known as the Convention of Cintra, had been signed in Portugal allowing the French army, defeated by the Anglo-Portuguese forces under Sir Arthur Wellesley, to peacefully evacuate the country in British ships. Back in Britain this was seen as an own goal; an English triumph had been turned into a French escape. Four years later, in *Childe Harold's Pilgrimage*, Byron described how 'Britannia sickens, Sintra! at thy name.' The Spanish and Portuguese had been scandalously betrayed by the English army, and Wordsworth, for whom there was no cause greater than that of Liberty, began a tract in support of 'the hopes and fears of suffering Spain'. Coleridge's politics coincided with his own, and the 10,000-word pamphlet Wordsworth eventually produced was the fruit of long discussions between the two men. De Quincey, seizing the opportunity to collaborate with the collaborators, threw himself into Spanish and Portuguese affairs. As a long-time admirer of Edmund Burke – whose prophetic style was being used by Wordsworth as a model – he was in a position to advise the poet on the construction of his first political essay.

Apprenticing himself to Wordsworth, De Quincey began his tenure as a journeyman. As his brother William had done with Loutherbourg, Thomas would study at the feet of a master. During this time De Quincey considered himself 'more intimately connected' with Wordsworth 'than any other person, not being a member of his family, can pretend to have been'. He was closer to Wordsworth even than Coleridge, who was either in bed or sweating over *The Friend*, so that 'by day or by night he rarely walked'. De Quincey and Wordsworth regularly walked both by day and by night. In order to collect the newspaper and catch up with the latest events in Spain, they would leave the house at midnight and walk four miles to Dunmail Raise to meet the carrier that brought the London newspapers. Beneath the vault of stars, Wordsworth would place his ear to the road and listen for the sound of the wheels 'groaning along at a distance'. Perhaps this was the origin of De Quincey's false memory of the scene in

'Aladdin' where the magician places his 'ear to the earth' and 'fastens his murderous intention upon the insulated tread' of the small Arab boy.

One night, when Wordsworth was 'slowly rising from this effort, his eye caught a bright star that was glittering between the brow of Seat Sandal and of the mighty Helvellyn. He gazed upon it for a minute or so, and then, upon turning away to descend into Grasmere, he made the following explanation: "I have often remarked, from my earliest days, that if. . . the attention is energetically braced up to an act of steady observation, or of steady expectation, then, if this intense condition of vigilance should suddenly relax, at that moment, any beautiful, any impressive visual object. . . falling upon the eye, is carried to the heart with a power not known under other circumstances".'. This was precisely the kind of insight that De Quincey looked for in the man who knew the secrets of the universe. No matter that he pushed De Quincey off the road as they walked back to Allan Bank with their copy of the *Courier*, or that his legs were too short for his torso – Wordsworth had proved himself a sorcerer.

Since their move to Allan Bank in the spring of 1808, Dove Cottage had lain empty and Dorothy suggested that De Quincey take over the tenancy for the next seven years. This was the greatest honour she could have bestowed on him and more than he had dared to hope for – the cottage was as sacrosanct to Dorothy as the vale was to Wordsworth: 'They who are dwellers in this holy place,' the poet had proclaimed in 'Home at Grasmere', 'must needs themselves be hallowed.' The offer was not made entirely out of friendship. One benefit of having De Quincey as their neighbour was that his vast book collection, as Dorothy put it, would prove 'a solid advantage to my brother'. Wordsworth was forever complaining about his 'lack of commerce with passing literature, especially bulky works, for we have no neighbour that buys them', and when new books did appear he had to wait his turn while they were passed around the neighbourhood. There were solid advantages to Dorothy as well. With De Quincey as their tenant, she could keep the house and garden in her life. 'We have now almost a home still,' Dorothy informed her friend Jane Marshall, 'at the old and dearest spot of all.' She set about preparing the cottage: De Quincey would need plenty of bookcases (deal, she insisted, and not his preferred mahogany, which was too expensive), as well as new rugs and calico curtains. De Quincey, meanwhile, sent his mother and sisters a plan of his six rooms, and asked Jane to send him a similar plan of the house they were now building in Wrington, Somerset. 'I am,' Jane replied, 'a little surprised at such a requisition from you – a metaphysician and an architect! A monstrous incongruity!' De Quincey's pursual of abstract thought in a room he had measured with a ruler might appear paradoxical, but it had a clear logic: the more infinite his world became, the more he took down its dimensions.

Surmising from her brother's letters that Miss Wordsworth had a significant role in his current happiness, Jane teased him about consulting the taste of 'that beautiful and wild-hearted girl', who will be the 'best judge of what will please herself'.

In the heat of mutual enthusiasm another decision was made: De Quincey agreed to oversee the production of Wordsworth's 'Cintra' pamphlet in London. His expertise in punctuation confirmed him as the ideal candidate for the task. For Wordsworth, the appearance of this tract was part of his duty as poet; he was writing as a 'man speaking to men'. As a spokesman for freedom, his mission was to teach the people to 'guard their own liberties', and explain that war determines the destiny not only of nations, but of humanity itself.

The Convention of Cintra had been signed the previous summer and it was now late February 1809; public interest in the affair was fading and in order for Wordsworth's efforts not to have been wasted, his pamphlet needed to appear quickly. The next few months showed both Wordsworth and De Quincey in their worst lights, and brought to an end any promise of long-term intimacy. At the centre of the problem was Wordsworth's dislike of writing; he found 'penmanship. . . unendurable', prose far more so than poetry, and Dorothy, who had formerly relieved him of the strain by working as his secretary, now had her hands filled with nephews and nieces. De Quincey, who thought he had been elevated to the position of editor in a partnership of equals, took on, as far as Wordsworth was concerned, the feminine role of faithful domestic. Had Wordsworth been less arrogant and more understanding of the strain he was placing on De Quincey, had De Quincey been less in awe of Wordsworth and more experienced in the ways of writers and writing, and had communications between Grasmere and London been swifter, the experience might not have been as traumatic.

De Quincey took rooms in Great Titchfield Street, the road on which, six years earlier, he had waited in vain for Ann to appear. He hoped, perhaps, to see Ann's face in the crowd and be relieved of the guilt he felt towards her. His time was spent waiting for Wordsworth to deliver fresh pages and for printers to prepare proofs. No sooner had the proofs appeared, than Wordsworth wanted rewrites: De Quincey was deluged with orders, in the poet's illegible script, for corrections, additions, insertions, emendations, further research and footnotes. Progress was torturously slow and De Quincey was hopelessly unconfident. When one of Wordsworth's sentences was incomplete, rather than add the missing words he returned the leaf to Grasmere for the author's correction. Thus another week was wasted. More time was lost when a near-hysterical Wordsworth ordered De Quincey to '*stop the press*' in order to incorporate a minor change, and on 26 March, De Quincey received from Wordsworth no less than four separate letters detailing changes which had to be made. On 28 March, Wordsworth was still concerned that his 'meaning' was 'undeveloped'.

Meanwhile the compositor, who was drunk a good deal of the time, allowed the first set of proofs to be filled with 'monstrous errors', and De Quincey was forced to ask for 'a dozen' further sets before the errors disappeared. More weeks were wasted, and the news was now filled with the scandal of the Duke of York and his mistress, Mrs Clarke. To keep the pamphlet up to date with developments in Spain, Wordsworth asked De Quincey to compose a footnote on the French victory at Saragossa which De Quincey laboured over as though it were an examination. Wordsworth then breezily rejected what De Quincey produced on the grounds that his assistant's thoughts did not (unlike those of Coleridge) coincide with his own. It was over this sensitive point that De Quincey snapped, complaining to Dorothy 'of the very great injustice which he has done me'. Their opinions on Saragossa, he stressed, were precisely the same; his careful work – the first occasion on which he had written anything for publication – had been barely read, and what Wordsworth did read he had misread. For De Quincey, there could be no greater insult. His own pride was immense, but not as great as that of Wordsworth whose pride was a realm of its own: 'Never describe Wordsworth as equal in pride to Lucifer', he later wrote. 'No; but, if you have occasion to write a life of Lucifer, set down that possibility, in respect to pride, he might be some type of Wordsworth.'

Ticked off by Dorothy, Wordsworth apologised to De Quincey after his own fashion: 'it gives me great concern, to find that after all your fatigue, confinement, and vexation, you should have suffered such mortification. . . but I must quit the subject, my penmanship is very bad, and my head aches miserably'. Wordsworth's usual response to complaints about his own behaviour was to announce, De Quincey later learned, that he 'will have nothing to do with fending and proving'. Dorothy's letters could not have been more different. 'You must take it as proof of my affection that my penmanship is so bad,' she wrote in early May, 'for in proportion as my Friends have become more near and dear to me I have always been unable to keep my pen in such order as to make it write decently.'

Throughout the spring, Dorothy and Mary, desperate to get the pamphlet out of their lives, smoothed the path, calming Wordsworth in his irritation with De Quincey, thanking De Quincey for his hard work – 'you have indeed been a Treasure to us. . . having spared my Brother so much anxiety and care' – and reassuring him, again and again, that they were all, especially young Johnny, looking forward to his return. Sara Hutchinson, in a postscript to a particularly mortifying letter from Wordsworth, wished that De Quincey could see 'your orchard just now, for it is the most beautiful spot upon earth'. Dorothy was upset that the laurels in his orchard had been 'cruelly mauled' by a gardener, and now looked like 'dismembered creatures'. Mary, writing to thank him for his labours, added that 'the workmen are now very busy about your cottage'. 'Your cottage is painted,' wrote Dorothy in June, 'and I hope will be ready by the end of the next week or the beginning of the week after.' Even Wordsworth grudgingly added, at the end of a long complaining missive, that 'your house is in great forwardness and very neat'.

Amongst the correspondence currently heaving its way between London and Grasmere was a letter from De Quincey to Johnny, who wanted to be a printer. It is written with such care and charm that we can see in an instant why Dorothy felt such affection for her new friend. Wordsworth venerated childhood but was a distant and severe father; De Quincey had a clear affinity with children; he entered immediately into Johnny's world and allowed him access to his own. His letter contains a Piranesian picture of De Quincey's visits to the printer whose tardiness was causing him so much trouble:

When I get to the house where this man lives, I go first into a very dark passage, then I come to a stair-case which goes round and round and keeps getting darker and darker till at last it is so very dark that they are obliged to have a candle burning there all day long, even in the very middle of the day. When I am at the top of this stair-case, then I push against a door which opens and then shuts again of its own self – as soon as I have gone in – without my touching it I got through this door; and then I get into a large room full of men all printing; then I go into another room still bigger where there are more men printing; and in one corner of this room, a little wooden house is built with one window to it and one door – the least little place you ever saw; there is only room for about 2 men to sit down in it.

There is nothing patronising in his description of the building: De Quincey gives the stairs, doors and rooms exactly as he experienced them himself, and his 'sweet letter', said Dorothy, brought 'perfect joy in the house'. In other letters to Johnny he enclosed pictures he had drawn for the child's bedroom wall, and promised to teach him how to swim, fly a kite, walk on stilts and sail a boat. It was the adult world De Quincey found hard to engage with. He confessed in a letter to Wordsworth that he felt 'guilty of a crime' in not replying to Dorothy for 'so long a time'.

The Cintra pamphlet was finally ready for the printers in early May, at which point Wordsworth, in a sudden panic that he was to be thrown into Newgate prison, wanted it read for libel. Another week was wasted with De Quincey underlining any passage he felt was vulnerable, and the press eventually ran on 15 May. In a 'paroxysm of joy', De Quincey dispatched the first four finished copies to Grasmere. Wordsworth, who had now lost interest in the venture, responded with neither pleasure nor gratitude, but a list of errata: there were misquotations, incorrect words, the punctuation might have been improved, and one potentially libellous passage about Lord Wellesley which Wordsworth had ordered De Quincey to cancel was still there. As far as Wordsworth was concerned, De Quincey had failed in his task. Cornered and pointed at, De Quincey was indignant: 'About the supposed libel. . . I am anxious to be acquitted on this point – on which I am not at all in fault.' Quick to side with Wordsworth was a gleeful Coleridge: De Quincey's collaboration with the poet had ended, as his own had done in *Lyrical Ballads*, by his work being unacknowledged and his voice silenced.

Coleridge, who understood De Quincey all too well, expressed to Daniel Stuart, editor of the *Courier*, his 'vexation and surprise that Wordsworth should have entrusted anything to him beyond the mere correction of the Proofs'. He had, said Coleridge, 'both respect and affection for Mr De Quincey, but saw too much of his turn of mind, anxious yet dilatory, confused from over-accuracy, & at once systematic and labyrinthine, not fully to understand how great a plague he might easily be to a London Printer, his natural Tediousness made yet greater by his zeal & fear of not discharging his Trust, & superadded to Wordsworth's own Sybill's Leaves blown about by the changeful winds of an anxious Author's Second-thoughts.'

De Quincey's natural tediousness would increase with time. Forty years later his editor would describe how, when asked by a printer to confirm whether his use of the word 'caligraphy' should have one 'l' or two, De Quincey sent a note explaining that 'according to all analogy I should have expected the word to be written with a single "l", the adjective κ α λ σ ς being so uniformly spelt with a single λ; and resting upon this consideration I had in one of the proofs, and in one single instance, altered the whole to *caligraphy*. But, feeling some doubt, I consulted three or four different lexicons, all of which doubled the λ. And I have since met the word written *callig*. in a most carefully edited MS of Porson.' De Quincey never gave a printer a correction without including a lengthy explanation, which explanation, he then further explained in a spidery marginal script, should not be included in the printed text.

———

He remained in London after the pamphlet appeared, paralysed by the future. There had been a suggestion that he accompany Wordsworth and John Wilson on a trip around Ireland, which he let slide. Wilson then proposed that he and De Quincey visit Spain in September: this also never happened. His continuing silence was making Dorothy anxious: 'Sometimes we fancy that you are on the point of setting off to Grasmere, and therefore have delayed writing, and at times I, being of a fearful temper, fancy that you are ill. . . We have been so long used to receive your letters regularly that we take very ill to this long privation of that pleasure.'

Once again De Quincey was on the run from Wordsworth, but he was also nervous about his developing relationship with Dorothy. Added to which, the thought of 'his' cottage – its windows newly curtained, walls freshly painted, and deal bookcases standing empty – filled him with terror. His sister Jane wrote on 17 May to remind him that he had promised some time ago to be with them in ten days. 'I observe you always say ten days, a distance which as regularly recedes so that it is constantly at the same standing.' The only news they had of Thomas came 'from your favoured friend, Miss Wordsworth. . . When shall we hear anything more of this beautiful cottage? I can't approve of the sitting-room being upstairs.' Jane's letters to her brother were always teasing. 'I should like to know,' she said of his future in Grasmere, 'how you will pass your time – whether you mean to bury yourself in total seclusion, or only in an elegant retirement, embellished with every unsophisticated pleasure. I can tell you that you will never endure it alone for two months.' The only news she had from home was that Hannah More had published a novel called *Coelebs in Search of a Wife*, 'which we have read; – very good advice to masters and misses, but quite out of your way'.

De Quincey's time in London was currently spent bingeing on opium and books, both great stoppers of clocks. The thought of boxing up his new volumes – he had accumulated 300 more in the last few months – made him torpid. Coleridge described how any duty, once opium had been taken, would 'in *exact proportion*' to its '*importance* and urgency. . . be neglected', and similarly how 'in exact proportion, as I *loved* any person or persons more than others, & would have sacrificed my life to them', they would be 'barbarously mistreated by [my] silence, absence, or breach of promise'. De Quincey claimed that he was, at this point, still 'a dilettante eater of opium' but the evidence suggests he was more than this, and that opium was becoming preferable to reality. His inertia led to guilt, guilt led to opium, opium led to inertia, inertia led to guilt: he later described how the 'oppression of inexpiable guilt' lay upon him with 'the weight of twenty Atlantics'.

On Saturday nights he would douse himself and make his way across the city, walking far beyond his known boundaries, 'for an opium-eater is too happy to observe the motion of time'. He found himself in 'knotty problems of alleys' with 'enigmatical entries, and such sphinx's riddles of streets without thoroughfares, as must, I conceive, baffle the audacity of porters, and confound the intellects of coachmen'. These he imagined to be *terrae incognitae*, of which he was the 'first discoverer'. He paid 'a heavy price in distant years' for his metropolitan excursions, 'when

the human face tyrannised over my dreams, and the perplexities of my
steps in London came back and haunted my sleep'. Now, when he slept,
he saw Piranesian cities and palaces, and 'silvery expanses of water',
from seas and oceans to 'translucent lakes, shining like mirrors'.

In his sentient hours, De Quincey visited another peripatetic:
Walking Stewart. This was the same bushy-haired traveller he had
observed in Bath, and who, in his diary, he had compounded with the
ancient mariner to form an impression of Coleridge. Stewart, a figure
in the semi-mythical mould of Sir John Mandeville, had apparently
walked through India, Persia and Turkey, across the deserts of Abyssinia
and Arabia, through northern Africa, into every European country as
far east as Russia, as well as over to the new United States and into the
upper reaches of Canada. Whether his peregrinations were real or metaphorical it is hard to know – sometime he referred to them as journeys
of the mind. In his essay, 'Walking Stewart', De Quincey repeated some
advice the old man had given him about the preservation of books: 'he
recommended to all those who might be impressed with a sense of their
importance to bury a copy or copies of each work, properly secured
from the damp, &c, at a depth of seven or eight feet below the surface
of the earth; and on their death beds to communicate the knowledge of
this fact to some confidential friends, who, in their turn, were to send
down the tradition to some discreet persons of the next generation'.

Burying books was a gratifying thought for a man like De Quincey,
who imagined himself being buried beneath them. Some years later,
parting from Walking Stewart at Somerset House on the Strand before
making his way through Soho to Tottenham Court Road, De Quincey
recalled that he 'stopped nowhere, and walked fast; yet so it was that
in Tottenham Court Rd I was not overtaken by (that was comprehen-
sible), but overtook, Walking Stewart'. There must, De Quincey said,
'have been three Walking Stewarts in London', as he overtook him
again and then again. Walking Stewart was as multiple as the figure of
the artist in the Piranesi print.

Duplication was in the air. In the spring of 1809, De Quincey's brother
Richard reappeared after six years at sea. Having run away aged fourteen,
Richard had joined the navy, been captured first by pirates and then by the
Danes, and was now coming home as part of a prisoner exchange. Making
his way down Greek Street one evening, Thomas ran into a family friend

called John Kelsall who had come to London to legally confirm Richard
De Quincey's identity, but found himself barred from doing so when the
young man declared himself not well enough for visitors. Richard's reluctance to see visitors threw Mrs Quincey into a panic: this was a sign, she
believed, that the released prisoner was not her son at all but a 'pretender'
assuming his position in order to claim his inheritance. The 'real' Richard
would have come straight home to his loving mother rather than secrete
himself in London; this filial ingratitude was most unnatural. The 'real'
Richard, she surmised, had 'probably lost his life' in a mutiny and this other
person was a sailor 'assuming his name and character'. The bundle of letters
she had believed to be from Richard were, Mrs Quincey now concluded,
'forgeries'. It is a bewildering story which reveals something of the mindset
of the family, and puts into a different perspective De Quincey's own anxieties about counterfeit and multiple identities. Was his fear of identity fraud
inherited from his mother, who had given the family a false name?

De Quincey alone understood that Richard was who he said he was,
and that he needed to adjust to shore life before reintroducing himself
to the mother from whom he had run away. 'It is a great satisfaction to
me that my Feelings and actions are intelligible to you,' Richard wrote
to Thomas, adding that 'There seems to be something very whimsical
in Mr K[elsall]'s ideas of my non-identity.'

De Quincey eventually left London in July, and made his way not to
Grasmere but to the wooded vale of Wrington, twelve miles from Bristol,
where his mother had spent £12,500 (the equivalent of £700,000) on
a house called Westhay, for which she was planning radical improvements. His sisters, who had been amused by De Quincey's request for a
floorplan, were equally amused by his comments on the floorplans they
sent to him: 'We could not help laughing when we observed the truth
of your remark as to all the rooms at Westhay being 12ft by something,
for we have never remarked the circumstance before.' He arrived to find
the usual chaos of builders and carpenters, and he described the scene
to Dorothy as though it were one of his dreams:

> when I first came here we had below stairs only one room habitable,
> besides the kitchen. . . and in every other part of the house and even after
> the bedrooms were finished, it was impossible to make use of them in the
> daytime; for there being no front stairs yet erected – and there being no

road to the backstairs but through the hall which the workmen used as a workshop, there was no getting upstairs without displacing all their benches, etc, which was a complete ceremony and process; and, being up one was a complete prisoner – which did not suit me at all: – since then we have migrated successively into a parlour of the neighbouring farmhouse; – into a greenhouse with no floor; – into a room with a floor but no ceiling; – into a closet 6 feet by 6; – and finally, after having been hunted round the house by painters and paperers, we have resolved into our original sitting-room. . .

While De Quincey was in a greenhouse with no floor, and a room with a floor but no ceiling, Dorothy was 'musing' in the moss hut behind Dove Cottage. Always concerned about the maltreatment of trees – '*malice* has done the work', she wrote to De Quincey of the felling of ancient trees under Nab Scar – she was dreaming of the continued life of her garden. 'Pleasant indeed it is,' she mused in her reply, 'to think of that little orchard which for one seven years at least will be a secure covert for the Birds, and undisturbed by the woodman's axe. There is no other spot which we may have prized year after year that we can ever look upon without apprehension that next year, next month, or even tomorrow it may be deformed or ravaged.' Dorothy's suggestion was that De Quincey was to be custodian of her memories rather than tenant of the cottage. The house was still in every sense hers, and the orchard remained her 'perfect paradise'.

While her son was rearranging his life around the Wordsworths, Elizabeth Quincey was rearranging hers around Hannah More, whose own home, Barley Wood, was now less than a mile away. More's fame had reached the next level with *Coelebs in Search of a Wife,* which was the topic of all fashionable conversation. De Quincey, who had been unable to get beyond page forty, saw her regularly throughout the summer and described his visits in satirical letters to Dorothy. Hannah and her sisters, who were for Napoleon and against Wordsworth, sparred with De Quincey on all subjects. He 'tormented them to the utmost of my power' or so he said, and gave 'extreme pain to all the *refined* part of the community here'. But De Quincey remained a favourite of the More household, who thought he had the makings of a bishop; one of the sisters referred to him afterwards as 'that sweet young man', which suggests that they had been charmed rather than pained by their guest.

A month ago, wrote Dorothy to De Quincey on 1 August 1809, you had 'talked of being at Grasmere in three weeks'. 'When are we to see you?' a despairing Mary asked him on 12 September. 'All has been in readiness for you, and everyone of us wishing to see you for a long long time.' But Richard had arrived at Westhay on 8 September to be reunited with his siblings. The sailor was brimful of stories, some of which De Quincey relayed in a letter to Johnny:

> He has been in cold Countries where there is no daylight for many many weeks. He has been amongst great Forests where there were only Lions and Bears and Wolves. And up Rivers and Lakes where nobody lived. And amongst many nations of Black men and men that are the colour of copper. He has also been past the country where Giants live: they are called Patagonians. He has been in Battles and seen great Towns burning: And sometimes the men that he fought against caught him and put him in prison. Once he was in that Island where Robinson Crusoe and his man Friday lived: I dare say your Mother or your Aunt has told you about them.

It was another six weeks before he caught the mail to the north and opened the door to the cottage. 'It was,' De Quincey recalled, 'on a November night, about ten o'clock, that I first found myself installed in a house of my own – this cottage, so memorable from its past tenant to all men, so memorable to myself from all which has since passed in connexion with it.' Wordsworth had lived here during 'perhaps, the happiest period of his life – the early years of his marriage, and of his first acquaintance with parental affections'. De Quincey would do the same, but 'in that very house', he confessed, 'the second birth of my sufferings began'.

Wordsworth, 'The Deserted Cottage', frontispiece
illustration by Birket Foster

'. . . Margaret
Went struggling on through those calamitous years
With cheerful hope . . .'

Residence in Dove Cottage and the Revolution

I could not always lightly pass
Through the same gateways, sleep where they had slept,
Wake where they waked, range that enclosure old,
That garden of great intellects, undisturbed.

Wordsworth, *The Prelude*, Book Third

His sufferings began almost immediately. Until a permanent house-keeper could be found, Dorothy had arranged for thirteen-year-old Sally Green, whose parents had perished in the snow on Easedale, to come in and cook De Quincey's breakfasts, but he dismissed the 'little orphan maiden' and returned to Allan Bank.

What could have gone so wrong with Sally Green that De Quincey, who had kept his distance from Wordsworth for the past six months, now placed himself once again under the poet's roof? Dorothy, how-ever, was delighted to have him back. 'Mr De Quincey,' she said in a letter to a friend, 'has been above a month with us, and is like one of our own Family.' While he perched at Allan Bank, a procession of wagons and carts, all advancing in measured movements, delivered his cargo of books to the lawn of Dove Cottage. 'I can tell you that he has already received 9 or 10 chests,' wrote Dorothy of the volumes dumped like loads of coals, 'and that 19 more are on the road.' The bulk of the books would need to remain in their chests, she realised, 'on account of the smallness of the house'.

Despite his fascination with the death of Sally's parents – 'in so brief a period as one fortnight', De Quincey enthused in 'Lake

Reminiscences', the Green family 'came to be utterly broken up'– he thought the girl 'lazy, luxurious and sensual'. Sally was also being employed as a nurse for little Catherine Wordsworth, and as far as De Quincey was concerned more of her time was spent thinking about boys than protecting her 'youthful charge'. He had always entertained powerful fantasies around servants: his first sister, De Quincey believed, had been killed by a servant, while Elizabeth had died after being taken to visit a servant's father.

His dislike of Sally Green was not the only problem. De Quincey was uncomfortable in the cottage for a number of reasons. Jane had said that her brother would be unable to manage on his own for more than two months, and we know from his time in Everton that De Quincey threw himself on people – almost anyone – in order to break his solitude. Possibly the house, emptied now of children, felt eerie; quite possibly he saw himself as an intruder and needed reassurance from the Wordsworths that he was welcome; almost certainly he was overwhelmed by the responsibility he had been handed. When his family lived in North Parade it had not been at the personal invitation of Edmund Burke, and nor had Burke been concerned with whether his former home was being treated by its new occupants with sufficient respect. In many ways, it was De Quincey who was now the housekeeper at Dove Cottage, and he was made aware of his lowly position.

Added to which, he had a quite different perspective on the place to the one shared by the Wordsworths. For William and Dorothy, Dove Cottage epitomised the picturesque, but to De Quincey it was, like all houses, sublime. Compare their descriptions of the hill on which the cottage was built: Wordsworth's 'little domestic slip of mountain' was De Quincey's 'vast and seemingly never ending series of ascents'. The Wordsworths saw the exterior walls as 'embossed' with flowers, and De Quincey saw them as 'smothered'. For the Wordsworths the cottage was a hidden nest; for De Quincey there was nowhere from which it could not be seen. He had gazed towards it from Oxford Street in 1803, he had looked down on it from the gorge of Hammerscar in 1805, its 'glare' wheeled into view around bends in the road, and gleamed like a lighthouse amongst the rocks and stones and trees.

During the autumn De Quincey helped John Wilson to write an essay for *The Friend* called 'The Letter to Mathetes', in which a student explores his need for a Wordsworthian moral guide. It was De Quincey who came up with the signature 'Mathetes', meaning follower of Christ. By Christmas, Dorothy had found a replacement for Sally Green and De Quincey was reinstalled in his home. His new housekeeper, Mary Dawson, had originally worked for the Wordsworths and then moved on to Brathay where she cooked for Charles Lloyd and his family. She was, Dorothy enthused, a 'proud and happy Woman' who 'will suit the place exactly, and the place exalts her to the very tip-top of exaltation'. De Quincey enthusiastically suggested that the Wordsworth household – including Coleridge and the enormous John Wilson – return to the cottage for Christmas dinner, but the number proved too many for the parlour and the feast was moved to Elleray. Wilson, an ebullient entertainer who, the previous summer, had hosted a week-long fishing party for thirty-two men at Wast Water, would not have flinched at the last-minute change of plan. De Quincey opened up the cottage instead for the new year, when he put on a firework display for the children of the vale. 'Mr de Quincey's House was like a fair,' wrote the ever-watchful Sara Hutchinson.

———

The year 1810 was a good one for De Quincey and a bad one for Coleridge. De Quincey settled into cottage life and found his pace. He taught Latin to Johnny, read everything he could find about circumnavigating the globe, and played with the toddler, Catherine, who possessed, according to her Aunt Dorothy, 'not the least atom of beauty', but for De Quincey was the 'impersonation of the dawn'. In April, while being tended to by Sally Green, Catherine ate raw carrots and began to vomit. This, De Quincey felt, was 'criminal negligence' on Sally's part. A fit of convulsions followed which left the child's left hand and leg partly paralysed.

De Quincey and Wilson stood godfather to the Wordsworths' new baby (born on 12 May), a boy called William and known as Willie; De Quincey and Wilson climbed mountains together, explored the valleys together, and attended *soirées dansantes* hosted by the Lloyds – the tall man and the small man cultivating the relationship that would last for the rest of their lives. Wilson would be, De Quincey later said, 'the only very intimate friend I ever had'.

With Lloyd, De Quincey spent happy hours by the River Brathay listening to the water rising from the rocky bed, like 'the sound of pealing anthems. . . from the open portals of some illimitable cathedral'. When he was alone he read, drank laudanum, night-walked and night-watched. As dusk fell he would leave his fireplace to 'trace the course of the evening through its household hieroglyphics from the windows which I passed or saw'. Gazing into 'blazing fires shining. . . in nooks far apart from neighbours' and 'in solitudes that seemed abandoned to the owl', he caught 'the sounds of household mirth; then, some miles further. . . the gradual sinking to silence of the house, then the drowsy reign of the cricket'. And he was in 'daily nay hourly intercourse' with Wordsworth, who granted him the privilege of reading *The Prelude*, which he planned to be published only after his death. Then referred to as the 'Poem to Coleridge', or 'the poem on the growth of my own mind', De Quincey found here a work whose power went beyond anything he had hitherto read by Wordsworth.

Growth, intellectual and otherwise, was his absorbing preoccupation, and one of the attractions of opium was that it allowed De Quincey to observe the growth of *his* own mind. To see a thing grow was to catch it in a state of grace: writing, De Quincey observed in his 'Letters to a Young Man Whose Education Has Been Neglected', is not a 'piece of furniture to be shifted; it is a seed which must be sown, and pass through several stages of growth'. The difference between Edmund Burke and Dr Johnson, was that Burke grew 'a truth before your eyes' while Johnson's truths came fully formed. Burke's motion was 'all a going forward' while in Johnson there was 'no process, no evolution, no movement of self-conflict or preparation'. Similarly, De Quincey reprimanded Maria Edgeworth for misunderstanding the all-important lines from Book Four of *Paradise Lost*: 'And in the lowest deep a lower deep/ Still opens to devour me.' 'If it was already the lowest deep,' Edgeworth wondered, 'how the deuce. . . could it open into a lower deep?' 'In carpentry,' De Quincey replied, 'it is clear to my mind that it could not. But, in cases of deep imaginative feeling, no phenomenon is more natural than precisely this never-ending growth of one colossal grandeur chasing and surmounting another, or of abysses that swallowed up abysses.'

The Prelude, reworked over a forty-year period, was a poem which grew before your eyes, a never-ending growth of one colossal grandeur. A two-part version had been written in 1798–9; a five-book version had been given to Coleridge to take to Malta, and by the time Coleridge returned it had expanded to thirteen books. This was the version that Wordsworth had recited at Coleorton in the winter of 1807/08. Each section of the poem was given a title:

Book First – Introduction – Childhood and School-Time
Book Second – School-Time (continued)
Book Third – Residence at Cambridge
Book Fourth – Summer Vacation
Book Fifth – Books
Book Sixth – Cambridge and the Alps
Book Seventh – Residence in London
Book Eighth – Retrospect – Love of Nature Leading to Love of Mankind
Book Ninth – Residence in France
Book Tenth – Residence in France and French Revolution
Book Eleventh – Imagination – How Impaired or Restored
Book Twelfth – Same Subject (continued)
Book Thirteenth – Conclusion

Continually revised, the poem was eventually published as fourteen books in 1850. It is now possible to read the 1798, 1805 and 1850 versions as different poems sharing a genetic heritage. Even then, as its title suggests, *The Prelude* had been intended only as a prologue to a larger work. The original plan had been for Wordsworth to compose an extensive 'Philosophical Poem' to be called 'The Recluse', of which *The Prelude* would form one part and *The Excursion*, on which Wordsworth was currently working, another part. The relation between *The Excursion* and *The Prelude* was compared by Wordsworth to that of 'the Ante-chapel' and the 'body of a Gothic Church'. Dorothy, adopting the same metaphor, described *The Prelude* as a 'sort of portico to "The Recluse", part of the same building'. Despite, or because of, its mighty foundations, 'The Recluse' would never be completed.

In his 'Lake Reminiscences' De Quincey claimed to have memorised *The Prelude*, which he had not seen 'for more than twenty years',

but in 1848 he confessed that when the manuscript was in his possession he had copied it into five notebooks. This was without the poet's
knowledge. It will have been a slow and absorbing task, and one which
allowed him to concentrate his full attention on Wordsworth's thought.
We can imagine that these five notebooks were read again and again by
De Quincey before being buried in mountains of further notebooks,
which eventually piled up to the point where he was no longer able to
get inside the room in which they were stored.

What De Quincey found here was a quest narrative – the quest for
times past – in which the poet wrote about himself as though he were
inside a dream, seeing only 'a prospect in my mind'. The poem begins
with Wordsworth's leaving the 'bondage' of London and embracing his
homelessness:

> What dwelling shall receive me? in what vale
> Shall be my harbour? underneath what grove
> Shall I take up my home?

Wordsworth recalls his childhood as 'one long bathing of a summer's
day'; certain views of Westmorland, particularly the sea, gave him such
pleasure that he wondered if his soul might have learned to love such
sights during a previous existence. De Quincey read about the poet's
night-wanderings as a boy, how he stole a boat and felt the 'huge cliff'
rise up and stride behind him, how he plundered a nest and heard

> Low breathings coming after me, and sounds
> Of undistinguishable motion, steps
> Almost as silent as the turf they trod.

He read of how the poet found the grave of a man who had murdered
his wife, and saw a dead body emerge bolt upright from the bottom of the
lake. Wordsworth's favourite childhood book, De Quincey learned, was
'a slender abstract of the *Arabian Tales*', and when he understood that his
'little yellow, canvas-covered' volume contained only a fraction of the stories which had been 'hewn from a mighty quarry', he determined to purchase the whole thing. But however much he 'hoarded up/ And hoarded
up', Wordsworth was never able to complete his infinite task. De Quincey

read of how Wordsworth, then a schoolboy, had waited for the horses that would bring him home to his dying father, about his years at Cambridge, his time in revolutionary France, his walking tour of the Alps, and his first experience of London, described as 'a dream,/ Monstrous in colour, motion, shape, sight, sound!' where men live 'not knowing each other's names' and the face of 'every one/ That passes by me is a mystery!' The Inns of Court were 'labyrinths', individuals were 'melted and reduced to one identity'. The streets teemed with 'all specimens of man. . . the hunter Indian; Moors, Malays, Lascars, the Tartar and Chinese', coaches 'whirled' across the avenues with 'rash speed' and 'horn loud blowing'. De Quincey read about Wordsworth's visit to 'the giddy top' of 'the Whispering Gallery of St Paul's' and other 'churches numberless'.

Coleridge would mournfully describe Wordsworth's achievement in *The Prelude* as 'in substance, what I have been all my life doing in my system of philosophy', and the poem became quite literally the story of De Quincey's life. As in 'Tintern Abbey', Wordsworth moved backwards and forwards from the quiet present to the turbulent past, reflecting not only on his 'two consciousnesses' – he was both 'conscious of myself and of some other being' – but on the nature of consciousness itself. Visionary moments, in which 'what I saw/ Appeared like something in myself, a dream,/ A prospect in my mind,' would interrupt his childhood play. It was from *The Prelude* that De Quincey learned the use of dual time schemes; he too would describe himself as belonging to both the present and the past; he too would depict his younger self as haunted by an echo of a time which ghosts this one. Wordsworthian memory would become the subject of De Quincey's own autobiographical writing. 'Each man,' wrote Wordsworth, 'is a memory to himself', and the line might serve as De Quincey's epitaph.

He was as much of an insider now as he would ever be. Added to which, nearly all the sources of happiness he had listed in his diary five years before could be ticked off. De Quincey had a 'fixed and not merely temporary residence in some spot of eminent beauty' and was in charge of 'the education of a child'; he enjoyed 'health and vigour', the 'interchange of solitude and society', and 'emancipation from worldly cares' (i.e. enough money to live on); he was able to indulge in 'abstraction and reverie', and he had books galore. Over 5,000 volumes now crowded the shelves and the floors, and climbed in pillars up the walls. Still urgently to be achieved were the cultivation of 'some great intellectual project' and 'the consciousness of a supreme mastery over all unworldly passions (anger – contempt – and fear).'

———

While De Quincey was becoming indispensible to the Wordsworths, Coleridge was making himself impossible. He was soldiering on with *The Friend*, determined not to give it up. With the aid of Sara Hutchinson he worked in manic bursts, and was able to write – or rather dictate – a whole issue in two days. The first edition of the new year carried his attack on the 'garrulous' style of 'Modern Biography', composed of silly anecdotes, 'worthless curiosity' and 'unprovoked abuse'. The modern biographer, Coleridge argued, was a house-breaker who introduced 'the spirit of vulgar scandal, and personal inquietude into the Closet and the Library, environing with evil passions the very Sanctuaries, to which we should flee for refuge from them'. It was a pertinent image: Coleridge, currently violating the sanctuary of Allan Bank, had borrowed 500 books from De Quincey's library, and De Quincey was keeping his own evil passions in check while he inhabited Wordsworth's former closet.

Coleridge's routine, Dorothy complained, was out of kilter with the rest of the household. His fire needed lighting when the servant was busy elsewhere, and his bed had always 'to be made at an unreasonable time'. Not so long ago an unmade bed would not have provoked a crisis in their friendship, and the Wordsworths would have indulged Coleridge's unconventional hours. Time was, Coleridge had arrived at Dove Cottage in the moonlight and eaten a mutton chop beneath the stars. In those days he had been in love with Dorothy and William; but now he fantasised about himself and Sara cosseted 'in the cottage style in good earnest'. De Quincey, living Coleridge's dream, instead wanted what Coleridge had: a great intellectual project, and a woman by his side.

But Sara had had enough of Coleridge, and in February she moved temporarily to Wales to keep house for her brother. Without Sara Hutchinson, *The Friend* folded and Coleridge ceased to function. 'A candle in its socket,' he wrote in his diary, 'with its alternate fits and dying flashes of lingering Light – *O God! O God!*' Dorothy confessed to Catherine Clarkson that Sara's departure had come as a relief ('we

are all glad that she is gone') because Coleridge 'harassed and agitated
her mind continually, and we saw that he was doing her health perpetual injury'. As for Coleridge, Dorothy concluded, 'we have no hope
of him'.

> If he were not under our Roof, he would be just as much the slave of stimu-
> lants as ever; and his whole time and thoughts, (except when he is reading,
> and he reads a great deal), are employed in deceiving himself, and seek-
> ing to deceive others. He will tell me that he has been writing. . . when I
> *know* he has not written a single line. This Habit pervades all his words and
> actions, and you feel perpetually new hollowness and emptiness. . . He lies
> in bed, always till after 12 o'clock, sometimes much later, and never walks
> out. Even the finest spring day does not tempt him to seek the fresh air;
> and this beautiful valley seems a blank to him. He never leaves his own
> parlour except at dinner and tea, and sometimes supper, and then he always
> seems impatient to get back to his solitude – he goes the moment his food
> is swallowed. Sometimes he does not speak a word, and when he does talk
> it is always very much and upon subjects as far aloof from himself and his
> friends as possible.

Dorothy, usually so loyal to Coleridge, begged Mrs Clarkson to
'burn' this letter. But in such a mood she must also have confided in De
Quincey, who was keeping his own laudanum habit quiet and could
anyway see for himself the state of things in Allan Bank.

Unaffected by Coleridge's habits, Wordsworth was enjoying a burst of
creativity. He had returned to 'The Recluse', abandoned in 1806, and written an introduction to a collection of local views painted by the Reverend
Joseph Wilkinson. The paintings were, Wordsworth said, intolerable, but
his introduction was tremendous and later republished as Wordsworth's
Guide to the Lakes. Here he laid out his philosophy of landscape, his views
on rural architecture, and his famous hatred of larches.

———

Grasmere was emptied out in the summer of 1810. Dorothy visited friends
in Lincolnshire, De Quincey went to stay with his mother and sisters in
Westhay, and Wordsworth looked in on Sara in Wales, the thought of

which filled Coleridge with misery. Sara had written to the Wordsworths but not to Coleridge and he found himself sloping back to his own family at Greta Hall. Mary was now, for the first time in her marriage, left alone in the house (as alone as you can be with five children under seven years old) and Wordsworth took the opportunity to correspond with her privately. Their letters – only discovered in 1977 – add another dimension to the domestic goings-on in the vale. Wordsworth and Mary had a secret: their marriage was not a workaday partnership for the raising of offspring, and nor was Mary simply her husband's helpmeet and housekeeper. De Quincey was wrong in seeing Wordsworth as incapable of romance; he and Mary shared what Wordsworth now celebrated as the 'lively gushing thought-employing spirit-stirring passion of love', an ardour 'very rare' in 'married life. . . even among good people'. Wordsworth, who described himself as having an 'almost insurmountable aversion from letter writing' revealed that he could 'write on' to his wife 'to the end of time'.

The woman he compared in his poetry to 'a phantom', an 'apparition', a 'spirit', and a 'dancing shape' was, we now know, seen by him as flesh and blood. Despite sharing every moment of every day, Wordsworth's desire for Mary had to be held at bay for fear of distressing Dorothy, who believed that her brother's marriage included her. Dorothy, wrote Wordsworth, would find their letters 'obnoxious', and he instructed Mary to hide them away. But 'fail not to write to me without reserve', he implored. 'Never have I been able to receive such a letter from you, let me not be disappointed, but give me your heart that I may kiss the words a thousand times!' As for Mary, William's words – so new, so unexpected – had left her 'whole frame. . . overpowered with Love & longing. Well was it for me that I was stretched upon my bed, for I think I could scarcely have stood upon my feet for excess of happiness and depth of affection.'

That October, Basil Montagu, a friend who was passing through the Lakes, invited Coleridge to return with him to London and consult a doctor. Coleridge, it was agreed, would stay with Montagu until he had recovered his health. So he left Greta Hall in Montagu's coach, but by the time they arrived in the capital the offer of hospitality had been withdrawn. Wordsworth, it seems, had warned Montagu that

Coleridge was an 'absolute nuisance' as a houseguest. A version – the Wordsworth version – of what happened was given to Catherine Clarkson by Dorothy:

> William used many arguments to persuade M[ontagu] that his purpose of keeping Coleridge comfortable could not be answered by their being in the same house together – but in vain. Montagu was resolved. 'He would do all that could be done for him and have him at his house.' After this, William spoke out and told M[ontagu] the nature of C's habits (nothing in fact which everybody whose house he has been in for two days has not seen for themselves) and Montagu then perceived that it would be better for C to have lodgings near him. William intended giving C advice to the same effect; but he had no opportunity of talking with him when C passed through Grasmere on his way to London. Soon after they got to London Montagu wrote to William that on the road he had seen so much of C's habits that he was convinced he should be miserable under the same roof with him, and that he had repeated to C what William had said to him and that C had been very angry.

Coleridge's problem was houses. 'Being in the same house together', 'have him at his house', 'everybody whose house he has been in for two days', 'under the same roof'. Southey agreed: Coleridge's habits were 'so murderous of domestic comfort that I am only surprised that Mrs C is not rejoiced at being rid of him. He besots himself with opium, or with spirits, till his eyes look like a Turk's who is half reduced to idiocy by the practice – he calls up the servants at all hours of the night to prepare food for him – he does in short all things at all times except the proper time – does nothing that he ought to do, and everything which he ought not.'

Reporting back to Coleridge what Wordsworth had told him in confidence was a peculiarly destructive act on Montagu's part, and Coleridge was destroyed by it. 'O this is cruel! This is *base!*' he cried when Wordsworth's remarks reached him. In his notebooks he wrote: 'W authorised M to tell me, he had no hope of me! – O God! What good reason for saying this,' and he repeated the dreadful words: 'Sunday Night. No Hope of me! Absolute nuisance! God's mercy it is a dream.' Coleridge now found himself 'whirled about without a center – as in a nightmair – no gravity – a vortex without a centre'. The catastrophe had 'forced me to perceive – No one on earth has ever LOVED me.' It was as though, Coleridge said, he had been hit 'with the suddenness of a flash of lightning'.

In this state, with the 'never-closing. . . Wound of Wordsworth and his Family' still 'festering', Coleridge began to prepare for another set of lectures, this time on Shakespeare and Milton, to be given at the Philosophical Society on Fetter Lane during the winter months.

———

By 1811 De Quincey had exhausted his inheritance. In April he asked if his brother might repay a £2 loan, as 'my present income is so limited that every shilling is important to me'. In the late summer of that year, his mother and sisters made a much-postponed visit. Always well dressed, their 'scarlet cloaks and silk pelisses', noted by Sara Hutchinson, gave the impression that their neighbour was still a wealthy man. The fashionable De Quincey women contrasted sharply with the threadbare Wordsworth women: in one of her recent letters to William, Mary had described being mistaken for a pauper as she carried her newborn son around Grasmere Vale. 'I have become,' she said, 'like nobody in my looks and appearance.'

For the next two months Grasmere became a version of Jane Austen's Netherfield: the De Quincey ladies drank tea with the Wordsworth ladies, the Wordsworth ladies drank tea with the De Quincey ladies, the Wordsworths and De Quinceys were invited to drink tea with the Clarksons, Wordsworth interrupted a letter because 'the Misses De Quincey have just called, and I must walk with them to the Waterfall at Ghyllsode'. Mary De Quincey gave Wordsworth a gift of two birch trees; Wordsworth reciprocated with the roots of the fern *Osmunda regalis*, and Mrs Quincey brought along donations from Hannah More for the Sunday school being set up by Dorothy and Mary. The two households walked, picnicked, talked garden philosophy and read poetry; the visit was considered a great success by all. After they left, Mrs Quincey wondered if Mary Dawson might be tempted to leave her son's employ and cook for her.

Writing to her brother on 7 December, one month after they had returned to Westhay, Mary De Quincey reported that she had been ill and in her delirium found herself transported back to 'your sweet country'. On one occasion she dreamed that she was at the tarn of Watendlath with De Quincey and Jane, where 'we sat down by the warm stream, and ate the same mutton-bone which erst we gnawed on the descent into Borrowdale'. In another dream she 'walked with Miss Wordsworth through Tilberthwaite on the beautiful winding road which charmed us so much'. She asked to be remembered to the Wordsworths, and for Thomas to tell Mr Wordsworth that the *Osmunda regalis* was planted. De Quincey's orchard, she said, had inspired them to make improvements in their garden at Westhay, and in imitation of the moss hut they were building their own 'little rural hut of roots and moss and pieces of knotted trees, in a warm ever-green corner'.

Mrs Quincey, who had erected greenhouses when they were all the rage, was inevitably drawn to the rustic charm of Wordsworth's moss hut, which he had built with his own hands two years into his marriage. It was, Wordsworth informed his brothers, 'a charming little Temple in the Orchard. . . with delightful views of the Church, Lake, Valley etc., etc.'. The simple structure, 'circular' like a 'wren's nest', built of branches 'lined with moss. . . and coated on the inside with heath', was the perfect Romantic dwelling – in *Lyrical Ballads*, the huntsman Simon Lee lives in a similar 'moss-grown hut'. It was here that Dorothy and William came to escape from the babies: 'We are now sitting together in the moss-hut,' Dorothy wrote to Catherine Clarkson; 'William goes on rapidly with "The Recluse".' The moss hut became his study, and it was 'from the moss hut at the top of my orchard' that he had written to Sir George Beaumont on 3 June 1806 to say that he had completed *The Prelude*: 'the sun is sinking behind the hills in front of the entrance and his light falling upon the green moss of the side opposite me. A linnet is singing in the tree above. . . The green fields in the level area of the vale, and part of the lake, lie before me in quietness.'

But on 3 December, four days before his sister informed him that they were building a hut of their own, De Quincey had carried his woodman's axe up to the orchard and plunged it into the green mossy side of Wordsworth's charming little temple, slashing at its structure until it was nothing but a ruin. He then 'razed the ash tree in the orchard and the hedge of holly, hackberry, and hazel that had screened the spot,' wrote Sara Hutchinson, 'and all for the sake of the apple trees', which he over-pruned and left half-naked so 'instead of its being a little wood, as it used to be, there is neither shade nor shelter'. 'Dorothy is so hurt and angry,' Sara reported, 'that she can never speak to him more: and truly it was a most unfeeling thing when he knew what store they set by that orchard.'

His defence would be that he was gardening. But to destroy the poet's hut, entrusted to his safe-keeping by Dorothy, was evidently an act of iconoclasm. De Quincey knew how Dorothy felt about her orchard; he knew the lines in 'To a Butterfly', from *Poems, in Two Volumes*:

> This plot of orchard ground is ours;
> My trees they are, my sister's flowers.

But he also knew the lines in 'Nutting', where Wordsworth had, inexplicably:

> . . . dragged to earth both branch and bough, with crash
> And merciless ravage: and the shady nook
> Of hazels, and the green and mossy bower,
> Deformed and sullied.

What had inspired De Quincey's outburst? A year before, he was running out of ways of pleasing the Wordsworth family. He did not record the incident, which we only know about through Sara Hutchinson, and nor do his biographers pay it much attention. Some fail to mention it at all, while others trivialise it as the 'storm in the apple orchard'. Yet it was an act of tremendous symbolic importance which altered forever the relationship between De Quincey and the Wordsworths.

Would De Quincey have destroyed the moss hut had he not read *The Prelude*? He and Coleridge were the only people outside Wordsworth's immediate family to have seen the manuscript, and it had a devastating effect on them both. Coleridge, in his last great poem, 'To William Wordsworth, Composed on the Night after His Recitation of a Poem on the Growth of an Individual Mind', described himself as having 'culled in wood-walks wild' his own 'genius' and De Quincey's response was to do some woodland culling of his own. He decided now that he too would write a major philosophical work, to be called *De Emendatione Humani Intellectus* (*On the Correction of the Human Intellect*), which would proclaim Thomas De Quincey as 'the first founder of a true Philosophy'. This project, only marginally more ambitious than the one described by Wordsworth for 'The Recluse', was left similarly unrealised.

De Quincey was determined to be more than disciple-in-residence at the Wordsworth museum, custodian of a monument 'crowned' with 'historical dignity'. Not only did he also want to write but he wanted a home of his own, and if that meant making a style statement then so be it; he was used to his aesthetic interventions being greeted by the poet with what De Quincey called 'inhuman arrogance'. One of Wordsworth's most unappealing characteristics was his ownership of the 'whole theory of picturesque beauty', and any opinions offered by De Quincey were 'treated almost as intrusions and usurpations'. Nothing was more guaranteed to offend Dorothy or insult William than De Quincey's imposing his own taste in Dove Cottage, and nothing was more significant to De Quincey than the emotion attached to houses.

He had always been clear on this subject: in his 'Sources of Happiness' De Quincey explained that his home should be a place of stability to allow for 'the growth of local attachment'. Currently he was unattached to anything except the Wordsworths; every experience he had was related in some way to the Wordsworths. It was impossible to make an imprint on a house whose purpose was to preserve the hallowed imprint of another, especially such an other. De Quincey later wrote that the 'little cottage was Wordsworth's from the time of his marriage and earlier. . . Afterward, for many a year, it was mine.' His lightness of touch disguises the effort that went into achieving that personal pronoun.

A coastal shelf of indignation had built up inside him. De Quincey lived for the Wordsworths, he was forever running errands on their behalf; he was used as a library, a babysitter, a tutor, a secretary, and even at times, when Mary needed ready cash, as a bank. Any intellectual ambitions of his own had been discarded; he would never be anyone so long as he was Wordsworth's courtier, and it had not occurred to Wordsworth that De Quincey might have any other ambition. Despite treating Wordsworth with 'more than filial devotion' a friendship had not 'sprung up' between them like 'a wildflower'. De Quincey had tried rationalising his way to forbearance: 'I have been ill-used to a certain extent; but do I think *that* a sufficient reason for giving up all my intimacy with a man like Wordsworth? If I do *not*, let me make no complaint. . . The result. . . if I pursue this matter, will be to rob me of Wordsworth's acquaintance. . . I will, therefore, rest contentedly where I am.' The poetry and not the poet, he sadly conceded, contained the visionary gleam. This realisation put him 'in a strange sort of contradictory life; feeling that things were and were not in the same instant; believing and not believing in the same breath'.

Even before the orchard episode, De Quincey's bid for independence had been noted by Sara Hutchinson, who complained that he 'reads the newspapers standing, or rather stooping with [the infant] Catherine on his back – he is very fond of her but yet does not like to be plagued with her when he feels anything like a duty which as he has engaged to teach her to read etc., towards her – but he will contrive somehow or other to shake this off for he lives only for himself and his books. He used to talk of escorting Mary into Wales but I do not believe that she will have his company.'

It does not seem too great a crime to read a newspaper in the presence of a child, but De Quincey had similarly complained about Sally Green's lack of attentiveness to Catherine. This was a child-centred community. So offended was the mild-mannered Mary by De Quincey's new 'selfishness' that she refused to have him accompany her into Wales on a visit to her brother: the Wordsworth women, who moments before had taken tea with his mother and sisters, were now united against their former friend. The sea change in De Quincey's relations with them had been brought on by *The Prelude* but also by his family visit; the presence of his mother had acted like a trip switch, and we are left to imagine what went on beneath the surface of those late summer tea parties. Doubtless he found the collision of his real and his adopted families stressful in the extreme, and De Quincey's sisters would have been on the lookout for signs of romance between Thomas and his 'sweetheart', Miss Wordsworth. Perhaps they pushed their teasing too far and touched a nerve in their brother; perhaps Dorothy was embarrassed by the interest she excited in Mary and Jane De Quincey. Perhaps De Quincey, realising that his relations with Dorothy might look dangerously like a courtship, decided to sever once and for all any intimacy between them.

Whatever happened during the two months that De Quincey shared Dove Cottage with his mother and sisters, rather than bolt from his life in Grasmere when things began to go wrong, he decided to stake his claim and instead he pushed away the Wordsworths. The destruction of the moss hut took reckless courage, and it must have shocked De Quincey as much as it did Dorothy.

Between themselves the Wordsworth women now referred to De Quincey as 'Peter Quince'. It was an insightful joke, doubtless the work of Sara Hutchinson. Quince, the bookish carpenter in *A Midsummer Night's Dream*, directs 'the rude mechanicals' in his play 'Pyramus and Thisbe', a parody of the lament behind a locked door. There is a great deal that was Quince-like about De Quincey, who always enjoyed the idea of the play within a play, and who belonged, of course, in a midsummer dream.

ESCAPE of IOHN TURNER, by the SHEETS Knotted together;
after he had seen one of the Murderers plundering the dead bodies.

John Turner, journeyman, suspended from the bedroom window.
'Like chorus and semi-chorus, strophe and antistrophe, they work against each other.
Pull journeyman, pull murderer.'

Residence in London and Grasmere

Year follows year, the tide returns again,
Day follows day, all things have second birth;
The earthquake is not satisfied at once;
And in such way I wrought upon myself,
Until I seemed to hear a voice that cried
To the whole city, 'Sleep no more.'

Wordsworth, *The Prelude*, Book Tenth

On 7 December, the day that Mary De Quincey wrote to her brother about the moss hut they were planning for the garden at Westhay, Timothy Marr and his household were slaughtered in the draper's shop at 29 Ratcliffe Highway. 'Horrid and Unparalleled Murders', announced the *Morning Chronicle* the following Monday. 'We almost doubt,' reported *The Times*, 'whether, in the annals of murders, there is an instance on record to equal the atrocity of those which the following paragraphs will disclose.' Journalism was a rapidly developing trade; by 1811 over 240 different newspapers were in circulation in the country; the number had doubled since De Quincey's childhood and his appetite for them was insatiable. As a schoolboy he had translated them into Greek, as an adult he had read them while he carried Catherine on his back. He loved the animation of the *Courier* building with its iron-framed hand presses, and the romance of the mail-coach was bound up in its distribution 'over the face of the land, like the opening of apocalyptic vials, the heartshaking news of Trafalgar, of Salamanca, of Vittoria, of Waterloo'. It was, De Quincey found, possible to watch a news story grow before your eyes, and thus he watched the growth of events on the Ratcliffe Highway.

On 10 December *The Times* reported that 'a large shipwright's mallet, its head weighing from two to three pounds, and its handle about three feet long' had been found at the crime scene, along with 'a ripping chisel; and a wood mallet about four inches square, with a handle of about 18 inches long, made of iron, and is such as is generally used for ripping sheathing off from ships'. Marr's house backed onto a yard, beyond which lay an area of common land which led into the other back yards. On 'being alarmed by the ringing of the bell' the murderer went through the small yard at the back of the house and got over the gateway into the enclosed space of ground. After this, 'all trace' of him 'was lost'.

Twenty-nine Ratcliffe Highway had instantly become a tourist sight. On 11 December, *The Times* reported that 'the sensation excited by these most ferocious murders has become so general, and the curiosity to see the place where they were committed so intense, that Ratcliffe Highway was rendered almost impassable by the throng of spectators before ten o'clock yesterday morning'. The washed, re-clothed and decaying bodies of the Marr family and their young apprentice were laid out in the bedrooms for the traffic of visitors (a tradition which continued well into the twentieth century). The inquest into their deaths took place on 12 December and occupied a whole column of the paper. Margaret Jewell's testimony was printed in full:

> I lived servant with Mr Marr. I went to the counter to my master, who was behind it; he gave me a pound note; it wanted a few minutes to twelve; I left him busy behind the counter; I went out of the door, and turned to the left to Taylor's; they were shut up, and I returned again past the window, and still saw him behind the counter; I went to St John's hill, to pay the baker; they were shut-up likewise; I went with the intent to get some oysters, but found the shops were shut up; I returned again to the door of my master's house. I found it closely shut up, and no light to be seen; I think I was out about twenty minutes; I rang at the bell, and no one answered; I rang repeatedly; whilst I was at the door, the watchman went by on the other side of the way, with a person in charge; I certainly heard someone coming down stairs, which I thought was my master coming to let in me; I am certain I

heard the child cry very low; I rang again, and knocked at the door with my foot repeatedly, when a man came up to the door and insulted me: I thought I would wait till the watchman came, which he shortly did, and called the hour of one, at the same time desired me to move on, not knowing who I was; I said I belonged to the house, and thought it very strange I should be locked out; he then observed they had not fastened the pin of the window; the watchman then knocked, rang at the bell, and called Mr Marr through the keyhole; Mr Murray, the next door neighbour, then came out and asked what was the matter, the watchman then told him that I was locked out. I continued at the door with the watchman till Mr Murray came out again, and said there was a strong light backwards, while another watchman, who had joined the first, made an alarm; Mr Murray got into the house backwards and opened the street door, when the watchman and myself entered.

Mr Murray's testimony was then quoted in the third person:

About 10 minutes past 12 on Sunday morning [8 December] he was sitting at supper, and heard a noise in the shop-floor of the next house, which resembled the falling of a shutter, or the pushing of a chair: he also heard the sounds of a human voice, as if proceeding from fear or correction; the voice he thought to be that of a boy or woman. All this happened in one minute. A little before one o'clock he heard a continued ringing at Mr Marr's bell; this ringing continued till nearly half past one; he at length went to the door to know what was the matter; the watchman said, that the pin was not fastened, and that the girl was shut out; he told the watchman still to ring the bell, and that he would go to the other side, and make them open the door; he did go backwards, and called Marr three or four times, but got no answer; he then went again to the front of the house, told the watchman that he saw a light on one of the back windows, and that he would endeavour to get in backwards; he got over the fence, and finding the yard door open, he went in; he went up one pair of stairs, and he took the candle in his hand, which was on the landing place; the two doors of the chamber in which Mr Marr usually slept were open . . .

As more information was gathered it became possible for De Quincey to build up a picture of the crime scene. Marr was improving his shop and builders had recently replaced the front window. A Mr Pugh, supervising the work, had borrowed an iron chisel from a neighbour for the use of his carpenter, Cornelius Hart. By the time Hart had finished his job, three weeks previously, the chisel had been lost. Hart claimed to have last seen it on the premises, but Marr had painstakingly searched the house and found nothing. At twenty inches long, it was an easy enough object to spot. The next time the chisel was seen, *The Times* revealed, was the 'morning of the fatal massacre when it was found lying by the side of Mr Marr's body', its head matted with hair and blood. After the inquest nine men were taken into custody, including Cornelius Hart himself and a drunk who had already incoherently confessed to all four murders.

On 13 December the *Morning Chronicle* ran a long report on Coleridge's *Romeo and Juliet* lecture and the adjacent column carried a brief update on the murder investigation. It transpired that the mother and sisters of Mrs Marr had come in from the country to visit the new baby on Sunday 8 December; it was only when they arrived for lunch that they heard the horrific news: 'The effect which the intelligence had on them it would be vain to describe.' The suggestion now, from 'the print of some feet in the yard', was that two men were involved. 'The footsteps are marked with blood and sawdust, which is accounted for by there being some carpenters at work in the shop on the same day, and the sawdust mixing with the blood, it is supposed, stuck to the shoes of the murderers.' Three men had apparently been seen near Marr's drapery on the night of the murders, one of whom was observed looking through the new shop window. He was 'a tall' and 'lusty' man, dressed in a long coat. The other was smaller and scruffier, in a torn blue jacket and with a small-brimmed hat, while the third had no remarkable features at all.

The subject of Coleridge's lecture on the evening of Thursday 19 December was *A Midsummer Night's Dream*. That night, Mr and Mrs Williamson, who held the licence of the King's Arms at 81 New Gravel Lane, a narrow street which ran at a right angle to the Ratcliffe Highway in the direction of the docks, were closing the tavern. John Williamson was fifty-six, his wife, Elizabeth, was sixty; they shared their home with a lodger, John Turner, their granddaughter, Kitty Stillwell, aged four-teen, and their fifty-year-old servant, Bridget Harrington. One house in eight on New Gravel Lane was an inn, but the King's Arms was

more respectable than the rest. The Williamsons had been the proprietors for fifteen years; they kept the noise down, shut before midnight, and served a regular and reputable clientele. At eleven o'clock,
Mr Anderson, who lived next door but one, left the taproom with a
pot of beer and Williamson put up the shutters; twenty minutes later,
having finished his beer, Anderson returned for a quick second pot, but
found the tavern in a state of commotion.

Hanging from a second-floor window on two torn sheets which
had been knotted together, was the half-naked figure of John Turner.
'Murder, Murder!' Turner cried, before dropping eight feet into the arms
of the night watchman. A crowd had gathered around the scene; they
knocked at the Williamsons' front door but there was no answer. Several
men then began to beat down the entrance while others prised open the
cellar window on the front pavement. It was on the cellar stairs that they
found Williamson, his head crushed by an iron bar and his throat cut.
Mrs Williamson and Bridget Harrington were both in the tap room,
their skulls shattered and throats slashed to the neck bone. At the back of
the house was an open window through which the murderer had made
his escape onto the sloping clay wasteland which ran down to the docks.

John Turner, who had lodged with the Williamsons for eight months,
gave his account to the coroners of what had taken place. He returned
home that night, having eaten supper with his brother, at twenty to
eleven. Mrs Williamson was at the front door, Mr Williamson was
by the fire in his great chair, the servant was in the back room; Kitty
Stillwell was asleep in bed. He joined his landlord, who was told by a
customer that a stout man wearing a very large coat had been peering
through the inner glass door in the passage. Williamson, a burly man
himself, lifted the candlestick and went to look. He returned saying
that 'he could not see him, but if he did see him, he would send him
where he ought or would not like to go'. Mr Anderson then went home
with his first pot of beer and John Turner went upstairs to bed. Five
minutes later, Turner

heard the front door being banged: very hard. Immediately afterwards I heard
the servant exclaim 'we are all murdered' or 'shall be murdered' two or three
times. . . I heard two or three blows, but with what weapon I cannot say. Shortly
afterwards I heard Mr Williamson cry out, 'I'm a dead man.' I was in bed still.

> After two minutes I got out of bed, and listened at the door, but could hear
> nothing. I went down to the first floor, and from below I heard the sound of
> three heavy sighs. I heard some person walk across the middle of the room on
> the ground very lightly. I was then half way down the last pair of stairs, and
> naked. I went to the bottom of the stairs, and the door stood a little on the jar.
> I passed through the opening, and by the light of a candle which was burning
> in the room, I saw a man, apparently near six feet in height, in a large rough
> Fleming coat, of a dark colour, which came down to his heels. He was standing
> with his back to me, apparently leaning over some person, as if in the act of
> rifling their pockets, as I heard some silver rattle, and saw him rise and open his
> coat with his left hand and put his right hand to his breast, as if to put some-
> thing in his pocket. I did not see his face, and I only saw that one person.

Turner leapt back up the stairs in his bare feet. When he reached his
bedroom he pushed the bed against the door, stripped off the sheets,
tied them together and attached them to the bedpost. He then opened
the window, threw out the sheets and lowered himself down. Tucked
up in bed next door, young Kitty Stillwell lay fast asleep. In his haste,
John Turner had forgotten all about her.

The murderer's second set of victims were another married couple and
those who lived with them. Again, the target was not an individual but
a household, the house had been both a home and a place of work and
the intruder had apparently walked in through an open door and locked
it behind him. Again, nothing of significance had been stolen and there
was no clear motive for the killings; again, the exterminations had been
achieved in a matter of moments and the killer, interrupted by a pounding on the front door, had escaped through the back of the building.
Again there was a terrified survivor unrelated to the victims who could
be seen on the immediate outside: Margaret Jewell on the outside of the
door, John Turner suspended in mid-air from the bedroom window.

———

Christmas was coming and the killer was still at large; the Ratcliffe Highway
and surrounding streets were being manned by a night beadle and a team
of elderly night watchmen. The woeful inadequacy of the system of polic-
ing was creating a national outcry. Even in Grasmere, De Quincey later

wrote, panic had set in. A widowed neighbour of his 'never rested until she placed eighteen doors, each secured by ponderous bolts, and bars, and chains, between her own bedroom and any intruder of human build'. The occupants of smaller houses with fewer doors 'more than once died upon the spot, from the shock attending some suspicious attempts at intrusion upon the part of vagrants'. While these reports are evidently fantasies, Southey told a friend that: 'No circumstances which did not concern me ever disturbed me so much. I . . . never had mingled such a feeling of horror, indignation, and astonishment with a sense of insecurity too.' Also at Greta Hall that winter was Percy Bysshe Shelley, who had run away with his child bride, Fanny. For Southey and Shelley, the murders reflected the state of a nation which hovered on the edge of revolution; but for De Quincey they revealed the state of one man's soul.

Meanwhile the Wordsworths, no longer speaking to De Quincey, had not realised that Coleridge was no longer speaking to them. Wordsworth, aware of Montagu's indiscretion but not of its impact, had offered Coleridge neither an explanation for his comments nor an apology for the hurt caused. It is unlikely that De Quincey knew anything about the lull in the Coleridge–Wordsworth relations, but we can imagine him taking advantage of the lull in his own relations with the Wordsworths to increase his laudanum intake and follow the reports of the Williamson murders: shortly after the slaughters two men had been seen running up the lane towards the Ratcliffe Highway, the shorter of whom appeared to be lame.

Every man in Wapping, it seemed, was presumed guilty and forty false arrests had been made. Then on Sunday 22 December, a twenty-seven-year-old sailor called John Williams was apprehended in his lodgings, a public house called the Pear Tree, close to the river in Old Wapping. Described by *The Times* as 'about 5 feet 9 inches in height' and 'of an insinuating manner', John Williams was by all accounts over-familiar and intrusive; he had, for example, been seen to lean over the bar of a tavern and laughingly remove money from the till. Nothing was known about his family; on land he lived at the Pear Tree where he shared a room with two other men and drank away his wages. He belonged to Wapping's fluid community of wanderers.

The evidence against Williams was thin. He had been seen at the King's Head at seven o'clock on the night of the Williamson murders, and on his

return to the Pear Tree – at around midnight – he had asked one of his fellow lodgers, a German sailor called John Frederick Richter, to put out the
candle. Added to which his clothes were stained, and he had in his pocket
fourteen shillings, a pound note and two pawn tickets. Further evidence,
about to appear, was that the bloodstained maul had been traced back
to the Pear Tree. It belonged to a ship's carpenter called John Peterson,
currently at sea, who was storing his tools at the house. In his defence,
John Williams explained that he was a friend of the Williamsons, that his
pocketful of cash was due to having pawned his shoes, and that after leaving
the King's Arms he had visited a doctor about a cure for his leg, which had
been giving him problems as a result of an old wound (Williams walked
with a limp). He had told Richter to put out the candle not because he
didn't want to draw attention to the house, but to prevent a fire.

Witnesses described seeing a large figure in a long coat in the vicin-
ity of both murders. A man of this description had been seen staring
in through the front window of 29 Ratcliffe Highway on the night of
7 December, and through the glass inner door of the King's Head on
the night of 19 December. A similar figure, accompanied by two other
men, had been seen on the Ratcliffe Highway soon after the murders,
and also on New Gravel Lane, with a companion who was lame. Turner
had seen a large man in a long coat by the corpse of Mrs Williamson,
pocketing some change. John Williams, of medium height and without
an ankle-length coat, bore no relation to this 'lusty fellow' but may have
been one of his companions. In which case, where was his accomplice?
From lodgers in the Pear Tree it transpired that the Marrs' carpenter,
Cornelius Hart, was one of William's drinking friends. Hart at first
denied knowing him, but then admitted to dispatching his wife to the
Pear Tree to have it confirmed that Williams had indeed been arrested.

On Christmas Eve John Williams was taken to Coldbath Fields
Prison, and on Boxing Day his body was found hanging in his cell –
an apparent suicide. The court proceedings continued regardless and
Londoners, frantic for justice, found the dead man guilty.

The body was removed from the prison and taken to a watchhouse
at the London Docks. The following day, the last of the old year, it was
dressed in blue trousers and an open-necked white, frilled shirt and
placed in a cart on a specially raised and slanted platform with the maul
and the ripping chisel displayed on either side of its broken neck. In an
unprecedentedly bizarre piece of theatre, the cart was paraded through

the parish led by a procession of grey horses on which rode, in hier-
archical order, the constable, the Collector of King's Taxes, the baker,
the coal merchant and the Superintendent of Lascars in the East India
Company's service. They were followed by constables and beadles on
foot. This ceremony was watched by 10,000 spectators who crowded
the streets and leaned from the windows of the houses lining the route.
It was, said the MP and playwright, Richard Brinsley Sheridan, 'an
unseemly exhibition' which 'fed the worst appetites of the mob'.

The cart stopped outside 29 Ratcliffe Highway where Williams's
head, which had fallen to the side, was turned around so that his dead
eyes could take in the sight of the now empty house, and the convoy
then continued to New Gravel Lane where it halted in a similar fashion outside the King's Arms. The body was then pulled to a crossroads
above St George in the East, where it was bent in half and thrown into
a hole four feet deep. Using the still bloodied maul, a stake was ham-
mered through his heart. The residents of Ratcliffe Highway greeted
the dawn of 1812 with the tense relief that follows the impact of a sudden explosion. Action had been taken, revenge was achieved.

That night, in his last lecture of the year, Coleridge talked about
Iago, later memorably described by him as a 'motiveless malignity'. For
De Quincey, John Williams was another such character.

———

Coleridge's first lecture of 1812, on 2 January, was on *Hamlet*. The
ghost of the murdered king reveals to his son the cause of his death and
'what is the effect. . . ? Instant action and pursuit of revenge? No: endless reasoning and hesitating – constant urging and solicitation of the
mind to act. . . ceaseless reproaches of himself for sloth and negligence,
while the whole energy of his resolution evaporates in these reproaches.'
For Hamlet, Coleridge propounded, 'the external world' was 'comparatively dim' and of no interest in itself. It became interesting only when
it was 'reflected in the mirror of his mind'. 'Prompted' by 'heaven and
hell' to avenge his father's murder, he instead unpacked his 'heart with
words'; the prince had the 'aversion to action which prevails among
such as have *a world in themselves*'.

Presenting Hamlet as a Romantic hero, Coleridge changed forever
the way the play was seen while painting for his audience an enduring

portrait of his own condition. He too inhabited a word-packed world within his mind, and when his lecture had ended, a member of the audience, turning to Henry Crabb Robinson, whispered 'This is a satire on himself.' 'No,' Crabb Robinson replied, 'it is an elegy.'

———

'How do I do?' De Quincey asked in his *Confessions*. 'Well, pretty well thank you, reader. I never was better in my life than the spring of 1812.' His ship, however, was sailing into the iceberg. In March we find him back in London vaguely pursuing a career as a lawyer. He took up his old rooms in Great Titchfield Street and made daily visits to Coleridge, who was living with the Morgans in nearby Berners Street, Soho. It was now that he heard the grim tale of Wordsworth's advice to Montagu – 'as ought not', De Quincey grandly concluded, 'to have proceeded from the hands of a friend'. Wordsworth, he learned, was Coleridge's 'bitterest Calumniator', and De Quincey had his own Wordsworth miseries to share. That he was still raging about the reaction to the moss hut is clear from an incident at a party. A guest mentioned that Mary Wordsworth had said something about 'possession of the house', at which point De Quincey 'took fire... and retired... in great indignation'.

Amongst his book purchases that spring it is likely that he now treated himself, for sixpence each, to four rapidly produced pamphlets whose contents he studied closely. The first: 'Fairburn's Account of the Dreadful Murder of Mr Marr and Family, at their House in Ratcliffe Highway on Saturday Night, December 7, 1811, including the Whole Investigation before the Coroner's Inquest, etc etc.', contained a picture of 'The Pen Maul, used by the Murderers' and retold the story De Quincey knew already from *The Times*.

The second, 'Fairburn's Account of the Inhuman Murder of Mr and Mrs Williamson and their Woman Servant at the King's Arms, New Gravel Lane, Ratcliffe Highway, on Thursday Night, December 19, 1811', opened with a cartoonish illustration of John Turner descending from his bedroom window, and contained the deposition of Turner, accounts of the events given by various witnesses, and the coroner's report in which he described the Ratcliffe Highway as riddled with 'the lower classes of the community', 'strangers and seamen discharged from. . . the East and West India and London Docks' and 'foreign sailors from all parts of the globe'.

The third pamphlet, 'Fairburn's Account of the Life, Death and Interment of John Williams, the Supposed Murderer of the Families of Marr and Williamson, and Self Destroyer', contained a plate of Williams's body as it appeared on the platform before being thrown into the pit at the crossroads, and a cobbled-together biography. His name was not Williams at all, it transpired, but John Murphy and while he tried to pass himself off as Scottish it was supposed that he was from Banbridge, near Down Patrick in County Down. 'The prejudice of the hour,' a furious Richard Brinsley Sheridan informed the House of Commons, 'would have him an Irishman.' The reaction to the murders became entangled in anti-Irish hysteria:

> Whether he was in his native country at the time of the unhappy troubles of 1798 can only be a matter of conjecture, but it is certainly not unnatural to suppose, that a monster capable of committing the late atrocities must early in life have lost that innate horror of bloodshed, which forms so striking a feature in the moral constitution of man. In the dreadful paths of rebellion, probably it was that he was first tempted to embrue his hands in the blood of his fellow-creatures; and, amidst those terrible scenes of midnight murder, which that unhappy country then afforded, might his sinful conscience have been seared to every feeling of repentance and remorse.

John Murphy, aka John Williams (as De Quincey continued to call him), aged around thirty, had until recently been at sea, a career he was 'driven' into as a result of 'former bad conduct'. Having served on several East Indiamen, including the *Henry Addington* and the *Nottingham*, he was laid up for some time at St Thomas's hospital with a leg injury. In April 1808 he sailed on the *Dover Castle* under Captain George Richardson, returning in July 1810. Employed as the captain's personal servant on the same voyage was Timothy Marr.

> The conduct of the two formed, it is said, a striking contrast: Marr was sober, diligent, peaceable, and obliging; and by his services gained so greatly the esteem of his master, that on their return to England, the captain, in conjunction with another friend, supplied him with the means of taking the house in Ratcliffe Highway, and of commencing business. Williams, on the contrary, was idle, drunken, dissolute, and quarrelsome, and so continually

involved in disgrace, that, on his quitting the ship, the captain is said to have prophesied that he would come to an untimely end.

Reckless Williams was before the mast while mild Marr cleaned the captain's clothes: they sound like rival brothers in a fairy tale. When the *Dover Castle* docked in Wapping, Marr married his sweetheart, Celia, and set up shop, while Williams, now going by the name of 'John Williamson', got himself a berth on board the *Roxburgh Castle* bound for the Brazils. The ship was possessed of a 'very bad crew', who, on reaching Surinam, mutinied. One of the three leaders of the revolt was William Ablass, known as Long Billy, a large man with a limp who had been seen drinking with Williams in the *King's Arms* on the night of the Williamson murders. Ablass had already been 'apprehended on suspicion of being concerned with Williams in the late murders; but discharged on the deposition of a woman, who, it now appears, was interested in his fate'.

The pamphlet, which contained a detailed account of the murder investigation, built up a case against John Murphy/Williams/Williamson. Would he have been convicted had he lived to face trial? 'Of his real guilt, there can, we think, be no doubt; but that there was sufficient *legal proof* of it, is not so easy to determine.' The night before he took his life, Williams had asked for a pen and ink, 'and it is much to be regretted, that the request should have been denied him, as in the state he then was, his conscience might have prompted him to make a full confession of his guilt: whether or not he had any accomplices remains to be discovered'.

The fourth pamphlet bought by De Quincey – his future essays suggest that he knew it well – was called 'The Substance of the Horrid Murders in Ratcliffe Highway and Gravel Lane', and contained the transcript of a sermon given on Sunday 29 December 1811 at the chapel of the influential Reverend Rowland Hill. The reverend made no attempt to disguise his ghoulish pleasure in the horrid murders: the sainted Marrs, he boomed from the pulpit, had been 'butchered like so many brute beasts!. . . Robbery and Rapine stalk abroad at noon-day! Murder, cold-blooded Murder, seeks us in our very dwellings; and, to use the emphatic language of the Coroner, "Our houses are no longer our castles; we are no longer safe in our beds!"' He railed against the slanderous suggestion that the government might be responsible for the lawless state of the country: 'how could Government have prevented the commission of these dreadful deeds? What mere mortal preoccupations could possibly have guarded against them?. . . Maniacs and Murderers, as they are out of the pale of common humanity, are also out of the reach of human prevention. . . my beloved Brethren, I repeat it again and again, the best system of Police in the world could not have prevented the late dreadful occurrences.' As for the killer himself,

> Here we see a wretch, going coolly and deliberately into the house of a man with whom he had been intimate, and butchering him, his wife, his servant and a child; not as it should appear, from any blood-thirsty spirit of revenge, but purely and solely, that he might be enabled to rob and plunder, in greater security! Having failed in this his first attempt, the universal horror excited by the event is not subsided, before he, with equal coolness and deliberation, commits three more murders, whose diabolical atrocity is only equalled by the former!

The preacher's fantasy of the murders as accomplished with 'coolness and deliberation' whetted De Quincey's appetite. So too did his invitation to imagine the murderer's last night alive: 'Alone, in the dark, left a prey to his own dreadful thoughts, and suffering the intolerable stings of a guilty conscience. . . He has escaped the gallows, it is true, but how will he escape God? He has fled from the Judges of the world, but where can he flee from the Judge of Heaven and Earth?' His cell resounded as loudly as the Whispering Gallery of St Paul's. As for the worry over whether the murderer had any 'accomplices in his hellish work' we can only hope, the reverend concluded, that 'no other heart could conceive, no other hand execute, the dreadful scheme!'

In May 1812, Wordsworth arrived in London with what he called a '*determination* to confront Coleridge and Montagu upon this vile business'. (He felt no such determination to confront the vile business with De Quincey.) Crabb Robinson acted as go-between and Wordsworth signed a document swearing that he had not 'commissioned' Montagu to tell Coleridge he was a hellish houseguest or a 'rotten drunkard'. Coleridge was pacified, but it was a plaster over an infected wound. He later told Thomas Poole that his former love for Wordsworth could never return. The damage to their friendship was irreparable, and one of the tragedies of his life.

On 11 May, in the midst of their negotiations, there was another murder and this time at the heart of government: the prime minister Spencer Perceval was shot dead in the foyer of the House of Commons. It was as though the king himself had been slain, and in his own castle. His assassin, a Liverpool merchant-broker called John Bellingham, acted with striking coolness and deliberation. Having taken himself to Parliament after visiting an exhibition of paintings (his father had been an artist), Bellingham shot Perceval with a single bullet to the chest and then sat on a bench to wait for his arrest. For once, De Quincey was on the scene: John Williams might be lying beneath the crossroads with a stake through his heart, but murder still stalked abroad. Bellingham was a handsome and articulate man whose story was utterly dismal. He had been imprisoned for four years in Russia, where he had travelled for business, and had subsequently been refused government compensation. 'Recollect, Gentlemen,' he told the court in his trial, 'what was my situation. Recollect that my family was ruined and myself destroyed, merely because it was Mr Perceval's pleasure that justice should not be granted. . . I demand only my right, and not a favour; I demand what is the birthright and privilege of every Englishman.' Coleridge, immediately drawn in, offered to report on the murder for the *Morning Chronicle* and the next day he visited a London pub to take down the local reaction. He found here no pity for Perceval, leader of an unrepresentative government, and total sympathy for his avenger: Bellington was a popular hero.

So while Parliament mourned the death of the prime minister, the rest of the country celebrated the execution of a tyrant and anticipated further such deaths. 'These were the very words,' Coleridge reported from the tavern: '"This is but the beginning" – "More of these damned Scoundrels must go the same way & then the poor people may live."' What Coleridge heard was the revolutionary fervour of 1790s France. 'The country is no doubt in a most alarming situation,' Wordsworth wrote home to an anxious Dorothy, 'and if much firmness be not displayed by the Government, confusion & havoc & murder will break out and spread terribly.'

The next household wreck, however, was to be his own.

The tension between De Quincey and Dorothy was broken exactly a month later when, on 11 June, he received a letter. 'My dear Friend,' Dorothy ominously began: 'I am grieved to the heart as I write to you – but you must hear the sad tidings – Our sweet little Catherine was seized with convulsions on Wednesday night. . . the fits continued till ¼ after 5 in the morning, when she breathed her last.' Later that day, Wordsworth appeared on his doorstep in the company of Crabb Robinson, who noted that De Quincey 'burst into tears' on seeing them and 'seemed to be more affected than the father'.

The fact that Dorothy had written immediately to De Quincey while Wordsworth went out of his way to pay him a visit shows that they were concerned about how he would take the news, but De Quincey's grief – described by an appalled Crabb Robinson as 'puling and womanly weakness' – was beyond anything they could have expected. 'Nobody,' De Quincey replied to Dorothy,

> can judge from [Catherine's] manner to me before others what love she shewed to me when we were playing or talking together alone. On the night when she slept with me in the winter, we lay awake all the middle of the night – and talked oh how tenderly together: When we fell asleep, she was lying in my arms; once or twice I awoke from the pressure of her dear body; but I could not find [it] in my heart to disturb her. Many times on that night – when she was murmuring out tender sounds of endearment, she would lock her little arms with such passionateness round my neck – as if she had known that it was to be the last night we were ever to pass together. Ah pretty pretty love, would God I might have seen thy face and kissed thy dear lips again!

Mary Dawson, De Quincey added, had a burden on her conscience for the way in which she sometimes spoke to Catherine.

One of the meanings of the Latin word *plagiarius*, from which 'plagiarism' derives, is the theft or seduction of another man's child. In this sense, De Quincey plagiarised Catherine Wordsworth. For as long as he could remember he had nurtured thoughts of kissing a dead girl as he parted from her for the final time, and his eroticisation of Catherine is intensified by the fantasy, expressed in his letter to Dorothy, that she knows this night together will be their 'last'. De Quincey later described himself as having had a presentiment, on leaving for London, that Catherine's life would end, which was confirmed when a dog howled three times outside his door. He went on to tell Dorothy that he was fixated by the image of the 'idle gazers' who will have crowded into her room to look 'at our darling's face' as she lay lifeless on the bed prior to her burial, while 'her father, her mother, and I should have been allowed to see her face no more'. Her aunt is not included in this line-up of intimates, but then Dorothy, as De Quincey knew, had never shown much fondness for Catherine's face.

Crabb Robinson, who saw De Quincey over the next few days, thought he was hamming up his pain and in De Quincey's next letter to Dorothy, he laboured over his expressions of sorrow, producing three drafts before he was satisfied: 'Oh that I could have died for her or with her! Willingly dear friend I would have done this.'

His anguish was such that residents of the vale assumed De Quincey must be Catherine's father. 'The grounds for this fiction,' he explained, 'were the plainness of the child's appearance,' Wordsworth's 'indiffer- ence' to and 'want of fondness' for 'the little thing', and De Quincey's own 'grief for its death'. He was evidently on the verge of a breakdown. Wordsworth was not indifferent to Catherine's death, which in part destroyed him. 'Surprised by Joy', written for his daughter, describes a sudden moment of delight which he instinctively turned to share with her, before remembering that she was 'long buried in the silent tomb':

> Love, faithful love, recalled thee to my mind –
> But how could I forget thee? – Through what power,
> Even for the least division of an hour,
> Have I been so beguiled as to be blind
> To my most grievous loss? – That thought's return
> Was the worse pang that sorrow ever bore,
> Save one, one only, when I stood forlorn,
> Knowing my heart's best treasure was no more;
> That neither present time nor years unborn
> Could to my sight that heavenly face restore.

Wordsworth's grief for Catherine was pure. De Quincey's was en- tangled in guilt – about reading the newspapers when she wanted to play, about being in London when she died, about having destroyed the moss hut and culled the orchard and thus damaged relations between the two houses. Added to which, De Quincey and Catherine had entered the Wordsworths' world at the same time, and in this sense they were twinned: her departure coincided with his own. As long as the children still loved him, De Quincey had a link to the family; good relations were unlikely to be resumed now that Catherine had gone.

But there was another dimension to the story as well: the death of Wordsworth's daughter reactivated De Quincey's grief for Elizabeth. Catherine had died in midsummer, twenty years – almost to the day – after De Quincey's sister. Catherine had vanished in 'early dawn, just as the first gleams of morning began to appear above Seat Sandal and Fairfield', and she thereafter 'assumed a connection . . . with the summer sun, by timing her immersion into the cloud of death with the rising and setting of that fountain of life'. Her death triggered memories of other tragic maids, like Ann of Oxford Street and the nameless child with whom De Quincey had curled up in the freezing house on Greek Street. Wherever in the country he ran, De Quincey was pursued by the same scenes. Not only had he been unable to save Jane, Elizabeth and Catherine from the deadly hands of ungrateful servants, but he had, as far as the Wordsworths were concerned, become an ungrateful servant himself.

Catherine also recalled Wordsworth's Lucy. Both girls were three when they died – 'Three years she grew in sun and flower', Wordsworth wrote of Lucy – and the narrator of this 'Lucy' poem had, like De Quincey, insisted on being the girl's sole tutor:

This Child I to myself will take;
She shall be mine, and I will make
A lady of my own.

The dead Lucy was a 'Maid whom there were none to praise/ And very few to love', and the death of Catherine, De Quincey later wrote, was 'obscure and little heard of. . . amongst all the rest of the world'.

Catherine's death allowed De Quincey to reclaim his Wordsworthian credentials. His relationship with Wordsworth had begun with the wise child in the churchyard in 'We are Seven', and this is where it ended. Aged fourteen, De Quincey had seen himself in Wordsworth's maid who played by her brother's gravestone and now, aged twenty-six, he went one stage further, 'stretching' himself 'every night, for more than two months running' upon the earth where Catherine lay. In *Suspiria de Profundis*, the sequel to *Confessions of an English Opium-Eater*, De Quincey explained his 'passion for the grave': he did not see a 'grave as a grave' but 'as the portal through which . . . some heavenly countenance', a 'mother or sister', might be pulled back again.

In daylight hours he had visions of Catherine walking through fields of foxgloves carrying a basket on her head (recalling one of *The Prelude*'s spots of time, the 'girl who wore a pitcher on her head'), and by the autumn De Quincey began to feel that his 'life could not be borne'. He left Grasmere and travelled to Liverpool, Birmingham, Bath and Bristol in search of medical help.

It was in Bristol that he recovered. As suddenly as it came, his grief left his body in the form of a 'peculiar sensation' from the 'knee downwards', making it hard for him to move. It was as though he had drunk from 'Lethe or a river of oblivion'. All memories of Catherine now 'vanished from my mind. . . she might have been dead for a thousand years, so entirely abolished was that last lingering image of her face or figure'. Her grave now became a memorial not to her brief life but to 'the dire internal physical convulsion' by which De Quincey had been 'shaken and wrenched' at the news of her death. It was Catherine, of course, who had experienced the dire internal physical convulsions, but Catherine was now as abstracted to De Quincey as John Williams himself. De Quincey had no idea what, apart from raw carrots, had caused the child's strange fit of passion, but he gave to his own condition a name: 'nympholepsy'.

The word, first used in the late eighteenth century, is from the Greek, *nympholeptos*, meaning possessed by nymphs. It refers, in De Quincey's usage, to the 'frenzy' of longing suffered by those in pagan times who caught a glimpse of a nymph or goddess in the forest. The 'nympholept' himself is then 'doomed to die', its being impossible to live after seeing such beings. In the wake of Nabokov's 'nymphets' we now associate nympholepsy with paedophilia, and while De Quincey sexualised (dead) girls, he used the term to describe a longing for any unobtainable object. A boy in the vale killed himself, he wrote, after 'languish[ing] with a sort of despairing nympholepsy after intellectual pleasures'; De Quincey's own early relationship with Wordsworth was a 'nympholepsy which had seized upon me', and then attached itself, by proxy, to 'the very lakes and mountains, amongst which the scenery of this most original poetry had chiefly grown up and moved'. He also experienced the 'sublime attractions of the grave' as a form of 'nympholepsy', and saw in the 'Lucy' poems Wordsworth's particular expression of the malady.

Any chances of Dorothy once again becoming De Quincey's daily companion were now destroyed by the actions of a servant. Mary Dawson had proved a worse housekeeper than Sally Green. She was a 'foolish, selfish and ignorant old maid', who gave herself 'unlimited power in all which regarded the pecuniary arrangements of my house'. De Quincey had a longstanding arrangement with Dorothy that during his periods of absence the Wordsworths were free to use the cottage. Despite its having become a tender subject for both parties, the offer still stood. But when De Quincey was away in London, probably during the spring of 1812, Dorothy was turned from the door by Mary Dawson on the grounds that her 'master' had left instructions to let no one in. 'Any real friend of mine,' De Quincey stormed when he heard what had happened, would have seen through Mary Dawson – who enjoyed having the cottage to herself – but the Wordsworths were all too ready to believe they had been turned away from 'their own' house. They had already lost control of the orchard; this was considered the next step in De Quincey's takeover bid. Accused of bolting the door against them, De Quincey – who prided himself on his generosity – was too wounded to defend his own honour. Besides, who would believe that he had been wronged? The word of Mary Dawson, a longstanding retainer and, most importantly, a native of the vale, would hold more weight than anything an 'intruder' had to say. So De Quincey 'sate down half-contentedly under accusations which, in every solemnity of truth, applied less justly to myself than to any one person I knew amongst the whole circle of my acquaintance. The result was that ever after I hated the name of the woman at whose hands I had sustained this wrong.'

The year 1812 was a terrible one for the Wordsworths who, six months after the death of Catherine, lost their son Thomas to measles. 'Pray come to us as soon as you can,' Wordsworth wrote to De Quincey on the night of the boy's death, ending his summons: 'Most tenderly and loving, with heavy sorrow for you, my dear friend.'

The Corsican Crocodile dissolving the Council of Frogs.

'I was kissed, with cancerous kisses, by crocodiles.'

II

The Recluse

> . . . a mighty city – boldly say
> A wilderness of building, sinking far
> And self-withdrawn into a wondrous depth,
> Far sinking into splendour – without end!

Wordsworth, The Excursion

In 1813 De Quincey went to sleep in Dove Cottage, and while he slept 'a theatre seemed suddenly opened and lighted up' in his brain 'which presented nightly spectacles of more than earthly splendour'. In his dreams the house 'swelled, and was amplified to an extent of unutterable infinity', the walls expanded and the floors dissolved, the dark wainscoting unfolded like a Japanese flower in water and the stone flags crumbled into desert sands: 'I seemed every night to descend,' he wrote, 'not metaphorically, but literally to descend, into chasms and sunless abysses, depths below depths.' Like Milton's Satan, he was 'hurld headlong flaming from th' Ethereal Skie', to a 'bottomless perdition'.

Time, too, unfurled itself; he seemed sometimes 'to have lived for 70 or 100 years in one night; nay; sometimes had feelings representative of a millennium passed'. Childhood episodes, long forgotten and the length of eternity, paraded themselves before him, and the featureless figures of his London walks returned 'upon the rocking waters of the ocean. . . the sea seemed paved with innumerable faces, upturned to the heavens: faces, imploring, wrathful, despairing, surged upwards by thousands, by myriads, by generations, by centuries'. He became the heaving ocean; he found himself in China, a country in which he had often thought he would 'go mad'. In scenes of 'unimaginable horror' he was oppressed by 'birds, beasts, reptiles' and every tropical tree and plant.

> I was stared at, hooted at, grinned at, chattered at, by monkeys, by paroquets, by cockatoos. I ran into pagodas: and was fixed, for centuries, at the summit, or in secret rooms; I was the idol; I was the priest; I was worshipped; I was sacrificed. I fled from the wrath of Brama through all the forests of Asia: Vishnu hated me: Seeva laid in wait for me. I came suddenly upon Isis and Osiris: I had done a deed, they said, which the ibis and the crocodile trembled at. I was buried, for a thousand years, in stone coffins, with mummies and sphinxes, in narrow chambers at the heart of eternal pyramids. I was kissed, with cancerous kisses, by crocodiles; and laid, confounded with all unutterable slimy things, amongst reeds and Nilotic mud.

Adopted by cartoonists to symbolise Napoleon, the 'cursed crocodile' was the creature that terrified De Quincey the most. In his dreams he escaped from the reptile's great green jaws to find himself trapped in Chinese houses whose furnishings 'soon became instinct with life'. He lay under 'the weight of incubus and nightmare', cursing 'the spells which chain[ed] him down from motion'. Powerless as a child, he was imprisoned by sleep.

To have asked De Quincey whether he had taken opium on 'any particular day' was the equivalent of asking 'whether his lungs had performed respiration'. His daily consumption of laudanum rose to 8,000 drops; a considerable amount but still only half of what Coleridge was taking. 'He can do nothing,' Dorothy noted of De Quincey. 'He is eaten up with the spirit of procrastination; but if once in two or three years he actually does make an effort, he is so slow a labourer that no one who knows him would wish to appoint him to it.' Johnny, to whom De Quincey was once again teaching Latin, he now saw 'for a *nominal hour* every day. . . This said nominal hour is generally included in the space of twenty minutes; either the scholar learns with such uncommon rapidity that more time is unnecessary, or the Master tires.'

———

This was a momentous year for De Quincey's Lakeland neighbours. John Wilson, now married, lost his fortune and left Elleray for his home town of

Edinburgh. Despite being on his uppers, De Quincey gave Wilson £200 ('Will £200 be enough?' he asked). Mary Dawson announced that she was pregnant – the fruits of her time in the cottage while the master was away – which left De Quincey without a servant, and Wordsworth was offered the lucrative position of Distributor of Stamps for Westmorland, which allowed the family to move into a handsome pile called Rydal Mount, on the road to Ambleside. After thirteen years, the Wordsworths were no longer residents of Grasmere. 'I was the last person who left the house yesterday evening,' Dorothy wrote to Jane Marshall of their final night in the hamlet. 'It seemed as quiet as the grave; and the very church-yard where our darlings lie, when I gave a last look upon it seemed to cheer my thoughts. There I could think of life and immortality – the house only reminded me of desolation, gloom, emptiness, and cheerless silence.'

The following year, 1814, *The Excursion* was published. In the first part a figure known as 'The Wanderer' tells the story of Margaret, a Lakeland girl deserted by her husband when he runs away to join the army. Impoverished and depressed, her cottage crumbling around her, Margaret waits for him to return. 'My spirit clings/ To that poor Woman,' says the Wanderer:

> – so familiarly
> Do I perceive her manner, and her look,
> And presence; and so deeply do I feel
> Her goodness, that, not seldom, in my walks
> A momentary trance comes over me. . .

Two miles from Grasmere, on the edge of Rydal Water, there stood, and still stands, an ancient farmhouse called The Nab. Low and white with mullioned windows, the building, in possession of the same family for generations, was the home of a farmer called John Simpson, whose seventeen-year-old daughter was another Margaret. A courtship began between this strapping young woman and the battered incumbent of Dove Cottage, who serenaded her, so a watchful Dorothy informed Mrs Clarkson, 'at the up-rouzing of the Bats and the Owls'. Wilson, visiting from Edinburgh, reported that he had 'walked to De Quincey's, which I reached at half-past one o'clock in the morning: he was at The Nab, and when he returned about three o'clock, found me asleep in his bed'. She will have been nine when De Quincey first arrived in the vale, but he did not encounter Margaret Simpson until now, at which point he described himself as falling in love with her simplicity (she thought *The Vicar of Wakefield* was a history book). But as we know from his Everton journals, De Quincey was plagued by his sex drive.

In August 1814, his youngest brother, Henry, arrived in Grasmere but found no one at home. After two days of knocking, Henry reported, he 'gave up the ghost, for I perceived that at least nothing more than your ghost made its appearance'. There were a few telling glimpses of De Quincey that year. Crabb Robinson saw him in London at the house of Charles Lamb, where he talked 'about Wordsworth with the zeal and intelligence of a well-instructed pupil'. His style was a 'mixture of pedantry and high-flown sentimentality', his conversation did not 'flow readily', and he was 'too much of a disciple and admirer to have anything of his own'. 'Pedantry and high-flown sentimentality': Crabb Robinson's observation recalls that of Coleridge, who described De Quincey's working style as 'anxious yet dilatory'. His distance from Wordsworth had not improved his confidence; De Quincey was as unsure now as he had been eleven years earlier about what 'character' to present to the world. But in Edinburgh, where he visited John Wilson that same year ('Quince has gone off to Edinburgh at last with Mr Wilson,' reported Sara Hutchinson), his talk was remembered differently. Here, in the company of James Gibson Lockhart, Regency beau and fledgling biographer of Sir Walter Scott, James Hogg, Ettrick shepherd and poet, Sir William Hamilton, philosopher, and the Germanist R. P. Gillies, De Quincey was more at his ease. His voice, remembered Gillies, was 'extraordinary, as if it came from dreamland', and his talk leapt 'at will from the beeves to butterflies, and thence to the soul's immortality, to Plato, and Kant, and Schelling, and Fichte, and Milton's early years and Shakespeare's Sonnets, to Wordsworth and Coleridge, to Homer and Aeschylus to St Thomas of Aquin, St Basil and St Chrysostom'. He would 'recount profound mysteries from his own experiences – visions that had come over him in his loneliest walks among the mountains, and passages within his own personal knowledge, illustrating, if not proving, the doctrines of dreams, of warnings, of second sight and mesmerism. And whatever the subject might be, every one of his sentences (or one of his chapters, I might say) was woven into the most perfect logical texture, and uttered in a tone of sustained melody.'

Later that year, Wilson, Hogg and De Quincey formed an awkward party at Rydal Mount. On a night of spectacular beauty, when a belt of stars stretched across the sky, Hogg raised his glass. 'Hout, me'em!' he said, 'it is neither mair nor less than joost a triumphal arch in honour of the meeting of the poets.' Wordsworth, taking De Quincey's arm and 'leading the little opium-chewer aside' muttered in his ear, 'Poets? Poets? – What does the fellow mean? Where are they?' De Quincey, pleased to display his intimacy with Wordsworth, mischievously reported the insult to Hogg. Two years later, Hogg avenged himself with a send-up of 'The Recluse' called 'The Stranger', which appeared in an anonymous collection of parodies called *The Poetic Mirror*. A traveller arrives at a tarn where his horse 'breaks propriety' with a snort 'like blustering canon':

> The boy was stunned – for on similitude
> In dissimilitude, man's sole delight,
> And all the sexual intercourse of things,
> Do most supremely hang.

In Grasmere, the sexual intercourse of things was disturbing Wordsworth, who did what he could to prevent the blossoming of his neighbour's affair with Margaret Simpson. Thus De Quincey now found, when he roused himself with the bats and the owls, that Wordsworth, like Gil-Martin in Hogg's future novel, *The Private Memoirs and Confessions of a Justified Sinner*, appeared by his side. 'It drove me crazy then, it drives me crazy now,' he recalled in a passage later removed from his 'Lake Reminiscences'. The stalker was himself being stalked. 'I found myself in the same situation almost every night,' De Quincey railed. Wordsworth was 'possessed' by 'a malicious purpose', and De Quincey felt 'almost a hatred' for him. How, unless he had 'corresponded with fairies', had Wordsworth known where De Quincey was going? 'He could not: it was impossible. I am sure it was.' De Quincey hid his love life from his family, but in September 1815 Wordsworth wrote to Mrs Quincey to inform her not only that her son was 'about to marry' (which was not true) but that his bride was from the lower orders. Margaret may, although De Quincey furiously denied it, have replaced Mary Dawson as his servant; it was whispered that De Quincey's wife 'had often made his bed before she ascended it'. This would explain why he stressed, in his *Autobiographic Sketches*, that the position of housekeeper to the cottage had been competed for by many fine and highly respectable young ladies.

Their courtship caused consternation up at Rydal Mount. Dorothy, who had known 'Peggy' Simpson all her life, described her as a 'stupid heavy girl' who had been 'reckoned a Dunce at Grasmere School', and she and William mocked De Quincey's lyrical accounts of her 'beauty', 'good sense' and 'angelic sweetness'. Clearly jealous, Dorothy spoke of Margaret as a rival and consistently ridiculed De Quincey's affection for her. The mockery got back to De Quincey who later said that: 'Nothing causes a greater rankling in the heart, than to find that you have laid open its finer feelings and have got laughed at for your pains.' De Quincey was in love, but he was also falling apart. Two months later Sara Hutchinson wrote that 'Quince was often tipsy and in one of his fits had lost his gold watch. . . He doses himself with Opium and drinks like a fish and tries in all other things to be as great a gun as Mr Wilson.'

———

While De Quincey was dreaming by day and courting by night, Napoleon was defeated at Waterloo and in June 1815 over twenty years of war came to an end. The emperor was exiled to the island of St Helena, and Charles Lloyd, suffering a mental breakdown, was institutionalised. All the local houses that De Quincey had once loved now lay empty. When he walked in Lloyd's former garden he could hear the voices of his young family 're-echoed', and lying by the river De Quincey listened once more to the music of the water, rising like 'choral chanting – distant, solemn, saintly'.

Reality and reverie took on the same texture in De Quincey's current twilight world. An intruder in his dreams was a wanderer he called the Dark Interpreter, whose role, like that of a Greek chorus, was to recall the dreamer 'to his own lurking thoughts'. The Dark Interpreter repeated in the cryptonyms of dream language the words that De Quincey had spoken during the day, but it was not only in dreams that the figure made his appearance: at times the Dark Interpreter was 'outside, and in open sunlight'. De Quincey seemed now to 'live, and to converse, even when awake, with. . . visionary companions much more than with the realities of life'. One Easter morning he stepped from his cottage and, blinking in the light, saw before him 'the domes and cupolas of a great city'. Grasmere had become Jerusalem, and sitting in the garden, tears streaming down her face, was Ann. 'So I have found you at last,' De Quincey said and suddenly there they were, back in the lamplight of Oxford Street.

'Mr De Quincey has taken a fit of solitude,' Wordsworth wrote to R. P. Gillies in April 1816. 'I have scarcely seen him since Mr Wilson left.' His remark suggests that Peter Quince now only visited Rydal Mount in the company of that great gun, Mr Wilson. Later that year, Lloyd escaped from his asylum in York and walked to Grasmere where he threw his arms around De Quincey and wept. His pursuers were close at hand; he would be captured and returned; he knew he would be safe in Dove Cottage but refused to stay. 'I dare say,' he told De Quincey, 'you think you know me; but you do not, and you cannot. I am the Author of all Evil; Sir, I am the Devil. . . I know also who you are: you are nobody, a nonentity, you have no being.' Lloyd revealed to De Quincey that 'his situation internally was always this: it seemed to him as if on some distant road he heard a dull trampling sound, and that he knew it, by a misgiving, to be the sound of some man, or party of men, continually advancing slowly, continually threatening, or continually accusing him'. He tried to rid his mind of this sound but it returned again and again, 'still steadily advancing, though still at a great distance'.

At about this time another visitor knocked on the door, also needing sanctuary. 'There is a sort of demon downstairs,' De Quincey was informed by his servant, who was probably Margaret Simpson. Standing in the hall in a turban and loose white trousers was a Malayan man with 'sallow and bilious' skin, 'veneered with mahogany by marine air', and 'tiger-cat' eyes which were 'small, fierce, and restless'. His 'gestures and adorations' were 'slavish' and he 'worshipped' De Quincey 'in a most devout manner'. The man knew no English and De Quincey knew only the Arabic for barley and the Turkish for opium. Wanting rest, the Malay lay down on the stone floor and slept. He awoke refreshed, and to cheer him on his way De Quincey presented him with a large piece of opium which the stranger ate whole in one mouthful. 'The quantity was enough to kill three dragoons and their horses, and I felt some alarm for the poor creature; but what could be done?' Did the Malay survive the opium? The man 'fastened upon my dreams, and brought other Malays with him, worse than himself, that ran "a-muck"'.

Did this event, recorded in *Confessions of an English Opium-Eater*, really take place? Could De Quincey have even answered that question? The figure came out of the *Arabian Nights* and De Quincey's Oriental nightmares, but he was also a version of the Arab on a dromedary in the dream described by Wordsworth in *The Prelude* – a mysterious personage making his lonely way to an unknown destination.

Visiting Rydal Mount soon after staying with his mother in Westhay, De Quincey was able to pass on to Wordsworth the compliment that Hannah More approved of *The Excursion*. 'As usual,' purred Sara Hutchinson, 'Peter is very entertaining, now that he is fresh.' When Crabb Robinson visited Grasmere in the summer of 1816, he reported that the tenant of Dove Cottage was looking 'very much an invalid'. De Quincey was 'dirty, and even squalid. I had read a bad account of him from Wordsworth. . . It appears that he has taken to opium, and, like Coleridge, seriously injured his health. I understand, too, though Wordsworth was reserved on the subject, he has entangled himself in an unfortunate *acquaintance* with a woman.' Crabb Robinson also understood, as he made his way between Grasmere and Rydal Mount, that Wordsworth and De Quincey were now avoiding one another. 'De Quincey still praises Wordsworth's poetry,' he noted in his diary, 'but he speaks with no kindness of the man.'

The year 1816 was known as the year without a summer. A volcanic eruption on an Indonesian island had created enough ash in the atmosphere to block out the sun, and in a villa on the shores of Lake Geneva, Byron, Shelley and Mary Shelley took advantage of the darkness to hold the ghost story competition which resulted in the birth of *Frankenstein*. In May, at the request of Byron, three fragments by Coleridge were published in a slim volume. The first was 'Christabel', the ballad about a Sapphic vampire that Wordsworth had excluded from the *Lyrical Ballads*; the second was 'Kubla Khan: or, A Vision in a Dream', an opium reverie heard entirely as music; and the third was 'The Pains of

Sleep', described by Coleridge as 'an exact and most faithful portraiture
of the state of my mind under influences of. . . Opium'. The movement
of the trilogy – from pleasure to pain – went to the heart of the opium
experience, and the preface to 'Kubla Khan' became mythical.

In the summer of 1797, explained Coleridge, he 'had retired to a
lonely farm-house between Porlock and Linton, on the Exmore con-
fines of Somerset and Devonshire'. To cure 'a slight indisposition',
opium had been prescribed and he fell asleep while reading the following sentence from 'Puchas his Pilgrimage': 'Here the Khan Kubla com-
manded a palace to be built, and a stately garden thereunto. And thus
ten miles of fertile ground were inclosed with a wall.'

> The author continued for about three hours in a profound sleep, at least of the
> external senses, during which time he has the most vivid confidence that he could
> not have composed less than from two to three hundred lines; if that indeed can
> be called composition in which all the images rose up before him as *things*, with a
> parallel production of the correspondent expressions . . . On awaking he appeared
> to himself to have a distinct recollection of the whole, and taking his pen, ink, and
> paper, instantly and eagerly wrote down the lines that are here preserved.

The writing was interrupted by a knock on the door and Coleridge 'was
unfortunately called out by a person on business from Porlock'. When
he returned, 'with the exception of some eight or ten scattered lines
and images' the dream had vanished from his mind like 'the surface of
a stream in which a stone has been cast'.

Margaret Simpson, like Mary Dawson, had become pregnant and in
November she gave birth to a boy whom they named William, after
De Quincey's late brother. 'Such,' Wordsworth wrote loftily to Lamb,
'are the fruits of philosophy ripening under the shelter of our Arcadian
Mountains. A marriage is expected by some; but from the known pro-
crastination of one of the parties, it is not looked for by others till the
commencement of the millennium.' But the great tomorrower married
Margaret Simpson in Grasmere church on 15 February 1817. 'Mr De
Quincey is married,' Dorothy told Catherine Clarkson, 'and I fear I
may add he is ruined.' The newlyweds, she added, were 'spending their

honeymoon at *our* cottage at Grasmere'. De Quincey had by this point been tenant for seven years. 'I am very sorry for Mr De Quincey,' commiserated Mary Lamb from London. 'What a blunder the poor man made when he took up his dwelling among the mountains.'

While there is no cache of letters to prove that De Quincey's marriage was the same 'lively gushing thought-employing spirit-stirring passion of love' enjoyed by William and Mary Wordsworth, there is no reason to doubt it. De Quincey left a wonderful description of himself and Margaret, 'hand locked in hand', descending the fells on their way home one night, 'thinking of things to come at the pace of a hurricane; whilst all the sleeping wood about us re-echoed the uproar of trampling hoof and groaning wheels'. He had probably not planned on making Margaret his wife – the delay in the nuptials suggests a hesitation on his side – but he would be appalled at the prospect of abandoning a pregnant girl. He might ruin himself with drugs, but he would not be the cause of a woman's destruction. Plus he adored children and had longed for a family. It was De Quincey's wife for whom Mary Lamb should have felt sorry; a depressive by nature, Margaret had, before she met De Quincey, attempted suicide, and her husband's extended absences would drive her again to the edge of despair.

The bride and groom found in one another, as lovers always will, antidotes to their parents. In Margaret, De Quincey embraced a spouse who differed in almost every way from his mother. And Margaret took a husband whose politics were the polar opposite to those of her father, a silent man described by his son-in-law as 'a rank Jacobin'. When De Quincey looked up he saw a nurturing and sweet-tempered woman with no notion of the land beyond the vale; when Margaret looked up (or down) she saw a gentle, generous, raddled, emaciated, drug-addicted dreamer, who had squandered his inheritance, wasted his health, lost his friends, blown his social standing, and was being kicked around by the Wordsworths like – as he put it – a 'mere football of reproach'. Margaret married De Quincey when he was at his least eligible and his most vulnerable. She saw in him a man-child filled with stories, who unswervingly, unreservedly, needed to love and be loved; and he saw in her an incarnation of a Wordsworthian heroine.

De Quincey was now consuming 10,000 drops of laudanum a day and Margaret nursed him through the worse stages of his addiction, wiping his forehead and pressing water to his black-baked lips as he lay, to use Carlyle's memorable phrase, 'invisible in bed'. Margaret, like Ann of Oxford Street, saved De Quincey's life. When he 'awoke in struggles, and cried aloud, "I will sleep no more",' his lady was by his side, asking in her gentle voice: 'Oh, what do you see, dear? What is it that you see?' De Quincey saw many brain-sickly things. Sometimes 'a city of sepulchres', lying like a 'purple stain upon the horizon' rose before him, trembling 'through many changes, growing into terraces and towers of wondrous altitude'. Rising on every side were 'vast sarcophagi', 'towers and turrets that strode forward with haughty intrusion, that ran back with mighty shadows into answering recesses'. He was in a carriage hurtling headlong down the aisle of an 'infinite cathedral' – St Paul's, Bath Abbey, St Mary Redcliffe – forty leagues, seventy leagues they ran; in the 'little chapels and oratories to the right hand and left of our course, the lamps, dying or sickening, kindled anew in sympathy with the secret world that was flying past'. He was at the funeral of his sister, where the golden organ 'threw up columns of heart-stopping music' and a voice from the heavens issued a decree: 'Let there be no reflux of panic – let there be no more fear, and no more sudden death!'

When he closed his eyes he was in hell, but his waking hours were happy ones: 'Candles at four o'clock, warm hearthrugs, tea, a fair tea-maker, shutters closed, curtains flowing in ample drapery on the floor, whilst the wind and rain are raging audibly without.' When baby William learned to stand he would stack up the philosophy books and fire at them with his bow and arrow; his father sometimes joined him. Another baby, a girl called Margaret Thomasina, was born on 5 June 1818 – in the same midsummer week that Catherine Wordsworth and young Elizabeth Quincey had both died. Little Margaret would later refer to her father's 'medicine' as '*yaddonum*'.

Like Wordsworth, De Quincey was beginning his life as a husband and father in the wainscoted rooms of Dove Cottage, but unlike Wordsworth he had married the mother of his illegitimate child. The similarity, and difference, between the two situations was doubtless noted in Rydal Mount. Also noted was De Quincey's likeness to Coleridge: an unfortunate marriage, a love affair with yaddonum. But rather than feel relieved that the fragile De Quincey was in the care of a good woman, the Wordsworths never ceased to condemn his choice and to rehearse amongst themselves the impertinence of his having brought such a figure to their former home. Mary and Dorothy, who had once poked fun at Sarah Coleridge for seeming conventional, made it plain that they would not take tea with the new mistress of Dove Cottage, and nor should Mrs De Quincey expect to take tea with them. De Quincey was just able to bear the arrogance of the Wordsworths when he was the target, but he would not suffer their 'criminal' rudeness to his wife. And this from the very people who praised the nobility of rustic life and stressed the superiority of those who were native to the vale. The Wordsworths, who accused De Quincey of barring them from his house, now barred their own front door to his sainted wife.

———

The newlyweds lived like pariahs, rarely going beyond their gate. The coffers were now empty; Elizabeth Quincey sent £100 which was swallowed up by debts. De Quincey was in no state to keep on top of the accounts; without Margaret, 'all records of bills paid, or to be paid, must have perished: and my whole domestic economy. . . must have gone into irretrievable confusion'. The debtors' prison beckoned, but in 1818 Wordsworth recommended De Quincey as editor of the new Tory paper, the *Westmorland Gazette,* founded, in advance of the local election, to oppose the Whig *Kendal Courier.* In backing the appointment of De Quincey, Wordsworth admitted to the paper's proprietors that their new editor did not do well 'on the score of punctuality', and a good deal has been made of De Quincey's general lack of qualification for a position of this sort. But in many ways running his own newspaper could not have been a more suitable job. De Quincey now belonged in the world of journalism, and he brought to the post the freshness and flavour he injected into all his writing. Each edition of the *Gazette* came roaring bare-fisted into the ring, ready for combat with the *Courier.*

Politics aside, the *Gazette* allowed De Quincey's readers access to his obsessions. Selecting his news from the London press, he might report on the discovery of a feral child in a German forest, an 'Incombustible Man' who chewed burning coal and licked red-hot pokers, the Stockholm labourer who used his wife's dead body as bait for wild animals (successfully trapping one wolf and two foxes), or the suicide who walked into a barber's and asked for his throat to be cut. One

Saturday he described the attempt by Dr Ure of Glasgow to galvanise, with electronic rods, the corpse of a murderer: 'Every muscle in his countenance was simultaneously thrown into fearful action; rage, horror, despair, anguish, and ghastly smile.' For a dying man bitten by a rabid dog, 'a drop of liquid was as difficult as the ocean, and a breath of air as terrible as a blast of Simoon'. As newspaper editors tend to do, De Quincey justified his choice of content on moral grounds. If he prioritised all things sensational, he patiently explained, it was in order to monitor the national morality. Lingering lovingly over the details of macabre deaths, De Quincey's *Gazette* resembled *Blackwood's Edinburgh Magazine*, where John Wilson was now based and where, in August 1818, Wilson had published a tale called 'Extracts from Gosschen's Diary' about a man who murders his mistress. 'Do you think there was no pleasure in murdering her?' the killer confesses on the eve of his execution. 'I grasped her by that radiant, that golden hair, – I bared those snow-white breasts, – I dragged her sweet body towards me, and, as God is my witness, I stabbed, and stabbed her with this very dagger, ten, twenty, forty times, through and through her heart. . . My joy, my happiness, was perfect.' Here, years before De Quincey made the subject his own, Wilson presented a killer who gloried in his crime as an artist glories in the execution of an image, or a poet in a poem.

As an editor, De Quincey was pugnacious, eccentric, opinionated and unpredictable, and he accordingly reduced his laudanum intake to between 1,000 and 4,000 drops a day. If his work was not sufficiently appreciated, he scolded the readers. His report on Queen Caroline's funeral, De Quincey complained, 'had cost the Editor a whole day's labour – with no reward in prospect beyond the hope of furnishing an interesting subject of reading for one winter's evening to the cottagers of Westmorland'. Sometimes he fell out with his readers altogether: 'The Editor of the *Gazette* differs in many points from many of his correspondents, in some respects perhaps from all of them.' Both schoolmasterly and childish, he exercised his 'anxious yet dilatory' characteristics. His job was made more difficult because he lived eighteen miles from the paper's offices in Kendal, a commute De Quincey did as rarely as possible due to his growing fear of death. He assumed during this time that a headache meant hydrocephalus, while a dog bite was the onset of hydrophobia. Working from 'beneath a drift of paper cuttings', he sent his copy to the press on Thursday nights for printing on Friday and distribution on Saturday. If he missed the mail-coach from Ambleside, more or less anything would need to be found by the subeditor, John Kilner, to fill the empty pages. The appearance of the *Gazette* increasingly depended on the reliability of Kilner, who was paid £109 by De Quincey out of his own annual earnings of £160.'

At times the *Gazette* ran news stories about De Quincey himself. He kept his readers informed about his health, for example, especially when he was suffering from a particularly 'painful indisposition', and on 28 January 1819 he reported that 'an accident occurred at the house of Mr De Quincey in Grasmere, which providentially terminated without injury to any member of his family'. In the early hours of the morning, while his wife and children were asleep and he was busy preparing the paper, a 'great fork of flames' sprung up from the hearth, 'extending to a place of about four feet distant'. It was in the pages of the *Westmorland Gazette* that De Quincey's life as a confessor began.

His attitude to journalism was always vexed. Deadlines, De Quincey later reflected, 'drive a man into hurried writing, possibly into saying the thing that is not. They won't wait an hour for you in a Magazine or a Review; they won't wait for truth; you may as well reason with the sea, or a railway train. . .' The prospect of errors horrified him just as the prospect of horrors electrified him, and in one particularly unbuttoned *Gazette* editorial De Quincey described how:

> more than once, under anxiety at the recollection of some error uncorrected or some thought left open to misconstruction (which being sent off by Friday morning's post would be sure to face him in print the following day) he has fervently wished that some Eastern magician would, a few hours before publication, loosen the 'Gazette' Office from that rock on which we trust it is built – raise it into the air with all its live and dead stock – and would transport it for one week, – not – (as angry people are apt to say) into the Red Sea, but some comfortable place on its shore, Arabia Felix for instance.

It was not a literary style that Westmorland cottagers would be used to, but in a few years' time De Quincey's flights of fancy would make him famous.

Deadlines created anxiety, but they also enabled him to write. Without the limits they imposed De Quincey's essays would possibly never stop, and certainly never start. Deadlines allowed him to 'express himself rapidly', to create a 'more burning logic, a perfect life of cohesion, which is liable to be lost or frozen in the slow progress of careful composition'. The transitory nature of journalism both excited and alarmed him. 'A newspaper is not like a book in its duration,' De Quincey explained in one of his distinctive editorials. 'Books are immortal; for some of them last for ten or even fifteen years: but newspapers must content themselves with an existence almost literally ephemeral.' His letter of resignation, written after eighteen months at the *Westmorland Gazette,* was accepted and following De Quincey's departure, John Kilner was appointed editor.

———

By 1820 the cottage felt weighed down by books and babies – Mary was expecting her third child, Horatio, who would be known as Horace – and De Quincey took a six-month lease on a larger house, Fox Ghyll, one mile north of Ambleside. 'Mr De Quincey's Books have literally turned their master & his whole family out of doors,' mocked Sara Hutchinson. His move set the pattern for the rest of his life: De Quincey accumulated paper in its various forms until the space became, as his daughters put it, 'snowed-up' and there was no longer room in which to sit, stand or open the door, at which point he started again somewhere else. He did not relinquish the lease on Dove Cottage; instead the house became a cupboard.

When Wordsworth visited Fox Ghyll he described the downstairs rooms as so dark that they resembled 'a well or dungeon'. This is the only image we have of the interior of De Quincey's new home. As for the exterior, during the family's residence there, Dorothy said, the windows were 'always blinded, or with but one eye to peep out of'. The house was isolated, the only neighbours being an old woman and her daughter, and because De Quincey had pawned his wife's watch, they had no means of telling the time. Sara Hutchinson predicted that De Quincey would stay here for the duration, 'unless unsettled by an earth-quake or a second accumulation of books'. He stayed until 1825, returning to Dove Cottage only when he needed to retrieve something. But while De Quincey no longer inhabited the cottage, the cottage still inhabited him. It was 'endeared' to his 'heart so unspeakably beyond all other houses' that, years after leaving, he revealed that 'I rarely dream through four nights running that I do not find myself (and others besides) in some one of those rooms, and, most probably, the last cloudy delirium of approaching death will re-install me in some chamber of that same humble cottage.'

———

In December, at the invitation of John Wilson, De Quincey travelled to Edinburgh to meet William Blackwood, proprietor and clandestine editor of *Blackwood's Edinburgh Magazine*. '*Maga*', as it was known by its contributors (from Blackwood's way of calling it, in his Scottish accent, the '*Mahga*zine') had been founded to rival the *Edinburgh Magazine* and Wilson was one of its stars. Also in the constellation were Hogg, Lockhart, and a lethal young Irishman called William Maginn.

Sir Walter Scott called *Blackwood's* the 'mother of mischief'; Mary Russell Mitford called it 'a very libellous, naughty, wicked, scandalous, story-telling, entertaining work'; and more recently the critic Karl Miller described it as a journal of *squabash*, *bam* and *balaam*. 'Squabash' meant putting people down or cutting them up. A 'bam' was a trick or a leg-pull. And 'balaam' meant 'rejected or unsolicited material (slush in the common parlance)'. One of the earliest editions, in 1817, opened with a hatchet job by Wilson on Coleridge's *Biographia Literaria* before presenting something called 'The Chaldee Manuscript'. Written in the language of the Book of Daniel, and posing as a found document of the sort rescued by Chatterton from St Mary Redcliffe, the Chaldee Manuscript was a piece of nonsense cooked up by Wilson, Lockhart and Hogg in which Blackwood, 'the man whose name was of ebony' and Constable, proprietor of the *Edinburgh* and 'the man which is crafty', wrestle for mastery. Its appearance offended everyone – Church, Whigs, Tories, ladies – and Blackwood was forced to publish an apology. Sales of *Maga* duly soared to 10,000.

Parody, personality and headlong jollity summed up the *Blackwood's* manifesto, while imitation, masquerade and double-bluff lay at the heart of the *Blackwood's* personality. The contributors imitated both one another and themselves. John Wilson adopted the persona of Christopher North, *Blackwood's* elderly editor, and behind this mask, so Wilson's biographer puts it, he could 'abuse Wordsworth anonymously in an article, and, in a later number of the magazine, attack with scorn the author of his own article, and write a stern letter against himself for libelling so great a poet – then, in the following number, round off this Protean transaction with another vigorous onslaught on the Lake Poets'.

Blackwood's squabash and bam came to the boil in the 'Noctes Ambrosianae', a literary symposium which ran from 1822 until 1835 in which, as Hogg complained, the personality of each was '*eemetawtored*'. An in-joke composed of further in-jokes, the effect of the 'Noctes' was to invite the reader to look through a window at a party to which they were not invited. Together with Christopher North, the sketches featured Morgan Odoherty, modelled on Maginn (whose pseudonym was otherwise Sir Morgan O'Doherty, Bart), the Shepherd, based on Hogg, and Timothy Tickler, the pseudonym of Wilson's Tory uncle, Robert Sym (Tickler being the name of William Blackwood's dog). Walk-on parts included Lord Byron, various characters from John Galt's novels, and a German called 'Kempferhausen', modelled on R. P. Gillies. The companions would meet at Ambrose's Tavern – a real place – to consume vast quantities of food and drink and debate the issues of the day. Their discussions usually ended up being about *Blackwood's* itself. It was the very sublime of fun, and nothing so brilliant has ever been repeated in the British press.

Not only did De Quincey need the money, but he was perfectly placed to become a Blackwoodsman, as the cohort were known, and had been edging towards this manner of journalism in his editorship of the *Gazette*. There was one subject on which he was currently an expert, and he suggested that he write a piece for *Blackwood's* on opium. Blackwood welcomed the idea and looked forward to the finished product. The article never appeared; all Blackwood received from De Quincey were high-handed letters in which he described himself as 'the atlas of the magazine' and as 'hard at work, being determined to save the Magazine from the fate which its stupidity merits'. 'I *do* "keep my word",' De Quincey stormed in a further letter to his long-suffering editor, '– not "once" merely, but always – when I am aware that it is pledged'. Bewildered by De Quincey's self-importance, Blackwood replied that as far as the magazine was concerned, 'it will be quite unnecessary for you to give yourself further trouble'.

While De Quincey was busy not writing for *Blackwood's*, another drama was brewing. In January 1820 an English journal called the *London Magazine* had launched, with the aim of countering the power of the Scottish publications. It was here that Hazlitt's *Table Talk* and Lamb's *Essays of Elia* first appeared. The editor, a Scot called John Scott, was soon at loggerheads with the pseudonymous Blackwoodsmen for attacking all his friends, including Keats and Leigh Hunt, and for using, as he put it, 'the most licentious personal abuse' to 'lure. . . one class of readers, and the veriest hypocritical whine, on matters of religion and politics' as 'bait for another'. *Blackwood's*, said Scott, made a 'common joke of common honesty'. Such claims, Wilson told De Quincey, had only one response: Scott '*must be a dead man*'. Ready to challenge him were Lockhart and Wilson himself, 'so Scott had no chance'. While *Blackwood's* feigned deep hurt, Scott would not retreat and De Quincey, whose 'abhorrence' of Scott was 'deep – serious – and morally grounded', stoked the fire by goading Wilson to 'Lampoon him in songs – in prose – by night and day – in prosperous and adverse fortune. Make him date his ruin from Nov 1st 1820 – Lash him into lunacy.' De Quincey's cheerleading had only just begun: 'I am burning for vengeance. I do so loathe the vile whining canting hypocrisy of the fellow, that I could myself contribute any price of labour to his signal humiliation.' In February 1821, Scott challenged Lockhart – who he believed to be the editor, Christopher North – to a duel. In the masquerade that was *Blackwood's*, Lockhart was represented by his friend, Jonathan Christie, who shot Scott through the abdomen. Nine days later, aged thirty-six, Scott was indeed a dead man. And Lockhart, Maginn proudly proclaimed, was 'wet with the blood of the Cockneys'.

———

What De Quincey did next was all too predictable: he took his opium article to the *London Magazine*. Armed with a letter of introduction from Wordsworth – this was the second time since De Quincey's marriage that the poet had come to his rescue – he met the new editors, John Taylor and James Hessey, and secured himself a commission. Nothing was known at the *London* about his support for *Blackwood's* in the fatal row, and De Quincey lived in terror of his duplicity being revealed.

In order to write his opium piece he stayed in the city during the summer of 1821, but rather than return to his former lodgings on Great Titchfield Street he installed himself in John Scott's former rooms at 4 York Street (now Tavistock Street), Covent Garden. Five months earlier, Scott had left this building feet-first. Only De Quincey could have sought such a domestic arrangement: having quarrelled with William Blackwood, he secretly aligned himself with another man who had quarrelled with Blackwood and been killed as a consequence. By now he openly identified with Scott. 'To speak conscientiously', whispered De Quincey to Wilson, he could not 'wholly approve of everything' that *Blackwood's* had done in the duel business. He referred, in particular, to the magazine's 'contemptuous' treatment of Keats, who had died in Rome in the same week that Scott had died in London; 'snuff'd out', said Byron, by a bad review. Keats's *Endymion* had been described by *Blackwood's* as 'imperturbable drivelling idiocy'. De Quincey himself thought the poem 'the very midsummer madness of affection'.

That summer, De Quincey, his daily laudanum intake down to 300 drops, scuttled through the London streets in a state of high anxiety, revealing to Taylor that he 'had a sort of feeling or ominous anticipation, that possibly there was some being in the world who was fated to do him at some time a great & unexpiable injury'. Taylor assumed that 'Wilson might be the man.' Withdrawal from opium released his paranoia, but De Quincey's fears were, as ever, not entirely ungrounded. John Wilson was a dangerous beast, and De Quincey's betrayal of *Blackwood's* was bound to have repercussions. 'These things Wilson can never forgive,' he told his new friend, a lawyer called Richard Woodhouse. 'They will rankle in his mind: and at some time or other I am sure he will do what he can to injure me. I care not for myself, but there are quarters through which he can injure me.' These quarters referred to Margaret, alone and unprotected in Grasmere while her husband was alone and unprotected in the capital. De Quincey worked throughout August so that the article could appear in the September edition of the magazine, and he could return home to the bosom of his family.

———

Writing in haste in the former rooms of the murdered editor, De Quincey produced 'Confessions of an English Opium-Eater: Being an

Extract from the Life of a Scholar'. The story had been forming itself
in his mind for years: a man returns to London where, in his youth, he
had undergone terrible sufferings. These became the cause of his later
trials as an opium addict. His early sufferings had been external – he
was cold, hungry and homeless – while those he experienced as an adult
were internal, and revealed themselves in dreams. De Quincey hoped
that his narrative would prove 'useful and instructive' but the nobility
of this intention was undermined by his announcement that opium
was the 'true hero' of the tale. Amongst other things, 'Confessions' is a
fan letter addressed to opium itself.

The *London* paid him well (his fee was 'ultramunificent') but as De
Quincey was now renting three homes – Dove Cottage, Fox Ghyll and
4 York Place – the money did not go far. In desperation, he asked if
Coleridge might now return the £300 he had loaned him in 1807. It
was not to be. 'I feel,' Coleridge apologised, 'that I am lingering on the
brink.' So too was De Quincey. In the week of his thirty-sixth birthday
he was threatened with arrest for an unpaid bill and so hid himself in
the 'tumult of coffee houses'. He was penniless, ill, and waiting to be
bludgeoned to death by *Blackwood's*. It will not have gone unnoticed
by him that he had reached the same age as Scott when he died, and
that little had changed between the life he was currently leading and
the past he was writing about: De Quincey had been on the run then
and he was on the run now. Meanwhile, his narrative was expanding
and required a second instalment. The first part – an account of how
he ran away from school, wandered in Wales, and came to London –
was completed at the end of August and appeared anonymously in a
twenty-page spread buried deep in the magazine.

The readers loved this strange story. 'Everyone who noticed the magazine at all is interested in the Fate of the Opium-Eater,' announced the
delighted Taylor, who was praised by Shelley's publisher for having '"the
best prose writer in England" as a contributor'. The first instalment
proved so popular that the second instalment was presented as the lead
article for the October issue. It was divided by De Quincey into three sections: 'The Pleasures of Opium', in which the author described the happiness he had discovered on that wet Sunday afternoon; 'Introduction
to the Pains of Opium', which contained the appearance of the Malay;
and 'The Pains of Opium', where he compared the 'architecture' of his

dreams with those of Piranesi. The sections replicated the movement from euphoria to nightmare of Coleridge's 'Christabel', 'Kubla Khan', and 'The Pains of Sleep'. He concluded by (falsely) assuring his readers that while he was still 'agitated, writhing, throbbing, palpitating', 'shattered' and 'racked', the worst of his addiction was now over.

While Carlyle, when he had finished the 'Confessions', concluded that it would be a 'thousand times better' to '*die* than have anything to do with such a Devil's own drug', the lawyer Sir James Mackintosh responded with 'more delight than I know how to express'. One reviewer condemned the author's 'secret, selfish, suicidal debauchery', and another – for the *Edinburgh Review* – accused him of lifting the appearance of the Malay from a scene involving a visiting Highlander in Hogg's short story 'The Adventures of Basil Lee'. The other notices were glowing. The Opium-Eater was a writer of 'first-rate talents', declared the *Imperial Magazine*. *The United States Literary Gazette* thought his language 'sometimes powerful and magnificent in the extreme'. Who, readers wondered, could have written such a thing? The painter and poisoner, Thomas Griffiths Wainewright, unmasked himself as the author; Edgar Allan Poe declared it was the work of Juniper, his pet baboon. Coleridge, who knew exactly whose confessions they were, felt 'unutterable sorrow' when he read them. With 'morbid vanity', he wrote, De Quincey had 'made a boast of what was my misfortune'. De Quincey's celebration of opium was in opposition to Coleridge's condemnation, and his focus on the pleasure principle was a criticism of Coleridge's denial that he had ever used opium for anything other than medicinal purposes. Addicts typically compare and contrast their addictions, and Wordsworth suggested that in order to exonerate himself, De Quincey had simply transferred his own guilt onto the figure of the conveniently sinking mariner. It was only Crabb Robinson who saw that De Quincey's 'fragment of Autobiography' was written 'in emulation of Coleridge's diseased egotism'.

De Quincey promoted himself as the first to sing a hymn to the poppy's intellectual pleasures as opposed to its curative qualities, but everyone knew, from Coleridge's own preface, that 'Kubla Khan' was the product of an opium dream. De Quincey's only reference to his precursor in the 'Confessions' was to note the high 'quantity' of Coleridge's consumption, which 'greatly exceeded' his own; the high quality of Coleridge's opium-saturated imagination is not mentioned.

The importance of Coleridge as the first literary opium-eater is confirmed in the essay by Elia (Charles Lamb) called 'Witches, and Other
Night Fears', which immediately followed the second instalment of De
Quincey's 'Confessions'. As a child, Elia confessed, he saw 'fiendish
faces' looking down at him as he slept but in adult life he was 'morti-
fied' by the poverty of his dreams. 'They are never romantic, – seldom
even rural. . . I have travelled along the Westmorland fells – my highest
Alps, – but they were objects too mighty for the grasp of my dreaming
recognition.' How was it, Elia asked, that his friend Coleridge was able
to 'solace his night solitudes' with 'icy domes, and pleasure houses for
Kubla Khan, and Abyssinian maids, and songs of Abara, and caverns
"Where Alph, the sacred river, runs"', while he himself was unable to
'muster a fiddle'? The answer, of course, was that Coleridge ate opium.

———

The 'Confessions' appealed as an account of dreams and an account
of addiction, but principally as an account of the author himself.
Autobiography – although the word was not yet in general circulation – was the current charging the literature of the first half of the nineteenth century, and De Quincey was to be its consummate practitioner.
'Egotism is the spirit of the age,' wrote one of the 'Confessions' reviewers, 'and the object of every author is to describe his own thoughts, his
own feelings, his own passions.' 'Egotism,' wrote Thomas Colley Grattan
in his parodic 'Confessions of an English Glutton', which appeared in
Blackwood's in January 1823, 'has become as endemical to English literature as the plague to Egypt or the scurvy to the northern climes.' When
Wordsworth proclaimed of *The Prelude* that it was 'a thing unprece-
dented in literary history that a man should talk so much about himself'
he was echoing Rousseau, whose *Confessions*, published in 1784, had
opened with the assertion that 'I have resolved on an enterprise which
has no precedent, and which, when complete, will have no imitator.' De
Quincey, who imitated everyone, declared in the opening pages of his
own 'Confessions' that there were 'no precedents' that he was 'aware of'
for the type of 'impassioned prose' he employed. He described his writing as 'self-accusation' and contrasted it with the 'self-abuse' of 'French
literature'. One of the many ironies woven into the dense fabric of his
'Confessions' is that while De Quincey opened with an attack on the

'spurious and defective sensibility of the French', it is this sensibility that he impersonated. And it was to be in France, through *Les Paradis artificiels*, Charles Baudelaire's 1860 translation and adaptation of De Quincey's *Confessions*, that he would find his most sympathetic readers.

But De Quincey did more in his 'Confessions' than describe his own thoughts, feelings and passions: as a confessor he gave himself personality, and the Opium-Eater would take on a life of his own. 'What can be done without personality?' asked Christopher North in the 'Noctes' in March 1822. Personality was not the *London* house style: 'everything that can fairly be called *personality* should be avoided', Scott had ruled when setting up the magazine, by which he meant the sort of arrogance and buffoonery that *Blackwood's* promoted. Personality meant celebrity, and De Quincey's celebrity was sealed when a reviewer of the 'Confessions' said he was unsure if the 'character in which the Opium-eater speaks be real or imaginary'. *Blackwood's* writers all passed themselves off, so the Shepherd puts in the 'Noctes', as 'sometimes for real, and sometimes for fictitious characters', but since the days of his youth De Quincey had been anxious about attacks on his 'veracity,' added to which the power of the recovery memoir has always rested on humility and truth. He thus responded to this particular reviewer's 'impeachment' of his identity in a letter to the *London Magazine*. 'The entire "Confessions",' he wrote, 'were designed to convey a narrative of my own experience as an opium-eater, drawn up with entire simplicity and fidelity to the facts.' He now promised a third part which would redress the 'overbalance' various reviewers had noted 'on the side of the *pleasures* of opium' at the expense of the 'pains'. This much trumpeted final instalment never appeared.

Now that opium has reverted to the realm of myth, we read De Quincey differently. We see him as one of us, a voice anticipating our own age of recreational drug use, but this is not how he was read in 1821. While De Quincey pronounced himself 'the only member' of 'the true church on the subject of opium' the congregation, as he knew very well, was bursting through the doors of the cathedral. The 'Confessions' alludes to some of the more illustrious consumers – 'the late dean of – ; Lord – ; Mr –, the philosopher' – but the whole country was marinated in opium, which was taken for anything from upset stomachs to sore heads. Hannah More's great friend, the saintly Wilberforce, was an addict; middle-class women collapsed on their sofas in its haze; even dogs and children were dosed up with it. The miraculous effects of opium were no more mysterious to De Quincey's contemporaries than the miraculous effects of aspirin are to us today; everyone who had ever taken opium to sedate a sore tooth knew what De Quincey was describing. Those few who remained unaware of the drug's effect on dreams now gave it a try. Southey had his first taste of opium 'for the sake of experiencing the sensation which had made De Quincey a slave to it'. Branwell Brontë did the same. Dorothy, in her later years, also became addicted (her dosage was 35–40 drops a day), while Wordsworth remained remarkable in living eighty years without letting opium pass his lips. 'Many persons,' wrote the author of *Advice to Opium-Eaters*, 'greatly injured themselves by taking Opium experimentally, which trial they had been enticed to make by the fascinating description of the exquisite pleasure attendant on the taking of that drug, given in a recent publication on the subject.' De Quincey, however, scoffed at the suggestion that he was the nation's drug-pusher: 'Teach opium-eating!' he exclaimed. 'Did I teach wine-drinking? Did I reveal the mystery of sleeping? Did I inaugurate the infirmity of laughter?'

Subscribers to the *London Magazine* would have enjoyed the exaggerated romance of De Quincey's first trip, the outrageous irony of posing as the only floating Londoner, the comically soaring prose – 'eloquent opium! that with thy potent rhetoric stealest away the purposes of wrath, and to the guilty man, for one night givest back the hopes of his youth, and hands washed pure of blood' – and the chutzpah involved in recasting a household habit as a personal and unique transgression. The genius of his *Confessions*, as the cultural historian Mike Jay puts it, is that 'De Quincey was not so much breaking a taboo as deliberately creating one by recasting a familiar practice as transgressive and culturally threatening. It was a Byronic double game: baiting the moralists and middlebrow public opinion while delighting the elite with the invention of a new vice.'

It was a complicated ruse, but nothing De Quincey wrote was ever straightforward. A fearless ironist, his mischief worked in curious ways, and playfulness, venom, ambition, revenge and self-perception were built into every brick of his *Confessions*.

So too was his response to Wordsworth, whose voice can be heard throughout. De Quincey took Coleridge's subject matter and clothed it in

Wordsworthian garb. Like *The Prelude*, De Quincey's *Confessions* was a work the author had 'hesitated' about 'allowing' to 'come before the public eye, until after my death (when, for many reasons, the whole will be published)'. And as in Wordsworth's 'Tintern Abbey', De Quincey was concerned with the maturing self. To explore the newly discovered mansion of his mind he returns to the streets of London rather than the 'hedge-rows, hardly hedge-rows' of the Wye Valley, and the 'sense sublime' located by Wordsworth in 'setting suns and the round ocean and the living air' is found by De Quincey in the bottle he buys on Oxford Street. His impersonation of 'Tintern Abbey' can be heard in the very rhythm of his sentences. Addressing himself to his wife, 'beloved M., dear companion of my later years', De Quincey reveals at the end of Part I that 'these troubles are past', and brings us into the present moment:

> Meantime, I am *again* in London: and *again* [my stress] I pace the terraces of Oxford-street by night, and oftentimes, when I am oppressed by anxieties that demand all my philosophy and the comfort of thy presence to support, and yet remember that I am separated by three hundred miles and the length of three dreary months, – I look up the streets that run northwards from Oxford-street, upon moonlight nights, and recollect my youthful ejaculation of anguish: – and remember that thou art sitting alone in that same valley, and mistress of that very house to which my heart turned in its blindness nineteen years ago. . .

'The length of three dreary months' echoes 'Tintern Abbey's' 'the length of five long winters'. The incantation of 'again. . . again' repeats Wordsworth's:

> and again I hear
> These waters . . .
> . . . Once again
> Do I behold these steep and lofty cliffs . . .
> . . . Once again I see
> These hedge-rows, hardly hedge-rows . . .

By Wordsworth's side, we discover at the end of the poem, is his 'dear, dear Sister' and the sudden appearance of De Quincey's Margaret, sitting by Dorothy's former hearth, plays a similarly healing role.

But the Opium-Eater assumed, in a way that Wordsworth did not, his reader's intimacy: 'And how do I find my health after all this opium-eating? In short, how do I do? Why, pretty well, I thank you, reader.' Opium is not a voluble or a social drug and his visionary descents took him into soundless worlds, but De Quincey talks to us in the way people talk after dinner, several bottles down, when the table is cleared and the night is young. He confides more than he confesses, and is generous in his confidences; he anticipates our responses, fears our boredom, and likes our company. At least, this is how he appeared in his writing.

———

It is possible to see the Opium-Eater in his first flush of fame because his new friend Richard Woodhouse kept a record of their conversations. John Taylor and James Hessey, who bought the *London* after the death of John Scott, hosted regular dinners, in the style of the 'Noctes', to which their contributors were invited and De Quincey, an object of great fascination, was a frequent guest. Here he appeared 'sallow-looking' and 'very much an invalid', being often too ill to add to the table talk. He would, however, sit up afterwards with Woodhouse smoking 'segars'. 'I was astonished at the depth and *reality*, if I may so call it, of his knowledge,' Woodhouse said of the man for whom reality had become a distant memory. He was also astonished by De Quincey's capacity to gossip, stir and sow the seeds of discontent. Speaking in what Carlyle would describe as his 'slow sad and soft voice', De Quincey insisted that Wordsworth and Dorothy were in fact not having sexual relations, that it was simply Wordsworth's habit to kiss his sister whenever he saw her. Always attuned to the voices of others, De Quincey described how when Wordsworth read his own poetry his face assumed a 'conventicle appearance, and his voice a methodistical drawl that is quite distressing. Southey mouths it out like a wolf howling. Coleridge lengthens the vowels and reads so monotonously, slowly, and abstractedly, that you can scarce make out what he says.' As for the fatal affair with *Blackwood's*, Wilson was 'the principal person concerned', the man who should have come forward to Scott and revealed his identity. But De Quincey also described to Woodhouse the effect of first reading 'We Are Seven': 'How deep must a man have gone below the thoughts of the generality,' he mused, 'before he could have written such a ballad.'

It was at one of the dinners hosted by Taylor and Hessey that De Quincey found himself in the company of a man who turned out to be 'a murderer, and a murderer of a freezing class; cool, calculating, wholesale in his operations'. This was the young artist and critic, Thomas Griffiths Wainewright, who contributed to the *London Magazine* under the *noms de plume* Janus Weathercock, Egomet Bonmot and Cornelius van Vinkbooms. Sixteen years later Wainewright was accused of poisoning his uncle, mother-in-law and sister-in-law, the latter because she had 'very thick ankles'. Wainewright was, said De Quincey, a snake who slithered 'over the sleeping surfaces of confiding household life'. De Quincey was too unwell to partake in the conversation, but 'if I had known this man for the murderer that even then he was. . . what sudden growth of. . . interest, would have changed the face of that party!' Wainewright's case struck De Quincey as remarkable for two reasons: 'for the appalling revelation which it makes of power spread through the hands of people not liable to suspicion', and for the contrast 'between the murderer's appearance and the terrific purposes with which he was always dallying'. He and Wainewright wrote for the same journal – 'this formed a shadowy link between us; and, ill as I was, I looked more attentively at him than at anybody else'.

To De Quincey's horror, John Wilson appeared in London that October, where he offered his services as a writer for the *London*. Hessey suspected that it was a *Blackwood's* plot. De Quincey, expecting to become a '*dead man*' once Wilson revealed whose side he had been on in the magazine wars, agreed. To protect himself, he blackened his friend's name. Wilson, De Quincey said, had the 'happy knack' of 'catching & making use of the thoughts of other people', with 'no opinions of his own on any subject', no 'originality', 'no principles' and 'no judgment'. It was Wilson who penned 'the most objectionable' of the *Blackwood's* articles. 'His character is represented to be a compound of cruelty and meanness. He will domineer over those authors who have as yet no reputation in the world, he will grudge them their fair degree of credit, he will abuse them, & strive to keep them back, & even to crush them. But to those who are established in reputation. . . he will be abject & cringing.' And at the same time as slandering him, De Quincey plotted with Wilson his return to *Blackwood's*. Crabb Robinson, that perfect recorder of the De Quinceyan temperature, called on him and found him 'querulous', 'in ill health', 'very strongly impressed with his own excellence, and prone to despise others'.

By December 1821, De Quincey could no longer endure the separation from his family and he returned to Fox Ghyll in time for the New
Year celebrations. He had been away for seven months, and was now
the self-appointed 'Pope of Opium'.

In 1822 he did, in a manner of speaking, return to *Blackwood's* when he
made his debut as the Opium-Eater in the community of the 'Noctes'.
'Pray, is it true, my dear Laudanum,' asks the doddery Christopher
North, 'that your "Confessions" have caused about fifty unintentional
suicides?' 'I should think not,' replies the Opium-Eater. 'I have read of
six only; and they rested on no solid foundation.' 'And now,' continues North, 'that you have fed and flourished fourteen years on opium,
will you be persuaded to try a course of arsenic?' The Shepherd then
describes his own response to the Opium-Eater's 'desperate interesting
confession':

> It's perfectly dreadfu', yon pouring in upon you o' oriental imagery. But nae
> wunner. Sax thousand draps o' lowdnam! It's as muckle, I fancy, as a bottle
> o'whusky. I tried that experiment mysel, after reading the wee wud wicked
> wark, wi' five hunner draps, and I couped ower, and continued in ae snore
> frae Monday night till Friday morning. But I had naething to confess.

The Shepherd had 'naething at least that wad gang into words', his
opium experience being just 'clouds, clouds, clouds hovering round
and round'. He is told by North that he should write a book about
the clouds anyway. Moving the conversation forwards, the Shepherd
asks 'But how's Wudsworth?' 'I have not seen him since half-past two
o'clock on the 17th September,' replies the Opium-Eater.

It is doubtful that he was amused by his 'Noctes' persona. Teased
by Lamb about his *Confessions*, De Quincey had reacted badly. There
were, he grandly explained, 'certain places & events and circumstances,
which had been mixed up or connected with parts of my life which
have been very unfortunate, and these, from constant meditation &
reflection upon them, have obtained with me a sort of sacredness'.
Should they be referred to 'by others in any tone of levity or witticism'

it seemed to him 'a sort of desecration & harrowing, analogous to the profanation of a temple'.

It was through the 'Noctes' that *Blackwood's* poached the Opium-Eater from the *London Magazine* and turned him into their own creation. De Quincey's 'personality' was further embedded in the culture of *Maga* with the appearance of the parodic 'Confessions of an English Glutton'. Like the Opium-Eater, the English Glutton finds that in 'profess[ing] himself a slave to gluttony – the commonest failing of all!' he is alone of his kind. The way to ensure immortality, he learns, is to 'pour' his 'fatal story' into the 'confiding and capacious bosom of the public' as 'the Wine-drinker, the Opium-Eater, the Hypochondriac, and the Hypercritic' have all done (the Wine-drinker referred to Charles Lamb's 1813 essay – republished by the *London* in 1822 – 'Confessions of a Drunkard'). A glutton since 'August 1764' when he was 'precisely two years and two months old', he is now an eater of everything (except opium). A plate of pork, he confesses, 'smoking in his rich brown symmetry of form and hue', plunges him into '*media res*. Never shall I forget the flavour of that first morsel – it was sublime!' Thus De Quincey's rainy Sunday afternoon becomes a steaming Sunday roast. Discarding both knife and fork, the Glutton thrust the beast 'wholesale' into his mouth 'until at last my head began to swim – my eyes seemed starting from their sockets. . . a fullness of brain seemed bursting through my skull – my veins seemed swelled into gigantic magnitude – I lost all reason and remembrance, and fell, in that state, fairly under the table.' These horrors, however, are now behind him. 'Forty-two years have passed since that memorable day – forty thousand recollections of that infernal pig have flashed across my brain.' As for his 'dreaming hours', the Glutton suffered 'quotidian repetitions of visions, each more hideous than the former. I dreamt, and dreamt, and dreamt – of what? Of pig – pig – pig – nothing but pig.' He saw ham in the landscape and ham in the clouds. Pursued by Hogg (the pun was intended), he 'tumbled headlong down thousands of thousands of fathoms, till I was at length landed in a pig-stye, at the very bottom of all bottomless pits'.

The parodies of the Opium-Eater were tributes rather than attacks: *Blackwood's* revenge came later, and when it was least expected.

Gill's Hill Cottage, where the corpse of William Weare was hidden in a pond.

'The murder is a good one, and truly gratifying to every man of correct taste.
Yet it might have been better.'

Imagination, Impaired and Restored

> Like one, that on a lonely road
> Doth walk in fear and dread,
> And having once turned round walks on
> And turns no more his head,
> Because he knows a frightful fiend
> Doth close behind him tread.

Coleridge, 'The Ancient Mariner'

Debt swallowed debt, like one deep calling to another. Home in Grasmere in 1822, De Quincey's time was spent beating back the butcher, the grocer, the wine merchant, the haberdasher, the butterman, the dressmaker, the landlord, all demanding payment. He would dread the sound of knocking, and the suspense in the house when knocking was expected. His current income was around £250 a year, composed of £100 from Elizabeth Quincey – now suffering the indignation of being known as the Opium-Eater's mother – £100 from his Uncle Penson, and the rest made up from his writing. It was equivalent to the income of a country parson. Frugality was essential, but De Quincey understood only excess; during his worst excesses he spent £150 a year on laudanum. Excess was in the blood; his mother's extravagant property speculations and repeated home improvements had drained her own coffers, leaving her reliant on the generosity of her brother.

At the core of De Quincey's personality were his addictions. Opium was one and debt was another; his relationship to both was a manifestation of the same fear. Without the insulation they offered, he was faced with the ordinary tide of human affairs. Opium and debt allowed De Quincey to live a second life, apart and with himself alone. They removed him from the crowd and had him trapped: just as opium cured the effects of opium, the solution to debt was to borrow. A credit-based economy is a catastrophe for an addict, but the logic of debt made sense to De Quincey. 'You know there is such a thing,' he once explained, 'as buying a thing and yet not paying for it.' De Quincey was at home in the realm of indebtedness, intellectual or financial. Despite his fascination with political economy – a subject he chewed over for the *London Magazine* in thousands of indigestible words – money would always remain for him an abstract idea. When little Paul Dombey asks his father, in Dickens's novel, what money is, Mr Dombey replies: 'Gold, and silver, and copper. Guineas, shillings, half-pence,' as he jingles them in his pocket. Money was never so solid for De Quincey; any coins in his pocket disintegrated like a rope of sand. Money frightened him: lethal, insidious, invisible, it circled around his person, pursuing him in its absence like footsteps on the road. When it came his way he quickly passed it on to friends, ridding himself of the evidence. De Quincey's primary expenditure, apart from opium, was on books: book-buying was another addiction. He bought hungrily, greedily, avidly, regardless of cost and then, because he had nowhere to store his booty, he paid rent for rooms he could not afford. He was well trained in the business of bolting when reality began to bite.

His laudanum intake now swerved between 160 and 300 drops a day. Battling with 'infantine feebleness' and 'a torpor of the will', he reduced it to 130 drops; for a month it 'plunged' to 80 drops, and then to 60. For ninety hours in the summer of 1822, De Quincey took no laudanum at all. The results were sleeplessness, restlessness, excessive sweating, 'unspeakable, unutterable misery of mind' and 'the wretchedness of a lunatic'. A benefit was that, momentarily, his powers returned: 'I have a greater influx of thoughts in one hour at present than in a whole year under the reign of opium,' he wrote. Those thoughts 'which had been frozen up' now 'thawed' and streamed in on him. But he soon resorted to his usual levels of ingestion, and the drug once again 'aggravated the misery which for the moment it relieved'. And so the wheel turned. What he wrote under the influence afterwards filled him with self-loathing. Opium-writing became, he explained to Mary Russell Mitford, 'overspread with a dark frenzy of horror', as though 'wrapt' in a 'sheet of consuming fire – the very paper is poisoned to my eyes. I cannot endure to look at it, and I sweep it away into the vast piles of unfinished letters or inchoate essays.'

In November 1822 Margaret gave birth to their fourth child, a son called Francis. On 9 December he returned to London with the aim of clearing his debts. '*Why am I now in London?*' he raged to Hessey and Taylor from his rooms opposite their Fleet Street offices, 'Are you aware – 1. Of the enormous sacrifice I am making in *personal happiness* by staying at a distance of 300 miles from my own family? 2. . . of the *price in money* at which I am doing this? 3. Have you ever asked – *whose interests* this residence in London was meant to serve?' It was a confused rage, directed mainly at himself. Without his editors on his doorstep, nothing would get written, and if nothing was written there would be no payment. De Quincey was also aware – as were all the *London* contributors – that *Blackwood's*, to whose editor he had been similarly obnoxious, was the superior publication.

His rooms were described by a visitor as a 'German Ocean of Literature', with volumes 'flooding all the floor, the table and the chairs, – billows of books tossing, tumbling, surging open'. This ocean found its way into De Quincey's writing. In his 'Letters to a Young Man Whose Education Has Been Neglected', which appeared in the *London* between January and July 1823, he described his oceanic feeling for books. In his youth, he 'never entered a great library, suppose of 100,000 volumes, but my predominant feeling was one of pain and disturbance of mind' that there were not years in a lifetime in which to read everything. Books were reduced to nothing but counting: De Quincey could 'extract the honey' from one-twentieth of this hive; 'subtracting' works of reference, such as dictionaries, there 'would still remain a total of not less than twelve hundred thousand books over and above what the presses of Europe are still disemboguing into the ocean of literature'. A Portuguese monk, he continued, had shown how, 'with respect to one single work, viz: *The History of Thuanus*', that to 'barely. . . read over the words (allowing no time for reflection) would require three years labour, at the rate of (I think) three hours a-day'. Reading at the rate of 400 pages a day – 'all skipping being barred' – meant that the most a man could hope to accomplish in thirty years was 10,000 volumes. A sixty-year lifespan allowed him to 'travel through' only 20,000, 'a number not, perhaps, above *five per cent* of what the mere *current* literature of Europe would accumulate in that period of years'. His 'gluttonism' for books, De Quincey explained, turned what should be a pleasure into a 'torment'; the excess of it all tipped him into 'madness'. Meanwhile, his landlord was after the rent and so he absconded to a local inn and hid for a while beneath an alias.

In May 1823, Hazlitt published his own confessions, *Liber Amoris*. One of the strangest books ever written, Hazlitt's subject was his obsessive love for a servant girl, and De Quincey, who knew about obsession and had married his servant, was one of the book's few sympathetic readers. The two men occasionally walked home together after a late-night party, and in their only recorded conversation (recorded by De Quincey) their talk turned to the Duke of Cumberland's servant, who had been found with his throat cut. The coroner's jury concluded that the victim had tried to kill the duke and then killed himself, but rumour had it that the duke himself had murdered the servant, who had discovered him in bed with his valet. De Quincey the royalist stood by the official verdict, while Hazlitt the Jacobin 'would hear no reason', insisting that 'all the princely houses of Europe have the instinct of murder running through their blood'.

After eight months in London, De Quincey scraped together the fare back to Grasmere where he arrived in time to celebrate his thirty-eighth birthday in August 1823. In September, the *London* ran his magical essay on 'Walking Stewart', the 'sublime visionary' last seen by De Quincey in 1812 when he had been overtaken by three simulacra of Walking Stewarts on his way through Soho. That same month, from the chaos of Fox Ghyll, De Quincey wrote a paper on Malthus's 'Essay on Population'. Malthus described a populace veering out of control. The human race was doubling, trebling, quadrupling itself and hurtling towards extinction: it was a theory calculated to thrill De Quincey. Much of what he said in his essay, however, had been anticipated by Hazlitt himself, who complained to the editors that while he did 'not wish to bring any charge of plagiarism', 'credit' was due. In two sweating pages of self-defence, published in the *London*, De Quincey drew on the question of "'running away' with the credit of another'. The concept of credit was close to his heart, he teasingly explained, and 'Mr. Hazlitt must permit me to smile when I read that word used in that sense: I can assure him that not any abstract consideration of credit, but the abstract idea of a creditor. . . has for some time past been the animating principle of my labours.'

Having brushed Hazlitt's accusation aside, De Quincey broached the subject that had long been on his mind. It came through his reflections on *Macbeth*.

———

'From my boyish days,' he began, 'I had always felt a great perplexity on one point of *Macbeth*: it was this: the knocking at the gate, which succeeds to the murder of Duncan.' 'On the Knocking at the Gate in *Macbeth*', as this next paper was called, focused on Act 2, Scene 3, where, hungover, the porter grumpily responds to the early morning arrival of Macduff:

> [knocking within]
> PORTER: Here's a knocking, indeed! If a man were Porter of Hell Gate,
>   he should have old turning the key. [knocking] Knock, knock, knock.
>   Who's there, i'th' name of Beelzebub?

Readers of the *London* would be all too familiar with the scene, which has come down to us as the first 'knock, knock' joke: while productions of *King Lear* had been cancelled because of King George III's madness, *Macbeth*, warning of the dangers of regicide, had been a staple of the war years. The knocking, De Quincey went on, 'reflected back to the murder a peculiar awfulness and a depth of solemnity: yet, however obstinately I endeavoured with my understanding to comprehend this, for many years I never could see *why* it should produce such an effect'. It was only when John Williams 'executed those unparalleled murders which have procured for him such a brilliant and undying reputation' that De Quincey at last understood his childhood perplexity. Eleven years had passed since Williams 'made his *debut* on the stage of Ratcliffe Highway', and De

Quincey reminded his readers that preceding the servant girl's discovery
of the bodies of the Marr household, this 'same incident [of a knocking
at the door soon after the work of extermination was complete] did actually occur'. Through the coincidence of Coleridge's lectures, the Ratcliffe
Highway murders had, for De Quincey, segued from the very start into
scenes from Shakespeare, and so it was perhaps inevitable that he would
blend the figure of John Williams into that of Macbeth.

Shakespeare needed to create a device, De Quincey suggested, by
which the familiar, work-a-day human world disappeared for a moment
to allow for the appearance of a 'fiendish' world in which Lady Macbeth
was unsexed and Macbeth forgot that he was born of woman: 'The murderers, and the murder, must be insulated – cut off by an immeasurable
gulph from the ordinary tide and succession of human affairs – locked
up and sequestered in some deep recess: we must be made sensible that
the world of ordinary life is suddenly arrested – laid asleep – tranced –
racked into a dead armistice: time must be annihilated; relation to things
abolished; and all must pass self-withdrawn into a deep syncope and sus-
pension of earthly passion.'

With the knocking, the 'pulses of life' begin to 'beat again' as 'the
world of darkness' passes away 'like a pageantry in the clouds' and we
are made 'profoundly sensible of the awful parenthesis' which has taken
place. This parenthesis had allowed us to access the mind of the murderer. It is Macbeth rather than Duncan with whom the audience is
asked to sympathise – 'of course I mean a sympathy of comprehension,
a sympathy by which we enter into [Macbeth's] feelings, and are made
to understand them – not a sympathy of pity or approbation'. And
to encourage our sympathy, the murderer must have an interior existence. There must be 'some great storm of passion, – jealousy, ambition,
vengeance, hatred, – which will create a hell within him'.

A certain 'amateur' on the subject of sudden death, De Quincey
went on, had recently commented on the current absence of any good
murders, 'but this is wrong: for it is unreasonable to expect all men to
be great artists, and born with the genius of Mr Williams'. De Quincey's
sympathy had always been with Williams. He spared no pity for the
Marrs and their young apprentice, or the Williamsons and their age-
ing servant, all of whom were figures without faces. His reverence for
Williams was presented as ironic but his irony tapped into a truth, the

full force of which would be realised later in the century in the distinction accorded to Jack the Ripper, whose own debut took place not far from the Ratcliffe Highway.

The Opium-Eater, Charles Lamb conceded when he finished reading 'On Knocking', had 'written a better thing about *Macbeth* than anything I could write; – no – not better than anything I could write, but I could not write anything better.'

‘On the Knocking at the Gate in *Macbeth*’ appeared in the October 1823 edition of the *London Magazine*, and one week later a very good murder indeed took place in the Hertfordshire town of Radlett. Few murders, in fact, would create a greater sensation. The Ratcliffe Highway murders had generated panic because the killer remained at large, but the response to the Radlett murder, whose perpetrators were instantly apprehended, was undisguised pleasure in sensation. For three months the newspapers indulged in the story with such abandon that, for the first time in legal history, it was feared that a jury would be swayed by the media.

John Thurtell, the son of a Norwich alderman, was a failed cloth merchant turned prize-fighter and gambler. Tall and athletic, he had pockmarked skin and feline eyes. William Weare was a well-known cardsharp who reputedly carried a sum of £2,000 on his person. Thurtell, who believed himself cheated of £300 by Weare, invited him to Radlett for a weekend of shooting and gaming; they were to be the guests of a friend of Thurtell's, called William Probert, who was renting a cottage called Gill's Hill.

On the night of Friday 24 October, Thurtell and Weare set off together from London in a hired gig. The plan was for Thurtell to meet Probert and a third party called Joseph Hunt at the cottage, where they would murder Weare: like *Macbeth*, this was a tale of lethal hospitality. But before the two men had reached their destination, Thurtell took out his pistol and shot Weare in the face. The bullet only grazed the cheekbone; jumping from the gig, Weare ran screaming down the lane. Thurtell finished the job by dashing his gun through his victim's skull until his brains stuck to the nozzle, and slitting his throat in two places. Dumping the body and the murder weapons in a field, he continued his journey to Gill's Hill Cottage where he boasted to Probert and Hunt that the deed was done. The three men then removed Weare's corpse from its present position, stripped it of clothes and valuables (the £2,000 turned out to be only £15), tied it in a sack, dragged it to the cottage garden and threw it in the pond where it refused to sink until being weighed down by stones. Thurtell presented the blushing Mrs Probert with a gold chain taken from the corpse, after which the party enjoyed a supper of pork chops followed by a sing-song and a round of cards. The next day they thought better of leaving their quarry so close to home, and so Weare was fished out of the pond and carted to another pond, this time on the road to Elstree.

The murder of William Weare opened the door to an underworld of fallen privilege, thuggery and gaming. Between the discovery of his corpse and the conviction of his killers, no other news story was worth following. While Probert and Hunt were described in the papers as possessing only 'the lineaments of human beings', Thurtell was granted the glamour of a vampire. His thirst for blood was seen as insatiable; he was implicated by the press in the deaths of any number of women, clergymen and business associates. The body count grew by the day as Thurtell-mania took over the country. The son of the journalist William Cobbett learned to read by following the news on Thurtell; for those who could not afford a paper, Weare's murder was vividly recorded in broadsides such as *The Hertfordshire Tragedy; or, the Fatal Effects of Gambling*:

> The hapless man sprung from the gig,
> And strove the road to gain,
> But Thurtell pounc'd on him, and dashed
> His pistol through his brains.
>
> Then pulling out his murderous knife,
> As over him he stood,
> He cut his throat, and, tiger-like,
> Did drink his reeking blood.

For Londoners, a documentary drama called *The Gamblers*, which re-enacted the events, opened on 17 November. It included, in Act 2, the appearance of 'THE IDENTICAL HORSE AND GIG *Alluded to by the Daily Press*'; after Thurtell's trial, the props extended to the 'TABLE AT WHICH THE PARTY SUPPED, the SOFA as DESCRIBED to having been SLEPT on, with the Other Household Furniture'. In the play's final scene, when Thurtell and his accomplices were depositing the body in the pond, the audience watched as Weare, not quite dead, rose out of the water to condemn his killer.

The gloomy cottage itself became a tourist site, despite the fact that the murder took place elsewhere. A pilgrimage, which took in the various locations in which Weare's body had been dumped and the grave in which it now lay, attracted further crowds. Kitchen utensils and other household goods were sold by the Gill's Hill landlord as souvenirs; murder tourists could also purchase maps, books, pottery figures of Thurtell and Weare, plates and mugs illustrating Weare's death, and scraps of the sack in which his corpse had been stuffed. Those unable to afford such relics took home twigs from the cottage shrubbery.

The trial took place on 4 and 5 January 1824, and Thurtell took the stand in a plum-coloured frock coat. Blaming the murder on Hunt and Probert, he defended himself with what the *London Magazine* described as 'theatrical' eloquence. 'I have been presented by the Press,' Thurtell began, having learned his speech by heart,

> – as a man more depraved, more gratuitously and habitually profligate and cruel, than has ever appeared in modern times. I have been held up to the world as the perpetrator of a murder, under circumstances of greater aggravation, or more cruel and premeditated atrocity, than it ever fell to the lot of man to have seen or heard of. I have been held forth to the world as a depraved, heartless, remorseless, prayer-less villain, who had seduced my friend into a sequestered path, merely in order to dispatch him with the greater security – as a snake who has crept into his bosom only to strike a sure blow – as a monster, who, after the perpetration of a deed from which the hardest heart recoils with horror, and at which humanity stands aghast, washed away the remembrance of my guilt in the midst of riot and debauchery.

Thurtell went on to tell the courtroom, now warming to his presence much as they had warmed to that of John Bellingham, the story of his life: how he came from a respectable and God-fearing family; how he shed blood for his country in the war; how he was incapable of an ignoble act. It was, said Charles Dickens, 'a capital speech'. He had, in the words of the *London Magazine*'s reporter Edward Herbert, 'worked himself up into a great actor. . . such a performance, for a studied performance it assuredly was, has seldom been seen *on* the stage, and certainly never *off*'. Thurtell was commonly understood to be an artist possessed of a certain genius. The previous year, De Quincey had noted in his 'Letters to A Young Man Whose Education has been Neglected', that no man speaks better than when he is on the scaffold because, like the journalist, his faculties are sharpened by the advancing deadline.

Thus the serpentine Thurtell was metamorphosed into the strong, desperate, heroic Thurtell. The analogy between the noble Othello and the ham-fisted killer of Gill's Hill cottage was noted by a number of writers, including Edward Herbert himself. When the jury reluctantly sentenced Thurtell to death, the condemned man drew gasps of admiration by taking a pinch of snuff.

During Thurtell's trial, the *Morning Chronicle* had extended its pages from four to eight. After the verdict, the *Observer* and *Bell's Illustrated London Life* each ran an 'execution' double bill. Fifteen thousand people turned out to see Thurtell's neck broken, some of whom went on to the theatre afterwards for a performance of *The Gamblers*. He appeared on the scaffold dressed in a great brown coat with a velvet collar, light breeches and gaiters, and a waistcoat glistening with gilt buttons. Before the noose was put around his neck, Thurtell 'looked at the crowd, and made a slight bow; instantly every head was uncovered, and many muttered "what a Gentleman"'. His appearance at that moment, reported Edward Herbert, was 'affecting beyond description'. The nation mourned for the murderer. 'Thurtell being hanged last week,' wrote Carlyle, 'we grew duller than ever.'

Thurtell's posthumous confession, *A Warning from the Tomb, or J. Thurtell's Caution to the Youth of Great Britain*, was sold on the streets as a tale about the dangers of gambling; his skeleton was stored in the Royal College of Surgeons; his likeness was exhibited in Madame Tussaud's; his name turned up in novels by George Eliot, William Thackeray and Robert Louis Stevenson. Dickens was haunted by Thurtell (the murder of Montague by Jonas Chuzzlewit bears a striking resemblance to the murder of Weare), and a hundred years later the repetition of 'Thurtell was a murdered man' was used in schools for handwriting practice.

De Quincey had written to James Hessey in November, remarking that 'the murder is a good one, as you observe, and truly gratifying to every man of correct taste: yet it might have been better, if [Thurtell] would have thrown in a few improvements that I could have suggested – I speak *aesthetically* – as the Germans say, of course: morally, it is a damnable concern. You must allow me to look at these things in 2 lights. Perhaps it is yet too recent to be looked at by the aesthetic critic.' Hessey clearly agreed. Edward Herbert, who covered the Thurtell story for the *London Magazine*, was not an aesthetic critic. His exhaustive report appeared in the issue for February 1824, following De Quincey's translation of 'Analects of Jean Paul Richter'. 'I fear you will have become heartily wearied of the names of Thurtell, Probert and Hunt,' Herbert began before noting how, apart from the solitary natures of the location and the victim, everything else associated with the crime – the 'actors, the witnesses, the murderers, the merry party at the cottage. . . the gigs, the pistols, even the very knives, were in clusters!' The irrelevance of the observation inevitably found its way into the 'Noctes' where the party in Ambrose's Tavern enjoyed a discussion of 'Tims', as Herbert was named (Tobias Tims the barber is a recurring figure in the 'Noctes') over a tripe supper.

'Tims on Thurtell!!' mocked Timothy Tickler. 'What a most ludicrous thing it would have been had Thurtell assassinated Tims!. . . What small, mean, contemptible Cockney shrieks would he have emitted! 'Pon my honour, had Jack *bona fide* Thurtellised Tims, it would have. . . thrown such an air of absurdity over murder.' 'That's ae way indeed,' replied the surly Shepherd, 'o' making murder ridiculous. . . What kind o' a Magazine can that o' Taylor and Hessey be, to take sic writers as Tims? I hope they don't run in clusters.'

The clusters non sequitur was the cause of great mirth, and the response to Edward Herbert's praise of Thurtell's courtroom speech was unanimous: 'Ha! ha! ha! ha! ha! ha! ha! ha! ha! ha! ha!' 'I dinna ken the time,' concluded the Shepherd, 'I hae laucht so muckle.'

In a story written in 1838 called 'How to Write a Blackwood Article', Edgar Allan Poe has the editor propose to a would-be contributor, Signora Psyche Zenobia, that she kill herself in order to describe 'the sensations'. William Blackwood refers Miss Zenobia to an article called

'The Dead Alive', which contains a record, 'full of tastes, terror, sentiment, metaphysics, and erudition', of a man who was buried while still
breathing: 'You would have sworn,' he says admiringly, 'that the writer
had been born and brought up in a coffin.' Alternatively, Blackwood
suggests that she use as a model 'The Man in the Bell', the record of the
writer's 'sensations' as he was driven slowly mad by the tolling of the
church bell under which he was sleeping.

The Thurtell case allowed *Blackwood's* to indulge its love of the
macabre. 'We are certainly a blood-thirsty people,' noted Tickler,
'and the scaffold has been mounted, in this country, by first-rate
criminals.' Some of the more recent 'malefactors', Christopher
North agreed, included butlers 'quite unaccountably' cutting the
throat of their masters (a reference to the Duke of Cumberland
case), magistrates throwing their wives over bridges and into coal
pits, 'blue-eyed young maidens' poisoning their families 'with a
mess of pottage' (in 1815, servant girl Eliza Fenning was hanged
for putting arsenic in her employers' dumplings), and any 'decent
well-dressed person' you might meet on an evening stroll, who 'after
knocking out your brains with a bludgeon, pursues his journey'.
Tickler noted the 'beautiful variety of disposition and genius' which
saved the 'simple act of slaughter' from accusations of sameness. You
might be killed by a knife, dagger, pistol, club, mallet, hatchet, or
apothecary's phial; you might find yourself huddled out of a garret
window, impaled on spikes, put in a hot oven, 'gagged with a floor-
brush till your mouth yawns like a barn-door', boiled in lime in your
back court, cut up like bacon, and pickled, salted and barrelled. You
might escape from 'the murderer of the Marrs', Christopher North
added, 'through a common sewer'. The wonder of it all was 'that in
a country where murder has thus been carried to such a pitch of cultivation, its 14 million inhabitants would have been set agape and
aghast by such a pitiful knave as Jack Thurtell killing and bagging
one single miserable sharper'.

Amongst the nation's 'first-class assassins' was Sarah Malcolm, who
dispatched an entire household. 'Sprightly and diligent, good-looking
and fond of admiration', she would, Tickler mused, have made an
admirable wife for 'Gentleman Williams', who had been 'pleasant
with his chit-chat' and fond of children, patting 'their curled heads

with the hand that cut an infant's throat in the cradle'. Everyone who met Williams 'delighted' in 'the suavity of his smile. But in his white great coat – with his maul – or his ripping-chisel – or his small ivory-handled pen-knife, at dead of night, stealing upon a doomed family, with long silent strides, while at the first glare of his eyes the victims shrieked aloud "We are all murdered!" Williams was then a different being indeed, and in all his glory.'

In July 1824, De Quincey returned to London, determined to meet his deadlines and clear his debts. On arrival he purchased the inaugural copy of a journal called the *John Bull* which contained an anonymous article in which 'the Opium-Eater' was lampooned as the 'Humbug of the Age'. De Quincey was 'a sort of hanger-on' of the 'Lake School', a man so desperate for celebrity that he was prepared to present his own infirmities 'for wonder or applause'. Referring to him as 'Quincy', the author charged his subject with being 'a humbug even to his name: he has no right whatever to the Norman De. His father was an honest shopkeeper, who lived and died Quincy, and his son might just as well designate himself Mr Quin Daisy as Mr De Quincy.' As for De Quincey's person: 'conceive an animal about five feet high, propped on two trapsticks, which have the size but not the delicate proportions of rolling pins, with a comical sort of indescribable body and a head of the most portentous magnitude, which puts one in mind of those queer big-headed caricatures which you see occasionally from whimsical pencils. As for the face, its utter grotesqueness and inanity is totally beyond the reach of the pen to describe. . .'

De Quincey was presented as a second-rate show-off, a fake and a groupie. But most wounding were the references to Margaret, who was described as having been his 'serving maid long before he married her'. 'Quincy' was challenged to present the public with 'an extract from his parish register, dating the birth of his eldest son, and also his marriage'. The author of the article was the Blackwoodsman William Maginn, and the source of his information was clearly John Wilson, the man from whom De Quincey had anticipated a 'great & unexpiable injury'. The following month the libel was reprinted by the *Westmorland Gazette*'s rival paper, the *Kendal Chronicle*, thus ensuring that Margaret De Quincey, currently suffering from depression, was also informed. Thus *Blackwood's* avenged itself on the Opium-Eater.

———

'Do you live in Fox Ghyll?' Elizabeth Quincey asked her son in January 1825. 'How many children have you?' Her own children were almost all lost to her, Henry having died aged twenty-six in 1819, the year before Mary died in childbirth and Richard disappeared at sea. Only Jane was still living at Westhay, where De Quincey now never came.

His mother might well have asked where he was living: still in London, De Quincey was sleeping – so his new friend Charles Knight, the former editor of a journal called *Knight's Quarterly* to which De Quincey had contributed, observed – under hayricks in Hampstead, 'in retired doorways or upon bulkheads, after the fashion of poor Savage the poet'. One evening De Quincey met John Clare, a poet who 'studied for himself in the fields, and in the woods, and by the side of brooks'. Clare noted the Opium-Eater's 'little artless simple seeming body' stealing 'gently among the company' at parties, hat in hand and 'a smile turning timidly', looking 'something of a child over grown in a blue coat and black neckerchief'. His dress, Clare said, was 'singular'.

During these particularly rudderless London days De Quincey wrote an essay on a murder case which he described as 'amongst the most remarkable events of our times'. In 1816 the battered corpse of William Coenen, from Enfield, was found in the River Rhine, and in 1822 a German spirits merchant called Peter Anthony Fonk was charged with his death. In a documentary account of the background to the case, De Quincey questioned Fonk's guilt. The English, German and French, he reflected, operate different systems of justice, but 'it is possible that no system whatsoever would have sufficed to illuminate the guilty darkness of this transaction'. The essay, a sober piece of investigative journalism, was submitted but never published: Taylor and Hessey had left the *London*, and the new editor now dispensed with De Quincey's services.

With no income, De Quincey wrote some pieces for a paper called the *New Times* but the work fizzled out. 'To fence with illness with the one hand,' he complained to Wilson in February 1825, 'and with the other to maintain the war with the wretched business of hack author, with all its horrible degradations, – is more than I am able to bear.' He had nowhere to hide; he yearned to 'slink into some dark corner' and 'show my face to the world no more'. His abject state amused his fellow writers: referring to the booksellers, Payne and Foss, Lamb – famous for his puns – suggested the Opium-Eater 'should have chosen as his publishers, *Pain* and *Fuss*'.

Charles Knight came to the rescue and gave De Quincey a room in his house on Pall Mall. Here he stayed, in great embarrassment, during the summer of 1825 while waiting for his mother to direct him some money. Knight described his ragged guest as 'constantly beset by idle fears and vain imaginings' and 'helpless' in relation to 'every position of responsibility'. Not wanting to inconvenience the servants, De Quincey prefaced the smallest request with an apology of baroque elaboration.

Meanwhile, his wife and children, 'starving on the scanty produce of his scribble' as Carlyle put it, were forced out of Fox Ghyll when the house was sold to a friend of the Wordsworths. They took refuge at The Nab, from where Margaret sent her husband heart-rending letters. Still he did not return to Grasmere. Instead he resorted to begging Dorothy – of all people – to pay Mrs De Quincey a visit lest her 'grief' should grow to the point where she became ill. 'Oh Miss Wordsworth,' he wrote on 16 July, 'I sympathised with you – how deeply and fervently – in your trial 13 years ago: – now, when I am prostrate for a moment – and the hand of a friend would enable me to rise before I am crushed, do not refuse me this service.' The death of Catherine Wordsworth in the summer of 1812 was increasingly on his mind, but it was she and William, as Dorothy must have recollected, who had then deeply and fervently sympathised with De Quincey.

Mrs Quincey, once again making alterations to her house, managed to find a spare £300 to send to her exasperating son. It was three times the amount he was expecting, but still he failed to return to his family or to clear his debts. Bidding Knight farewell, De Quincey headed south rather than north, finding himself lodgings on the Surrey side of the Thames. He was hiding his face; he had slunk into a dark corner. 'Wife and children', he said, were 'a man's chief blessings' but 'also create for him the deadliest of anxieties'. He was, De Quincey later confessed, perpetually haunted by the desire to fly from himself and the double life, which had long been a necessity, was the reward of both opium and debt. Whether his disappearance from the world was mental or physical, De Quincey needed a home from which to escape, just as a man needs a wife to whom he can be faithless. As in the winter of 1802/03, he now dallied around the London streets doing very little. He had no work, and nor would he work in London again; his relationship with the metropolis had come to an end.

When Margaret De Quincey next saw her husband, in October 1825, he had turned forty. 'The poor little man is returned,' wrote Wordsworth's daughter, Dora. Her salty aunt, Sara Hutchinson, was typically sceptical about their neighbour's condition. 'He tells Miss W,' Sara wrote, 'that he had entirely left off opium before he came hither, but has been obliged to have recourse to it again: "as he has *no Shoes* to walk in & without exercise he is obliged to take it". I suppose it is *easier* to send to the Druggists than to the Shoe Maker.' De Quincey was immediately arrested for the sum of £90, after which he cleared floor space in Dove Cottage and, after an absence of six years, returned with his sprawling family to the hallowed site. His five young children – Margaret had given birth to a fourth son, called Paul Frederick – now lived inside what was effectively a warehouse; De Quincey's books were used as stools, tables, stepping-stones and building bricks, the covers stained with spillages, the pages scribbled on and torn. Writing was impossible, but he had no commissions anyway. Without an income or the possibility of an income, De Quincey's mood in the summer of 1826 was one of 'heart-withering depression', and his health was 'pretty uniformly = o'.

De Quincey had swallowed his pride when he begged Dorothy to call on his wife; he now swallowed it again and asked Wilson, the man he had believed was out to kill him, if there was anything with which he 'might assist Mr Blackwood at this moment?' Wilson was encouraging and so in September 1826, De Quincey exchanged the University of the Lakes for the Athens of the North, taking a room in the Wilsons' freshly built house at 6 Gloucester Place, a few moments walk from the Royal Circus.

'What a wonderful city Edinburgh is!' exclaimed Coleridge to Southey when he came here in 1803. 'What alteration of Height and Depth! – a city looked at in the polish'd back of a Brobdignag Spoon held lengthways – so enormously *stretched-up* are the Houses!' Built on volcanic rock, Edinburgh is crested by a castle and bordered by cone-shaped mountains and a ship-filled sea. Two cities in one, the Old Town was a warren of winding streets and squalid hovels and the New Town, where Wilson lived, was a place of cool elegance and neo-classical order. The subterranean vaults and chambers of the Old Town housed the underworld, while the New Town was home to the city's philosophers, lawyers and businessmen. During his years here on the run, De Quincey would inhabit both realms.

He had arrived in the land of Macbeth, but Scotland's ancient fascination with ghosts and witchcraft had been tempered by the Edinburgh professors, David Hume, Adam Smith and Dugald Stewart, under whose tutelage the city turned into a hub of rational thought. In 1820, Wilson added his name to the pillars of the Scottish Enlightenment when he was appointed, to general surprise, chair of moral philosophy at the university, a post previously occupied by Dugald Stewart. As the panel had been looking to appoint a Tory, Wilson's position turned out to be more political than philosophical. Professor Wilson was required to give 120 lectures a year on a subject about which he knew nothing and on which De Quincey, who had long planned to write a *magnum opus* which would synthesize all the philosophies, knew everything. To compensate for their lack of content, Wilson delivered his lectures in thunderous rhetoric, stressing words such as 'this' and 'of', and running his finger down his nose at the end of each paragraph. De Quincey's impersonation of the act was thought very good. 'The man is a fool,' observed one of his students, 'and if he was na sic a big fool, he would be laughed at.'

The two men had long been interdependent: while De Quincey drew on Wilson for cash, Wilson drew on De Quincey for credibility. Did De Quincey have any books about 'Socrates, Plato, Aristotle, &c or their system,' asked Wilson? Could he 'write me some long letters about either, or their philosophy?' What, in De Quincey's opinion, might 'constitute moral obligation? – and what ought to be my own doctrine on the subject?' Could De Quincey phrase the answer to these questions as though he were writing 'chapters' in his 'own work' so as

not to provoke suspicion, and 'contrive to give [his] letters a less mysterious outward appearance?' De Quincey made a point hereafter of
never praising his friend's intellect.

Together with Lockhart, Wilson established a drawing-room annual
called *Janus*, to be published on 1 January 1826. Only one copy of
'the double-faced old gentleman', as Wilson called it, appeared but it
was an appropriate title. A fake philosopher by day and the fictitious
Christopher North by night, Wilson, like Chatterton, employed a
shadow self. Added to which, Edinburgh was the city of doubles: forty
years earlier a local locksmith called Deacon Brodie had doubled up as
a moonlight burglar, using wax impressions of his customers' keys to
rob their homes. Robert Louis Stevenson – an admirer of De Quincey –
based *Dr Jekyll and Mr Hyde* on Brodie's two selves, but only after James
Hogg had provided the blueprint in *The Private Memoirs and Confessions
of a Justified Sinner*. De Quincey never mentioned Hogg's novel, which
appeared in 1824, but it was of profound interest to him. Hogg's title
was a reference to the Opium-Eater's own *Confessions*, and themes from
the novel would find their way into De Quincey's later writing.

———

Confessions of a Justified Sinner is narrated twice: first by an unnamed
'editor' and then by the sinner himself. The story begins in 1687 with
the marriage of a wealthy bride to the Laird of Dalcastle. Their union
is unhappy, and they soon live in separate parts of the house where
Lady Dalcastle spends her time in consultation with her spiritual
adviser, a Calvinist zealot called the Reverend Robert Wringhim, while
the laird enjoys the company of his bonny mistress. Lady Dalcastle's
first child, George, lives with the laird and her second child, understood to be the son of the clergyman whose name he is given, lives
with his mother. George grows into a popular young man while young
Wringhim becomes a joyless bigot. The brothers meet for the first time
at a tennis match in Edinburgh, where George proclaims Wringhim
the spawn of 'the crazy minister' from Glasgow. From that moment,
George is stalked by Wringhim. There is nowhere that Wringhim does
not appear: in the mist on Arthur's Seat, George sees a giant apparition of his brother, a 'halo of glory' around his head; turning around

he finds Wringhim behind him. George is then murdered and a witness claims that Wringhim, together with a companion resembling one of George's friends, did the deed. Here the editor's narrative ends and Wringhim's confession begins: we enter the hellish mind of the murderer.

He killed his brother, Wringhim reveals, under the malevolent influence of a shape-shifting stranger called Gil-Martin, who convinces him that as one of the elect his salvation is assured. Wringhim is himself being stalked by Gil-Martin, who at times becomes his mirror image. 'I am wedded to you so closely,' says Gil-Martin, 'that I feel as if we were the same person. . . I am drawn to you as by magnetism, and wherever you are, there must my presence be with you.' Other murders take place – including that of his pious mother – of which Wringhim has no memory. He suffers blackouts and loses all sense of time; it becomes unclear whether the events being described are internal or external. Unable to shake off the shadow of Gil-Martin, Wringhim flees: 'O that I had the wings of a dove, that I might fly to the farthest corners of the earth, to hide from those against whom I have no power to stand.' Having penned his confession, he hangs himself.

In the final pages of the book we return to 1823 where the 'editor', reading August's edition of *Blackwood's*, comes across a letter from Hogg about a suicide's grave: 'So often had I been hoaxed by the ingenious fancies displayed in that Magazine, that when this relation met my eye, I did not believe it.' The letter bore, however, 'the stamp of authenticity in every line'. It was indeed authentic, in the sense that it was really published in *Blackwood's*, in August 1823. Titled 'A Scots Mummy' and addressed to 'Sir Christy North', Hogg's letter described the digging up of an ancient grave by two shepherd boys. The resurrected corpse, buried in 1712, had been miraculously preserved, with dimpled cheeks and 'fine yellow hair about nine inches long'. The editor, contacting Lockhart, requests a meeting with the elusive Ettrick Shepherd. He and Lockhart then open Wringhim's grave where they find on his body the sodden manuscript of *The Private Memoirs and Confessions of a Justified Sinner*. Busy with matters of law and literature, Lockhart passes the pages over to the editor, who then presents them to the world.

Throughout the winter of 1826/27, De Quincey lived at 6 Gloucester
Place in much the same way that Coleridge had lived in Allan Bank
in 1808. Eating specially prepared meals in his room, he drank laudanum all night and slept all day; coming downstairs in the morning,
Wilson would pass his guest, candle in hand, retiring to bed. 'Hang
you!' he erupted on one occasion. 'Can't you take your whisky toddy
like a Christian man, and leave your damned opium slops to infidel
Turks, Persians and Chinamen?' Wilson's children became used to the
dishevelled figure comatose before the fire, his head resting on a book,
and the cook became used to De Quincey's daily bulletins detailing his
gastric state. She must be sure, De Quincey instructed her in reverential tones, to slice his mutton 'in a diagonal rather than a longitudinal
form'. 'A' this claver aboot a bit mutton nae bigger than a prin!' she
declared, shaking her head.

Meanwhile, it was Dorothy who once more took care of Margaret
and the children. 'Mrs De Quincey seemed on the whole in good spirits,' she reported to De Quincey, 'but with something of sadness in her
manner, she told me you were not likely very soon to be at home.' Why
did he not move his family to Edinburgh, Dorothy quite reasonably
asked, where 'lodgings are cheap' and 'provisions and coals not dear'?
This is where the remaining correspondence between De Quincey and
Dorothy Wordsworth comes to an end.

———

A *Blackwood's* article, explained Edgar Allan Poe in 'How to Write a
Blackwood Article', should be written in the '*tone laconic*, or *curt*'. It
'can't be too brief. Can't be too snappish. Always a full stop. And never
a paragraph.' Or else it should be written in the '*tone elevated, diffusive,
and interjectional*' where the 'words must be all in a whirl, like a hum-
ming-top, and make a noise very similar, which answers remarkably well
instead of meaning'. On the other hand, 'the *tone metaphysical* is also
a good one. If you know any big words this is your chance for them.'
De Quincey, who could do any of these tones, had sent Blackwood his
account of the murder of William Coenen by Peter Anthony Fonk.
Neither snappish, whirling or metaphysical, the article did not appear
and from now on, De Quincey employed for *Blackwood's* the tone

ironic. 'Pleasant it is, no doubt, to drink tea with your sweetheart,' he wrote in a review of Robert Gillie's *German Stories*, 'but most disagreeable to find her bubbling in the tea urn.'

John Wilson also had an essay spiked by *Blackwood's*. During the summer of 1823, he prepared a piece called 'Murderers', whose subject matter remains unknown. 'I am not very sure,' Blackwood responded, 'if these horrid details are the kind of reading that the general readers of "Maga" would like to have.' *Blackwood's* were currently running a more elevated series called 'Lectures on the Fine Arts'. De Quincey, still living under Wilson's roof, now interwove murder with the fine arts to produce his mock lecture 'On Murder Considered as One of the Fine Arts', which appeared in *Blackwood's* in February 1827. The lecture is framed by a letter 'To the Editor of *Blackwood's Magazine*' from 'XYZ' (one of De Quincey's *noms de plume*) informing him of a 'Society of Connoisseurs in Murder' in which murders are evaluated like works of art. As evidence of this unholy assemblage, XYZ enclosed for publication the purloined script of 'The Williams Lecture on Murder, Considered as One of the Fine Arts'. The author of the paper is the chair of the society, a position previously held by John Thurtell.

'Something more,' the lecturer insists, denouncing the talents of Thurtell (whose 'principal performance, as an artist, has been much overrated'), 'goes into the composition of a fine murder than two blockheads to kill and be killed – a knife – a purse – and a dark lane. Design, gentlemen, grouping, light and shade, poetry, sentiment, are now deemed indispensible to attempts of this nature.' The master of the art was, of course, John Williams, who raised murder to 'a point of colossal sublimity; and, as Mr Wordsworth observes, has in a manner "created the taste by which he is to be enjoyed"'. The reference is from Wordsworth's 1815 'Essay Supplementary to the Preface to the *Lyrical Ballads*': 'Every author, as far as he is great and at the same time *original*, has had the task of *creating* the taste by which he is to be enjoyed.'

Coleridge also got his dues: the pleasure of a good murder, the lecturer suggests, is akin to the pleasure we get from other catastrophes. Years before, he remembered, during an evening spent around the tea urn with Coleridge in Berners Street, their talk was interrupted by cries of 'Fire! Fire!' and the party rushed into Oxford Street to find a piano factory in flames. 'As it promised to be a conflagration of merit,' the lecturer regretted being unable to stay until the blaze reached its crisis. He later enquired of Coleridge 'how that very promising exhibition had terminated. "Oh, sir," said he, "it turned out so ill, that we damned it unanimously."' Coleridge, 'too fat to be a person of active virtue' but nonetheless a 'worthy Christian', had left his tea and talk, it transpired, for nothing.

After guiding the reader through 'the great gallery of murder' from 'Cain to Mr Thurtell', the lecturer considered the question of murdered philosophers. 'It is a fact, that every philosopher of eminence for the last two centuries has been either murdered, or, at the least, been very near it.' The excursus on the connections between philosophy and murder was chiefly, he confessed, a means 'of showing my own learning'. While Descartes was 'all *but* murdered', Spinoza died in suspicious circumstances – 'how was it possible that he should die a natural death at forty-four?' – while Hobbes, 'on what principle I could never understand, was not murdered'. Malebranche was murdered by Bishop Berkeley, Leibniz died from the fear of being murdered, and Kant had a narrow escape on a journey, the murderer preferring to kill 'a little child, whom he saw playing on the road, to the old transcendentalist'. The fate of the present incumbent of Edinburgh University's chair of moral philosophy was not discussed.

Thus the lecturer arrived at the Augustan age of murder, spanning the seventeenth to the nineteenth centuries. This included the cases of Sir Edmondbury Godfrey, Sir Theophilus Boughton, and Mrs Ruscombe of Bristol, murdered in her College Green bedroom by Highwayman Higgins, the man whose skeleton De Quincey knew so well. While the merits of the Ratcliffe Highway murders, 'the sublimest and most entire in their excellence that were ever committed', are deserving of a lecture in themselves, 'or even an entire course of lectures', the lecturer remained unimpressed by the Radlett murders: 'as to Mr Thurtell's case, I know not what to say'. Along with the rest of the populace, he had been 'carried away' with 'enthusiasm' about the dispatch of William Weare, a murder which occasioned 'the fullest meeting of amateurs that I have ever known since the days of Williams'. Out of their beds crawled the connoisseurs, 'on every side you saw people shaking their heads, congratulating each other, and forming dinner-parties for the evening'. But the truth, as one of their more respected members complained, is that there 'was not an original idea in the whole piece'. Thurtell's style was 'as hard as Albrecht Dürer, and as coarse as Fuseli'. The murder of Weare was 'mere plagiarism'.

Riding one day in Munich, the lecturer continued, he ran into a distinguished amateur of the society who had left British shores in order to 'practise a little professionally'. His debut, this amateur informed him, had recently taken place at Mannheim where his lodgings faced those of an overweight baker whose 'vast surface of throat' he fancied. One evening, after the baker had shut up shop, the amateur 'bolted in after him', 'locked the door' and, addressing him with 'great suavity, acquainted him with the nature of my errand'. Drawing out his tools, the murderer was 'proceeding to operate' when the baker, throwing himself into a boxing attitude, proudly announced that he 'would not be murdered'. Their fight began. 'For the first thirteen rounds, the baker positively had the advantage'; by round nineteenth, he 'came up piping'. By the twenty-seventh round, the baker had become 'a log on the floor' and the murderer was able, at last, to complete his task. The brave Baker of Mannheim, De Quincey's finest fictional creation, fixed himself in his author's imagination.

The lecture concluded with three rules to ensure an aesthetically satisfying murder. Firstly, the victim must be a good man, for 'how can there be any pity for one tiger destroyed by another tiger?' Secondly, he must be a private figure because public figures, such as the Pope, are seen as 'abstract ideas' rather than flesh and blood. Thirdly, he must be young enough to not yet be dyspeptic. While 'severe good taste' would demand that the victim leaves behind a family of dependants, 'I would not insist too keenly on this condition.'

'On Murder' was a rich brew. Edward Herbert's – 'Tims' – account of Thurtell as a 'great actor' was a main ingredient, but De Quincey added to the pot a sprinkling of Coleridge's lectures on the fine arts, Burke's theory of the sublime, and the current craze for brotherhoods and clubs. The boxing match between the amateur and the Mannheim baker was a parody of Hazlitt's 1822 essay, 'The Fight', and in the Society of Connoisseurs of Murder we see a version of the Blackwoodsmen in Ambrose's Tavern. The murderer's pleasure in his task recalls that described by Wilson in his *Blackwood's* story, 'Extracts from Gosschen's Diary', and De Quincey's tone throughout is in tune with the 'Noctes' celebration of the 'genius' apparent in the current variety of murder methods. He was also parodying his own persona: the man who hailed opium as the hero of his tale now proclaimed the murderer to be an artist. Ticking all the boxes, De Quincey had demonstrated How to Write a Blackwood Article.

But there was more to the conception of this essay than parody and imitation. There was design, grouping, light and shade: De Quincey had opened the door to a room in his own mind. The artist as murderer was a seed first sown by Richard Savage and confirmed by Thomas Wainewright, but the target here was Wordsworth. Suggesting that the Ratcliffe Highway murderer had created the taste by which he was enjoyed, De Quincey inoculated John Williams onto William Wordsworth: the murderer was a poet, the poet was a murderer.

———

Between now and 1830, De Quincey shuttled to and fro between Edinburgh and Grasmere. In November 1827 his exhausted wife gave birth to her sixth child, a daughter called Florence, and the two eldest children, William, aged eleven and Margaret Thomasina, nine, moved to Edinburgh to be educated by their father. That same month, in Tanner's Close in the city's Old Town, an army pensioner died in the home of an Irishman called William Hare. With the help of his friend, William Burke, Hare removed the fresh corpse from the coffin (replacing it with wood) and sold it for seven shillings to a professor of anatomy called Robert Knox, who used the body for dissection. When Hare's lodger fell ill a few days later, he and Burke helped him on his way by holding his nose and covering his mouth. Because there were no incriminating marks, the victim appeared to have died of natural causes and Burke and Hare again sold his carcass to Knox. They had stumbled upon a foolproof murder method: those people deemed worthless in their lifetime were of value after death. Burke and Hare similarly dispatched fifteen further Edinburgh citizens, inviting the victims into their homes, giving them enough alcohol to pass out, and then smothering them. The stream of bodies was delivered in tea chests to an apparently unsuspecting Knox. The ruse was not apprehended until November 1827, at which point Knox was presumed innocent,

Hare turned King's evidence and went to Ireland, and Burke was condemned to death.

It was Wilson who wrote about Burke and Hare for *Maga*, insert-
ing them into the 'Noctes' in March 1829. Having visited Hare in his
cell, Christopher North apparently found him 'Impenitent as a snake –
remorseless as a tiger'. Was he, asked the Shepherd, 'a strang Deevil
Incarnate?'

> Naebody believes in ghosts in touns, but every body believes in ghosts in
> the kintra. Let either Hare or Knox sleep a' night in a lanely wood, wi' the
> wund roaring in the tap branches o' the pines, and cheepin' in the side anes,
> and by skreich o' day he will be seen flyin' wi' his hair on end, and his een
> jumpin' out o' their sockets, doon into the nearest toon, pursued, as he
> thinks, by saxteen ghaists a' in a row. . . demandin' back their ain atomies.

The Shepherd later confuses an ornate monologue on Edmund Burke's
theory of fear with the fear generated by Burke, Hare and Knox.

De Quincey meanwhile, riding high on the success of 'On Murder
Considered as One of the Fine Arts', wrote a follow-up. Again composed
as a letter to William Blackwood, 'XYZ' describes himself as having been in
Germany at the time that his lecture appeared in 'your far-famed journal'
(in his haste, De Quincey had forgotten that in his original article XYZ
was not the lecturer but the correspondent who sends Blackwood the transcript of the Williams Lecture). He invites Blackwood and Christopher
North to join one of the banquets held by the Society of Connoisseurs
in Murder: 'Pray do not be alarmed by any superannuated old assassins
who you may see lounging about our ante-chambers, for they are as good
as muzzled.' It is the job of his servant, XYZ continues, to provide for his
weekend's reading 'the best murders that can be had in the public journals
of the empire'. Should the newspapers fail him, copies of the *Newgate
Calendar* and *God's Revenge against Murder* will do. And in the event of
this servant wanting to do 'a little in the murderous line' himself, his master explains that from murder 'you will soon come to highway robbery,
and from highway robbery it is but a short step to petty larceny. And when
once you are got to *that*, there comes in sad progression Sabbath-breaking,
drunkenness, and late hours; until the awful climax terminates in neglect
of dress, non-punctuality, and general waspishness.'

Defending himself from accusations of nationalism by praising only English murder, XYZ singles out the case of William Coenen and Peter Fonk – 'the most eminent German murder that has been produced for the last 50 years' – and the murder in Paris in 1720 of Jean Baptiste Savary. Savary, an 'unmarried man of dissipated life', was slaughtered in his home by a man 'of polished manners and elegant appearance', who had been admitted as a guest. His valet was then killed in the wine cellar, and his cook dispatched in the kitchen. The bludgeoned bodies were discovered 'pretty much in the same way as in the case of the Marrs: a person called in the evening, and knocked long and loud for above a quarter of an hour'. The motive was apparently revenge, but the murderer, 'an amateur of the finest genius', was believed to have been of such high rank that the affair was simply hushed up. As far as the French were concerned, 'the great Williams' owed everything to this Parisian murder: he was no more than a 'filthy plagiarist'. The essay was rejected by Blackwood who evidently felt that the joke had run its course.

Leaving Gloucester Place, De Quincey moved with his children into lodgings on Pitt Street, on the coast of the Firth of Forth, where he injected his energies (to the tune of around eighty-five articles) into a Tory newspaper called the *Edinburgh Evening Post*, edited by a trio of hard-line Presbyterian ministers. The family then moved to Porteus's Lodgings, 19 Duncan Street, in the Newington area of the city, where Wilson described finding De Quincey one day dressed in an army coat four times too large for him, and with nothing on beneath. 'You may see I am not dressed,' said De Quincey. 'I did see it,' replied Wilson.

An unlikely friendship blossomed with the newly married Thomas Carlyle, whose German translations De Quincey had bludgeoned in a review for the *London Magazine*. He 'grew pale as ashes at my entrance', Carlyle reported of their first encounter, 'but we recovered him again'. De Quincey was 'essentially a gentle and genial little soul', 'washable away', whose present existence was as a 'kind of "hostage" to his creditors'. The two of them should form, Carlyle suggested, a 'Bog School' to counter the 'Lake School'. 'What wouldn't one give to have him in a Box,' exclaimed Jane Carlyle, 'and take him out to talk!' When she questioned De Quincey's eldest son about his education, William explained that 'his father wished him to learn [Greek] through the medium of Latin and he was not entered in Latin yet because his father wished to teach him from a grammar of his own which he had not yet begun to write'.

Placing Horace and Francis in school at Rydal, Margaret De Quincey, who had never before left her native mountains, now made the journey to Edinburgh with her two youngest children. Here, in the granite city, she became so unhappy that her life was thought to be in danger.

De Quincey's next piece for *Blackwood's*, an essay on 'Rhetoric', was praised by Wordsworth who, despite noting that it contained 'some things from my Conversation', reported to Crabb Robinson that it proved that 'whatever [De Quincey] writes is worth reading'. The London *Athenaeum* considered it good enough to qualify De Quincey for the chair of logic at London University. The position, which De Quincey would have liked, was never offered, and in his 'Sketch of Professor Wilson', written for the *Edinburgh Literary Gazette* in 1829, he made plain his opinion of his friend's philosophical credentials.

The 'Sketch of Professor Wilson' is a summation of De Quincey's style as a biographer. Giving himself the central role, he focused on the opening scene in which he and Wilson were introduced by Wordsworth in the study used by Coleridge: one great literary partnership brought forth another. His description of Wilson's strapping physique was prefaced by a lengthy digression on his own dislike of physical descriptions; on one occasion De Quincey had been shocked to hear Coleridge describe a certain philosopher as 'chicken-breasted'. Wilson's long strides and arched instep eventually received their due praise, along with his masterly management of a runaway bull. As for his features, Wilson's complexion 'was too florid', his yellow hair was 'of a hue quite unsuited to that complexion; eyes not good, having no apparent depth, but seeming mere surfaces'. His house at Elleray was a 'silent commentary' on his 'state of mind': 'At first sight there was an air of adventurousness, or even of extravagance about the plan and situation of the building.' Of Wilson's academic credentials, the university presumably imagined 'that they filled the chair with some peculiar brilliance'.

'I wish you would praise me as a lecturer in Moral Philosophy,' Wilson complained to De Quincey when he read the first instalment. 'That would do me good; and say that I am thoroughly logical and argumentative – for it is true, not a rhetorician, as fools aver.'

———

In February 1829, De Quincey returned to Grasmere. He had agreed to share the mortgage of The Nab with Margaret's father, John Simpson, who owed £900. De Quincey wanted to do something to make his wife happy, but it was a complex arrangement which left him paying interest on a mortgage of £1,400. His attitude to house ownership was relaxed: 'Paying only the annual interest,' De Quincey wrote blithely to Charles Knight, who had expressed surprise at his friend's improved fortunes, 'is what *I* do, can do, and will do.' Margaret reassured the lawyer guaranteeing the loan that: 'from the love that we all bear the place there need be no doubt that we will all of us make any sacrifice rather than engender its loss'.

The eight De Quinceys squeezed into the farmhouse with the nine Simpsons, and Margaret gave birth to her seventh child, a boy called Julius. Taking with him a handful of his progeny, De Quincey decamped to Dove Cottage. He claimed during this time to have written a 400-page novel called *The New Canterbury Tales*, but such a thing was never published and nor has a manuscript been found. In May 1830, after a year of 'milk, milk, milk – cream, cream, cream', De Quincey left his family behind and returned to Edinburgh for good.

At Rydal Mount, Dorothy had collapsed with intestinal pains and it seemed unlikely that she would survive. 'Were she to depart,' said Wordsworth, 'the phasis of my moon will be robbed of light to a degree that I have not courage to think of.' A version of her lived on, but she was no longer the exquisite Dorothy who De Quincey had known. She lost her mind, and for the next thirty years remained a prisoner inside her attic bedroom.

What role did Wordsworth now play for De Quincey? Both men had found fame: Wordsworth's was slow to arrive and De Quincey's had roared in against the tide like the hysterical River Dee. But while De

Quincey had once been rich and Wordsworth poor, the Wordsworths now lived like country gentry and the De Quinceys starved. For want of any other occupation, little Johnny – these days stiffly addressed by De Quincey as Mr John Wordsworth – had become vicar of a parish in Leicestershire. Neither Johnny nor Willy were academically inclined, but Willy, according to his tutor, Hartley Coleridge, was 'a bore'. Dora, Wordsworth's favourite child, replaced Dorothy as amanuensis and virgin sacrifice, and finding themselves unemployed, Dorothy and Sara referred to their home as 'Idle Mount'.

Two letters to Wordsworth survive from this period, in both of which De Quincey apologises for having not received him when he called. In the first, sent from Fox Ghyll in 1823, he blames his 'strange' behaviour on the 'load of labour', and in the second, sent from The Nab in 1829, he blames a fever contracted on the mail-coach from Edinburgh. In both cases Wordsworth was evidently left standing outside while De Quincey cowered in a back room. The litanies of excuses recall those he employed in 1806, when he was dabbling in laudanum and postponing his first encounter with his hero. 'Mr de Quincey, I am sorry to say admits no one on account of illness,' Wordsworth now explained, unaware that he had been dropped as a friend. 'This grieves me much, as he is a delightful Companion and for weightier reasons, he has a large family of young Children with but a slender provision for them.' 'Father called on Mr de Quincey the other evening but was not admitted,' wrote the more sensitive Dora, adding that De Quincey had promised to return the call, but his 'tomorrow' has 'not yet arrived'.

So Wordsworth's role for De Quincey had not changed. An object of terror to begin with, an object of terror he remained. The only difference was that after twenty years, Wordsworth was left knocking on the door.

Holyrood Abbey, where De Quincey lived like 'the ghost of one whose
body had not received the clod of earth to entitle it to rest in peace'.

Same Subject (continued)

> . . . attired
> In splendid clothes, with hose of silk, and hair
> Glittering like rimy trees, when frost is keen.
>
> Wordsworth, *The Prelude*, Book Third

Apart from his friends and relatives and the relatives of his friends, De Quincey owed money to fifty-one tradespeople, including the tin-plate maker, the dance-master, the cobbler, the grocer, the poulterer, the cow-feeder, the brazier, the schoolmaster, the coalman, the confectioner, the glazier, and several booksellers and landlords. For debtors, Edinburgh was the best of towns and the worst of towns. The best because, by ancient Scottish law, Holyrood Abbey offered sanctuary to the pursued, and the worst because, also by ancient Scottish law, the debtor was first 'put to the horn' – a public humiliation whereby, with three blasts of a horn, he was denounced in the market place as a rebel to the king. If he could not then satisfy his creditors, he faced imprisonment – or sanctuary. For De Quincey, who was put to the horn on nine occasions, Holyrood Abbey became a home.

In late May 1830, however, we find him back in John Wilson's house. According to Wilson's daughter Mary, De Quincey turned up in a storm wanting a bed for the night and stayed for a year. She exaggerated: he stayed for six months.* During this time De Quincey wrote like a fury,

---

* Referring to this passage of Mary Wilson Gordon's *Memoir of John Wilson*, Emily Dickinson wrote to her cousins, Louise and Frances Norcroft, 'I wish I could make you as long a call as De Quincey made North.'

piling up pieces for Blackwood who paid him ten guineas per sheet –
a sheet was equivalent to sixteen printed pages – with the promise of
more money if the copy arrived early, which it never did. The Opium-
Eater's appearance in June's 'Noctes' gives us a sense of how Wilson
found his friend's company. 'Mr De Qunshy,' says the Shepherd,

> you and me leeves in twa different warlds – and yet its wunnerfu' hoo we under-
> staun ane anither aes weel's we do – quite a phenomena. When I'm soopin'
> you're breakfastin' – when I'm lyin' doon, after your coffee you're risin' up – as
> I'm coverin' my head wi' the blankets you're pitting on your breeks – as my
> een are steekin' ike sunflowers aneath the moon, yours are glowin' like twa gas-
> lamps, and while your mind is masterin' poleetical economy and metapheesics,
> in a desperate fecht wi' Ricawrdo and Cant [Ricardo and Kant], I'm heard by
> the nicht-wanderin' fairies snorin' trumpet-nosed through the land o' Nod.

Carlyle once described De Quincey's talk as consisting of a 'diseased *acuteness*' and this is precisely what is caught in the 'Noctes'.
'Mr De Qunshy' is an earnest expounder of Coleridgean philosophy
and Wordsworthian wisdom, delivered in a black letter English of
antiquated deliberation and politeness. While he bores the Tickler to
sleep, the Shepherd goads him on – 'I would like to hear ye, sir, con-
versin' wi' Coleridge and Wordsworth – three cataracts a' thunderin''
at once!' – and Christopher North keeps up an academic interest:
'You have been touching, my dear Opium-Eater, on abstruse matters
indeed, but with a pencil of light.' Wilson further teased De Quincey
in a scene where the four friends debate the Wordsworthian crime of
nest-robbing. 'Some one of my ancestors,' says the Opium-Eater, '– for
even with the deepest sense of my own unworthiness, I cannot believe
that my own sins – as a cause – have been adequate to the production
of such an effect – must have perpetrated some enormous – some
monstrous crime, punished in me, his descendant, by utter blindness to all birds' nests.' 'Maist likely,' responds the Shepherd. 'The De
Qunshys cam owre wi' the Conqueror, and were great Criminals –
But did you ever look for them, sir?' 'From the year 1811,' replies the
English Opium-Eater, '– the year in which the Marrs and Williamsons
were murdered – till the year 1821, in which Bonaparte the little – vul-
garly called Napoleon the Great – died of a cancer in his stomach. . .
did I exclusively occupy myself during the spring-months, from night

till morning, in searching for the habitations of these interesting creatures.' De Quincey's preoccupation with the Ratcliffe Highway murders had now become a *Blackwood's* joke.

Back in Grasmere, Margaret and the children had, for reasons unknown,
moved out of The Nab and were now installed in a farm called Lingstubbs
near Penrith, whose landlady had a bevy of children of her own. The infants
squabbled, the rent was late, the bills went unpaid, and Margaret wrote to
her husband threatening to kill herself if he could not settle what was owed.
The most he could earn from *Maga* was £100 a year; in response to her
threat De Quincey sent William Blackwood one of his infamous begging
letters, by which he made everyone other than himself responsible for his
woes: 'She assures me peremptorily that, if I do not hold out some immediate prospect of relief in my promised letter of tomorrow night, her present
application shall be the last letter she'll ever write.' Handed the responsibility of Margaret's continued life, Blackwood advanced the necessary funds –
a practice to which he became accustomed.

In December 1830 De Quincey's wife and bairns arrived in Edinburgh
where they moved into 7 Great King Street, in the New Town; 'a house',
De Quincey blithely explained to Lockhart, 'of that class which implies
a state of expenditure somewhat above the necessities of a needy man
of letters'. The rent was £200 a year. It was here that his three-year-old
daughter Florence was 'first awakened', as she later recalled, to the fact
that she 'had a father'.

———

His frozen debts began to thaw and De Quincey found himself in a fast-
flowing river. In May 1831 a bookseller took action against him for the
sum of £37 16/ 6d. The repayment was somehow made – presumably by
Wilson. On 1 February 1832, De Quincey wrote to Wilson's brother asking for £30 to cover another debt: 'My extremity is complete, for unless in
6 days of course I pay this bill, I am put to the horn.' Again, the debt was
settled, presumably by Wilson's brother. The water company now threatened to cut off his supply unless he paid their bill; De Quincey borrowed
£110 from his sister, and by the summer of 1832 the family had downsized
to a slate-grey Georgian terrace at 1 Forres Street. The new address was kept
secret but De Quincey's whereabouts was discovered, and before dawn on
his forty-sixth birthday he went into hiding to escape arrest. This was the

start of a decade of flight and disappearance as he evaded his pursuers; like all debtors, De Quincey saw himself as a victim of injustice while those to whom he owed money were villainous persecutors. 'It would be dangerous to me, that any servant should know where I am,' he explained to Blackwood, adding that any correspondence sent to Forres Street would be delivered to his secret abode by his twelve-year-old son, Horace.

The man who had once gazed through windows at shining fires was now himself spied upon: a solicitor called William Muir had Forres Street watched for four hours one day, but De Quincey was nowhere to be seen; the next day Muir had the neighbourhood searched but could still 'obtain no trace of him'. Some sources suggested that the debtor might be 'at the Lakes, and others that he was in the environs of Edinburgh'. Officers followed up every report of sightings 'at different times of the day & upon different days, but did not fall in with him'. One officer, having waited a 'whole day in the Meadows where in the Twilight he discovered a person corresponding to the marks given him of Mr De Quincey. . . followed and watched through many turns & windings & finally lost sight of him about the South end of Clerk Street'. Like Poe's 'Man in the Crowd', De Quincey had disappeared into the tumultuous sea of human faces. He was eventually arrested 'near the top of Montague Street'. It is the great inconvenience of poverty, as Hazlitt observed, that it makes men ridiculous.

In September 1832 De Quincey was put to the horn for the first time, for the £10 owed to the landlord of his former lodgings on Duncan Street. Unable to repay the full sum – Wilson had evidently put his foot down – he found himself imprisoned in the Canongate Tolbooth, a damp, black and airless Elizabethan jail at the end of the Royal Mile. He wrote nothing about this experience but within hours he had exploited the loophole of the sick bill, by which prisoners who were dangerously ill could be released on condition that they stayed within the boundaries of the city. He was arrested again the following month, but this time managed to repay the debt.

———

Throughout this hellish year De Quincey produced a roster of essays for *Blackwood's* as well as the Radcliffian novel *Klosterheim; or, The Masque*, which Blackwood published in a single volume – making this the first independent book, as opposed to journalistic paper, that De Quincey wrote. Were *Klosterheim* to succeed, he believed, 'it will deliver me from an abyss of evil into which few have ever descended'.

As a novelist, De Quincey is generally regarded as having failed. 'He cared nothing for delineations of character,' his daughter Florence observed, 'and I do not think he cared much for pictures of modern life.' He was mystified by the Brontës and by Charles Dickens, themselves great admirers of De Quincey, and avoided meeting Thackeray when given the chance. He diagnosed his own disease as one of meditating too much and observing too little; Virginia Woolf put it differently: De Quincey needed to adjust his fictional perspectives 'to suit his own eyesight'; in a De Quinceyan landscape, nothing must 'come too close'. While his heroines were lifeless – literally so, for the most part – and his dialogue dead on the page, De Quincey's plots have propulsion and an anarchic energy gives his narratives a nervous pulse rate. *Klosterheim* centres on the 'purloining' of a 'long and confidential letter' – the idea was to inspire Poe's 'The Purloined Letter' – and the labyrinthine city in which the dramas take place becomes a metaphor for the Opium-Eater's mind. In the novel's midnight masquerade, De Quincey propels us into a 'life below a life' where 'all was one magnificent and tempestuous confusion, overflowing with the luxury of sound and sight'. What distinguishes De Quincey's fiction is its reflection of inward states. From the preface to the *Lyrical Ballads* he learned that the feeling 'gives importance to the action and situation, and not the action and situation to the feeling'. If Southey's poems were Gothic tales in verse, with 'so many lines written before breakfast', De Quincey's Gothic tales were poems, whose length he measured with a ruler. Would Blackwood like another chapter, De Quincey asked? It would be no trouble to dash one off and fling it over to him.

Coleridge admired *Klosterheim* for its 'purity of style and idiom', and told Blackwood that De Quincey had reached 'an excellence to which Sir W. Scott. . . appears never to have aspired'. He would like, Coleridge said, to write to his 'old friend, De Quincey', to tell him so.

————

By 1833 De Quincey had no credit in any shops and was two years in arrears for the rent of Dove Cottage. Losing this house with its hold on the past was too much to bear, and to placate the landlord, John Benson, he offered to pay double the rent, or purchase the place for £130. Benson insisted he leave, and De Quincey, consulting lawyers, won the right to 'stay' until Candlemas 1834. 'For the last fifteen or sixteen days,' he told Blackwood, 'having a family of 12 persons absolutely dependent upon me, I have kept up with the demands upon me for mere daily necessities of warmth – light – food, etc., by daily sales of books at the rate of about 30 for 1s. In that proportion have been my sacrifices; and I have now literally no more to sacrifice that could be saleable.' He did, however, have something more to sacrifice: during this period one of De Quincey's children was kidnapped until a particular debt had been honoured.

On 10 February, Carlyle informed his brother that De Quincey was 'said to be in jail' but, 'at all events', remained 'invisible', and on the 22nd of that month Margaret gave birth to her eighth and final child, Emily. On 29 March, Carlyle told his brother that 'Dequincey [sic], who has been once seen out this winter, sent me word he would come and see me; he will do no such thing, poor little fellow: he has hardly got out his *cessio bonorum*.' *Cessio bonorum* was a declaration of bankruptcy, enabling the debtor to purchase immunity from prison in exchange for yielding up his worldly goods to his creditors. De Quincey's *Cessio bonorum* calculated his goods at £762 9/, and his debts at £617 16/; he included in the list of monies due that Coleridge had owed him £300 since 1807, plus £393 interest. In April, Carlyle told John Stuart Mill that De Quincey had seen 'no man, except Bailiffs, it appears, for the last eighteen months; he is said to be in the uttermost, unaidable embarrassment; bankrupt in purse, and as nearly as possible in mind . . .' De Quincey was, Carlyle added, one of the 'most irreclaimable Tories now extant, despising Poverty with a complete contempt'.

On 23 May both De Quincey and Margaret were put to the horn for the non-payment of rent on 1 Forres Street. The money was found, and two days later the family moved into Caroline Cottage in Doddington, on the edge of the city. Here the unbearable stress of their lives was alleviated by moments of joy. Florence remembered her father, on 'bright summer mornings. . . capturing my baby sister, fresh from the bath. . . and dancing her about the garden, the child with its scanty white raiment and golden head, looking like a butterfly glowing among the trees'. On 14 August, the day before his forty-eighth birthday, De Quincey went 'suddenly' into hiding, 'in expectation of a process of arrest', and remained invisible until

2 September. A few days later, the De Quinceys' youngest son, Julius, died in his mother's arms. Most wretched of all for Margaret was that she believed the boy's fever had broken and had not realised that his struggles, 'which she had supposed to be expressions of resistance to herself, were the struggles of departing life'. She never ceased to reproach herself for having appeared, when Julius last looked up at her, displeased with him. There was nothing, De Quincey afterwards said, more painful than the death of a child between three and five years old; it was vital to believe that the lives of those who died young had been happy ones, and that they departed this world knowing they had been loved. This had not been the case with Julius; De Quincey was haunted by the discovery, 'which but for the merest accident I never *should* have made – that [Julius's] happiness had been greatly disturbed in a way that afflicted me much'.

With Julius in the churchyard laid, the De Quincey children were now seven. On the day of the funeral De Quincey had to flee Caroline Cottage to avoid arrest and later that month The Nab was sold by auction. Inevitably, he had missed his first mortgage repayment; his mother sent £180 to cover the second and third repayments, subtracting the sum from her son's regular allowance, and De Quincey came up with madcap schemes to enable the Simpsons to keep their home. Foreclosure, however, was inevitable. In a vicious letter, Margaret's brother accused De Quincey of 'swindling' them all, and the house that had been in the Simpson family for generations was now lost to them. Within weeks, Margaret had lost both her child and her childhood home. Shortly afterwards her mother also died, and Margaret's father and half-witted uncle joined the De Quincey household in Edinburgh.

In November De Quincey was put to the horn once more, this time for non-payment of his daughters' music lessons. That month he took advantage of sanctuary and placed himself in accommodation with Mr Brotherton, landlord of one of the hovels in the precincts of Holyrood Abbey. It was the second time in his life that De Quincey had made his home in a monastery.

To live without money, said Hazlitt in 'On the Want of Money', 'is to live out of the world'. Holyrood was a world outside the world; it had its own government, its own court, its own prison, its own economy, its own streets and shops and small-town life; it even had its own wild terrain – Holyrood Park contained one half of Duddingston Loch and all of Arthur's Seat, a dormant volcano with a panoramic view of the city. Having paid the bailie (or governor) two guineas, the inmates – known as the 'Abbey lairds' – could roam within a radius of six miles, and from midnight on Saturday until midnight on Sunday they were free to leave the precinct without fear of arrest, frequently returning in full flight from their creditors as the clock struck twelve. Architecturally, Holyrood resembled the Priory but in other ways the life of an Abbey laird was like that of an Oxford undergraduate, not least because the university operated a similar curfew. In a rare sighting of him inside the abbey, William Bell Scott described De Quincey as resembling 'the ghost of one whose body had not received the clod of earth to entitle it to rest in peace'. Meanwhile, De Quincey's 'growing son' – most likely William – was 'getting well into his teens like an uncared-for dog'.

Caroline Cottage was on the edge of the abbey boundary, but to avoid harassment De Quincey did not return during his first few weeks in Brotherton's lodgings. We find him back home in the spring of 1834, but after being horned once more he returned to Holyrood. Sanctuary did not come free: De Quincey needed to find twelve guineas a month to cover the rents for Brotherton and for Caroline Cottage, and both fell into (or rather, began in) arrears. He was now unable to buy either ink or opium and could not leave Holyrood 'without very urgent danger' as 'emissaries are on the watch in all directions'. In April 1834 he was put to the horn again – for an unpaid book bill – and sued by a servant for her wages. In June he was sued by the grocer, and he exchanged Brotherton's lodgings for 'miserable' rooms with Miss Miller, where his vast family, to save on rent, joined him. To write in peace, De Quincey rented another set of rooms within the abbey from a Miss Craig. On two occasions in 1834 he was sued in Holyrood's own court for non-payment of rent to Miss Miller and Miss Craig, and he only narrowly avoided the shame of being imprisoned within the sanctuary itself.

On the eve of the 1832 Reform Act, William Tait, the radical son of a builder, launched a journal to rival *Blackwood's*. The purpose of *Tait's*

Edinburgh Magazine was to provide a voice for the new electorate: while *Blackwood's* was for the educated elite, *Tait's* was for the common man. Despite his aversion to Jacobins, De Quincey – nothing if not Janus-faced – approached Tait, and it was Tait who encouraged his new author to write about himself. Blackwood, who continued to commission De Quincey, turned a blind eye to the Opium-Eater's duplicity.

His first essay for *Tait's*, which appeared in December 1833, was an anonymous sketch of 'Mrs Hannah More', who had died, aged eighty-eight, in August that year. 'I knew Mrs Hannah More tolerably well,' De Quincey began, 'perhaps as well as it was possible that any man *should* know her who had not won her confidence by enrolling himself amongst her admirers.' The low temperature of his praise was maintained throughout. 'Mrs H. More,' said De Quincey, was an egotist surrounded by fawning acolytes; himself impatient of such characters, he 'never paid her a compliment'. Nor did he express any interest in her works, and he 'appeared', in her presence, not 'to know that she was an author'. As a friend and neighbour of 'a lady' with 'whose family' De Quincey 'maintained a very intimate acquaintance', Hannah More had been introduced to him in Wrington in 1809; nothing was said about this 'lady' being the author's mother (one of the fawning acolytes) or about De Quincey's having first met Mrs H. More in Bath in 1798. Nor was there any reference to her as the person who had introduced De Quincey to Wordsworth's 'We Are Seven'. On the contrary, listed amongst Hannah More's crimes was her boast that she had 'foresworn' poetry along with 'pink ribbons', as though poetry were a childish indulgence rather than 'the science of human passion in all its fluxes and refluxes'.

Beneath the mockery of Hannah More lay depths of nostalgia. De Quincey's prose is propelled by his pleasure in returning to the subject of his youth, his pride in having rubbed shoulders with fame. The full texture of his tone only becomes apparent when we remember the conditions under which he was writing: this was a man in freefall recalling the days when he had nothing to lose.

In 'Tintern Abbey', Wordsworth had moved back and forth between the quiet present and the turbulent past. In Holyrood Abbey, De Quincey did the opposite. Liberated from *Maga's* macho pugilism, from now until the end of his life De Quincey's subject was a lost paradise.

In February 1834 he began a series of twenty-five essays which would run
in *Tait's* over the next seven years. Initially called 'Sketches of Men and
Manners from the Autobiography of an English Opium-Eater', they were
eventually known as *Autobiographic Sketches*. De Quincey's childhood was
a fairy tale: 'I was born in a situation the most favourable to happiness
of any, perhaps, which can exist; of parents neither too high nor too low;
not very rich, which is too likely to be a snare; not poor, which is often-
times greater.' His father was a merchant with a copious library and his
mother was well born; his boyhood days were passed in large houses with
an abundance of servants, and the family income was £6,000 a year. De
Quincey recalled his disruptive elder brother; how Greenhay had been
sold at a loss; how his guardians had 'grossly mismanaged' his fortune;
how his mother had moved to Bath; how, on the 'most heavenly day in
May', he 'beheld and first entered' the 'mighty wilderness' of London;
and how he had travelled across a turbulent Ireland.

De Quincey's most striking feature as an autobiographer was his
romanticisation of first times. Here he was in tune with the age he was
recalling. Coleridge's mariner had been 'the first that burst into that silent
sea'; Keats had described 'On First Looking into Chapman's Homer';
and Hazlitt had recorded in his 1823 essay, 'My First Acquaintance
with Poets', how, as a youth, he had walked ten miles in the mud to
hear, for the first time, Coleridge preach. The *Autobiographic Sketches*
contain a catalogue of first times – 'It was, I think, in the month of
August, but certainly in the summer season, and certainly in the years
1807, that I first saw [Coleridge]'; 'It was in the year 1801, whilst yet
at school, that I made my first literary acquaintance'; 'It was in winter,
and in the wintry weather of 1803, that I first entered Oxford. . .'; 'It
was on a November night, about ten o'clock, that I first found myself
installed in a house of my own – this cottage, so memorable from its
past tenant to all men'; 'It was at Mr Wordsworth's house that I first
became acquainted with (then Mr) Wilson, of Elleray'. De Quincey
described the first time he experienced loss as a child, his first coach
journey as a boy, the first time he read *Lyrical Ballads* and, for the first
time, he mentioned the death from hydrocephalus of his sister. It was at
that point, he revealed, that he had become a 'nympholept'.

He would write several versions of his autobiography, each one
more impassioned than the last. Here, in the pages of *Tait's*, there are

no wheels announcing the arrival of his dying father, and no zeniths, vaults, or Sarsar winds accompanying the death of Elizabeth, an event then seen as less important than the loss of the family income.

All of De Quincey's writing grew out of Wordsworth but it was *The Prelude* that provided the seed for his *Autobiographic Sketches*. De Quincey's theme, like that of Wordsworth, was the history of 'what passed within me'. Wordsworth's revolutionary France became De Quincey's revolutionary Ireland, the 'blank confusion' of Wordsworth's London defined De Quincey's chaotic city; De Quincey's essays on Oxford rework Wordsworth's 'Residence at Cambridge'. 'Writing where I have no books,' De Quincey confessed, 'I make all my references to forty years' course of reading, by memory'. A relic of English Romanticism imprisoned in Victorian Scotland, De Quincey's memories were in full flow when, in July 1834, he heard that Coleridge, his role model in failure, had died.

Since 1816 Coleridge had been living in the Highgate home of his doctor, James Gillman. Here his opium intake was monitored, he was pampered by Mrs Gillman, and he was whisked off by the family on seaside breaks. His friends had initially complained at his withdrawal from the world, but Coleridge needed a sanctuary. He would never be entirely free of opium, but under the Gillmans' loving care he reduced his intake and, piece by piece, let go of the past. For the last chapter of his life he experienced stability, and his thinking took on renewed energy. In 1819 his reputation was sealed by a review in *Blackwood's*. 'The reading public of England,' wrote Lockhart, '. . . have not understood Mr Coleridge's poems as they should have done.' Coleridge was 'the prince of superstitious Poets. . . he stands absolutely alone among the poets of the most poetical age'.

Visiting Coleridge in 1824, Carlyle had found 'a fat flabby incurvated personage, at once short, rotund, and relaxed, with a watery mouth, a snuffy nose, a pair of strange, brown, timid, yet earnest looking eyes, a high-tapering brow, and a great bush of grey hair'. From Highgate Hill, Carlyle later wrote, this figure looked 'down on London and its smoke-tumult like a sage escaped from the inanity of life's battle; attracting towards him the thoughts of innumerable brave souls still engaged

there'. Seeming twenty years older than he was, Coleridge had become
a legend of a bygone age. Admirers made their pilgrimage to Highgate,
just as De Quincey had made his own pilgrimage to Bridgwater. 'To
the raising spirits of the young generation,' said Carlyle, Coleridge 'had
this dusky sublime character; and sat there as a kind of Magus, girt in
mystery and enigma.'

When Lamb, his oldest friend, heard of the death of Coleridge, 'it
was without grief. It seemed to me that he had long been on the con-
fines of the next world – that he had a hunger for eternity. I grieved then
that I could not grieve.' Did De Quincey grieve, or did he grieve that he
could not grieve? He later claimed that he and Coleridge had not been
friends, 'not in any sense, nor at any time', but this was untrue. Only
two years before his death, Coleridge had described De Quincey to
Blackwood as his 'old friend'. A fragile early friendship had developed
into a relationship which was more strange and less easy to define. As
Richard Holmes puts it, De Quincey saw in Coleridge something 'dangerous and elemental, a demonic elder brother or *doppelgänger*'.

During his Shakespeare lectures at the time of the Ratcliffe Highway
murders, Coleridge had described how, at sunset or sunrise on the highest of Germany's Harz Mountains, climbers could see a giant spectre
surrounded by a glowing halo. The 'apparition of the Brocken', as the
spectre is called, is a vast projection, caused by light and cloud, of the
climber's own shadow: his terrifying vision is of himself. The experience,
Coleridge concluded, is akin to being in the audience of a Shakespeare
play: here too, 'every man sees himself, without knowing that he does
so. . . you only know it to be yourself by similarity of action'. He had
also described his own effect on De Quincey: when De Quincey looked
at Coleridge, he knew it to be himself by similarity of action.

De Quincey's most immediate reaction on hearing of Coleridge's
death must surely have been that the poet owed him money. He, who
had once helped Coleridge without waiting to be asked, was now
reduced to begging. While De Quincey was on the run from creditors, Coleridge's shirts had been laundered, his dinners cooked, and his
health fussed over by devoted friends in a handsome house overlooking
Hampstead Heath. However bad things became for Coleridge, there had
always been a mattress for him to fall upon. He had enjoyed the patronage of the Wedgwoods, the hospitality of the Morgans, the devotion of

the Gillmans. As Coleridge span around Germany and Malta and the British Isles, his wife and children were warm and comfortable at Greta Hall, being tended to by Southey. De Quincey, equally erudite, equally articulate, equally troubled, had never been supported by anyone, and his own wife and children had been snubbed by his friends.

The month after Coleridge's death, De Quincey's eldest son, William – the 'uncared-for dog' – was taken ill. First he lost his hearing and then he lost his sight; his eyes protruded and were covered by a 'film of darkness'. The feverish boy had terrible dreams where, De Quincey believed, 'the recollection of some family distresses seemed to prey upon his mind'. He died on 25 November 1834. De Quincey believed that William had hydrocephalus, but the surgeons who opened his skull were unable to diagnose the cause of death. He had only just turned eighteen, dying at the same age as the uncle he was named after. A scholar of Greek and a lover of books, William was the child who most resembled his father. 'Upon him,' De Quincey said, 'I had exhausted all that care and hourly companionship could do to the culture of an intellect.' He considered publishing his son's commentary on Suetonius but his 'heart retreated under the hopelessness' of the scheme. All said and done, William's accomplishments were no greater than those of young men 'of every generation for the last two centuries', who have had 'their names murmured over' before sinking 'into everlasting silence and forgetfulness'.

Instead, De Quincey threw himself into work: 'I believe that in the course of any one month since that unhappy day I have put forth more effort in the way of thought, of research, and of composition, than in any five months together selected from my previous life. Thus at least (if no other good end has been attained) I have been able to instruct my surviving children in the knowledge that grief may be supported.' One month before the death of William De Quincey, William Blackwood had also died, and the following year the death of James Hogg would bring to an end the golden age of the 'Noctes Ambrosianae'.

De Quincey's essays on Coleridge, which ran from September 1834 until January 1835, might have diverted from the theme of his *Autobiographic Sketches* but instead they continue the story, describing

how the Opium-Eater went from being a maker to a destroyer of icons.
It was here that De Quincey described his evening with Thomas Poole
in 1807, where Coleridge was unmasked as a man who presented the
ideas of others as his own. Having revealed Poole's doubts about the
originality of Coleridge's table talk, De Quincey provided his readers
with a lengthy list of further 'borrowings' from German philosophers
that he alone had been able to detect in Coleridge's works. He was
right about Coleridge's thefts – scholars still grapple with the reasons
why an intellect as magnificent as his should lean so extensively on the
thoughts of others – but to unmask him in this way was an act of violence on De Quincey's part, born of utter despair. Having desecrated
the church, however, he continued to worship: 'I will assert finally,
that, after having read for thirty years in the same track as Coleridge, –
that track in which few of any age will ever follow us, such as German
metaphysicians, Latin schoolmen, thaumaturgic Platonists, religious
Mystics, – and having thus discovered a large variety of trivial thefts, I
do, nevertheless, most heartily believe him to have been as original in
all his capital pretensions, as any one man ever as existed; as Archimedes
in ancient days, or as Shakespeare in modern.'

Moving from scholarly competitiveness to backstairs gossip, De
Quincey suggested that Coleridge had always preferred the company
of Dorothy Wordsworth to that of his own wife, Sarah. Dorothy, De
Quincey conceded, had 'no personal charms' but 'still, it is a bitter trial
to a young married woman to sustain any sort of competition with a
female of her own age, for any part of her husband's regard, or any share
of his company'. De Quincey himself, meanwhile, owed 'no particular
civility' to Mrs Coleridge, who had once 'insulted. . . a female relative
of my own', a woman vastly her 'superior' in 'courtesy and kindness'.
The relative was Margaret. De Quincey rolled relentlessly forward: 'I
am the last person in the world to press harshly or uncandidly against
Coleridge, but I believe it to be notorious that he first began the use of
opium, not as a relief from any bodily pains or nervous irritations – for
his constitution was strong and excellent – but as a source of luxurious
sensations.' Self-indulgence rather than physical suffering was therefore
the cause of Coleridge's addiction. As for his lectures on the fine arts,
his black-lipped performance at the Royal Academy 'was a poor reflection of jewels once scattered on the highway by himself'.

De Quincey told the truth about Coleridge and in doing so gave us an angel riven by demons, a figure in whom fatal weakness combined with preternatural power. Excepting Hazlitt, no one understood Coleridge's thought so well as De Quincey, who navigated without difficulty through the mists of the mariner's mind. In 1825 Hazlitt had published a collection of twenty-five portraits called *The Spirit of the Age*. Nothing was said, in his sketch of Coleridge, about Hazlitt's own friendship with the poet, which had turned sour over politics. Instead he gave a brilliant account of his subject's intellectual development which reached a devastating conclusion: 'What is become of all this mighty heap of hope, of thought, of learning and humanity? It has ended in swallowing doses of oblivion and in writing paragraphs in *The Courier*.' De Quincey, another mighty heap of hope reduced to hackery and the pursuit of oblivion, trumped Hazlitt by creating a likeness of such vibrancy that other portraits appear pallid by comparison. Coleridge had died a 'ruin', De Quincey concluded, but he was nonetheless irreplaceable: 'Worlds of fine thinking lie buried in that vast abyss. . . Like the sea it has swallowed treasures without end, that no diving bell will bring up again.' De Quincey's Coleridge is touching, troubled, haunted; he is a man you want to meet and who, for a moment, you feel that you have met.

The responses of Coleridge's family and friends were various. For Sara Coleridge – to whom De Quincey had betrothed himself when she was a little girl – her father's mind was '*too* much in the mirror of [De Quincey's] own'. Refusing to believe that he 'had any enmity' towards Coleridge, Sara praised De Quincey for characterising his 'genius and peculiar mode of discourse with great eloquence and discrimination. . . indeed he often speaks of his kindness of heart'. For her brother, Hartley, De Quincey was 'an anomaly and a contradiction. . . he steals the aristocratic "de"; he announces for years the most aristocratic tastes, principles and predilections, and then goes and marries the uneducated daughter of a very humble, very coarse, and very poor farmer. He continues to be, in profession and in talk, as violent a Tory and anti-reformer as ever, and yet he writes for Tait. He professed almost an idolatry for Wordsworth and for my father. . . and yet you see how he is treating them!' Thomas Poole himself complained that De Quincey's memory '*must be incorrect*' because he, Poole, had 'never considered Coleridge a plagiarist'. Southey, erupting in what Carlyle described as 'Rhadamanthine rage', denounced De Quincey as 'one of the greatest scoundrels living'. 'I have told Hartley Coleridge,' Southey fumed to Carlyle at a dinner party, 'that he ought to take a strong cudgel, proceed straight to Edinburgh, and give De Quincey, publicly in the streets there, a sound beating – as a calumniator, cowardly spy, traitor, base betrayer of the hospitable social hearth.' De Quincey's crime, according to Southey, was against hospitality. Wordsworth's response, expressed to Coleridge's literary executor, J. H. Green, was that De Quincey was a stalker: 'It is not to be doubted that [De Quincey] was honoured by Mr C's confidence, whose company he industriously sought, following him into different parts of England: and how he has abused that confidence, and in certain particulars, perverted the communications made to him, is but too apparent from this obnoxious publication.'

From his mother De Quincey received a scolding for writing 'in a disreputable magazine on subjects and in spirits afflicting to your real friends'. His lapse of taste, Mrs Quincey assumed, was down to 'opium delirium'.

De Quincey's final word on his relationship with Coleridge can be found buried in an essay for *Tait's* on 'Milton v Southey', which appeared in 1847. 'Any of us,' he wrote, 'would be jealous of his own duplicate; and, if I had a doppelgänger, who went about personating me, copying me, and pirating me, philosopher as I am, I might. . . be so far carried away by jealousy as to attempt the crime of murder upon his carcass. But it would be a sad thing for me to find myself hanged; and for what, I beseech you? for murdering a sham, that was either nobody at all, or oneself repeated once too often.'

The subject of this passage was ostensibly Wordsworth, who had no equal. 'If you show to Wordsworth a man as great as himself, still that great man will not be much like Wordsworth – the great man will not be Wordsworth's doppelgänger.' De Quincey, meanwhile, now had his own American duplicate, a man who went about personating, copying and pirating him. His name was Edgar Allan Poe.

———

Now resuming his *Autobiographic Sketches*, De Quincey explained that he had 'not mentioned, in the "Opium Confessions", a thousandth part of the sufferings I underwent in London and in Wales. . . Grief does not parade its pangs, nor the anguish of despairing hunger willingly count again its groans or its humiliations.' His current grief, anguish and despairing hunger were more real and far worse than anything he had known in 1802, but De Quincey would never describe them in his journalism.

He eventually gave up the lease of Dove Cottage in the summer of 1835. The house rendered up for him, he wrote, 'echoes of joy', of 'festal music' and 'jubilant laughter', the 'innocent mirth of infants' and the 'gaiety, not less innocent, of youthful mothers', but alongside the 'reverberation of forgotten household happiness' were the 're-echoing records of sighs'. Closing the door of the cottage after his final visit, De Quincey felt 'the weight of a world' fall from his shoulders. 'I now possess my mind,' he told Tait, 'heretofore I was under a possession.'

His precious books, papers and letters were taken to Lingstubbs, the Penrith farmhouse in which Margaret had been so unhappy, where they snowed up another set of rooms. Three years later, having despaired of receiving any rent, the landlord of Lingstubbs put them up for sale. De Quincey's letters to Margaret, and quite possibly his diary from Everton days, were perused by prospective purchasers, and his library was sold.

'Yet in the lowest deep,' he would write in his tale 'The Household Wreck', 'there yawns a lower deep.'

The death that year of Uncle Penson filled him with hope: he would surely be remembered in the old man's will. It was not to be. The £100 annuity he had already been receiving he continued to receive, added to which he inherited his uncle's clothes, household linen and crockery. Furious, De Quincey lashed out at his mother: 'Not only has she absorbed 2/3rds of my father's fortune, but she has intercepted the whole of a second, and almost the whole of a 3rd (my uncle's). All these it is true come eventually. . . to myself. . . Now if all men had mothers living to ages so excessive and mothers by strange coincidence of accident absorbing one estate after another, who would escape embarrassment?' For Tait, De Quincey submitted an uncharitable account of his time in Everton in the company of William Roscoe, James Currie and William Shepherd.

His family were back in Holyrood in November 1836 where Margaret caught typhus, commonly known as jail fever. On 7 August 1837, aged forty-one, she died; later that day, De Quincey was sued for the sum of £12 1/ 8½d. Florence, aged ten when she lost her mother, described her father as 'unhinged' by sorrow and by 'the overwhelming thought of being left with a family of such differing ages and needs, and with no female relative at hand to help him'. He had been drinking in Eton when Ann disappeared and taking laudanum in London when Catherine Wordsworth died: De Quincey was at least with his wife when her life ended in the debtors' sanctuary, miles away from her Lakeland home.

Margaret De Quincey, like Mary Wordsworth, has come down to us as a phantom wife. De Quincey leaves little sense of her character, but from Florence we have a moving description of her mother's effect on the few who knew her: 'Delicate health and family cares made her early withdraw from society, but she seems to have had a powerful fascination for the few friends she admitted to intimacy, from an old char-woman who used to threaten us, as though it were guilt on our part, "Ye'll ne'er be the gallant woman ye're mither was", to a friend who had seen society in all the principal cities of Europe, and who, with no reason for exaggeration, has told us he had never seen a more gracious or a more beautiful lady than our mother.'

Grief, De Quincey wrote in the introduction to his series of 'Letters from a Modern Author to his Daughters', cannot be shared. Like opium, it locks us up inside our own citadels. The sole consolation for 'those who weep in secret for the vanished faces of their household' is 'love'.

De Quincey's love was countered by guilt and Rhadamantine rage, which found expression in his now open hatred of Wordsworth. In a letter to Tait, he described how, twenty-five years ago, his voice had 'trembled with anger' toward this man 'because he could not see the loveliness of a fair face now laid low in the dust'. Wordsworth had been 'indifferent' to 'an angelic sweetness in that face and an innocence as if fresh from Paradise which struck my own eyes with awe as well as love. I may say that I perfectly hated him for his blindness.' He might have been talking about little Catherine Wordsworth, whose beauty he also accused Wordsworth of having been blind to: De Quincey's dead loved ones all blend into one angelic form. Margaret's life had been hard, but not because Wordsworth was blind to the loveliness of her face. Whether or not she took tea with Mary Wordsworth will have been of less concern to Margaret than whether her children had enough to eat, but De Quincey fixated on the idea that his wife's suffering was due to social exclusion. The contrast between Wordsworth's treatment of the abandoned Margaret in *The Excursion* and his treatment of her soul sister, Margaret De Quincey, was too much for De Quincey to bear. He now idealised his married life, seeing it as a lost Eden. He forgot that Dorothy had been kind to Margaret in her hour of need, and that Wordsworth had called on at least two occasions and been refused entry. All De Quincey remembered was that his wife had been cut and that he, who had shared in the Wordsworths' own family sorrows, received no consolation from Rydal Mount following the wreckage of his own household.

De Quincey was now on the run from Holyrood, where he owed rent to Miss Craig and Miss Miller, and from his filial responsibilities, 'a burden which I could not carry, and which yet I did not know how to throw off'. His eldest surviving child, eighteen-year-old Margaret Thomasina, took over the care of her siblings while her father hid in the second-floor apartment of 42 Lothian Street, the home of a Frances Wilson and her sister, Miss Stark. The building contained six similar apartments, accessible by a common staircase. From now on, the city of Edinburgh became De Quincey's sanctuary from the abbey. He was blessed in his new abode; Lothian Street was in a seedy part of the Old Town, composed of dwelling houses and worn-out shops, but Mrs Wilson and Miss Stark were cultivated and kind, and they treated their bereaved tenant with maternal tenderness. Left alone to write until six o'clock, De Quincey enjoyed 'insulated' evenings where, in 'the soft splendour' of lamplight, he sat in the company of his landladies. His month here was described by him as the happiest he had 'known in a long, long time'. For Florence, left behind in the Holyrood 'hole', her father had 'deserted' his family, escaping 'for his own enjoyment'. His whereabouts was eventually discovered by a former washerwoman at the abbey who 'pursued' De Quincey's son Fred through the streets. De Quincey did not reveal his next address to his children, 'for they have too little presence of mind and too little discretion'.

He found solace in blame, but also in writing. From his Lothian Street hideaway he poured his complex of emotions into 'The Household Wreck', which was published by *Blackwood's* in January 1838. The hero of the story, whose name we are not given, has a tall and 'dovelike' wife called Agnes who hails from the mountains. Described, using Wordsworth's phrase, as 'A perfect woman, nobly planned,/ To warn, to comfort, to command', Agnes is seventeen when they marry and the couple move to a town many miles from her home. They are as happy as Adam and Eve, and the husband, who owes 'no man a shilling', reads to his wife from *Paradise Lost*. But beneath their joy is unrest: he has 'never ridded myself of an overmastering and brooding sense, shadowy and vague, a dim abiding feeling. . . of some great calamity travelling towards me. . . perhaps even at a great distance, but already dating from some secret hour – already in motion upon some remote line of approach'. He describes this calamity as 'the juggernaut of social life', a thing which 'pauses not for a moment to spare, to pity, to look aside, but rushes forward for ever'. This juggernaut careered into their lives on a spring day when Agnes went into town to do some errands. In an hour, it 'accomplished the work of years'.

Waiting for Agnes to return home, her husband becomes increasingly anxious. Hours pass by until 'suddenly a sound, a step: it was the sound of the garden gate opening, followed by a hasty tread. Whose tread? Not for a moment could it be fancied the dread step which belonged to that daughter of the hills – my wife, my Agnes. No; it was the dull, massy tread of a man; and immediately there came a blow upon the door, and in the next moment, the bell having been found, a furious peal of ringing. . . Who will go to the door? I whispered audibly. Who is at the door?'

It is a policeman with the news that Agnes has been accused of stealing lace in a haberdashery. She is thrown into a Piranesian jail, 'vast, ancient, in parts ruinous', where debtors and criminals live cheek by jowl, and whose population is further swollen by the presence of the debtors' families. While she awaits trial, her husband contracts typhus from the mobs around the prison gates and sinks into a fever. During his two months of delirium their son dies of the same fever and his wife's fame grows to the point where all the world is talking of her case.

Did Agnes steal the lace? Theft, her husband reflects, is a crime of the lower classes which reflects badly on the man who should be the family's provider. Nonetheless he finds himself doubting her innocence. 'She is, or she is not, guilty,' he tells himself, 'there is no middle case.' The court finds her guilty and sentences her to ten years hard labour, but her then husband learns that Agnes was set up by a villain called Barratt whose sexual advances she had rejected. 'Wrath, wrath immeasurable, unimaginable, unmitigable' now burns at his heart 'like a cancer'. Aided by an under-jailer called Ratcliffe, he helps his wife to escape but she dies soon afterwards. Barratt then confesses his crime and is lynched by the mob. 'My revenge,' says the hero, 'was perfect.'

'The Household Wreck' is a tale of terror whose strength lies in the husband's half-conscious sense that it is he and not Agnes or Barratt who is the guilty party: the cause of his wife's suffering and death. In *Suspiria de Profundis*, De Quincey would describe how as a child 'the crime which might have been was in my mind the crime which had been' and the vertiginous possibilities of this scenario are dramatised here. Wanting to tell a tale of grief, he describes instead only impotence and rage; rather than protect his wife, his narrator wallows in self-pity: 'misery has a privilege,' he says, 'and everywhere is felt to be a holy thing'. He battles with the past 'as though it were a future thing and capable of change'. As in a dream, 'The Household Wreck' refigured the elements of De Quincey's waking life: Agnes is found guilty of the crime De Quincey had accused Coleridge of committing; when his wife needs him, her husband is absent, coming ham-fisted to her rescue only when it is too late. The presence of a man called Ratcliffe is a reference to the other household wrecks by which De Quincey was haunted.

Hamlet-like, the hero of 'The Household Wreck' is an avenger unable to act. De Quincey now wrote another tale for *Blackwood's* on the same theme, which he called 'The Avenger'. Here the hero, Maximilian Wyndham, returns to his native Germany from fighting at Waterloo. A series of vicious murders takes place in the city where he lives, one of the victims being Maximilian's own young wife, who is called Margaret. In each case the murderer enters the house of the victim and slaughters its occupants. With a killer at large, the fear of the locals is compared to 'that which sometimes takes possession of the mind in dreams – when one feels one's-self sleeping alone, utterly divided from all call or hearing of friends, doors open that should be shut, or unlocked that should be triply secured, the very walls gone, barriers swallowed up by unknown

abysses, nothing around one but rail curtains, and a world of illimitable night, whisperings at a distance, correspondence going on between
darkness and darkness, like one deep calling to another. . .'

Thus De Quincey brings the terror inward, turning it into an opium
trance. The murderer is revealed to be Maximilian himself, avenging
the slaughter of his Jewish family, carried out by the same dignitaries
many years earlier. As in 'The Household Wreck', the city has two faces;
what seems to its other inhabitants to be a 'perfectly average' place is
experienced by Maximilian as 'a place of dungeons, tortures and tribu-
nals of tyrants'.

———

While their father made himself invisible, De Quincey's children delivered his messages and manuscripts. They were instructed to be light on
their feet but on 'three separate times', he complained to Tait in April
1838, 'in three separate lodgings, I had been traced by the emissaries
of my creditors; and always through the carelessness of my children,
who suffered themselves to be followed unconsciously'. His winged
offspring became a familiar sight: one bookseller recalled how 'Mr De
Quincey's young, fair-haired English laddies' came on their father's
behalf to ask for loans, and his copy was delivered to Tait by a daughter
who would throw the package into the room and shout 'There!' before
rushing off.

What can it have been like to have De Quincey as a father? Florence,
on whom 'the main burden fell', left a vivid description. Running his
errands, she got to know the 'north and south banks of the Canongate,
George the Fourth Bridge, the cross causeway &c as hideous dreams,
my heart rushing into my mouth with the natural terrors of footsteps
approaching and rushing down again into my shoes when left to quiet
and the ghosts'. The fear he had of his children being followed was,
Florence felt, a source of pleasure to De Quincey. 'It was an accepted
fact among us that he was able when saturated with opium to persuade
himself and delighted to persuade himself (the excitement of terror
was a real delight to him) that he was dogged by dark and mysterious
foes.' This way her father absolved himself of guilt for absconding from
Holyrood, a 'home without any competent head where truly no home

should have been, and where as truly he could by no possibility have done any work had he remained'.

As far as De Quincey's children were concerned, there was no 'reality' to his 'groanings unutterable about creditors and enemies'. We know from the records that there was a great deal of reality to these groanings, but Florence's sense of things reminds us that, for those who knew him, De Quincey lived in a paranoid world of his own construction. This same love of 'concealment and lurking enemies', she believed, explained why her father would allow no help in arranging his financial affairs. Some of De Quincey's friends 'gave up under the impression things were too bad to be meddled with, others that there was nothing to be arranged, others – which was the truth – that he didn't like to have them arranged as it disturbed the prevailing mystery in which he delighted'.

Throughout these years, Wilson's life had been running alongside De Quincey's on parallel tracks. In the year that Margaret died, Wilson lost his own wife, after which he left Edinburgh, and from now on he and De Quincey saw one another only sporadically. For Florence, their friendship was 'an illustration of Coleridge's, "Alas, they had been friends in youth", each indebted to the other at critical periods of their improvident lives for kindly help, perhaps not admitted as generously as they might have been by Professor Wilson when he was the successful man'.

The January 1839 edition of *Tait's* opened with an essay called 'Lake Reminiscences, from 1807–1830, By the English Opium-Eater, No 1 – William Wordsworth'. Building on the success of his portrait of Coleridge, De Quincey now promised to provide his readers with 'sketches of the daily life and habits' of the whole Wordsworth circle. What followed would cross-pollinate biography with gossip, literary criticism and local history, but it was as autobiography that De Quincey saw his 'Lake Reminiscences', which he later grouped together in his collected work under the title *Autobiographic Sketches with Recollections of the Lakes*. A black comedy about a Messiah who rejects his disciple, the 'Lake Reminiscences' might be seen as a parodic inversion of Boswell's *Life of Johnson*.

It was now that De Quincey, the avenger, described the deep, deep
magnet of William Wordsworth, his longing to meet the poet, his delay
of four and a half years, his first sighting of Dove Cottage, the day on
which he saw his hero descending down the garden path and the night
that followed, 'the first of my personal intercourse with Wordsworth',
which was also 'the first in which I saw him face to face'. 'In 1807 it
was,' De Quincey's 'Lake Reminiscences' began, 'at the beginning of
Winter, that I first saw William Wordsworth.'

Autobiographic Sketches had borrowed *The Prelude*'s narrative frame,
but in 'Lake Reminiscences' De Quincey used his first-hand knowledge
of the poem to prove his intimacy with the poet. Despite Wordsworth's
current 'slovenly' appearance, wrote De Quincey, he had 'assumed the
beau' at Cambridge, donning silk stockings and powdering his hair,
and the first time he got 'bouzy' was when he visited the Christ College
rooms which had once been occupied by Milton. Wordsworth's own
college rooms, De Quincey revealed, had been above the kitchen, where
from 'noon to dewy eve, resounded the shrill voice of scolding from the
female ministers of the head cook'. These Boswellian details, presented
as the fruits of private conversations, were gleaned from 'Residence at
Cambridge', Book Third of the unpublished *Prelude*.

De Quincey's moment of glory was yet to come. 'And here I may
mention,' he revealed to the readers of *Tait's*, 'I hope without any breach
of confidence, that, in a great philosophic poem of Wordsworth's, which
is still in M.S., and will remain in M.S. until after his death, there is,
at the opening of one of the books, a dream, which reaches the very ne
plus ultra of sublimity.' He was referring to the dream of the Arab in
Book Fifth. In De Quincey's account of these lines the poet, reading
Don Quixote by the sea, falls asleep and dreams that coming towards
him across the sands is an Arab on a dromedary. In his hands are two
books. One is Euclid's *Elements* and the other 'is a book and yet not
a book, seeming, in fact, a shell as well as a book, sometimes neither,
and yet both at once'. Applying the shell to his ear, the dreamer hears
a prophecy that the world will be destroyed by flood. The Arab is on
a 'divine mission' to bury the books and thus save 'two great interests
of poetry and mathematics from sharing in the watery ruin'. Thus he
continues on his way, 'with the fleet of waters of the drowning world
in chase of him'.

De Quincey's readers will have found in his various writings versions of Wordsworth's dream before. The Malay who appeared at Dove Cottage was another Arab dream, while in the *London Magazine* De Quincey had recalled Walking Stewart advising him to bury his most precious books 'seven or eight feet below the surface of the earth'. De Quincey doubted that his betrayal of Wordsworth's trust, which today would land him in court, could 'in any way affect Mr Wordsworth's interests', but few things could be more irritating to the poet than to discover that the contents of his yet unpublished masterpiece had been stolen from him and spilled out in a piece of popular journalism.

The first of the 'Lake Reminiscences' ended with a cliffhanger: 'I acknowledge myself,' De Quincey revealed, 'to have been long alienated from Wordsworth. Sometimes even I feel a rising emotion of hostility – nay, something, I fear, too nearly akin to vindictive hatred.' His great 'fountain of love' for the poet and 'all his household' had dried up, and he found himself 'standing aloof, gloomily granting (because I cannot refuse) my intellectual homage'. On whose side did the fault lie? On Wordsworth's, 'in doing too little', or on De Quincey's 'in expecting too much'? Both were to blame, De Quincey suspected. He then announced that for the next instalment he would 'trace, in brief outline, the chief incidents in the life of William Wordsworth': few biographies have begun in such a manner.

De Quincey was not, like Hazlitt, a great hater. In his essay 'On the Pleasure of Hating', Hazlitt argued that 'Love turns, with a little indulgence, to indifference or disgust: hatred alone is immortal.' But had De Quincey felt hatred alone towards Wordsworth he could never have described his colossal ego with such clarity, nor could he have explored so well the impact of colliding with such a thing. His subject in the 'Lake Reminiscences' is not vindictive hatred but disappointed love. In one passage he described:

> The case of a man who, for many years, has connected himself closely with the domestic griefs and joys of another, over and above his primary service of giving to him the strength and the encouragement of a profound literary sympathy, at a time of universal scowling from the world; suppose this man to fall into a situation in which, from want of natural connections and from his state of insulation in life, it might be most important to his feelings

that some support should be lent to him by a family having a known place and acceptance, and what may be called a root in the country, by means of connections, descent, and long settlement. To look for this, might be a most humble demand on the part of one who had testified his devotion in the way supposed. To miss it might – but enough. I murmur not; complaint is weak at all times; and the hour is passed irrevocably, and by many a year, in which an act of friendship so natural, and costing so little, (in both senses so priceless,) could have been availing.

Wordsworth has never been granted the same biographical immediacy as Coleridge, and without De Quincey he would have remained for us a distant figure in a black coat. The comic details in the 'Lake Reminiscences' allow him that vital extra dimension: Wordsworth, De Quincey revealed, had not been an amiable child, and nor did he make a performance of gallantry around women: 'a lover. . . in any passionate sense of the word, Wordsworth could not have been'. There are memorable portraits of him slicing through the uncut pages of De Quincey's new copy of Burke with a buttery knife, beating down the rent of Allan Bank when the chimneys smoked, and growing prosperous on the back of benefactors, patrons, legacies and bequests. Any need for money, De Quincey noted, was met by a convenient death; when Wordsworth's family began to increase, a wealthy uncle, feeling 'how very indelicate it would look for him to stay any longer', promptly departed this world. Those standing in Wordsworth's way politely 'moved off', for fear of being bumped off. Wordsworth's business sense was immaculate: 'Whilst foolish people supposed him a mere honeyed sentimentalist, speaking only in zephyrs and bucolics, he was in fact a somewhat hard pursuer of what he thought fair advantages.' Hazlitt's sketch of the poet in *The Spirit of the Age* described, without De Quincey's personal animosity, the same chill arrogance ('He admits of nothing below, scarcely of anything above, himself'), the same dismissal of other writers ('He condemns all French writers. . . in the lump'), and the same disengagement with the world beyond nature ('If a greater number of sources of pleasure had been open to him, he would have communicated pleasure to the world more frequently'). Hazlitt was indifferent to Wordsworth's indifference towards him; his mastery lay in evaluating the poet's character as though it were lines of verse. De Quincey's own mastery lies in the vulnerability of his anecdotes, the friction between biographer and subject, the focus on himself as the receiving consciousness. For all his Greek, he was a born journalist. 'The truth and life of these Lake Sketches,' gasped Mary Russell Mitford when she put down her copy of *Tait's*, 'is wonderful.'

We are also indebted to De Quincey for the best portrait of Dorothy that we have. 'A happier life, by far, was hers in youth,' he rightly said, comparing the woman whose dawn had 'fleeted away like some golden age' to 'the Ruth of her brother's creation'. The man to whom Ruth had 'dedicated her days' had abandoned her, and De Quincey implies that Wordsworth did the same. 'Miss Wordsworth suffered not much less than Coleridge,' De Quincey boldly declared.

He was able to reveal a good deal about the Wordsworths, but there was a good deal De Quincey did not know. He was unaware of Wordsworth's French mistress, Annette Vallon, and his illegitimate daughter, Caroline; he knew nothing of Coleridge's love for Sara Hutchinson; he believed – wrongly – that Dorothy had spent much of her childhood with the royal family in Windsor Castle. He depicted himself as both inside and outside the magic circle: at one point he called himself Wordsworth's 'sole visiting friend' in the tight community of the vale, and at another he described the surfacing of a memory which brought with it a 'pang of wrath': walking with Wordsworth and Southey, the subject of Charles Lloyd, then seriously ill, had arisen. Wordsworth said something which De Quincey did not hear; when asked to repeat his comment, Wordsworth replied that 'in fact, what he had said was a matter of some delicacy, and not quite proper to be communicated except to *near friends of the family*. This to me! – O ye gods – to me. . .'

It is easy to imagine De Quincey alone in his Lake adventures, but he is accompanied throughout by a huge yellow-haired man who shares his every experience and mirrors his every attitude. Whether they were travelling together, sharing a room, or sharing a bed, De Quincey and Professor Wilson would fall into 'a confidential interchange of opinions upon a family in which we had both so common and so profound an interest'. 'Let me render justice to Professor Wilson as well as myself,' De Quincey writes after describing Wordsworth's ingratitude: 'not for a moment, not by a solitary movement of reluctance or demur, did either of us hang back in giving the public acclamation which we, by so many years, had anticipated. . .' 'I shall acknowledge then on my own part,' De Quincey says elsewhere, 'and I feel that I might even make the same acknowledgement on the part of Professor Wilson,' that while they both treated Wordsworth 'with a blind loyalty of homage' which had 'something of the spirit of martyrdom', to 'neither' has he repaid such 'friendship and kindness'. Of the poet's marriage, 'to us who. . . were Wordsworth's friends, or at least intimate acquaintances – viz., to Professor Wilson and myself – the most interesting circumstance. . . the one which perplexed us exceedingly, was the very possibility that it should ever have been brought to bear'. Of Dorothy: 'All of us loved her, by which *us* I mean especially Professor Wilson and myself. . .' It is with a tribute to the poet's sister that the essays on Wordsworth end: 'Farewell, impassioned Dorothy! I have not seen you for many a day – shall never see you again, perhaps; but shall attend your steps with tender thoughts, so long as I hear of you living: so will Professor Wilson.'

Wordsworth would claim not to have read De Quincey's recollections of him in *Tait's*, which ran between January and August 1839, and he was probably telling the truth. His response to their appearance was to state that De Quincey had forced himself upon the family from the start: 'My acquaintance with him,' said Wordsworth, flicking away an afternoon fly, 'was the result of a letter of his own volunteered to me.'

On a Sunday evening in the late summer of 1839, De Quincey called at the home of one of his creditors, a solicitor called McIndoe who lived at 113 Princes Street. Two of De Quincey's sons had lodged here from February to May that year, and he still owed the McIndoes rent. While Mrs McIndoe repaired their guest's torn coat, the men talked. By twelve o'clock the coat was not yet mended; it was too late to 'leap the boundary' of sanctuary and so De Quincey was given a bed for the night in a chamber next to the dining room.

The following month he was still there. Mrs McIndoe now sued him for the unpaid rent and De Quincey bolted back to Holyrood, where Miss Miller was also in pursuit of payments. Ricocheting between irate landladies, De Quincey returned to Princes Street with his hoards of books, letters and manuscripts – including 'about 8 separate works' by Giordano Bruno, bought back in 1809, and 'one or two' other books, 'equally rare' – where he stayed for the next three years. During this time he developed a horror of the McIndoes, whom he regarded as his jailers. The McIndoes felt equally trapped by De Quincey. Were he to have sold his editions of Bruno, De Quincey would have been a free man, but he would not part with them for 'a thousand guineas'.

While he described himself as 'persecuted' by McIndoe's 'hostile attitude' and his 'violent attempts' at 'ejection', McIndoe hung on De Quincey's promises of payment. So bitter were relations in the Princes Street household that at various points the two parties communicated only by letter, and in the third person. 'Mr McIndoe. . . requests that Mr De Quincey shall remove tonight for he is resolved that no further communication shall take place between them on this subject and that before 10 o'clock, so as to prevent any unnecessary steps being taken,' wrote McIndoe, pushing the missive beneath De Quincey's door. McIndoe's object, De Quincey explained in desperation to Blackwood's son, Robert, who was now editing *Maga*, was to 'possess himself of my papers, and hold those as a means of extracting money *ad libitum*'. It was stalemate. 'If I am to go away at this moment,' argued De Quincey, 'I should draw upon myself a sort of legal persecution which at present would be ruinous. I wish to stay a month longer.' And if McIndoe put him to the horn, De Quincey would simply bounce back into and out of sanctuary. De Quincey saw himself not as a betrayer of trust but as a victim of extortion: McIndoe received whatever money his tenant earned, often directly from Blackwood himself, but he always demanded more. 'I spend months after months in literary labour,' De Quincey told Blackwood in despair:

I endure the extremity of personal privations; some of which it would be humiliating to describe; (but by way of illustration I may mention – that having in a moment of pinching difficulty for my children about 10 months since pawned every article of my dress which could produce a shilling. I have since that time had no stockings, no shoes, no neck-handkerchief, coat, waist-coat, or hat. I have sat constantly barefoot; and being constitutionally or from the use of opium unusually sensible of cold, I should really

have been unable to sit up and write but for a counterpane which I wrap
round my shoulders).

Blackwood, 'pained beyond measure' by this letter, sent De Quincey
£4.

The McIndoes, on their own downward slope, were also pawning
their belongings: 'I suppose that a more absolute wreck of decent prosperity never can have been exemplified,' De Quincey grandly observed
of the couple. 'If I give him nothing, he will immediately take occasion
to write me a violent letter full of abuse. He will insist on my leaving his
house. No matter what rights I may afterwards establish in law, he will
obtain his immediate object of retaining my Papers – now a vast body,
far above portability.' Back in Holyrood, Miss Miller – 'for vindictive
purposes' – held out the same threat.

Tracing the growth of one of his debts as it is recorded in Miss
Miller's passbook, which contains records of De Quincey's accounts
between 3 May 1836 and 14 August 1840, Horace Eaton, the best of
his biographers on the business of money, allows us to watch a seed
sprout into Jack's beanstalk:

> Beginning with the small sum of £2 3s., small considering that De Quincey
> had apparently been living under her roof for two years, the amounts owed
> varied from month to month. It was increased by charges for milk and
> vegetables, by small loans, by the use of Miss Miller's credit with grocers
> when De Quincey's credit was nil. It reached £33 in April 1837, in spite of
> occasional payments; falling to £12 in May, rising through 1838 and 1839,
> until when the rooms were finally surrendered, it reached the not inconsid-
> erable sum of £175 4s. 2d. This debt troubled De Quincey until his death
> and was finally settled by his executor.

To get a sense of the scale of De Quincey's difficulties, we must imagine
acre upon acre of similar saplings.

'Caught and chained' by his papers, De Quincey dared not leave his
room. The scene is reminiscent of his childhood in Greenhay, when he
had been placed under arrest by his brother William ('Who could put
you under arrest?' he had then imagined his guardian saying; 'A child
like *you*?') A relative of the McIndoes, visiting their house as a girl,

remembered with awe the closed door behind which the mysterious tenant sat writing. 'The last body who went into that room,' the servants teased, 'was put up the lum [chimney] and never came out.' De Quincey's door creaked open only to receive his meals which, because his teeth were mostly gone, consisted of tea, coffee, sops of bread and tender slivers of mutton. Fascinated, the girl once managed to peep inside the room and see the famous ocean of paper. Meanwhile, Mrs McIndoe, whom De Quincey suspected of 'tampering with locks, listening, eaves dropping', shook any letters that arrived for him in case they contained money. One of these was from Branwell Brontë: affected by *Confessions* and himself now an opium-eater, Brontë sent De Quincey a poem and some translations of his own. The previous year Branwell had made the pilgrimage to Grasmere where he knocked on the door of Hartley Coleridge, the present incumbent of The Nab. Too preoccupied to take much notice of his young acolyte, De Quincey did not reply.

———

It was while he was imprisoned by the McIndoes that De Quincey returned to the subject of household murder. His 'Second Paper on Murder Considered as One of the Fine Arts', composed as a letter from XYZ to Christopher North, appeared in *Blackwood's* in November 1839, at the same time as *Tait's* was running De Quincey's 'Lake Reminiscences'. For those subscribing to both journals, the murder story and the Wordsworth story could be read alongside one another.

'A good many years ago,' XYZ began, 'you may remember that I came forward in the character of a *dilettante* in murder.' Few readers will have remembered De Quincey's first murder essay, written twelve years before. Fewer still will have remembered the Ratcliffe Highway murders to which he once again referred. XYZ reveals that he has a 'horribly ambitious' nephew who fancies himself 'a man of cultivated taste in most branches of murder'; the boy's ideas on the subject, says his uncle, are all 'stolen from me'. Not all murders, XYZ goes on to explain, are in 'good taste'; like statues, paintings and 'epic poems', they each 'have their little differences and shades of merit'. A career as a murderer is a downward path, 'for if once a man indulges himself in

murder, very soon he comes to think little of robbing; and from robbing he comes next to drinking and Sabbath-breaking, and from that
to incivility and procrastination'.

One of the connoisseurs, known from his misanthropical disposition as 'Toad-in-the-hole', despairs of modern murder: 'Even dogs are
not what they were, sir – not what they should be. I remember in my
grandfather's time that some dogs had an idea of murder. . . but now. . .'
Holding the French Revolution responsible for the degeneration in his
art, Toad-in-the-hole retires from society in 1811. It is widely assumed
he has hanged himself, but one morning in 1812 he is seen cleanly
shaved and gaily attired, 'brushing with hasty steps the dews away to
meet the postman'. The cause of his jollity is 'the great exterminat-
ing chef-d'oeuvre of Williams at Mr Marr's, No 29 Ratcliffe Highway'.
What took place twelve nights later, at Mr Williamson's, was by 'some
people pronounced even superior', but Toad-in-the-hole demurs. 'One,
perhaps, might suggest the Iliad – the other the Odyssey: what do you
get by such comparisons?' In celebration of Williams's achievement, a
splendid dinner is given by the society to which all the connoisseurs
are invited. Toasts are drunk to 'the sublime epoch of Burkism and
Harism', to 'Thugs and Thuggism', to the Syrian assassins, and the
Jewish Sicarii.

Jaded and depressed, De Quincey was recycling earlier work: returning to the paper turned down by Blackwood in 1828, he re-hashed his
joke about murder being the tip of the moral iceberg. In the rejected
paper, Williams had been described by a Frenchman as a 'plagiarist';
here it is the nephew of XYZ who steals his uncle's ideas.

But if 'On Murder Considered as One of the Fine Arts' had been
an imitation of a *Blackwood's* essay, De Quincey's 'Second Paper on
Murder' was an imitation of the first. The 'Second Paper' was no more
than nostalgia: his friendship with John Wilson was exhausted and
Christopher North, to whom XYZ's letter was addressed, belonged to
a bygone age. Like Toad-in-the-hole, De Quincey was looking back to
his golden years and in publishing the piece, *Blackwood's* was doing the
same. The jubilation of the connoisseurs following the Thurtell case,
described in 'On Murder', is repeated in the 'Second Paper' as jubilation at the Williams murders. The difference between the two published papers is plain: in 'On Murder' the murderer is a poet; in the

'Second Paper', the murderer is a plagiarist. No longer a portrait of Wordsworth, the murderer looked more like De Quincey himself, in his motiveless malignity.

———

Throughout 1840 De Quincey continued to write his 'Lake Reminiscences'. Having told the story of his first acquaintance with Wordsworth, Coleridge and Southey, he now wrote four essays on the 'Society of the Lakes', which appeared in *Tait's* between January and August. Here the vale described by Wordsworth as a maternal embrace was unveiled as an assemblage of 'afflicted households'. Along with De Quincey's account of Charles Lloyd's 'utter overthrow of happiness' are a litany of other grim Lakeland tales, including the story of a man named Watson who murdered his mother 'by her own fireside'; a Miss Smith who was saved from falling down a ravine by a figure in white who she assumed to be her sister but discovered was a ghost; and the dream described to De Quincey by a local woman in which 'a pale and bloodless' footman 'appeared to be stealing up a private staircase, with some murderous instruments in his hands, towards a bedroom door'. He told the tale of the Maid of Buttermere, seduced and abandoned by a fraud posing as 'The Hon. Augustus Hope', and explained that the mountainous landscape inspired some 'remarkable suicides', including that of a 'studious and meditative young boy, who found no pleasure but in books, and the search after knowledge'. The history which made the greatest impact on De Quincey was that of Sally Green's parents, who fell down a ravine on Easedale during a storm, leaving in the snow 'the sad hieroglyphics of their last agonies'. Six children were still living at home; and Sally, their twelve-year-old daughter, was taken on by the Wordsworths – fatally, so De Quincey believed – as a servant.

The 'Lake Reminiscences' end with the death of Catherine Wordsworth, whose 'nature and manners' contained a 'witchery', which made De Quincey 'blindly, doatingly, in a servile degree, devoted'. The child, he revealed to his readership, 'in a manner lived with me at my solitary cottage; as often as I could entice her from home, walked with me, slept with me, and was my sole companion'.

De Quincey's account of his estrangement from Wordsworth appeared not in the 'Lake Reminiscences' but as diversion in an essay for *Tait's* on 'Walking Stewart', which appeared later that year. By attaching himself so unthinkingly to his idol, De Quincey explained, he had 'committed a great oversight. Men of extraordinary genius and force of mind are far better as objects for distant admiration than as daily companions.' There were traits of Wordsworth's character which were 'painful and mortifying'. A man was entitled to his pride, but 'something there was, in the occasional expression of this pride, which was difficult to bear'. Wordsworth would allow no one's opinion but his own; on occasions when others spoke 'he did not even appear to listen'.

De Quincey was floundering. Refusing to recognise the role played by opium, he pinned the breakdown in relations on the business with Mary Dawson, his 'selfish housekeeper' who in 1812 had denied Dorothy access to the cottage during one of De Quincey's trips to London. How could the Wordsworths have believed these orders came from De Quincey himself? And 'why . . . upon discovering such forgeries and misrepresentations' did they not 'openly and loudly denounce them for what they were?' Having been falsely accused by the Wordsworths, De Quincey's innocence was never acknowledged. But then again, he conceded, 'after the first year or so' his friendship with Wordsworth had hardly developed anyway. Wordsworth had 'no cells in his heart for strong individual attachment', as 'poor Coleridge' also realised, whose rupture with his former collaborator was now described by De Quincey in detail and at length. Other reasons were proffered for the waning of his 'blind and unquestioning veneration': Wordsworth did not like Mrs Radcliffe's novels or Schiller's 'Wallenstein', he had not even read Walter Scott. De Quincey might, he concluded, have left Grasmere altogether were it not for Margaret Simpson.

This is the last he says, in any of his writings, about his adult life. De Quincey, whose experiences were always pre-scripted, had no script for what happened next. Having described his London adventures in his *Confessions*, his childhood and youth in his *Autobiographic Sketches*, and his early acquaintance with Wordsworth and Coleridge in his 'Lake Reminiscences', his tale now comes to a sudden end. It is as if, having reached the top of the stairs, he found himself looking down a void and from this point on he referred to himself in terms only of his dreams and reveries. The reason he says nothing more about the external world is because, from 1813, De Quincey no longer lived there: from now on he inhabited a word-packed world within himself and drowned in rivers of oblivion.

———

Edinburgh was killing him. In late February 1841, as the sky was beginning to crimson, he packed into a single trunk as many of his papers as would fit, hired a porter to help him with the load, and slipped like a fugitive out of the McIndoes' house. A free man at last, De Quincey launched himself into the dawn of a new day.

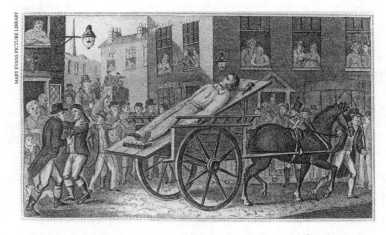

John Williams: connoisseur, dandy, aesthete and scourge of God.

14

Postscript

> Our meddling intellect
> Misshapes the beauteous form of things –
> We murder to dissect.
>
> Wordsworth, 'The Tables Turned'

De Quincey went fifty miles west to Glasgow. Here, in what its citizens called the second city of the British Empire, he hid in the home of John Pringle Nichol, professor of astronomy at the university. 'Address under cover, if you please,' De Quincey instructed Robert Blackwood. A month later he moved into the house of Edward Law Lushington, the university's professor of Greek. Lushington – who went on to become one of De Quincey's late, great, friends – had been a Cambridge contemporary of Tennyson and was now engaged to marry the poet's sister, Cecilia.

But two days after arriving at Lushington's, De Quincey was back in Edinburgh, arrested – under the name of 'T. E. Manners Ellis' – at the instigation of Frances Wilson, the landlady of 42 Lothian Street, the house in which he had been so well looked after. How many other names did De Quincey hide behind? We can assume that there were many. In April he was in Glasgow once more, this time in lodgings on the high street, and from here he took a 'mean room' in the house of a college officer called Thomas Youille at 79 Renfield Street, an austere avenue in the city centre. A kindly man, Youille was soon turned by his tenant into a second McIndoe. 'It is often shocking,' De Quincey observed of Youille and his wife, 'to witness the struggle between their good nature on the one side and on the other their failing power with their growing vexation.' During his two years at Renfield Street, De Quincey was ill with purpura, a condition in which blood haemorrhages into the skin. His legs turned scarlet and purple and he was unable to lift either arm; he existed, as one of his visitors noted, in a 'half torpid condition under opium'.

Meanwhile Mrs McIndoe had discovered his whereabouts, and De Quincey temporarily found movement enough in his limbs to flee. Undeterred, she tracked him 'from lodging to lodging, and took advantage of the hours when she knew I was not at home, to procure admission to my rooms'. He was being pursued by this irate woman, De Quincey shamelessly explained to Professor Nichol, as the result of a 'violent but hopeless attachment. . . which [he] could not reciprocate'.

In November 1841 he scrawled on a scrap of envelope: 'I am in the situation of a man holding on by his hands to the burning deck of a ship. . . This is the *End*.' In May 1843, Youille gave him an ultimatum: either pay the rent or go. Leaving his papers as promise of payment, De Quincey closed the door on another lodging.

———

The previous August his children had been ejected from Holyrood. Taking a lease on an eight-room cottage called Mavis Bush near Lasswade, seven miles outside of Edinburgh, they now took control of their lives. Here the sisters lived in what their father described as 'the most absolute harmony I have ever witnessed'. Using his annuity to pay off debts, Margaret Thomasina raised Florence, Emily and Paul Frederick, while Francis began an apprenticeship in Manchester and Horace, an ensign with the 26th Regiment (a position costing De Quincey a mighty £700), sailed to China to fight with the British in the Opium Wars. They described Mavis Bush as 'paradise', but their lives were not without stress. Writing in 1858, Charles MacFarlane remembered how De Quincey's abandoned children went 'begging about the village for food, and looking both sickly and hungry. . . The minister and his wife supplied their immediate wants, and then we raised a small fund for them in Edinburgh, where their father has had his hand in nearly every man's pocket.' Doubtless, concluded MacFarlane – who had 'lost all patience' with the man – De Quincey will spin 'eternal sentences about the strength, depth, and unimaginable vivacity of his paternal affections'. But from now on, De Quincey treated his daughters as idealised mothers, while he embraced old age as a second childhood.

For years Margaret Thomasina was plagued by creditors who, hearing that the family were no longer in sanctuary, beat a path to the door of Mavis Bush cottage, and as a result of these 'persecutors' though still in her twenties she suffered two haemorrhages. De Quincey feared his daughter would die, as he put it, from 'the misery of her situation. She is entirely guiltless of wrong; and I, unless I can do something effectual and sudden, shall feel myself in part the cause.' Margaret lived on, but at the end of 1842 he heard that Horace had died of sickness in Hong Kong. De Quincey's own opium wars now began.

Returning to Midlothian, he based himself at Mavis Bush where, for the third time in his life, he fell prostrate before his dark idol. Descending to a daily dose of 5,000 drops of laudanum, he could sink no further. 'Through that ruin, and by help of that ruin,' he afterwards wrote in a series of extraordinary letters to Lushington, 'I looked into and read the latter states of Coleridge. His chaos I comprehended by the darkness of my own, and both were the work of laudanum. It is as if ivory carvings and elaborate fretwork and fair enamelling should be found with worms and ashes amongst coffins.' It is a memorable image of the destruction of a delicate and finely cast mind. He was increasingly preoccupied by Coleridge; the poet had often 'spoken to me of the dying away from him of all hope. . . Then I partly understood him, now perfectly.' De Quincey imagined escaping from a 'maelstrom roaring for him in the distance'; in his dreams he saw through 'vast avenues of gloom those towering gates of ingress which hitherto had always seemed to stand open, now at last barred against my retreat, and hung with funeral crape'. The Dark Interpreter returned to his side, a 'symbolic mirror' reflecting the dreamer back to himself.

Reducing his daily drops, he fell 'from purgatory into the shades of a deeper abyss', but still he persisted. By November 1844 he was describing to Lushington 'the tremendous arrears of wrath still volleying and whirling round me from the retreating opium. Its flight is Parthian; flying it pursues.' On Christmas Day he recorded in his diary how, at 'about 7 p.m.,' it 'first solemnly revealed itself to me that I am and have long been under a curse. . . Oh dreadful! By degrees infinitely worse than leprosy.' His revelation echoes the belated discovery ten years earlier, on giving up the lease of Dove Cottage, that he had been 'under a possession'. Admitting that opium was 'at the root of all this unimaginable hell', he took the first steps towards recovery.

'Conquer it I must by exercise unheard of,' he told himself, 'or it will conquer me.' Addicts often use exercise as an aid to recovery, but De Quincey's feet gave way beneath him. Unable to walk as far as Edinburgh, he instead staggered round and round the garden, measuring his circuits; after ninety days he had completed, he estimated, one thousand miles. It has been convincingly suggested that De Quincey suffered from a neurological condition known as restless legs syndrome, characterised by a creeping sensation in the feet and calves and an urgent need for the legs to 'yawn', particularly at night. Today it is treated with gentle exercise, lifestyle changes and the drugs used for Parkinson's disease; De Quincey suppressed the symptoms with opium.

After eight months of steady reduction he discovered, he told Lushington, 'in the twinkling of an eye, such a rectification of the compass as I had not known for years'. Two days later he relapsed, 'but that no way alarmed me – I drew hope from the omen'. He returned to the image of the whirlpool; no longer 'carried violently by a headlong current', he was 'riding as if at anchor, once more dull and untroubled, as in days of infancy'. 'Silently, surely,' De Quincey 'descended the ladder'. He had in his hand the 'true key' to recovery, and 'even though a blast of wind has blown the door to again, no jot of spirits was gone away from me. I shall rise as one risen from the dead.'

In late 1844, De Quincey, now aged fifty-nine, jotted down preparatory notes for 'A New Paper on Murder as a Fine Art'. His murder essays always take us to the seabed of his psyche, and he now proposed that our most glorious murderers – like John Williams 'who murdered the baby' – should be commemorated as public statues. This thought flowed into another, aimed at Wilson: 'Note the power of murderers as fine-art professors to make a new start, to turn the corner, to retreat upon the road they have come.' De Quincey's concern in this paper was less with murder or plagiarism than poverty and the camouflage of the crowd. Obscurity, he continued, 'throws a power about a man, clothes him with attributes of ubiquity. . .

The privilege of safe criminality, not liable to exposure, is limited to classes crowded together like leaves in Vallombrosa' – the image is from Milton – 'for *them* to run away into some mighty city, Manchester or Glasgow, is to commence life anew.' Concealment was an art he had learned in 1802, as a grubby Romantic on the streets of London. In a riff about authorship as a criminal activity, he now imagined two writers – doubtless himself and Wilson – who were so prolific that 'at fifty they had forgotten much of their own literary villainies, and at sixty they commenced with murderous ferocity a series of answers to arguments which it was proved upon them afterwards that they themselves had emitted at thirty'. The lives of these 'self-replying authors' had come full circle: it was as though, he said, they had found themselves in 'the Whispering Gallery at St Paul's', where secrets committed to the walls were 'retaliated . . . in echoing thunders'.

In another terrifying idea, De Quincey suggested that there were, 'living at this moment', men who had 'figured in so many characters, illustrated so many villages, run away from so many towns, and performed the central part in so many careers, that were the character, the village, the town, the career, brought back with all its circumstances to their memories, positively they would fail to recognise their own presence or incarnation in their own acts and bodies'. He himself was one such man, Wilson was another.

De Quincey's line, or cycle, of thought was becoming clear: we cannot escape the past, but nor are we identical with the selves we once were.

In the most poignant of his notes for the 'New Paper on Murder', De Quincey tells the story of a sultan who dips his head into a basin of enchanted water and finds himself transposed to another world. Born into poverty, he marries for love, sires seven children, struggles to bring them up, goes through 'many persecutions', and eventually, walking on the beach, 'meditating some escape from his miseries' he bathes in the sea. 'Lifting up his head from the waves,' he finds himself 'lifting up his head from the basin'. The life he had just lived lasted for thirty-three seconds.

Leaving the paper unfinished ('opium-eaters', De Quincey once explained, 'though good fellows upon the whole, never finish anything'), he sent Robert Blackwood a review of the *Life of Samuel Taylor Coleridge*, by the poet's former doctor and landlord, James Gillman. 'There is a thing deader than a door-nail,' he began. 'Dead, more dead, most dead is Gillman's Coleridge – dead, deader, deadest, is volume the first.' Nowhere in these pages could De Quincey find the unequalled figure who had 'cruised over the broad Atlantic of Kant and Schelling, of Fitch and Oken'. Nor could he find a satisfying account of the effect of opium on the 'faculty of self-revelation'. Coleridge, De Quincey mocked, spoke of his opium-eating as both 'a thing to be laid aside easily and forever in seven days', but also as 'the scourge, the curse, the one almighty blight which had desolated his life'. It was neither so easily discarded nor so powerful a foe: 'Opium gives and it takes away. It defeats the *steady* habit of exertion; but creates spasms of irregular exertion.' Opium killed the poet in Coleridge, but it fuelled the philosopher. There was a great deal to say about the poppy's power in 'dealing with the shadowy and the dark', but neither Coleridge nor his biographer would say it. The task was left for De Quincey to complete.

For *Tait's*, he now wrote a critical assessment of Wordsworth. Next to 'On the Knocking at the Gate in *Macbeth*', 'On Wordsworth's Poetry' was to be De Quincey's finest piece of literary criticism. He began by warning against confusing the poetry and the poet: 'Put not your trust in the intellectual princes of your age', he intoned; it is 'safer to scrutinise the words of eminent poets than long to connect yourself with themselves'. The difference between Wordsworth's personal limitations and the boundless splendours of his writing would never cease to shock him. It was De Quincey's first disillusionment and would be his last; it was also his greatest critical insight. 'Form no connections too close,' he continued,

> with those who live only in the atmosphere of admiration and praise. The love or friendship of such people rarely contracts itself into the narrow circle of individuals. You, if you are brilliant like themselves, or in any degree standing upon intellectual pretensions, such men will hate; you, if you are dull, they will despise. Gaze, therefore, on the splendour of such idols as a passing stranger. . . but pass before the splendour has been sullied by human frailty, or before your own generous admiration has been confounded with offerings of weeds, or with the homage of the sycophantic.

Follow one thread in this knot of resentments and De Quincey suggests that it was not he who hated Wordsworth for being less than his poetry, but Wordsworth who hated De Quincey for being too brilliant. Follow another, and De Quincey implies that Wordsworth despised him for not being brilliant enough; a third thread leads to the proposal that it is

Wordsworth's frailty, rather than any frailty on his own part, which was the cause of De Quincey's disappointment.

Putting aside his own passions, De Quincey now assessed Wordsworth's treatment of such things. The poet's genius, he argued, lay in approaching passion indirectly, in 'forms more complex and oblique, when passing under the shadow of some secondary passion'. For example, 'We Are Seven' is a poem 'which brings into day for the first time a profound fact in the abysses of human nature – viz. that the mind of an infant cannot admit the idea of death, cannot comprehend it, any more than a fountain of light can comprehend the aboriginal darkness'. Wordsworth 'flashes upon' the girl who has lost two siblings, and 'whose fullness of life could not brook the gloomy faith in a grave', the 'tenderest of images of death'. He thus forces a connection between 'death and its sunny antipole'. The effect, De Quincey said, was the 'influx of the joyous into the sad, and of the sad into the joyous'.

He now moved on to the first part of *The Excursion*, in which Margaret's husband, due to what De Quincey described as 'mere stress of poverty', deserts his family. If 'We Are Seven' mirrored his childhood grief, here, laid out accusingly, was his married life, and De Quincey duly went to his own defence. Wordsworth's treatment of the abandoned Margaret is, he argued, 'in the wrong key' and rests 'upon a false basis'. In his excessive loftiness, the Wanderer managed to overlook the practical side of human sympathy. Rather than philosophising over her poverty, he might more usefully have given Margaret a guinea. And could he not have done something for her dying baby? The child lay crying, De Quincey drily noted, 'whilst the philosopher was listening at the door'.

De Quincey ends by rehearsing Wordsworth's former ignominy ('Forty and seven years it is since William Wordsworth first appeared as an author. Twenty of those years he was the scoff of the world. . .' etc.) and anticipating his death: 'He has entered upon his seventy-sixth year. . . he cannot be far from his setting; but his poetry is only now clearing the clouds that gathered about its rising.' As a 'meditative poet', De Quincey concluded, William Wordsworth has only one equal: William Shakespeare.

This same issue of *Tait's* contained an unsigned review of Edgar Allan Poe, whose poem 'The Raven', about a tapping at his chamber door, had that year appeared to acclaim. Poe, for whom the Opium-Eater was one of 'the first men in England', had praised *Confessions* as a feast in which 'the ludicrous is heightened into the grotesque: the fearful coloured into the horrible: the witty exaggerated into the burlesque: the singular wrought out into the strange and mystical'. *Confessions* is reworked in 'The Man of the Crowd'; *Klosterheim* inspired both 'The Masque of the Red Death' and 'The Purloined Letter'; Poe satirised the *Blackwood's* house style, and, in 'Diddling Considered As One of the Exact Sciences', he parodied the murder essays. He joked that the *Confessions* had been written by Juniper, his pet baboon, and in 'The Murders on the Rue Morgue', Poe aped De Quincey's obsession with the tigerish John Williams by unveiling his own murderer as an escaped orang-utan.

But it was in his 1839 short story 'William Wilson' that Poe tapped most unnervingly into the De Quinceyan mindset. 'William Wilson', whose name combines all the Williams in De Quincey's imagination – William Wordsworth, William Quincey, William De Quincey, John Williams, John Williamson and John Wilson – thinks his 'patronymic' (son of William) 'very common', and his first name 'plebeian'. To protect his identity, he is writing this personal history under a pseudonym which sounds like, but is not quite, William Wilson. Having been raised in an ancient house in England, he starts school on the same morning as another boy with the same name, who was born on the same day and imitates him in all things. Thus William Wilson is forced to hear twice as often the names he so despises. Horrified by the coincidence, he runs away and lives a drunken and debauched life during which he is stalked by his doppelgänger. At a masquerade ball where they appear dressed in the same outfit, William Wilson stabs the other William Wilson, who tells him that 'thou hast murdered thyself'.

If De Quincey read this story, he said nothing about it. Nor did he once mention Poe's name.

The 1840s saw colossal advances in steam, speed and light. A railway link had opened between Edinburgh and Glasgow, allowing De Quincey to experience the thrill of 'eternal hurry' as he journeyed between the two cities. Photography became a popular hobby, and De Quincey was the only Romantic known to have his photograph taken. In Nichol's

Glasgow observatory, he saw the theatre of the heavens through 'Lord Rosse's almost awful telescope'; he had seen infinity many times before but never through an instrument like this. Advances had also taken place in underground plumbing systems, and De Quincey now encountered his first basin with hot and cold running taps. As the water ran into 'the nearly brimful' bowl, recorded John Findlay, journalist on *The Scotsman* and his new friend, De Quincey 'stood paralysed. His alarm was lest the basin should overflow and deluge the room.' A drowned world had long been a feature of De Quincey's dreams.

He was living through what he described as a 'perilously centripetal' storm in need of balance by a counter impact in religion or philosophy. This centrifugal force he produced in 1845, in the form of a 'sequel' to the *Confessions*, entitled *Suspiria de Profundis* – 'Sighs from the Depths'.

'Of all the tasks I ever had in my life,' De Quincey told Robert Blackwood, the writing of *Suspiria* was 'the most overwhelming'. He intended the work to consist of thirty-two autobiographical fantasias or 'noonday visions' with titles such as 'The Dreadful Infant' and 'The Nursery in the Arabian Deserts'; some of these pieces were lost, some were burned in various fires at his desk, others were never written. The five papers that *Blackwood's* ran during the spring and summer of 1845 make up a fragment of the projected whole.

Employing his impassioned prose, De Quincey began with his fear that the agitations of modern life would destroy man's latent grandeur, which was found in solitude and dreams. The reason, he explained, that he was able to dream 'more splendidly than others' was because he 'took excessive quantities of opium'; and the reason he took excessive quantities of opium was because certain experiences in childhood 'had left a weakness in one organ which required (or seemed to require) that stimulant'. There was another, unstated, reason why he preferred dreaming to wakefulness: in dreams De Quincey could see the world once more through the eyes of a child. In his writing, the word 'dream' no longer meant simply the actions of the mind during sleep; De Quincey's dream world now resembled a place like Lewis Carroll's Wonderland or J. M. Barrie's Neverland. A boy who never grew up, De Quincey was the quintessential Peter Pan.

He had described in his *Confessions*, De Quincey revealed, only a fraction of what he had suffered. Preceding his days on the streets of London, an experience 'of intolerable grief' had driven 'a shaft for me into the worlds of death and darkness which never again closed, and through which it might be said that I ascended and descended at will'. A battered and bereaved old man, De Quincey now drew back the curtain on the opening scene of his life.

In the first of the essays, 'The Affliction of Childhood' (the title recalls Wordsworth's 'The Affliction of Margaret'), De Quincey returned to the midsummer afternoon in 1792 when he crept into his sister's bedroom to see her dead body beneath an open window. The midday sun was showering torrents of splendour onto her frozen eyelids, and a solemn wind began to blow. In that instant he was introduced to self-consciousness, loss and the sublime; he understood that 'life is finished', and knew for certain that his sister would 'rise again' to 'illuminate the hour' of his own death. Next came the doctors to open up Elizabeth's head, after which the door to her room was locked, 'the key was taken away – and I was shut out for ever'. From this day forwards, De Quincey was a figure on the outside.

Twelve years later, when he first became an opium-eater, memories which had lain dormant in his mind unveiled themselves before him. 'Again I was in the chamber with my sister's corpse – again the pomps of life rose up in silence, the glory of the summer, the frost of death.' The nurse who had been cruel to his sister, Jane, appeared 'dilated to colossal proportions', standing 'upon some Grecian stage'; with her hand uplifted 'like the superb Medea', she 'smote me senseless to the ground'. 'If there was one thing in this world,' De Quincey said of this younger self, 'from which, more than from any other, nature had forced me to revolt, it was brutality and violence.'

Addiction is now believed to be a shield against childhood trauma, but De Quincey made this link himself in *Suspiria* where he moved seamlessly from the death of his sister to the memory of his first debt – 'three guineas deep' – to the local bookseller.* A 'deep anxiety now began to oppress me as to the course in which this mysterious (and indeed guilty) debt would finally flow. . .' In a passage of dazzling insight, he reminded the reader that 'though a child's feelings are spoken of, it is not the child who speaks. *I* decipher what the child only felt in cipher.'

> An adult sympathises with himself in childhood because he *is* the same, and because (being the same) yet he is *not* the same. He acknowledges the deep,

---

*   In several languages, 'guilt' and 'debt' are the same word.

mysterious identity between himself, as adult and as infant, for the ground
of his sympathy; and yet. . . he feels the differences between the two selves
as the main quickeners of his sympathy.

The subject of *Suspiria* might be described as the double life, De
Quincey's abiding interest for over half a century. It is not only adulthood that splits us in two; the rational self will always operate alongside
the Dark Interpreter. We inhabit reality by day and dreams by night,
and our dreams replay our lives in hieroglyphics.

Suspiria, thought John Wilson, was superior by far to the *Confessions*.
De Quincey's words rose from the page like music; his genius was in full
bloom. Never moving from the subject of the two selves, De Quincey considered the nature of suffering, the structure of memory, and the amplification of space and elasticity of time under opium. Simulating the experience
of an opium dream, he presented the Victorians with a performance of
High Romanticism fuelled by spontaneous overflows of powerful feeling,
longings for the infinite and unbounded, fearless descents into the childhood imagination, and a deep knowledge of the numinous. 'Did you read
Blackwood?' Elizabeth Barrett asked a friend; 'And in that case have you had
deep delight in an exquisite paper by the Opium-Eater, which my heart
trembled through from end to end? What a poet that man is! How he vivi-
fies words, or deepens them, and gives them profound significance.' There
is nothing to compare with *Suspiria de Profundis*, although many writers
have since drawn on its helium quality. De Quincey, as Virginia Woolf put
it, had 'made a class for himself'. In the terminology of Wordsworth and
Coleridge, he had created the taste by which he was to be judged.

The second section, 'The Palimpsest', compares the workings of memory
to a parchment on which writing has been erased but not totally expunged.
'What else than a natural and mighty palimpsest is the human brain?
Everlasting layers of ideas, images, feelings have fallen upon your brain
softly as light. Each succession has seemed to bury all that went before.
And yet in reality not one has been extinguished.' Like water in water,
'endless strata have covered up each other in forgetfulness' and only death,
fever or opium can revive them. De Quincey had used the same image in
Confessions when he described the 'veil' dividing 'our present consciousness and the secret inscriptions of the mind'. A thousand accidents will
rend this veil away, but 'the inscription remains forever'. The image had

also appeared in a note by Coleridge to his poem, 'The Wanderings of Cain' – 'I have in Cain tried to recover the lines from the palimpsest tablet of my memory' – but De Quincey elaborated on it in such a way that the palimpsest became an essential and inevitable way of thinking about the mind. Men themselves, he suggested, could be palimpsests: Ralph Waldo Emerson, for example, was 'a palimpsest' of Thomas Carlyle. Palimpsests were another form of double: 'the traces of each successive handwriting', De Quincey explained, 'have, in the inverse order, been regularly called back: the footsteps of the game pursued, wolf or stag. . . have been unlinked, and hunted back through all their doubles'. It was the same image as the one he used to describe the task of the biographer.

The third, and most celebrated, section of *Suspiria* is a prose poem with the mythical title, 'Levanna and Our Ladies of Sorrow', and in the fourth section De Quincey broaches the Coleridgean topic of the 'Apparition of the Brocken'. 'At first,' he says of the spectral form that haunts the Harz Mountains, 'from the distance and the colossal size, every spectator supposes the appearance to be quite independent of himself. But very soon he is surprised to observe his own motions and gestures mimicked; and wakens to the conviction that the phantom is but a dilated version of himself.' Like the Dark Interpreter, like William Wilson, and like the satanic Gil-Martin in Hogg's *Confessions of a Justified Sinner*, the Apparition of the Brocken reflects to the world the things we bury within. The form was, De Quincey explained, 'solitary. . . in the sense of loving solitude' but it had 'been known to unmask a strength quite sufficient to alarm those who had been insulting him'. Herein lies De Quincey's finest self-portrait.

———

Great storms and driving mists dictate the moods of *Suspiria de Profundis*. In a sudden squall, De Quincey attacks those 'men that pass for good men', who 'degrade' other men of 'intellect or character'. Men such as these 'respect you: they are compelled to do so: and they hate to do so'. They co-operate with 'any unhappy accidents in your life', they 'inflict a sense of humiliation upon you, and. . . force you into becoming a consenting party to that humiliation'. Such men we are likely, in the hour of death, to 'salute with the valediction – Would God I had never seen your face'. Wordsworth was such a man but so too was Professor Wilson; both were indebted to De Quincey; both had philosophised a good deal during the worst stages of his poverty, but neither had given him a guinea.

Another man he could not forgive was William Maginn, who had slandered him in the *John Bull* as the first humbug of the age. De Quincey's appearance had been savagely mocked, his wife's virtue had been grossly insulted, his family's honour had been scandalously impugned, the nobility of the ancient De Quincey name had been challenged, De Quincey's son William had been humiliated; but what the Opium-Eater chose to publicly defend in *Suspiria* was the reality of the house in which he had lived during the winter of 1802. Maginn had doubted that a building such as this existed on Oxford Street, and De Quincey would not be seen as having lied about, or embellished, the wretchedness of his past suffering. The empty house had actually been, he revealed, on Greek Street. He was now at liberty to give the address because the attorney whose home it was had since died, and would therefore not recognise the description and be provoked into producing some counter *Confessions* of his own.

Amongst De Quincey's notes for future *Suspiria* was an account of a man called Symonds who, in revenge for a woman's scorn, 'committed several murders in a sudden epilepsy of planet-struck fury'. Symonds later confessed to the prison chaplain that 'as he rushed on in his hellish career, he perceived a dark figure on his right, keeping pace with himself'. He had been attended in his crimes, De Quincey noted, by the Dark Interpreter himself.

———

De Quincey would have a base in Mavis Bush cottage for the rest of his life, but for the most part he preferred not to be there. His habit of camouflaging himself in city crowds while his family resided in the country was ingrained, and he continued to rent rooms – the exact number is uncertain – in Edinburgh and Glasgow, which he loaded with treasure before moving on. In Mavis Bush itself, a tin bath being stored in his study was filled to the brim with papers which, under his strictest orders, were not to be moved. De Quincey was pursued, said James Hogg's son (also called James Hogg), 'by Chinese-like reverence for written or printed paper. Newspapers and magazines, which reached him from all parts of the world, he preserved with religious care.' He was also astonishingly careless. Two tea chests of papers were left for storage in a booksellers in Glasgow, the name and address of whom De Quincey promptly forgot, and candle fires turned many of his papers to ash (it was habitual for his daughters to point out to De Quincey, as he worked, that his hair was alight).

The chaos of his filing system was recalled by a Glasgow friend, Colin Rae Brown. In 1847 De Quincey, then residing in the city with a certain Mrs Tosh, had to leave when her daughter was struck suddenly with fever. What was he to do? Where on earth could he go? De Quincey was in a whirl. And then, '"Ah," he answered, putting his hand to his forehead, "that reminds me that I have been paying the rent of apartments in Renfield Street for a number of years. Many valuable books and papers are or should be still there." As he thus spoke,' wrote Rae Brown, 'I stared, almost agape, in downright amazement.' So back De Quincey went to his mean little room at the Youilles'.

In appearance he resembled a cartoon of poverty. He wore stockings without shoes or shoes without stockings, his ancient jacket was a size too large, his neck-tie looked like a piece of straw. During his daily walks De Quincey was mistaken for a tramp, and he became known in the two cities for what David Masson, his future biographer and editor, remembers as 'the absolute uncertainty of his whereabouts'. Scuttling through the night streets, invisible as a mole, the Opium-Eater made the occasional public appearance. In one account of his arrival at a dinner party, a commotion was heard in the hall 'as if some dog or other stray animal had forced his way in. . . What can it be? Some street boy of some sort?' Enter De Quincey, dressed in whatever he could get his hands on – a 'boy's duffle great-coat, very threadbare, with a hole in it, fragments of a particoloured belcher handkerchief. . . list shoes, covered with snow. . . and the trousers! – someone suggests that they are mere linen garments blackened with writing-ink'.

His conversation remained mysterious in tone and remarkable in range, the drawback being that De Quincey rose to his best when it was 'rapidly becoming tomorrow'. 'The first difficulty,' one of his admirers recalled, 'was to induce him to visit you. The second was to reconcile him to leaving.' As the guests departed for their beds, De Quincey stayed on at the table, sometimes for weeks at a time.

Elizabeth Quincey died in January 1846. 'She was above ninety-seven,' calculated her son. He had last seen his mother fourteen years before, although they had been in regular contact about money. Under the terms of her will, Thomas continued to receive his annual allowance. The rest of the estate was left to Jane, her other surviving child.

In America, where the British magazines were regarded as setting the highest possible standard, the Opium-Eater was considered a master. 'No Englishman cares a pin for De Quincey,' despaired Nathaniel Hawthorne. 'We are ten times as good readers and critics as they.' It was De Quincey whom Ralph Waldo Emerson, visiting Edinburgh in February 1848, most wanted to meet, expecting him to be 'some figure like the organ of York Minster'. During their conversation, De Quincey revealed to Emerson that he had copied Wordsworth's poem on the growth of his own mind into five notebooks. He also said that it had been the poet's habit to 'appropriate what another said so entirely as to be angry if the originator claimed any part of it'.

Later that year De Quincey penned what would be his final letter to Wordsworth, now Poet Laureate. His purpose was to introduce his former mentor to a certain 'Mr Neocles Jaspis Mousabines', an accomplished young Greek scholar who 'honours your name and services to this generation' and has been 'powerfully and unaffectedly impressed by the study of your works'. Would Wordsworth have any time in his schedule to 'converse' with this latest acolyte? Wordsworth's reply has not survived, but eighteen months later, on 23 April – the day on which Shakespeare was both born and died – the poet breathed his last. His widow now took from the drawer her husband's autobiographical poem, which she named *The Prelude*, and sent it to the publisher. It was an 'inappropriate' title, thought De Quincey; 'he designed it as the opening to a great poem, but as the great poem was never finished, the "Prelude" stands as an opening to nothing'.

In 1849 'The English Mail-coach' was published in *Blackwood's*. It would be De Quincey's last contribution to *Maga*, and the essay stands as the

crowning example of the effect of opium addiction on the imagination.
Divided into four parts, 'The Glory of Motion', 'Going Down with Victory',
'The Vision of Sudden Death' and 'Dream Fugue', De Quincey returned
to his love of velocity, in the days before trains, when the mail-coach, like
'some mighty orchestra' obedient 'to a supreme baton', distributed around
the land the news of Napoleon. As ever, the prose is driven by nostalgia –
'Even thunder and lightning, it pains me to say, are not the thunder and
lightning which I remember at the time of Waterloo' – and De Quincey's
subject is less the historical past than the life of his dreams, tyrannised even
today by the 'terror and terrific beauty' of the mail-coach.

In one of his most potent and brilliant diversions, De Quincey now
described the way in which dreams contain, in compound images, 'the
horrid inoculation upon each other of incompatible natures'. In dreams, he
suggests, images are injected into one another – the dragon, for example, 'is
the snake inoculated upon the scorpion'. The term was apt for a man who
inoculated himself with opium, but 'most frightful' of all these 'dream horrors' is that in which the dreamer finds *himself* inoculated with 'some horrid
alien nature'. What if this 'were his own nature repeated'? What if 'not one
alien nature, but two, but three, but four, but five, are introduced into what
he once thought the inviolable sanctuary of himself?' In his fantasy of escalating antibodies, De Quincey was back inside the Piranesian dreamscape,
endlessly climbing the stairs of his own Carceri.

He then, in 'The Vision of Sudden Death', recalls how coming home
many years ago after a visit to his mother, he had warmed himself with
'a small quantity of laudanum' and sat, as he liked to do, in the 'drawing
room' of the mail-coach next to the driver. This monster of a man had
only one eye and, in his hallucinogenic state, De Quincey watched the
lid flicker and shut as the charioteer fell into a deep sleep. Meanwhile
the horses thundered on into the dawn, led by the 'great saucer eyes of
the mail'. The woods and fields on either side were cloaked in silvery
mist, and despite the comatose state of his companion, De Quincey
felt as safe as a child in his older sister's arms. Suddenly he heard wheels
ahead. 'A whisper it was – a whisper from, perhaps, four miles off –
secretly announcing a ruin that, being foreseen, was not the less inevitable.' What could he do to 'check the storm-flight' of the 'maniacal
horses?' The slumbering Cyclops had the reins held tightly in his grip,
and De Quincey was unable to loosen them. They were coursing down

an avenue as straight as a 'cathedral aisle', at the end of which appeared a small gig, a tug in the line of a great cutter. On the bench sat a pair of cooing lovers, their heads bent towards one another. 'Between them and eternity' lay 'but a minute and a half'. De Quincey cried out in alarm and the couple took in the hurricane tearing towards them on the wrong side of the road. 'Fast are the flying moments, faster are the hoofs of our horses'; rising, the young man pulled hard on the reins but too late – the charging block on which De Quincey sat whirled, with the force of twenty Atlantics, past the tiny cart, clipping the back wheel: 'the blow, from the fury of our passage, resounded terrifically'. Rising 'in horror', De Quincey turned around to observe the wreckage: the carriage was trembling, the horse was standing still, the driver was 'like a rock. . . But the lady –'

> But the lady! Oh heavens! Will that spectacle ever depart from my dreams, as she rose and sank upon her seat, sank and rose, threw up her arms wildly to heaven, clutching at some visionary object in the air, fainting, praying, raving, despairing! Figure to yourself, reader, the elements of the case. . . From the silence and deep peace of this saintly summer night, – from the pathetic blending of this sweet moonlight, dawnlight, dreamlight, – from the manly tenderness of this flattering, whispering, murmuring love, – suddenly as from the woods and fields, – suddenly as from the chambers of the air opening in revelation, – suddenly as from the ground yawning at her feet, leaped upon her, with the flashing of cataracts, Death the crowned phantom, with all the equipage of his terrors, and the tiger roar of his voice.

The 'rapture of panic' and fantasia of guilt, which returned 'a thousand times' in his future dreams, is described in *Suspiria*'s final section, 'Dream Fugue', where De Quincey sees the terrified girl at the prow of a boat in the 'desert spaces of the sea', a frigate flying towards her while he, helpless, looks on. 'The deeps opened ahead in malice to receive her, towering surges of foam ran after her, the billows were fierce to catch her.' There she stands, 'sinking, rising, fluttering, fainting' through storms, 'through the darkness of quicksands, through fugues and the persecution of fugues'.

The unknown woman joined the gallery of girls whose deaths he had been unable to prevent.

In the autumn of 1849 he appeared at the offices of *Hogg's Instructor*, the journal founded by James Hogg the younger. From one pocket of his cape – a garment three sizes too large – De Quincey produced a roll of manuscript and from the other a small brush; uncurling the sheets he carefully brushed each one, placing them individually in the editor's hands, 'with a grave upward glance to see how [he] was getting on'. Thus he proposed himself as a new contributor, and from 1851 everything De Quincey wrote, including essays on the guilt of Anne Boleyn, the etymology of the Westmorland dialect, the opium trade in China, and a further autobiographical series called 'A Sketch from Childhood', would be published by Hogg. De Quincey's 'Sketch', the most magnificent version of his memories so far, now centred on the death of Elizabeth and opened with the following sentence: 'About the close of my sixth year, suddenly the first chapter of my life came to a violent termination.'

Hogg, an amiable and patient man, left a loving memoir of De Quincey in which he recalls the 'gifted, ingenuous and noble' author, aged seventy, ascending 'like a squirrel' a ravine on the Esk, and suffering 'unheard-of-misery' when invited out to dinner. On one occasion Hogg ran into Wilson who asked: 'Well, how is friend De Quincey?' He was, regretted Hogg, on his way to see him, rather complaining. 'Ah!' said the Professor, 'I hope it is only caused by one of those small matters about which he is so frequently worrying himself, such as the loss of a manuscript or some other trifle. . . Say to him when you call that I would be pleased if he would come and dine with me to-morrow at the usual hour. You know the difficulty of dragging him out to dinner. Say that we are to have no strangers, and that I will see to a dish of hare-soup *a la* De Quincey being on the table.'

It is unlikely that De Quincey took up the invitation. It was with Hogg that he now discussed the smaller matters of the day, from the thrill of boxing matches to 'a murder surrounded by mysteries'. When it came to the latter, Hogg noted, De Quincey was always able to 'track out the missing links in the chain of evidence'.

No sooner had De Quincey abandoned Tait for Hogg than *Tait's* ran a paper by the pathologist John Paget on 'The Philosophy of Murder'. The world is changing, argued Paget, and so too are murder methods. 'Crowbars, masks and dark lanterns are *outré* and behind the times. The highway-gentleman of the last century, dressed and curled. . . he too is passed away with the times he illustrated, and his place is filled by men of business – by march-of-intellect operators in chloroform and new and improved strangulators.' In order to execute the 'cool, nicely considered, artistic crime' the modern murderer employs arsenic or strychnine: 'Poisoning,' concluded Paget, '(the word crawls from the pen like a snake) is the prevailing style'; it is 'the kind of murder that even a lady might do with clean hands – that even Macbeth might have found some comfort in. "Out! Out, damned *spot*!"'

De Quincey's *oeuvre* was now, in the words of George Gilfillan, 'scattered in prodigal profusion through the thousand and one volumes of our periodical literature'. In America, a Boston firm of publishers called Ticknor and Fields took on the challenge of compiling a twenty-two-volume edition of his collected works, something De Quincey believed to be 'absolutely, insuperably, and for ever impossible'. This they achieved by going through thirty years' worth of journals and cutting out the essays signed XYZ, the Opium-Eater and Thomas De Quincey. Without Ticknor and Fields, 'hardly the sixth part of my literary undertakings, hurried or deliberate, sound, rotting, or rotten, would ever have reached posterity'. But there was unease as well in De Quincey's response to the project. 'It is astonishing,' he mused, 'how much more Boston knows of my literary acts and purposes than I do myself.' With this advantage over him, the Opium-Eater feared that 'if on any dark December morning, say forty or fifty years ago, I might have committed a forgery (as the best of men will do occasionally) Boston could array against me all the documentary evidence of my peccadillo before I should have time to abscond'.

De Quincey was now persuaded by Hogg to begin the Sisyphean task of putting together an English edition of his works, more extensive than its American sibling. All of his papers needed to be located; some had been burned by candles, others he vaguely remembered depositing in various lodgings. Miraculously, some of the dispersed manuscripts made their way back to him: when De Quincey was sheltering from a thunderstorm in the Royal Exchange Hotel, a waiter tapped him on the arm and politely handed over a bundle that had been left there for

storage several months before. Former landladies, who received payment for their trouble, appeared at Hogg's offices with cartloads of
packages; one of them – probably Mrs McIndoe – exploited the system
by returning what turned out to be several parcels of straw.

In letters to Hogg, De Quincey documented the pandemonium into
which he was now hurled: he was 'utterly in the dark' as to the whereabouts of the paper entitled 'Coleridge and Opium-Eating' – was it *chez
moi?* Or *chez la presse?* (I speak French, simply as being the briefest way
of conveying my doubt).' Should the lost paper be *chez moi*, it would
take him 'half a day' to find; 'as it is manifestly not on my table, I should
proceed to postulate that it must have been transposed to the floor'.
There was nothing De Quincey disliked more than the business of
having to 'stoop'. Referring to another mislaid essay, he despaired that
despite 'working through most parts of the night, I have not yet come
to the missing copy. . . I am going on with the search yet, being walled
in by superfluous furniture, in so narrow an area (not larger than a post-
chaise as regards the free space), I work with difficulty, and the *stooping*
kills me. I greatly fear that the entire day will be spent in the search.' As
for the papers themselves, George Gilfillan chanced to see one of De
Quincey's manuscripts and described the words as 'piled over each other's heads, two, three, and four deep – erasure after erasure'. As Wilson
said of De Quincey's style: 'the best word always comes up'.

The exercise allowed De Quincey not only to locate, collate and order
his writing but to rebuild it as well. Essays written under pressure were
returned to at leisure. Writing to deadline, he said, forced a man into 'saying
the thing that is not'. Hammering away on these hurried pieces, he now
added rooms, floors and staircases, higher attics and deeper cellars in an
ever-increasing number of notes, afterthoughts, second thoughts, reflections
and diversions. He chose as his title *Selections: Grave and Gay*: 'Selections'
reflected the incomplete nature of the project, and 'Grave and Gay' comes
from Book VI of *The Prelude* ('Strange rendezvous my mind was at that
time,/ A parti-coloured show of grave and gay'). Here was the parti-coloured
mansion of De Quincey's own mind, revealed for all to see. Volume one,
which appeared in May 1853, opened with *Autobiographic Sketches*. These
might be described as a palimpsest of his essays for *Tait's*, sections of *Suspiria
de Profundis*, and his recent 'Sketch from Childhood' for *Hogg's Instructor*.
Writing once again over the earlier versions of his youth, De Quincey cut

some passages, extended others, and divided the whole into thirteen sections, echoing the thirteen books of Wordsworth's 1805 *Prelude*. The titles he chose, after Wordsworth's own titles, were as follows:

The Affliction of Childhood
Introduction to the World of Strife
Infant Literature
The Female Infidel
I am Introduced to the Warfare of a Public School
I enter the World
The Nation of London
Dublin
First Rebellion
French Invasion of Ireland, and Second Rebellion
Travelling
My Brother
Premature Manhood

He was now alone of all his kind. In 1853 his daughter Margaret married and moved to Ireland, and in April 1854 John Wilson died. In the months before his friend's death De Quincey had considered enquiring after his health but was prevented from doing so by his real reason for writing, which was to retrieve, from one of Wilson's associates, a trunkful of books. 'My unfortunate chattels,' De Quincey explained to John Findlay, 'instead of being rescued from destruction, are plunged into a deeper and more hopeless oblivion than ever. This, you see, is what I want to know from Wilson, not, of course, where the books are placed, but the name of the gentleman to whom he introduced me.' Soon after Wilson's funeral, De Quincey remarked at a dinner party that the professor had surrounded himself with parasites 'who ministered to his vanity', and that 'the sickly, false sentiment of his works' had been mocked by the Wordsworths. He then entertained the company with a 'droll' impersonation of Wilson's style of lecturing.

The wind was in his sails; it was time to move on. 'I often', De Quincey told Findlay, 'feel an almost irresistible inclination to rush away and bury myself among books in the heart of some great city like London or Paris.' Taking only his coat, he left Mavis Bush, walked the seven miles to Edinburgh and returned to the rooms at 42 Lothian Street where, sixteen years earlier, he had written 'The Household Wreck'. Removing from the cupboard the set of clothes he had then left behind, his land-lady, Frances Wilson, unlocked the door to his lair. He was, he told Hogg, planning his own version of *Arabian Nights*, which in a sense was true. Mixing his opium with water, De Quincey began work on the fourth volume of *Selections: Grave and Gay*. Blending into one continu-ous essay 'On Murder Considered as One of the Fine Arts' and 'Second Paper on Murder as One of the Fine Arts', he now added a 'Postscript' which proved to be the finest murder essay of them all.

It was required of him, De Quincey's 'Postscript' began, to provide 'some account of Williams, the dreadful London murderer of the last generation' who, 'in one hour. . . exterminated all but two entire households'. The art-ist's performances were remarkable not only for their aesthetic value, but also for their continuing 'mystery': 'Had the murderer an accomplice?'

For his final piece of theatre, De Quincey's design, grouping, light and shade were all perfectly arranged. The Ratcliffe Highway was 'a public thoroughfare in a most chaotic quarter of eastern or nautical London'. There were as many turbans to be seen here as hats; 'every third man might be set down as a foreigner. Lascars, Chinese, Moors, Negroes, were met at every step.' The serpentine figure who 'forced his way through the crowded streets' on the night of 7 December 1811, his tools buttoned up in his oversized coat, stood five foot seven inches tall, and judging from De Quincey's plaster cast of his face, his features were 'mean'. John Williams had been at sea during the war, when the navy was composed of 'murderers and ruffians' and all types of men on the run; those who knew him noted his 'polished hatred of bru-tality' and the 'exquisite suavity' of his manners. A woman who had seen him at the Thames Police Office told De Quincey that the hair of Williams 'was the most extraordinary and vivid colour, viz, bright yel-low'. Ruminating on this information, De Quincey wondered if, hav-ing been in India, Williams had disguised its natural colour by dying it with paint used to decorate high-caste horses of the Punjab. This same woman also revealed that Williams had a ghastly pallor, as though 'green sap' rather than blood circulated in his veins.

Like Titian and Rubens, who practised their art in wigs and diamond buckled shoes, De Quincey imagined Williams setting out 'for a grand compound massacre' in full dress. 'It is really wonderful,' he mused, picturing the silken murderer clad in black stockings and pumps, gliding like a hellkite through the turbaned crowds, 'to pursue the successive steps of this monster, and to notice the absolute certainty with which the silent hieroglyphics of the case betray to us the whole process and movements of the bloody drama, not less surely and fully than if we had been ourselves hidden in Marr's shop.'

Watching the detective slither his way into the mind of the murderer is now a staple form of popular entertainment. But when De Quincey entered the interior of Williams, a man of 'snakey insinuation', he was going where only Milton had gone before when, in *Paradise Lost* Book IX, Satan penetrates the head of the sleeping serpent through his mouth.

The victim towards whose house Williams was aimed was an 'old and very intimate friend'. At least, Marr had 'originally had been a friend; but subsequently, on good cause arising, he had become an enemy. Or more probably, as others said, the feelings had long since languished which gave life to either relation of friendship or of enmity.' The two men had sailed to Calcutta together and quarrelled over the girl who eventually married Marr. This, at least, is what the public wanted to believe, De Quincey suggested; they preferred to think of Williams as a spurned lover rather than a hound from hell. Timothy Marr, a 'stout, fresh-faced young man of twenty-seven', had invested 'about £180' in refurbishing his small drapery at 29 Ratcliffe Highway. The unpaid bills were accumulating and he was alarmed by the prospect of debts; as he closed the shop that night he looked forward to resting his head on the breast of his wife, who was in the basement nursing the baby.

Leaving the house shortly before midnight to buy oysters for her master's supper, Margaret Jewell – who De Quincey renamed Mary – saw a figure in the shadows. The elderly watchman saw him too, peeping into the shop window. The servant girl had left and Marr was alone: Williams 'bolted' inside 'and by a dexterous movement of his left hand. . . turned the key'. 'Let us leave the murderer alone with his victims,' De Quincey now instructed, tip-toeing away. 'For fifty minutes let him work his pleasure. The front-door, as we know, is fastened against all help. Help there is none. Let us, therefore, in vision, attach ourselves to Mary; and, when all is over, let us come back with *her*, again raise the curtain, and read the dreadful record of all that has passed in her absence.'

It had turned midnight, and was now the morning of Sunday 8 December. Mary made her way down the coffin-narrow passageways, 'in an area of London where ferocious tumults were continually turning her out of what seemed to be the direct course'. The shops had shut, she was losing her bearings, and her mission had failed. Nothing remained 'but to retrace her steps'. A watchman with a lantern guided her back to the door of 29 Ratcliffe Highway. 'In many cities,' De Quincey paused to explain, 'bells are the main instruments for communication between the street and the interior of houses: but in London knockers prevail. At Marr's there was both a knocker and a bell. Mary rang, and at the same time very gently knocked.' She listened for the thud of footsteps coming up from the kitchen. Silence. One person in the household might possibly have fallen asleep during her absence, but surely not everyone – ? Had the child been taken ill? An 'icy horror' crept over her as she remembered 'the stranger in the loose dark coat, whom she had seen stealing along under the shadowy lamp-light, and too certainly watching her master's motions'. The silence deepened; Mary's heart was pounding. Then came a sound which filled her with 'killing fear'.

What was it? On the stairs, not the stairs that led down to the kitchen, but the stairs that led upwards to the single story of bedchambers above, was heard a creaking. . . Next was heard most distinctly a footfall: one, two, three, four, five stairs were slowly and distinctly descended. Then the dreadful footsteps were heard advancing along the little narrow passage to the door. The very breathing can be heard of that dreadful being, who has silenced all breathing except his own in the house. There is but a door between him and Mary. What is he doing on the other side of the door?. . . How hard the fellow breathes! He, the solitary murderer, is on one side of the door; Mary is on the other side. . . The unknown murderer and she both have their lips upon the door, listening, breathing hard; but luckily they are on different sides. . .

There was not a doubt in De Quincey's mind about the murderer's purpose. 'Quietly opening the door,' he would ask, in a whispering 'counterfeit' of Marr's voice, why Mary had been out for so long. Thus inveigling the girl into 'the asylum of general darkness', Williams would have 'perfected and rounded the desolation of the house'.

Behind the counter, Marr's body 'told its own tale'. He had been bludgeoned on the back of the head while reaching for a pair of unbleached cotton socks. Then, 'by way of locking up all into eternal silence', his throat had been cut. Hearing groans, Mrs Marr and James Gowan, the apprentice boy, made for the front rather than the back door, where the heavy swing of the murder's mallet stopped them in their tracks.

'I was myself at the time nearly three hundred miles from London,' De Quincey recalled, but even here 'the panic was indescribable'. Southey himself had been struck by the degree of terror felt across the nation, while Coleridge, delivering his Shakespeare lectures in London, noted there the 'many thousands of households, composed exclusively of women and children', and later drew De Quincey's attention to the many other households 'who necessarily confide their safety, in the long evenings, to the discretion of a young servant girl'. Should she find herself 'beguiled by the pretence of a message from her mother, sister, or sweetheart, into opening the door, there, in one second of time', goes the wreckage of the house. It was the murder twelve nights later of the Williamson household which revealed the 'absurdity of ascribing to [Williams] any ruralising tendencies'. A killer of this calibre would not 'abandon for a moment. . . the great metropolitan *castra stativa* of gigantic crime, seated for ever on the Thames'.

John Williamson, publican of the King's Head tavern on New Gravel Lane, around the corner from Ratcliffe Highway, had served his last customer when, at twenty-five minutes to midnight 'the house-door was suddenly shut and locked' by 'a crash, proclaiming some hand of hideous violence'. It is through the eyes of John Turner, the 'poor, petrified journeyman' who had retired for the night, that De Quincey now describes the events. Driven by the fascination of 'killing fear', Turner rose from his bed, opened the door and, 'quite unconscious of what he was doing, in blind, passive, self-surrender to panic, absolutely descended both flights of stairs'. Four steps from the bottom, he could

see directly into the blood-soaked parlour where, swathed in a coat of
the finest quality, Williams was pacing about in creaking shoes, decid-
ing which of the keys from Mrs Williamson's pocket would lead him
to the hidden treasure. Had the murderer been less occupied, he would
have heard the breathing of the journeyman who now leapt back up the
stairs, passing as he did so the door of the Williamsons' sleeping granddaughter. 'Every minute,' John Turner felt, 'brings ruin nearer to *her*.'
His 'first thought' had been to take the girl 'out of bed in his arms' but
what if she were to wake and cry out? She would endanger the lives of
them both. The only way to save the child was by first saving himself.
John Turner then pushed his bed against the door and began to rip the
bedding into shreds. Downstairs, Williams filled his pockets with coins
and his sack with plate. 'Murderer is working in the parlour; journeyman is working hard in the bedroom. . . Like chorus and semi-chorus,
strophe and antistrophe, they work each against the other. Pull journeyman, pull murderer.'

The murderer was certain to find another throat on the upper
storeys, but to loiter would hazard his night's work. He had to leave
in haste, shave off his yellow hair, blacken his eyebrows and return to
sea. But blood beckoned; rather than slip out of the house he began
his ascent. Still knotting his sheets together, the journeyman heard the
approaching tread. 'As the Alpine avalanches, when suspended above
the traveller's head. . . come down through the stirring of the air by a
simple whisper, precisely on such a tenure of a whisper was now suspended the murderous malice of the man below.'

For De Quincey, writing involved the projection of the writer's 'own
inner mind'. Words, he wrote in an essay on 'Style', needed to 'pass
through a prism, and radiate into distinct elements, what previously had
been even to himself but dim and confused ideas'. Virginia Woolf, in
her essay on 'Impassioned Prose', put it more succinctly: De Quincey's
enemy was 'the hard fact'. Despite his knowledge of the background
and character of John Williams, garnered from the newspapers and
Fairburn's 'Accounts', De Quincey had no interest in the hard facts
of the case. What he understood was that a man calling himself John

POSTSCRIPT 333

Williamson had murdered a man called John Williamson; it recalled the time he was pursued by the shadow of Monsieur Monsieur De Quincy, or the time when Mrs Quincey believed that her son, returned from his own sea adventures, was not Richard De Quincey at all but an imposter calling himself Richard De Quincey.

In *The Maul and the Pear Tree*, their skilful re-examination of the Ratcliffe Highway murders, P. D. James and T. A. Critchley cast doubt on the guilt of John Williams and suggest that William – 'Long Billy' – Ablass, who had orchestrated the mutiny on the *Roxburgh Castle*, and Cornelius Hart, the carpenter for Marr's new shop front, were the killers. The murders, argue James and Critchley, were linked to the mutiny, 'and we think that the circumstances of that mutiny, could they now be traced, would bear out our own hypothesis'. De Quincey, for whom there was little difference between being guilty and seeming so, did not countenance the thought of Williams as having a collaborator. He had read about the tall man and the shorter man seen hurrying from the King's Head on the night of the Williamson murders; he knew that two or even three men had been seen loitering on the Ratcliffe Highway when Marr's household was slaughtered, but De Quincey's object was to prove that Williams was an actor, a connoisseur, a dandy, an aesthete, a scourge of God who walked in darkness, a tiger, a man of snaky insinuation, and a domestic Attila. The murderer was, like Wordsworth's vision of the poet, a solitary artist, lonely as a cloud.

In the 'Postscript', facts stored in De Quincey's inner mind for forty-two years radiated and took on the grandeur of a dream. The wreckage of his own two households – the first when he was a child at Greenhay, the second when he was an adult in Edinburgh – unfurled before him. The draper's shop above which he was born returned as 29 Ratcliffe Highway; the former tavern, The Dove and Olive Branch, which had been first Wordsworth's and then De Quincey's home returned as the King's Head. His sister's body behind the locked door re-formed itself as the massacred families; his precious Margaret 'inoculated' upon Mary Dawson – whose name he had hated since she barred the door to Dorothy Wordsworth – to become Mary Jewell, the sole survivor of the household wreck. Coleridge, whose genius lay 'scattered like jewels on the highway', reappeared as the murdered man; De Quincey's lost brothers, William and Richard, his mentor, Wordsworth, his collaborator,

John Wilson, and his nemesis, Napoleon Bonaparte – with whom he shared a birthday – inoculated upon one another to form the faceless figure of the suave, yellow-haired sailor-poet skulking through a city which might have been Bath, or Bristol, or Baghdad, or Manchester, or Liverpool, or Edinburgh, or Paris, or Pandemonium, or even one of Piranesi's prisons; his object being to kill the former friend who lived on a street with almost the same name as De Quincey's favourite novelist and which sounded like St Mary Redcliffe, the Gothic church in which Chatterton had unlocked the door to the room at the top of the stairs and invented an alter ego called Thomas Rowley.

And in his dream fugue, Kitty Stillwell – whose age De Quincey remembered as nine rather than fourteen – is at the forefront of the journeyman's mind. A hard fact to swallow was that, in his desperation to escape from the house, John Turner had forgotten all about her.

In a letter to Florence, De Quincey described this latest volume of his works as containing 'one novelty, *viz*, an account of the murders perpetrated by Williams in 1812, which may a little interest you'. He had consistently misremembered the year of the Ratcliffe Highway slaughters, which was 1811. The difference between the two dates was crucial: in the spring of 1811 De Quincey had reached the peak of his intimacy with Wordsworth, who had lent him a copy of *The Prelude*. In the winter of 1811 he had taken an axe to the moss hut in the orchard, and relations between the two households had chilled; by the summer of 1812 he was sleeping on Catherine Wordsworth's grave. The Ratcliffe Highway murders marked the point where De Quincey's life broke in half: the figure of John Williams gazing through windows at household hieroglyphics and patting the head of the baby whose throat he was about to cut, represented De Quincey's last guilty scene.

In the twenty-seven years since 'On the Knocking at the Gate in *Macbeth*', De Quincey had approached the murders from the positions of Shakespearean critic, satirist, reporter, Gothic novelist and self-plagiarist. In 'Postscript' he told the story of John Williams from the position of biographer, and the figure he described was as freely invented as Chatterton's Rowley. He had also imagined the murders from the perspectives of all the key players, and whenever De Quincey was depressed, John Findlay would cheer him up with a game called 'What would the Baker say?' In 'On Murder Considered as One of the Fine Arts', was an account of the Mannheim baker who defended himself with his fists against his killer. Findlay and De Quincey, as Findlay put it, had 'established a queer sort of freemasonry' about this baker, who they saw as 'quite free from shilly-shally – always decided in his views, and with a certain ready activity in expressing them'. The effect of Findlay's question on De Quincey's spirits 'was perfectly magical. The drooping head was raised, the pallid face slowly wreathed into a half-aroused smile, which seemed to convey: "Well, that is a good idea. We have not yet considered what can be said and what can be done from that point of view."'

On 15 February 1855, De Quincey added a sentence to the end of a cheerful letter to Florence: 'On Tuesday last I saw the death announced of Miss Wordsworth at the age of eighty-four.' This is all he writes on the subject; De Quincey had bid farewell to his impassioned Dorothy many years before.

In Lothian Street, the Opium-Eater had become as celebrated a magus as Coleridge on Highgate Hill. Disciples came from afar to witness his dreamlike voice and antiquated manners. One such figure recalled how, during a night walk, De Quincey 'suddenly, casting a startled look behind, exclaimed, "My adversaries are in full chase of me; good-night"'. On another occasion, having been dragged out to dinner, De Quincey returned to his lodgings worse for wear and found himself locked out. He knocked and knocked, but failed to rouse the household. Climbing over a wall, he slept in a ditch. One night, concerned about his daughters, he dreamed that 'a door opened: it was a door on the *further* side of a spacious chamber'. He 'waited expectingly, not knowing *what* to expect. At length a voice said audibly and most distinctly, but not loudly – *Florence and Emily*, with the tone of one announcing an arrival. Soon after, but not immediately, entered Florence, but to my great astonishment, no Emily. . . A shadow fell upon me, and a feeling of sadness – which increased continually as no Emily entered at the door.'

Florence believed that her father's luxurious love of excitement eventually became burdensome to him, and that he settled down in his later years 'much like other people'. This was only relatively true. In 1856 another William was added to De Quincey's roll call: a man called William Palmer was convicted of poisoning a man called John Cook. 'Never for one moment have I doubted Palmer's guilt,' De Quincey announced in a long letter to Emily about the case, adding that 'I would habitually say to such criminals. . . For your own peace of mind, I counsel you to confess.' Preparing volume five of *Selections: Grave and Gay*, De Quincey was revising his own *Confessions*, which he allowed to grow to three times their natural size. Now, for the first time, he recorded his memories of the Whispering Gallery at St Paul's, of the 'huge charging block of waters' in the River Dee, and of the nameless woman who returned to the post office the bank draft for Monsieur Monsieur De Quincy. 'I long for the rest of De Quincey,' wrote Crabb Robinson, 'and yet I neither love nor respect the man: I admire only the writer.'

In 1857 he became absorbed in the case of Madeline Smith, a pretty young lady from Glasgow on trial for poisoning her lover. 'To me,' De Quincey concluded, 'it seems that from the very first Miss Smith has been cruelly treated.' So Paget had been right about modern murder methods: poison was the prevailing style. This same year De Quincey visited Margaret in Ireland, crossing the sea for the second time in his life. The journey from Dublin to Lisheen was taken by train, where he 'crept along at the tail of 666 wagons'. He now had a granddaughter – his 'little Tipperary thing' – the thought of whom gave him great pleasure. Florence had also become a mother, and was living in India where her husband, Colonel Baird-Smith, was involved in quelling a mutiny. 'I have no heart *now* for any one thought but what concerns poor insulated Florence and her baby,' De Quincey told Emily. Always terrified by the idea of India, every night he had the same dream: 'a vision of children, most of them infants but not all, the *first* rank being girls of five or six years old, who were standing in the air outside, but so as to touch the window, and I heard, or perhaps fancied I heard, always the same dreadful word, *Delhi*'. He would wake to find himself standing 'at the window, which is sixteen feet from the bed'. His nervous system had not suffered like this, De Quincey confessed, since 'the summer of 1812'.

After 1858 he barely left the house. Working on the edge of a groaning table, with mountains of newspapers climbing the walls and the floor beneath him swamped, De Quincey completed the fourteenth volume of *Selections: Grave and Gay*. He was now receiving royalties from both the American and the British editions of his work: at last, his writing was making money.

———

Towards midnight on 7 December 1859, De Quincey began to lose consciousness. 'Twice only was the heavy breathing interrupted by words,' recorded Emily. 'My dear, dear mother,' he murmured; 'Then I was greatly mistaken.' Mrs Quincey had been right, after all, to insist that her wayward son remain at Manchester grammar. In the last few days, he had also remembered his father, 'for a juster, kinder man never breathed'. This was one of the very few occasions that Emily had heard mention of her grandfather. Then, as the 'waves of death rolled faster and faster over him', Emily watched De Quincey rise from the 'abyss' and throw up his arms as if to greet a long lost friend: 'Sister! Sister! Sister!' he cried. Elizabeth had, as he knew she would, come to illuminate his final hour.

In another presentiment, recorded long before in his *Confessions*, De Quincey had declared that the 'last cloudy delirium of approaching death' would return him to Grasmere, where he would be reinstalled 'in some chamber of that same humble cottage'. In bed, her father looked, thought Emily, 'like a boy of fourteen'.

Thomas De Quincey, the last of the Romantics, died aged seventy-four on the forenoon of 8 December, exactly forty-eight years to the day after the wreckage of the Marr household at 29 Ratcliffe Highway. He was buried next to Margaret in the kirkyard of St Cuthbert's, beneath the castle rock, and two bowshots from the statue of John Wilson in Princes Street Gardens.

Thomas De Quincey, who lived through enormous
advances in speed and light, was the only
Romantic to have had his photograph taken.

The Tables Turned

'May I quote Thomas De Quincey? In the pages of his essay, "On Murder Considered as One of the Fine Arts" I first learned of the Ratcliffe Highway deaths, and ever since that time his work has been a source of perpetual delight and astonishment to me.'

Peter Ackroyd, *Dan Leno and the Limehouse Golem*

'I wonder,' said Jorge Luis Borges, 'if I could have existed without De Quincey?' Many people could not have existed without De Quincey. The last of the Romantics, in all other things he came first. *Confessions of an English Opium-Eater* spawned two genres: the recovery memoir, and what Terence McKenna has called the 'pharmo-picaresque' literary tradition. In 1822 the *Confessions* were translated into Russian, and in 1828 Alfred de Musset produced the first French 'translation', which he furnished with a further 5,000 words, including a section in which De Quincey rediscovers Ann of Oxford Street bejewelled in a ballroom, hanging on the arm of a baron. Musset's version of the *Confessions* inspired the nightmarish programme music of Berlioz's *Symphonie fantastique* (1830), in which the despairing hero tries to poison himself with opium, only to suffer visions in which he believes he has murdered his beloved, been condemned to death, and witnesses his own execution and funeral, marked by a witches' sabbath, and equally Balzac's novella *Massimilla Doni* in 1837. Twenty years later Fitz Hugh Ludlow's *The Hasheesh Eater* appeared in America: 'And now, with time, space expanded also. The whole atmosphere seemed ductile, and spun endlessly out into great spaces surrounding me on every side.' One hundred and thirty years on, in William Burroughs's *The Place of Dead*

Roads, Kim Carson 'opens the door to go out of the druggist's shop' just
as 'some one comes in with a puff of fog and cold air. Boy about eighteen, angular English face. . . rather like the young De Quincey.'

Reading De Quincey, wrote Baudelaire, affected 'my whole emotional
and aesthetic orientation' and he described, in his 1860 translation of
Confessions in *Les Paradis artificiels*, the solipsism of the Opium-Eater
as 'an appalling marriage of man to himself'. In Wilkie Collins's *The
Moonstone* (1868), the opium-addicted Ezra Jennings (a partial portrait
of Collins himself) recommends the London passages of the 'far-famed'
Confessions as an account of how a man can 'occupy himself actively,
and. . . move about from place to place under the influence of opium'.
In his opium stupors, Jennings has hellish dreams. In one, 'I was whirling through empty space with the phantoms of the dead, friends and
enemies together. In another, the one beloved face which I shall never
see again, rose at my bedside, hideously phosphorescent in the black
darkness, and glared and grinned at me.' For Jean Cocteau in *Diary of
an Addict* – based on his opium withdrawal in 1928 – 'Opium is the
woman of destiny, pagodas, lanterns.'

While the *Confessions* have ensured De Quincey's cult status, his
essays on murder anticipated our construction of, and obsession with,
Jack the Ripper. Alfred Hitchcock, who modelled his own dandy killers
on John Williams, described 'On Murder' as a 'delightful essay'. Murder,
Hitchcock counselled, was not the province of the 'underworld thug':
it 'should be treated delicately', and 'brought into the home where it
rightly belongs'. Both Dickens and Dostoevsky – who went into exile
with the *Confessions* in his pocket – used the motif of knocking as a way
of entering their murderer's minds. 'Suddenly,' Dostoevsky wrote of
Raskolnikov, outside the money-lender's flat in *Crime and Punishment*,
'he heard the careful placing of a hand on the handle of the lock and
the rustle of clothing close to the door and listening, just as he was
doing outside it, holding her breath and probably with her ear to the
door'. After murdering Tigg Montague in *Martin Chuzzlewit*, Jonas
springs from the wood 'as if it were a hell'. But it is no longer the wood
that Jonas fears; his fear has diverted 'to the dark room he had left shut
up at home. He had a greater horror, infinitely greater, of that room
than of the wood. . . His hideous secret was shut up in the room, and
all its terrors were there; to his thinking it was not in the wood at all.'

Stopping at an inn for a glass of beer, he hears 'a knocking within'. He imagines a similar knocking on the door 'of that infernal room at home', a knocking 'which would lead to rumour, rumour to detection, detection to death. At that instant, as if by some design and order of circumstances, the knocking had come. It still continued; like a warning echo of the dread reality he had conjured up. As he could not sit and hear it, he paid for his beer and walked on again.' In D. H. Lawrence's short story, 'The Prussian Officer' (1916), the orderly, having murdered his captain after giving him a tankard of beer, hides out in the woods. Sequestered in some deep recess, he hears a knocking – 'A great pang of fear went through his heart. Somebody was knocking.' It is a bird tapping a branch, the 'tap tap tap' a sign that the pulses of life were beginning to beat again.

In 'The Decay of Murder', published in the *Cornhill Magazine* in 1860, Leslie Stephen impersonated De Quincey's style to complain that the current spate of 'intelligent' detective fiction was like 'a drug in the market'. For Oscar Wilde, there was 'no essential incongruity between crime and culture', and in 'Pen, Pencil and Poison', his essay on Thomas Griffin Wainewright, Wilde included among his subject's artistic attributes his skills as 'a subtle and secret poisoner almost without rival in this or any age'. The heroine of Ibsen's *Hedda Gabler* counsels Eilert Lovborg to commit suicide with artistic grace: 'Do it beautifully'. In 'Decline of the English Murder', George Orwell complained that 'you never seem to get a good murder nowadays', and Jean-Paul Sartre included in *Saint Genet* a chapter called 'On Fine Art Considered as Murder'. 'The criminal kills,' Sartre observed; 'he is a poem; the poet writes the crime.' In Nabokov's *Despair*, Hermann Karlovich, who kills his doppelgänger (who in fact looks nothing like him), explains to the reader that 'An artist feels no remorse, even when his work is not understood, not accepted.' Truman Capote, in his 'nonfiction novel', *In Cold Blood*, describes how Perry Smith, who murdered the Clutter family in their home in Holcomb, Kansas, admitted that he had always wanted to make something artistic. 'And now, what has happened?' Smith says to Capote: 'An incredible situation where I kill four people and you're going to produce a work of art.'

Humbert Humbert's observation in *Lolita*, that you can 'count on a murderer for a fancy prose style', is the perfect De Quinceyan epigram, and Virginia Woolf found in De Quincey's fancy prose style a model for her own. The 'Time Passes' section of *To the Lighthouse* – in which Woolf experiments with the expansion and contraction of time in the rooms of the now empty house – was composed alongside her essay on 'Impassioned Prose'.

De Quincey's dreams are hailed by Borges as 'the best in literature', and we return to his opium descent in Alice's fall down the rabbit hole. In Wonderland, Alice drinks from a mysterious bottle similar to those found in apothecary shops, and talks to a caterpillar on a mushroom smoking a hookah. For J. G. Ballard, De Quincey was an inventor of dystopias; *Crash* might be seen as the twentieth-century equivalent of 'The English Mail-Coach'.

For Baudelaire, De Quincey was the first flâneur; for Guy Debord, his mapping of the mind onto the movements of the city made him the original psychogeographer; for Iain Sinclair psychogeography began with De Quincey's image of the north-west passage in *Confessions*.

As editor of *The Westmorland Gazette*, De Quincey anticipated our finest tabloid traditions, while an example of De Quinceyan memoirs might be *Sir Vidia's Shadow*, Paul Theroux's frank account of the break-down of his relationship with V. S. Naipaul and *Iris as I Knew Her*, A. N. Wilson's recollections of Iris Murdoch. De Quincey's portrait, in the 'Lake Reminiscences', of Dorothy and William Wordsworth as impassioned, fervent and feral inspired Emily Brontë's creation of Cathy and Heathcliff in *Wuthering Heights*: the Brontës were avid read-ers of the Edinburgh magazines. His 'Lake Reminiscences' were also the blueprint for Lytton Strachey's iconoclastic *Eminent Victorians*, the biography that punctured our reverence for the past. 'The first duty of the biographer,' said Strachey, is 'a becoming brevity. . . The second. . . is to maintain his own freedom of spirit. It is not his business to be complimentary; it is his business to lay bare the facts of the case, as he understands them.' It was from De Quincey that Lytton Strachey learned the fine art of character assassination.

'For years,' said Borges of Thomas De Quincey, 'I thought that the almost infinite world of literature was in one man.' But one almost infinite man, it seems, runs through a world of literature. We are all De Quinceyan now.

Notes

Abbreviations

Coburn – Kathleen Coburn (ed.), *The Letters of Sara Hutchinson, 1800–1835*, London: Routledge and Kegan Paul, 1954

'Confessions' – De Quincey, 'Confessions of an English Opium-Eater', in Barry Milligan (ed.), *Confessions of an English Opium-Eater and Other Writings*, Harmondsworth: Penguin, 2003

Diary – 'Diary, 1803' in Barry Symonds (ed.), *Writings, 1799–1820: The Works of Thomas De Quincey*, vol. 1, London: Pickering and Chatto, 2000

Eaton – Horace A. Eaton, *Thomas De Quincey: A Biography*, Oxford: Oxford University Press, 1936

Griggs – E. L. Griggs (ed.), *Collected Letters of Samuel Taylor Coleridge*, 6 vols, Oxford: Clarendon, 1956–57

H. A. Page – H. A. Page, *Thomas De Quincey, His Life and Writings, with unpublished correspondence*, 2 vols, London: John Hogg and Co., 1877

Hogg – James Hogg, *De Quincey and His Friends, Personal Recollections, Souvenirs and Anecdotes of Thomas De Quincey, His Friends and Associates*, London: Sampson Low, Marston and Company, 1895

Japp – Alexander H. Japp (ed.), *De Quincey Memorials, Being Letters and Other Records Here First Published*, 2 vols, London: Heinemann, 1891

Jordan – John E. Jordan (ed.), *De Quincey to Wordsworth: The Biography of a Friendship*, London: Cambridge University Press, 1962

Lindop – Grevel Lindop, *The Opium Eater*, London: J. M. Dent, 1981

'Mail-Coach' – De Quincey, 'The English Mail-Coach', in Milligan (ed.), *Confessions of an English Opium-Eater*

Masson – David Masson (ed.), *The Collected Writings of Thomas De Quincey*, 13 vols, London: A & C Black, 1897

Middle Years – Ernest de Selincourt (ed.), *The Letters of Dorothy and William Wordsworth, The Middle Years*, part 1, 1806–1811; part 2, 1812–1820, revised by Mary Moorman and Alan G. Hill, Oxford: Clarendon Press, 1967

Morrison – Robert Morrison, *The English Opium Eater: A Biography of Thomas De Quincey*, London: Weidenfeld and Nicholson, 2009

344   NOTES TO PAGES 1–6

'New Paper' – De Quincey, 'A New Paper on Murder as a Fine Art', in Robert
    Morrison (ed.), *On Murder*, Oxford: Oxford World's Classics, 2006
'On Knocking' – De Quincey, 'On the Knocking at the Gate in Macbeth', in
    Morrison (ed.), *On Murder*
'On Murder' – De Quincey, 'On Murder Considered as One of the Fine Arts', in
    Morrison (ed.), *On Murder*
'Postscript' – De Quincey, 'Postscript [to On Murder as One of the Fine Arts]', in
    Morrison (ed.), *On Murder*
Recollections – David Wright (ed.), *Recollections of the Lakes and the Lake Poets*,
    Harmondsworth: Penguin, 1970
'Second Paper' – 'Second Paper [on Murder as One of the Fine Arts]', in Morrison
    (ed.), *On Murder*
'Suspiria' – 'Suspiria de Profundis', in Milligan (ed.), *Confessions of an English Opium-
    Eater*

The Prelude

1 *Suppose the Earth. . .* Kathleen Coburn (ed.), *The Notebooks of Samuel Taylor
    Coleridge, 1794–1826,* Princeton University Press and Routledge, 1957–90, vol. 3,
    1808–1819.
2 *the hardest building to describe in London. . .* Ian Nairn, *Nairn's London,*
    Harmondsworth: Penguin, 2014, p. 111.
3 *closely shut up. . .* The Times, 11 Dec 1811, p. 3.
3 *I said I belonged to the house. . .* The Times, 11 Dec 1811, p. 3.
3 *Marr, Marr. . .* The Times, 11 Dec 1811, p. 3.
4 *The child, where's the child? . . .* The Times, 11 Dec 1811, p. 3.
5 *What is true of friendship. . .* Samuel Taylor Coleridge, *Seven Lectures on
    Shakespeare and Milton,* with an introductory preface by J. Payne Collier,
    London: Chapman and Hall, 1856, p. 93.
5 *Coleridge said in his advertisement. . .* Samuel Taylor Coleridge, *Biographia
    Literaria,* edited by James Engell and W. Jackson Bate, Princeton: Princeton
    University Press, 1983, I, p. 60n.
5 *the only man to whom. . .* Griggs, I, p. 334.
5 *scene of struggle. . .* Recollections, p. 293.
5 *Few writers . . . had so keen. . .* Peter Ackroyd, *Dan Leno and the Limehouse
    Golem,* London: Minerva, 1995, p. 38.
5 *the loveliest spot . . .* William Wordsworth, 'Farewell. Composed in the Year 1802'.
6 *the practice of putting the chain. . .* 'Postscript', p. 98.
6 *quite incapable of fear. . .* H. A. Page, I, p. 192.
6 *There must be raging . . .* 'On Knocking', p. 5. De Quincey's image of an inter-
    nal hell is lifted from Milton's description of the fallen Satan in Book IV of
    Paradise Lost: 'The hell within him; for within him Hell/ He brings. . .'

7   *Some of our contemporaries* . . . De Quincey, 'Some Thoughts on Biography',
    in G. Lindop (ed.), *The Works of Thomas De Quincey*, XXI, London:
    Pickering and Chatto, 2003, p. 26.
7   *We should not assert for De Quincey.* . . Hogg, p. 1.
8   *review-like essay.* . . Walter Bagehot, 'The First Edinburgh Reviewers',
    Literary Studies, London: Dent, 1911, 1.1–35, p. 4.
8   *one boundless self-devouring Review.* . . Thomas Carlyle, 'Characteristics',
    Edinburgh Review, 54, 1831.
8   *a bat . . . on the wings of prose.* . . Leslie Stephen, *Hours in a Library*,
    London: Smith, Elder & Co., 1892, I, p. 240.
9   *wearisome and useless.* . . De Quincey, 'A Sketch from Childhood', *Instructor*,
    Edinburgh: 1851, p. 147.
9   *We might imagine this descent.* . . Masson, X, p. 344.
10 *unfortunately diminutive.* . . *Middle Years*, pt 1, p. 255.
10 *I wish . . . he was not so little* . . . Carol Bolton and Tim Fulford (eds),
    The Collected Letters of Robert Southey, 1804–9, University of Maryland: *A
    Romantic Circles Electronic Edition*, Part 3, no. 1534.
10 *this child has been in hell.* . . Thomas Carlyle, *Reminiscences*, edited by
    James Anthony Froude, New York, Charles Scribner's Sons, 1881, p. 203.

Chapter 1: Books

13 *'suddenly' to a 'violent termination'.* . . Masson, I, p. 28.
13 *in the house of a labouring man.* . . Masson, I, p. 37.
13 *was rapidly approaching.* . . De Quincey, 'Sketches of Life and Manners',
    Tait's Edinburgh Magazine, 1834, p. 22.
13 *lady architect.* . . Masson, I, p. 404.
14 *The door so softly. . . deeper than the Danube.* . . Masson, I, p. 42.
14 *Nothing. . . a sorrow without a voice.* . . Masson, I, p. 9.
14–15 *on a summer day. . . on a summer day.* . . Masson, I, pp. 41–2.
15 *without fear. . . closed.* . . 'Mail-Coach', p. 230.
15 *shut out forever.* . . Masson, I, p. 43.
16 *sank back. . . clamorously for death.* . . Masson, I, pp. 44–8.
16 *burst of. . . open grave.* . . Masson, I, p. 50.
17 *a man, of elegant tastes.* . . Masson, I, p. 130.
18 *deep and memorable.* . . Masson, I, p. 132.
18 *clouds were dispersed.* . . Thomas Percival, *A Father's Instructions, Consisting
    of Moral Tales, Fables, and Reflections*, Robert Dodsley, 1775, p. 21.
18 *the finest. . . astonishment of science.* . . Masson, I, p. 35.
20 *How much the greatest Event.* . . Lord John Russell (ed.), *Memorials
    and Correspondence of Charles James Fox*, Blanchard and Lea, 1853, II,
    p. 361.

20   *With freedom, order and good government*. . . William Pitt, *The Speeches of the Right Honourable William Pitt*, edited by W. S. Hathaway, London: Longman, Hurst, Rees, Orme, and Brown, 1817, II, p. 36.

20   *the British turned Louis into a hero*. . . see John Barrell, 'Sad Stories', *Imagining the King's Death: Figurative Treason, Fantasies of Regicide, 1793–1796*, Oxford: Oxford University Press, 2000.

21   *summer and winter came again*. . . Masson, I, p. 34.

21   *terrific. . . evil and strife*. . . Masson, I, p. 35.

21   *anniversary of the battle of So-and-So*. . . David Masson, *De Quincey*, London: Macmillan, 1881, p. 107.

22   *What is to be thought of sudden death?*. . . 'Mail-Coach', p. 219.

22   *Wonderful it is. . . Perceptions. . . Recollections*, p. 259.

22   *'fugitive' spiders*. . . 'Suspiria', p. 130.

22   *the most upright man*. . . Masson, I, p. 26.

23   *circumstances of luxury*. . . Masson, I, p. 30.

23   *principal room*. . . Masson, I, p. 26.

23   *would have been able to. . . St Kitts*. . . Masson, I, p. 55.

23   *raising altars and burning incense*. . . 'A Sketch from Childhood', *Instructor*, 1851, p. 147.

24   *instant amusement*. . . Masson, I, p. 25.

24   *unusual solemnity*. . . Masson, I, p. 57.

24   *midsummer night's dream*. . . 'A Sketch from Childhood', *Instructor*, p. 174.

24   *the endless days of summer*. . .'Confessions', p. 83.

25   *omen of anticipation*. . . Eaton, p. 284.

25–6 *a perfect craze . . . choose to build*. . . Masson, I, p. 59.

26   *detested all books. . . dream upon it*. . . Masson, I, p. 62.

26   *slovenly and forlorn*. . . Masson, I, p. 70.

27   *What is this I hear, child?*. . . H. A. Page, I, p. 30.

27–8 *a most splendid. . . same hour*. . . Masson, I, pp. 116–19.

28   *a new book*. . . Masson, I, p. 115.

28   *Were the lamps of our equipage clean and bright?*. . . Japp, I, pp. 9–10.

29   *a mighty theatre. . . infinite review*. . . 'Suspiria', p. 151.

29   *Trial by jury, English laws of evidence*. . . Japp, I, p. 9.

29   *Had the Vatican. . . carry it off to sea*. . . 'Suspiria', p. 135.

29–30 *What a huge thing. . . crack of doom*. . . 'Suspiria', pp. 136–8.

30   *at the front door. . . set of ropes*. . . 'Suspiria', p. 141.

31   *Into a downright. . . yet a higher flight*. . . Masson, X, pp. 38–40.

31   *An infinite book*. . . see Jorge Luis Borges, 'The Thousand and One Nights', *The Georgia Review*, XXXVIII, No. 3 (Fall 1984), pp. 564–74.

32   *involutes*. . . Masson, I, p. 128.

32   *compound experiences*. . . 'Suspiria', p. 107.

32–3 *At the opening. . . corresponding keys*, Masson, I, pp. 128–9.

33   *the opening scene of 'Aladdin'*. . . De Quincey uses the image again in 'The Nation of London', where he describes how his visit as a boy to St Paul's

Cathedral was hampered by the vendor selling tickets to see the sights: 'I ask, does no action at common law lie against the promoters of such enormous abuses? Oh, thou fervent reformer – whose fatal tread he that puts his ear to the ground may hear at a distance coming onwards upon *every* road. . .'

Chapter 2: Childhood and Schooltime

35   *all the signs of the Zodiac*. . . Tobias Smollett, *The Expedition of Humphry Clinker*, Munich, 2005, p. 40.

37   *Another stupid party*. . . Claire Tomalin, *Jane Austen, A Life*, Harmondsworth: Penguin, 1997, pp. 171–2.

37   *mattermoney*. . . Smollett, *Humphry Clinker*, p. 352.

37   *cold reason*. . . Letter from Walpole to Mme Du Deffand, quoted in W. S. Lewis (ed.), *The Castle of Otranto*, Oxford: World's Classics, 1982, p. x.

37   *no one*. . . *poor judge of a novel*. . . Eaton, p. 467.

38   *purgatory*. . . Lindop, p. 23.

38   *decaying condition*. . . Masson, I, p. 288.

38   *crowds of inquirers*. . . Masson, I, p. 289.

39   *the very idea*. . . *hereditary poet laureate*. . . Thomas Paine, *Rights of Man*, edited by E. Foner, Harmondsworth: Penguin, 1969, p. 83.

39   *the age of chivalry*. . . *French excesses*. . . *Recollections*, p. 220.

39   *object*. . . *down their faces*. . . see Jenny Uglow, *In These Times, Living in Britain Through Napoleon's Wars, 1793–1815*, London: Faber, 2015, p. 21.

39   *decent drapery of life*. . . 'Confessions', p. 3.

40   *Suddenness . . . terror*. . . Edmund Burke, *A Philosophical Enquiry into the Origin of our Ideas of the Sublime and the Beautiful*, edited by Adam Philips, Oxford: Oxford University Press, 1990, pp. 76, 103, 53.

41   *Epigrammatic*. . . *quotations*. . . Jordan, p. 251.

41   *travelled*. . . *politeness*. . . Masson, XIV, p. 96.

41   *everyone of celebrity*. . . *Dr Johnson &c*. . . Jordan, p. 252.

42   *was honoured*. . . *extempore*. . . Masson, I, p. 152.

42   *I neither read*. . . *till Easter*. . . H. A. Page, I, p. 36.

43   *aged seventeen*. . . We cannot be sure of the date of William's birth, but it is likely to have been 1782.

44   *a contemplative dreamer like myself*. . . Masson, I, p. 115.

44   *no honours to excite one*. . . Japp, I, pp. 40–1.

45   *forty years*. . . *Bristol*. . . Masson, I, p. 393.

45   *despicable place*. . . *twenty*. . . John Dix, *The Life of Thomas Chatterton, including his Unpublished Poems*, London: Hamilton Adams, 1837, p. 175.

46   *fix his eyes*. . . Charles Bonnycastle Willcox, *The Poetical Works of Thomas Chatterton, with Notices on his Life, History of the Rowley Controversy and Notes illustrative of the Poems*, Cambridge: W. P. Grant, 1842, p. lxxiv.

46   *a miscellaneous. . . hieroglyphics. . .* Henry H. Jennings, *Thomas Chatterton: The Boy Poet of Bristol, A Biographical Sketch*, Bristol: St Augustine's Press, 1868, p. 13.

47   *the first modern attempt. . .* Walter Scott, introduction to *The Castle of Otranto*, Edinburgh, 1811, p. iii.

48   *Bristol's mercantile. . . miserable hamlet. . .* Sir Herbert Croft, *Love and Madness: A Story Too True,* London: G. Kearsly, 1780, p. 176.

49   *torn-up pieces of manuscript. . .* see Richard Holmes's compelling essay on Chatterton in *Sidetracks: Explorations of a Romantic Biographer*, London: HarperCollins, 2000, pp. 5–50.

49   *adventurer. . . by expedients. . .* Thomas Warton, *The History of English Poetry: From the Close of the Eleventh to the Commencement of the Eighteenth Century*, London: J. Dodsley, 1824, II, p. 477.

50   *murdered Chatterton. . .* Croft, *Love and Madness*, p. 172.

50   *Whom did he deceive. . .* Thomas De Quincey, 'Great Forgers, Chatterton, and Walpole, and Junius', in Alexander H. Japp (ed.), *The Posthumous Works of Thomas De Quincey*, London: Heinemann, 1891, I, p. 125.

50   *forbidden rooms. . .* In 1856, De Quincey's future editor, David Masson, published a novel called *Chatterton: The Story of a Year*, in which he described the last moments of Chatterton's life in a way that would have delighted De Quincey. Having climbed the narrow stairs to his room: 'He entered and locked the door behind him. The Devil was abroad that night in the sleeping city. Down narrow and squalid courts his presence was felt, where savage men seized miserable women by the throat and the neighbourhood was roused by yells of murder. . . Up in the wretched garrets his presence was felt, where solitary mothers gazed on their infants and longed to kill them.'

50   *ghost crab. . .* This image is used by Patrick Bridgwater in *De Quincey's Gothic Masquerade*, Amsterdam and New York: Rodopi, 2004, p. 63.

50–1   *carried. . . elder poets. . .* Masson, II, p. 58.

51   *if it be possible. . .* Japp (ed.), *Posthumous Works of Thomas De Quincey*, p. 128.

51   *Poor Chatterton. . . my friend. . .* Linda Kelly, *The Marvellous Boy: The Life and Myth of Thomas Chatterton*, London: Weidenfeld and Nicolson, 1971, p. 230.

51   *panegyric instead of satire. . .* Joseph Cottle, *Reminiscences of Samuel Taylor Coleridge and Robert Southey*, London: Houlston and Stoneman, 1847, p. 193.

52   *the greatest event. . .mind. . .* De Quincey remembers this as being 1799, but it is more likely to have been the spring or summer of 1798. *Lyrical Ballads* was published in the autumn of 1798, and it is unlikely that a manuscript of one of the poems would be in circulation after the book itself was available. James Losh of Bath, a friend of Wordsworth, remembered reading in manuscript 'a curious but fine little poem of Wordsworth's' during the spring of 1798. See Mary Moorman, 'Wordsworth's Commonplace Book', *Notes & Queries*, 202 (1957), p. 405.

53   *Nothing. . . my own being. . .* Jared Curtis, *The Fenwick Notes of William Wordsworth*, Bristol: Bristol Classical Press, 1993, p. 159.

53   *dark, cold place. . .* Coleridge, *Biographia Literaria*, I, p. 141.

53   *How deep. . . such a ballad!. . .* Hogg, p. 93.
53   *guidance. . .* Jordan, p. 37.
53   *religious fervour. . .* Coleridge, *Biographia Literaria,* II, p. 9.

Chapter 3: Schooltime (continued)

56   *the feeling therein developed. . .* R. L. Brett and A. R. Jones (eds), *Lyrical Ballads,* London and New York: Routledge, 2005, p. 293.
57   *language of conversation. . . awkwardness. . .* Brett and Jones (eds), *Lyrical Ballads,* p. 49.
58   *procrastination . . . too-lateness. . .* Japp, II, p. 142.
58   *full thirty years. . .* Masson, II, p. 59.
58   *an old quiz. . .* Masson, I, p. 393.
58   *the originality of the Lyrical Ballads. . .* see Robert Mayo, 'The Contemporaneity of the *Lyrical Ballads*' (*PMLA,* lxix, 1954, pp. 486–522). Mayo argues that the *Lyrical Ballads* conformed in many respects to the popular poetry of the magazines in the 1790s. It was 'experimental' less in its innovations than in the freshness and intensity it brought to already familiar traditions.
59   *The name of Wordsworth. . . contempt. . .* Masson, II, p. 60.
59   *poems from the first edition appeared in twenty-three separate papers. . .* Patricia Gael, '*Lyrical Ballads* in British Periodicals, 1798–1800', *Wordsworth Circle,* Winter 2013.
60   *in an element of danger. . .* Masson, I, p. 390.
60   *mere beds. . . shrubberies. . .* Masson, I, p. 283.
60   *This was a tender point. . . Black Letter period. . .* Masson, I, p. 168.
61   *the sublimity. . . gloom and uncertainty. . .* Masson, I, pp. 178–82.
61–2   *first view. . . greater distances. . .* Masson, III, p. 296. Readers of the Whispering Gallery passage in De Quincey's revised edition of *Confessions of an English Opium-Eater* have remarked that he misremembered its effect: the sound which begins in a state of muffled secrecy arrives not magnified but *clarified*. De Quincey's memory always tended towards amplification rather than elucidation.
62   *Depths. . . gloomy recesses. . .* G. Lindop (ed.), *Works,* 20, p. 337.
62   *exploding like minute guns. . .* Japp (ed.), *Posthumous Works of Thomas De Quincey,* I, p. 77.
62   *down into. . . able to describe. . .* Japp, p. 32.
63   *Dullness was the downside of sublimity. . .* see De Quincey, 'Schlosser's History of the Eighteenth Century', in John E. Jordan (ed.), *De Quincey as Critic,* London: Routledge, 1973, p. 314.
63   *Eleusinian mysteries. . .* Masson, I, p. 212.
63   *my profoundest sympathies. . .* Masson, I, p. 219.
63   *this morning. . . so are you. . .* Masson, I, p. 223.
64   *old Irish nobility . . . cornucopia. . .* Masson, I, p. 325.
65   *In England. . . microscope. . .* Japp, pp. 37–8.

65   *Reading, Hunting . . . elemental war. . .* Japp, I, pp. 28–9. The line, 'from
        some high cliff superior', is not from Shakespeare but Akenside's mid-
        eighteenth century didactic poem, *Pleasures of Imagination.*
66   *some victim. . . antique school-room. . .* Masson, I, p. 331.
67   *stir out of doors. . . conjured up. . .* Japp, pp. 53–5.
67   *trifling degree of cleanliness. . .* Friedrich Engels, *The Condition of the Working
        Class in England*, London: Swan Sonnenschein & Co., 1892, p. 53.
67   *Series of unfurnished . . . cauliflower. . .* Masson, III, pp. 247–52.
67   *worm-eaten passages. . .* Masson, III, p. 271.
68   *slumbering in the mind. . .* 'On Wordsworth's Poetry', in Jordan (ed.), *De
        Quincey as Critic*, p. 416.
69   *a profound secret. . .* Masson, II, p. 60.
69–70   *All good poetry. . . into neglect. . .* Brett and Jones (eds), *Lyrical Ballads*,
        pp. 291, 294.
70   *the most finished. . . fine arts. . .* 'Wordsworth and Southey, Affinities and
        Differences', in Jordan (ed.), *De Quincey as Critic*, p. 427.
70–1   *You need bring. . . introduce you. . .* Japp, I, p. 61.
71   *fraternisers. . . with ingratitude. . .* Masson, II, pp. 127–8.
71   *genius . . . of the highest class. . .* see Henry Roscoe, *The Life of William
        Roscoe*, London: Cadell and Blackwood, 1833, p. 233: 'With the little vol-
        ume of Mr. Coleridge's poems I have been greatly delighted – his genius is
        of the highest class. The characteristics of a fervid imagination and a highly
        cultivated taste are visible in every page.' For an excellent exploration of De
        Quincey's relationship with, and debt to, the Everton coterie see Daniel
        Sanjiv Roberts, 'De Quincey's Discovery of *Lyrical Ballads*, The Politics of
        Reading', *Studies in Romanticism*, 36 (Winter 1997), pp. 511–32.
72   *Bristol is not. . .* Roscoe, *Life of William Roscoe*, I, pp. 231–3.
72   *the manners of good sense. . .* Griggs, I, pp. 607, 2, 746.
72   *To me. . . of a divine art. . .* Masson, II, p. 129.
72   *hallowed to my own thoughts. . .* Masson, II, p. 139.
72   *searched east and west. . .* Masson, II, p. 139.
73   *a pretty duodecimo. . .* Masson, III, p. 312.
73   *ancient gothic monastery. . .* Masson, II, p. 11.
73   *Sir Robert's day. . . on its stage. . .* Masson, I, p. 409.
74   *Every human being. . . I govern you?. . .* Japp, I, pp. 73–4.
74   *transformation in a pantomime. . .* Uglow, p. 289.
74   *army with banners. . .* Masson, III, p. 289.
74   *he had been uniformly . . . power. . .* 'Confessions', p. 12.
74–5   *a sort of trance. . . upon the stairs. . .* Masson, III, p. 297.
75   *I dressed myself . . . archididasculus. . .* 'Confessions', pp. 12–14.
75   *deep, deep magnet. . .* Masson, III, p. 283.

Chapter 4: Residence in London

77   *hallowed character. . . embarrassment. . .* Masson, III, p. 284.

78   *Sphinx's riddle. . .* Masson, III, p. 287.

78   *confluent at the post office. . .* Masson, III, p. 286.

79   *what Wordsworth. . . heart-corroding doubt. . .* Masson, III, pp. 279–84.

79   *dazzling day. . . Whispering Galleries. . .* Masson, III, p. 300.

79–80   *What was it?. . . my fancied felony. . .* Masson, III, p. 310.

80   *total revolt. . .* Japp, I, p. 71.

80–1   *headstrong act. . . magnify. . .* Masson, III, pp. 312, 317.

81   *even the brooks . . . seeking in Wales. . .* Masson, III, p. 322.

81   *You must recollect, Betty . . .* Masson, III, p. 323.

82   *two and a half hours. . . this vagrancy. . .* Masson, III, p. 329.

82   *to fly where no man pursued. . .* Masson, III, p. 338.

83   *real suffering. . .* Masson, II, p. 55.

83   *the last brief. . . expiring lamp. . .* Masson, III, p. 343.

83–4   *whole atmosphere. . . and in darkness. . .* Masson, III, pp. 346–7.

84   *unhappy countenance. . . barely decent. . .* Masson, III, pp. 350–1.

85   *Radix God. . .* see Iain McCalman, 'Mystagogues of Revolution', in James Chandler and Kevin Gilmartin (eds), *Romantic Metropolis: The Urban Scene of British Culture, 1780 –1840*, Cambridge: Cambridge University Press, 2005, p. 192.

85   *corrector of Greek proofs. . .* 'Confessions', p. 28.

85   *extremities such as these. . .* 'Confessions', p. 19.

87   *ballad-singing confraternity. . .* John Thomas Smith, *A Book for a Rainy Day, Or, Recollections of the Events of the Years 1766–1833*, London: Methuen, 1905, p. 239.

87   *natural black frame. . .* Charles Lamb, 'Recollections of a Late Royal Academician' (1831) in *The Complete Correspondence and Works of Charles Lamb*, with an essay on his life and genius by Thomas Purnell, London: E. Moxton, 1870, III, p. 406.

87   *ceiled with looking glasses. . . enriched with trees. . .* Jerry White, *A Great and Monstrous Thing: London in the Eighteenth Century*, London: Bodley Head, 2011, p. 294.

88   *the outcasts and pariahs. . . sitting. . .* 'Confessions', p. 24.

88   *ragged dirty shoes. . . common to them all. . .* Francis Place, *The Autobiography of Francis Place*, edited with an introduction by Mary Thale, Cambridge: Cambridge University Press, 1972, p. 71.

89   *died on the spot. . .* 'Confessions', p. 26.

89   *by dreamy lamplight . . . shed tears. . .* 'Confessions', p. 27.

90   *fraud. . .* De Quincey, 'Some Thoughts on Biography', in Japp (ed.), *Posthumous Works of Thomas De Quincey*, I, p. 116.

90   *beauteous Wretches. . . the same circle. . .* 'An Account of the Life of Mr Richard Savage', in Donald Greene (ed.), *The Oxford Authors, Samuel Johnson*, Oxford: Oxford University Press, 1984, p. 145.

90   *nest-egg. . .* Japp (ed.), *Posthumous Works of Thomas De Quincey*, I, p. 114.

90   *on moonlight nights. . . fly to comfort. . .* 'Confessions', p. 40.

91   *many a charming family scene . . . Sophie in London, 1786; Being the Diary of Sophie v la Roche,* trans. from the German by Clare Williams, London: Jonathan Cape, 1933, p. 141.

91   *now in the occupation . . . cheerful and gay. . .* 'Confessions', p. 34.

92   *If she lived. . . meeting her. . .* 'Confessions', p. 38.

92   *stony-hearted stepmother. . .* 'Confessions', p. 39.

92   *concessions. . .* Diary, p.18.

93   *book that . . . does not permit itself to be read. . .* Edgar Allan Poe, 'The Man of the Crowd', in *Edgar Allan Poe, Thirty-Two Stories*, edited by Stuart Levin and Susan F. Levine, Indianapolis: Hackett Publishing, 2000, p. 129.

Chapter 5: Summer Vacation

95   *good and kind matron. . . under her roof. . .* Robert Syers, *History of Everton, Including Familiar Dissertations on the People, and Descriptive Delineations of the Several & Separate Properties of the Township*, Liverpool: J. and G. Robinson, 1830, p. 303.

96   *afloat in the heart of the town. . .* W. Jones, *The Liverpool Guide, Including a Sketch of the Environs*, Liverpool, Crane and Jones, 1801, p. 34.

96   *lost in thought . . . never passed away. . .* Diary, p. 25.

97   *the sentence hangs and turns. . .* Diary, p. 55.

98   *damnation to drink. . .* Diary, p. 55.

98   *talk about the war. . .* Diary, p. 53.

98   *as inferior beings. . .* Diary, p. 50.

99   *road down to hell. . .* Diary, p. 36.

99   *Chattertonian melancholia. . .* Diary, p. 13.

99   *I see Chatterton. . . at midnight. . .* Diary, p. 22.

99   *Edmund Spenser. . . NO. . .* Diary, p. 15.

100   *A few days ago. . . by my heart. . .* Diary, pp. 20–1.

100   *I image myself . . . not tell you. . .* Diary, p. 22

100   *second identity. . . Recollections*, p. 120.

101   *walked into the lanes . . . saved me trouble. . .* Diary, p. 22.

102–3   *Sir. . . lowly to prostrate myself. . .* Diary, pp. 28–30.

103   *I thought it . . . of their accomplishment. . .* Diary, p. 28.

103–4   *humble task. . . works might relate. . .* Francis Jeffrey, *Contributions to the Edinburgh Review*, London: Longman Brown, 1846, I, p. 11.

104   *Poetry has this much . . . call in question. . .* 'Southey's *Thalaba; a metrical Romance*', *Edinburgh Review* 1.1, October 1802, pp. 63–83.

104   *What is a poet?. . .* Brett and Jones (eds), *Lyrical Ballads*, p. 300.

104   *the face of a darling Child. . .* Richard Holmes, *Coleridge: Early Visions 1772–1804*, London: HarperCollins, 1989, p. 326.

104   *feeble, fluttering, ingenious. . .* Masson, II, p. 60.

105   *electrical . . . were all new. . .* Henry Cockburn, *Life of Lord Jeffrey: With a Selection From His Correspondence*, Edinburgh, A & C Black, 1852, p. 131.

105   *I was not . . . my going there. . .* Diary, p. 31.

105   *dying on an island. . .* Diary, p. 38.

106   *admits of humour. . .* Diary, p. 25.

107   *Southey. . . metrical pathos. . .* Diary, p. 54.

108–9 *I suppose that most men. . . interest and happiness. . .* Diary, pp. 40–2.

109   *These particulars I gathered. . . Wordsworth or Coleridge. . .* Diary, p. 44.

110   *of Coleridge. . . go to sleep. . .* Diary, p. 44.

110   *My imagination flies. . .* Diary, p. 55.

111   *fears and schemes were put to flight. . .* Jordan, p. 35.

Chapter 6: Residence at Oxford

113   *Let there be a cottage. . . Jasmine. . .* 'Confessions', p. 65.

114   *A remarkable instance. . . Middle Years,* pt 1, p. 180.

114   *it would be out of nature. . . all others. . .* Japp, I, p. 121.

114   *My friendship is not. . . very happy . . .* Japp, I, p. 121.

115   *a rare thing. . .* Mary Moorman, *William Wordsworth: The Early Years, 1770–1803*, Oxford and New York: Oxford University Press, 1957, p. 568.

115   *at your feet. . .* Moorman, *Early Years*, p. 568.

115   *Plant it. . . as yours. . .* Moorman, *Early Years*, p. 587.

115   *Your sincere friend. . .* Moorman, *Early Years*, p. 595.

115   *The Beau . . . his verses. . .* Moorman, *Early Years*, p. 184.

116   *In your poems. . . take no interest. . .* Mary Gordon, '*Christopher North': A Memoir of John Wilson*, Edinburgh: Edmonston and Douglas, 1862, pp. 26–32.

117   *Nothing in England . . .* W. A. Speck, *Robert Southey: Entire Man of Letters*, New Haven: Yale University Press, 2006, p. 101.

117   *a convulsive inclination. . .* Duncan Wu, *Hazlitt: The First Modern Man*, Oxford: Oxford University Press, 2008, p. 11.

117–18 *William Hazlitt. . . twang of the Bow-string. . .* Griggs, II, pp. 990–1.

118–19 *What foolish thing. . .good wishes to them both. . .* Jordan, pp. 34–5.

119   *It was Ann Radcliffe. . .* Masson, III, p. 282.

119   *heaviness of heart. . .* Griggs, II, p. 975.

119   *determined hater of the French. . .* William Knight (ed.), *Letters of the Wordsworth Family from 1787 to 1855*, Boston and London: Ginn and Co., 1907, I, p. 150.

120   *No longer. . . of the world. . .* Masson, II, p. 10.
120   *Singularly barren. . .* Jordan, p. 21.
120   *knew nothing. . . escaped. . .* Masson, II, p. 55.
120–1 *one hundred words. . . pompous. . .* Masson, II, p. 75.
121   *When you gave me permission. . . acquaintance. . .* Jordan, p. 36.
121–2 *Some years ago. . . converse with nature. . .* Jordan, p. 37.
122   *repent the notice. . .* Jordan, p. 41.
123   *wet and cheerless. . .* 'Confessions', p. 55.
123   *In an hour. . . mail-coach. . .* 'Confessions', p. 46.
123   *the majestic intellect. . .* 'Confessions', p. 47.
123   *torments. . .* 'Confessions', p. 47.
123   *shut him up.* . . George Gilfillan, *Second Gallery of Literary Portraits*, Edinburgh: James Hogg, 1852, p. 298.
124   *I sought him. . . bodily fashion. . .* 'Confessions', pp. 42–3.
124   *an absolute revelation . . . men. . .* 'Confessions', p. 46.
125   *without much regarding. . . north-west passage. . .* 'Confessions', p. 53.
125   *It was my disease. . .* 'Confessions', p. 54.
125   *a size too large. . .* Virginia Woolf, 'The English Mail Coach', in Andrew McNeillie (ed.), *The Essays of Virginia Woolf, 1904–1912*, New York: Harcourt Brace Javanovich, 1986, I, p. 365.
126   *But Mr Lamb. . . began our conversation. . .* Hogg, p. 71.
126   *began to inquire. . . waiting. . .* Recollections, p. 34.
127   *phantom-self. . .* Recollections, p. 120.
127   *spiritualised object. . . coal cellar in disguise. . .* 'Mail-Coach', pp. 197, 195.
127   *foolish panic. . .* Recollections, pp. 122–3.
128   *guilty weight. . .* 'Mail-Coach', p. 230.
128   *long silence. . . willingly recall. . .* Jordan, p. 42.
129   *the frost of death. . .* 'Suspiria', p. 143.
129   *one CRIME of OPIUM.* . . Molly Lefebure, *Samuel Taylor Coleridge: A Bondage of Opium*, London: Quartet, 1974, p. 40.
129   *Sources of Happiness. . .* Diary, pp. 72–3.
130   *look dreadful. . .* Michael Neve, 'Spaced', *London Review of Books,* III, No. 16, 3 Sep 1981.
131   *loveliest of landscapes. . . like a guilty thing. . .* Recollections, p. 122.

Chapter 7: Retrospect: Love of Nature Leading to Love of Mankind

133   *there was a limit. . .* Recollections, p. 124.
134   *to have not been original. . .* Recollections, p. 35.
135   *sent a carriage for him. . .* Recollections, p. 43.
135–6 *in height. . . mighty music. . .* Recollections, p. 46.
136   *not been a happy one. . .* Recollections, p. 51.
136   *rolling, rudderless. . .* Griggs, IV, p. 651.

136   *utterly changed. . . Middle Years*, pt 1, p. 78.

136   *current of my own. . .* Griggs, IV, p. 888.

137   *Sara! Sara! Love me!. . .* Seamus Perry (ed.), *Coleridge's Notebooks: A Selection*, Oxford: Oxford University Press, 2002, p. 96.

137   *perpetual struggle. . . poison-taking. . .* Griggs, II, p. 1178.

137   *idolatry of that family. . .* Kenneth Curry (ed.), *New Letters of Robert Southey, 1792–1810*, New York: Columbia University Press, 1965, I, pp. 44–9.

137   *under the full dominion. . . Recollections*, p. 43.

138   *gossiping taste. . . Recollections*, p. 154.

138   *a cruel sweat on the brow. . .* see Richard Holmes, *Coleridge: Darker Reflections*, London: HarperCollins, 1998, p. 96.

138   *besieged by decay. . . Recollections*, p. 56.

139   *Two faces. . . ever the same. . .* Ernest Hartley Coleridge (ed.), *Anima Poetae: From the Unpublished Notebooks of Samuel Taylor Coleridge*, London: Heinemann, 1895, pp. 176–7.

139   *drivelling to the common pile-wort . . . a sucking-pig. . .* For a selection of the reviews see E. Smith, *An Estimate of William Wordsworth by his Contemporaries, 1793–1822*, Oxford: Blackwell, 1932.

140   *routs, dinners, morning calls. . .* Mary Moorman, *William Wordsworth: A Biography, The Later Years, 1803–1850*, Oxford: Oxford University Press, 1966, p. 104.

140   *not a man in the Kingdom. . .* Lindop, p. 146.

140   *no doubt of the source. . .* Japp, 1891, I, p. 133.

141   *I never knew two pairs . . . stops growing. . .* Griggs, III, pp. 37–8.

141   *sudden shock. . . Recollections*, p. 127.

142   *apparition. . . cordial manner. . . Recollections*, pp. 127–8.

142   *stunned. . . expression of benignity. . . Recollections*, pp. 128–9.

142   *all fire. . . impassioned intellect. . . Recollections*, pp. 131, 188.

142   *fourteen steps. . . Recollections*, p. 134.

143   *showed him the universe. . .* Stopford Brooke, *Dove Cottage: Wordsworth's Home from 1800–1808*, London: Macmillan, 1894, p. 53.

143   *this sequestered nook. . .* Wordsworth, 'The Green Linnet'.

143   *What-like?. . . Recollections*, p. 135.

143–4 *Is it possible. . . depths below all depths. . . Recollections*, pp. 135–6, 139.

144   *only to laugh at it. . . Recollections*, p. 308.

144   *so very shy. . .* Knight (ed.), *Letters*, I, p. 325.

144   *whatever fate Befal me. . .* see Alethea Hayter, *The Wreck of the Abergavenny: The Wordsworths and Catastrophe*, Basingstoke: Macmillan, 2002, pp. 23–4.

145   *superior. . . self-contempt. . . Recollections*, p. 207.

145   *the forest of his genius. . . Recollections*, p. 139.

146   *enshrined Mr and Mrs Crump. . .* Moorman, *Early Years*, p. 441.

146   *at t'maist o' t' houses i' these parts.* . . Hardwicke Drummond Rawnsley, *Reminiscences of Wordsworth among the Peasantry of Westmoreland*, London: Dillon's University Bookshop, 1968, p. 20.

146   *good enough for me.* . . *Recollections*, p. 211.

147   *city tailor.* . . *Recollections*, p. 215.

147   *ancient fireside friends.* . . *Recollections*, p. 221.

147   *calumny and ingratitude.* . . Griggs, I, p. 298.

147   *we are by no means glad.* . . Moorman, *Early Years*, p. 140.

148   *at the zenith.* . . *Recollections*, p. 321.

148   *ridiculed. . .effeminate.* . . *Recollections*, p. 319.

148   *doomed household.* . . *Recollections*, p. 324.

148   *woman you admire.* . . Japp, I, p. 285.

148   *All of us loved her.* . . *Recollections*, p. 206.

149   *gift from God . . . not have had.* . . *Recollections*, p. 201.

Chapter 8: Home at Grasmere

151   *struggling with pain . . . in the highway by himself.* . . *Recollections*, pp. 77–9.

152   *Wordsworth the great poet.* . . Edwin W. Marrs (ed.), *The Letters of Charles and Mary Lamb*, Ithaca and London: Cornell University Press, II, p. 274.

152–3 *sloven. . . those he opposes.* . . Moorman, *Later Years*, p. 124.

153   *having been treated. . . expectations.* . . Jordan, p. 87.

153   *You have sent . . . before him.* . . Hogg, p. 102.

154   *I do therefore ask you.* . . Japp, I, p. 136.

155   *I have suffered considerable.* . . Japp, I, p. 138.

155   *Some of them. . . gloom of the hall.* . . 'Confessions', p. 78.

156   *aerial dungeon.* . . *Recollections*, p. 344.

156   *a chamber within a chamber.* . . *Recollections*, p. 251.

157   *he is loving, gentle and happy.* . . Knight (ed.), *Letters*, I, p. 425.

157   *Mr de Quincey has been here.* . . Jordan, p. 57.

157   *little Chinese maiden.* . . *Middle Years*, pt 1, p. 365.

158   *her sole tutor. . . gentle thoughts.* . . Knight (ed.), *Letters*, I, p. 436.

158   *a sixteen stoner.* . . William Maginn, 'John Wilson, Esq', *Fraser's Magazine*, 3 (Apr 1831), p. 364.

158   *balmy odours.* . . see Karl Miller, *Electric Shepherd: A Likeness of James Hogg*, London: Faber, 2003, p. 129.

158   *more brilliant . . . principles of poetry.* . . *Recollections*, p. 123.

159   *headlong nonsense.* . . H. A. Page, II, p. 175.

159   *the stormiest pleasures.* . . *Recollections*, p. 362.

159   *I abhor stairs.* . . Gordon, *Memoir of John Wilson*, p. 89.

159   *a most tempestuous youth.* . . Masson, V, p. 279.

160   *he rarely walked.* . . Jordan, p. 217.

161   *I have often remarked . . . circumstances.* . . *Recollections*, p. 160.

161   *no neighbour that buys them. . . Middle Years*, pt 1, p. 377.
161   *dearest spot of all. . . Middle Years*, pt 1, p. 376.
162   *A monstrous incongruity!. . .* Japp, II, p. 5.
162   *that beautiful and wild-hearted girl. . .* Japp, II, p. 285.
163   *stop the press. . . Middle Years*, pt 1, p. 294.
163   *the very great injustice . . .* Jordan, p. 132.
163   *Never describe Wordsworth . . . Recollections*, p. 381.
164   *it gives me great concern . . . Middle Years*, pt 1, pp. 317–18.
164   *fending and proving. . . Recollections*, p. 376.
164   *You must take it . . . decently. . . Middle Years*, pt 1, p. 339.
164   *much anxiety and care. . . Middle Years*, pt 1, p. 320.
164   *dismembered creatures. . . Middle Years*, pt 1, p. 337.
165   *When I get to the house. . .down in it. . .* Jordan, pp. 317–18.
165   *joy in the house. . . Middle Years*, pt 1, p. 314.
165   *at all in fault. . .* Jordon, p. 198.
166   *both respect. . . Second-thoughts. . .* Griggs, III, pp. 305–6.
166   *according to all analogy. . .* Hogg, p. 24.
166   *Sometimes we fancy. . . pleasure. . . Middle Years*, pt 1, p. 169.
167   *I observe you always say. . . out of your way. . .* Japp, II, p. 3.
167   *in exact proportion. . . promise. . .* Griggs, III, p. 927.
167   *twenty Atlantics. . .* 'Confessions', p. 85.
167–8 *the motion of time. . . haunted my sleep. . .* 'Confessions', p. 53.
168   *he recommended . . . the next generation. . .* Masson, III, p. 112.
168   *three Walking Stewarts. . .* Masson, III, p. 107.
169   *forgeries. . .* Japp, I, p. 262.
169   *my non-identity. . .* Japp, I, p. 256.
169   *We could not help laughing. . .* Japp, I, p. 283.
169–70 *when I first came here . . . sitting-room. . .* Jordan, p. 244.
170   *malice has done the work. . . Middle Years*, pt 1, p. 338.
170   *Pleasant indeed it is . . . ravaged. . . Middle Years*, pt 1, p. 337.
170   *perfect paradise. . . Middle Years*, pt 1, p. 369.
171   *in three weeks. . . Middle Years*, pt 1, p. 363.
171   *When are we to see you?. . . Middle Years*, pt 1, p. 371.
171   *He has been in cold Countries. . .* Jordan, p. 254.
171   *It was. . . on a November night. . . Recollections*, p. 301.

Chapter 9: Residence in Dove Cottage and the Revolution

173   *little orphan maiden. . . Recollections*, p. 301.
173   *one of our own Family. . . Middle Years*, pt 1, p. 374.
173   *I can tell you. . . smallness of the house. . . Middle Years*, pt 1, p. 376.
174   *lazy, luxurious and sensual. . . Recollections*, p. 269.
174   *youthful charge. . . Recollections*, p. 370.

174   *smothered. . . Recollections*, p. 294.
175   *tip-top of exaltation. . . Middle Years*, pt 1, p. 374.
175   *not the least atom of beauty. . . Middle Years*, pt 1, p. 370.
175   *impersonation of the dawn. . . Recollections*, p. 372.
176   *the only very intimate friend. . . Recollections*, p. 288.
176   *the sound of pealing anthems. . . Recollections*, p. 332.
176   *trace the course . . . reign of the cricket. . . Recollections*, pp. 228–9.
176   *a truth before your eyes. . .* Masson, X, p. 270.
176   *that swallowed up abysses. . .* Masson, X, p. 416.
177   *for more than twenty years. . . Recollections*, p. 169.
179   *in substance, what I have been all my life.* . . Hartley Coleridge (ed.), *Specimens of the Table Talk of the Late Samuel Taylor Coleridge*, London: John Murray, 1835, II, p. 71.
180   *we should flee for refuge from them.* . . 'A Prefatory Observation on Modern Biography', *The Friend*, Number 21, 1810, p. 337.
180   *to be made at an unreasonable time. . . Middle Years*, pt 1, p. 397.
180   *in the cottage style. . .* Griggs, III, p. 273.
180–1   *we are all glad. . . his friends as possible. . . Middle Years*, pt 1, pp. 398–9. *criminal negligence. . . Recollections*, p. 271.
182   *lively gushing thought-employing . . . people. . .* Beth Darlington (ed.), *The Love Letters of William and Dorothy Wordsworth*, London: Chatto and Windus, 1982, p. 59.
182   *end of time. . .* Darlington (ed.), *Love Letters*, p. 48.
182   *kiss the words a thousand times! . . .* Darlington (ed.), *Love Letters*, p. 42.
182   *whole frame. . . depth of affection. . .* Darlington (ed.), *Love Letters*, p. 210.
183   *William used many . . . been very angry. . . Middle Years*, pt 1, pp. 488–9.
183   *so murderous of domestic comfort. . .* Curry (ed.), *New Letters of Robert Southey*, I, p. 448.
183   *whirled about without a center. . .* Coburn (ed.), *Notebooks of Samuel Taylor Coleridge*, III, p. 3991.
184   *suddenness of a flash of lightning. . .* Griggs, III, p. 389.
184   *never-closing . . . Wound. . .* Griggs, III, p. 338.
184   *like nobody in my looks and appearance. . .* Darlington (ed.), *Love Letters*, p. 35.
184   *the Misses De Quincey have just called. . .* Moorman, *Later Years*, p. 114.
184–5   *your sweet country. . . ever-green corner. . .* Japp, II, p. 79.
185   *and all for the sake . . . set by that orchard. . .* Coburn, pp. 36–7.
186   *storm in the apple orchard. . .* Jordan, p. 219.
187   *inhuman arrogance. . . usurpations. . . Recollections*, pp. 375–6.
187   *little cottage was Wordsworth's. . . Recollections*, pp. 122–3.
187   *I have been ill-used. . . Recollections*, p. 377.
187   *a strange sort of contradictory life. . . Recollections*, p. 381.
188   *reads the newspapers standing . . . his company. . .* Coburn, pp. 37–8.

Chapter 10: Residence in London and Grasmere

191   *over the face of the land* . . . 'Mail-Coach', p. 192.

197   *never rested. . . part of vagrants*. . . 'Postscript', p. 98.

197   *No circumstances which did not concern me*. . . 'On Murder', p. xi.

198   *he had in his pocket fourteen shillings* . . . John Fairburn, *Fairburn's Account of the Life, Death and Interment of John Williams, the Supposed Murderer of the Families of Marr and Williamson, and Self Destroyer*, John Fairburn, Blackfriars, 1812, p. 6.

199   *an unseemly exhibition*. . . see P. D. James and Thomas A. Critchley, *The Maul and the Peartree*, London: Faber, 1986.

199   *what is the effect?*. . . Payne Collier, *Seven Lectures on Shakespeare and Milton*, introductory preface, p. 142.

199   *comparatively dim. . .aversion to action*. . . Payne Collier, *Seven Lectures*, introductory preface, pp. 141–2.

200   *proceeded from the hands of a friend*. . . *Recollections*, p. 380.

200   *in great indignation*. . . Alan G. Hill (ed.), *William and Dorothy Wordsworth: A Supplement of New Letters*, Oxford: Clarendon Press, 1993, p. 63.

200   *lower classes of the community* . . . *all parts of the globe*. . . John Fairburn, *Fairburn's Account of the Inhuman Murder of Mr and Mrs Williamson and Their Woman Servant at the King's Arms, New Gravel Lane, Ratcliffe Highway, on Thursday Night, 19 Dec 1811*, John Fairburn, Blackfriars, 1812, p. 3.

201   *Whether he was in his native country. . . remorse*. . . Fairburn, *Fairburn's Account of the Life, Death and Interment of John Williams*, p. 3.

201–2   *conduct of the two formed. . . untimely end*. . . Fairburn, *Fairburn's Account of the Life, Death and Interment of John Williams*, p. 4.

202   *apprehended on suspicion*. . . Fairburn, *Fairburn's Account of the Life, Death and Interment of John Williams*, p. 5.

202   *accomplices remains to be discovered*. . . Fairburn, *Fairburn's Account of the Life, Death and Interment of John Williams*, p. 7.

202   *the late murders. . . butchered like so many brute beasts!*. . . Rev. G. Williams, 'The Substance of a Sermon on the Horrid Murders in Ratcliffe Highway and Gravel Lane, which was Preached on Sunday December 29th, 1811, at the Chapel of the Rev. Rowland Hill', London: Fairburn, 1811, p. 2.

203   *determination to confront*. . . Knight (ed.), *Letters*, II, p. 3.

204   *Recollect, Gentlemen* . . . Andro Linklater, *Why Spencer Perceval Had to Die: The Assassination of a British Prime Minister*, London, Bloomsbury, 2012, p. 130.

204   *These were the very words* . . . Linklater, *Spencer Perceval*, p. 38.

204   *The country is no doubt in a most alarming situation*. . . Darlington (ed.), *Love Letters*, p. 148.

205   *I am grieved to the heart* . . . Knight (ed.), *Letters*, II, p. 9.

205   *more affected than the father*. . . Jordan, p. 210.

205   *puling and womanly weakness*. . . Morrison, p. 159.

205   *Nobody. . . can judge. . . dear lips again. . .* Jordan, p. 265.

206   *idle gazers. . .* Jordan, p. 266.

206   *Oh that I could have died for her. . .* Jordan, pp. 270–1.

206   *The grounds for this fiction. . .* Hogg, p. 23.

207   *early dawn . . . fountain of life. . .* Recollections, p. 372.

207   *obscure and little heard of . . .* Recollections, p. 369.

207–8   *for more than two months running. . .* Recollections, p. 372.

208   *life could not be borne . . .* Recollections, p. 373.

208   *peculiar sensation . . . wrenched. . .* Recollections, p. 374.

208   *nympholepsy. . .* Recollections, p. 374.

208   *despairing nympholepsy . . .* Recollections, p. 272.

208–9   *which had seized upon me. . .* Recollections, p. 119.

209   *sublime attractions of the grave . . .* De Quincey made the word his own,
        but he was not the only writer to use it. Byron wrote of 'The nympholepsy
        of some fond despair', and Edward Bulwer-Lytton, who called it 'the sad-
        dening for a spirit that the world knows not', believed 'nympholepsy' to
        be 'the most common disease to genius'. In a letter to Ruskin, Elizabeth
        Barrett Browning confessed that 'we are all nympholepts in running after
        our ideas', and George Moore, in *Memoirs of My Dead Life*, described it as
        'a disease that every one would like to catch'.

209   *foolish, selfish and ignorant. . .* Recollections, p. 377.

209   *Any real friend of mine. . .* Recollections, p. 378.

209   *sate down half-contentedly. . . this wrong. . .* Recollections, p. 379.

209   *Pray come to us as you can. . .* H. A. Page, I, p. 173.

Chapter 11: The Recluse

211–12 *a theatre seemed suddenly opened . . . Nilotic mud . . . instinct with life. . .*
        'Confessions', pp. 76–82.

212   *whether his lungs. . .* 'Confessions', p. 60.

212   *He can do nothing . . . Master tires. . .* Middle Years, pt 2, p. 665.

213   *I was the last person . . . cheerless silence. . .* Moorman, *Later Years*, p. 230.

213   *up-rouzing of the Bats and the Owls. . .* Middle Years, pt 2, p. 372.

213   *walked to De Quincey's. . .* Lindop, p. 209.

214   *'gave up the ghost'. . .* Japp, II, p. 162.

214   *pedantry and high-flown sentimentality. . .* Lindop, p. 210.

214   *Quince has gone off to Edinburgh. . .* Coburn, p. 88.

214   *extraordinary, as if it came from dreamland . . . melody. . .* R. P. Gillies,
        Memoirs of a Literary Veteran, London: Richard Bentley, 1851, II, p. 220.

215   *Hout, me'em . . . where are they?. . .* Miller, *Electric Shepherd*, p. 104.

215   *the sexual intercourse of things. . .* James Hogg, *The Poetical Works of James
        Hogg*, Edinburgh: Constable, 1822, III, p. 142.

215   *It drove me crazy then. . .* Jordan, pp. 226–67.

216 *made his bed before she ascended it...* William Maginn, 'Humbugs of the Age, No 1 – The Opium Eater', I, *John Bull Magazine and Literary Recorder* (1824), 21–3.

216 *stupid heavy girl...* Middle Years, pt 2, p. 372.

216 *Quince was often tipsy...* Coburn, p. 88.

216 *distant, solemn, saintly...* Recollections, p. 332.

216–17 *Dark Interpreter... visionary companions...* 'Suspiria', p. 162.

217 *So I have found you at last...* 'Confessions', pp. 84–5.

217 *a fit of solitude...* H. A. Page, I, p. 192.

217 *a nonentity, you have no being...* Hogg, pp. 78–9.

217 *his situation internally... distance...* Recollections, p. 326.

217–18 *enough to kill three dragoons... ran "a-muck"...* 'Confessions', pp. 62–3.

218 *an unfortunate acquaintance with a woman...* Lindop, p. 218.

219 *an exact and most faithful portraiture...* Griggs, III, p. 495.

219 *person on business from Porlock...* S. T. Coleridge, *Christabel, Kubla Khan, The Pains of Sleep*, London: John Murray, 1815, p. 53.

219 *the fruits of philosophy...* Hill (ed.), *Supplement of New Letters*, p. 162.

219 *Mr De Quincey is married...* Middle Years, pt 2, p. 372.

220 *I am very sorry for Mr De Quincey...* E. V. Lucas (ed.), *The Works of Charles and Mary Lamb*, VI, pp. 506–7.

220 *lively gushing thought-employing...'* Darlington (ed.), *Love Letters*, p. 89.

220 *hand locked in hand...* Recollections, p. 288.

220 *mere football of reproach...* Recollections, p. 240.

221 *invisible in bed...* J. A. Froude, *Thomas Carlyle: A History of the First Forty Years of his Life, 1795–1835*, Cambridge: Cambridge University Press, 2011, p. 427.

221 *I will sleep no more...* 'Confessions', p. 78.

221 *no more sudden death!...* 'Mail-Coach', pp. 240–1, 244.

221 *Candles at four o'clock...* 'Confessions', pp. 65–6.

222 *would not take tea with the new mistress of Dove Cottage...* Mary Wordsworth was similarly horrified when, in 1819, her brother George also married his pregnant servant, who was also called Margaret.

222 *irretrievable confusion...* 'Confessions', p. 74.

223 *rage, horror, despair, anguish, and ghastly smile...* Westmorland Gazette, 30 Jan 1819.

223 *Do you think there was no pleasure in murdering her?...* 'Extracts from Gosschen's Diary', *Blackwood's Edinburgh Magazine*, No. XVII, Aug 1818, I, p. 596.

223 *cost the Editor a whole day's labour...* Westmorland Gazette, 23 Jan 1819.

223 *The Editor of the Gazette differs in many points...* Westmorland Gazette, 9 Jan 1819.

224 *great fork of flames...* Westmorland Gazette, 30 Jan 1819.

224 *reason with the sea, or a railway train...* Masson, I, p. 6.

224   *more than once. . . Arabia Felix for instance. . . Westmorland Gazette*, 23 Jan
        1819.

225   *more burning logic. . .* Masson, I, p. 6.

225   *A newspaper is not like a book . . . Westmorland Gazette*, 26 Dec 1818.

225   *Mr De Quincey's Books . . .* Coburn, p. 209.

225   *always blinded. . .* Eaton, p. 294.

225   *second accumulation of books. . .* Coburn, p. 209.

226   *some chamber of that same humble cottage. . . Recollections*, p. 298.

226   *squabash, bam and balaam. . .* Miller, *Electric Shepherd*, p. 158.

226   *abuse Wordsworth anonymously . . .* Miller, *Electric Shepherd*, p. 131.

227   *the atlas of the magazine . . . further trouble. . .* Morrison, pp. 199–200.

228   *most licentious personal abuse. . .* Patrick O'Leary, *Regency Editor: Life of
        John Scott*, Aberdeen: Aberdeen University Press, 1983, p. 146.

228   *must be a dead man . . . no chance. . .* Hogg, pp. xix, 8.

228   *I am burning for vengeance. . .* O'Leary, *Regency Editor*, p. 148.

229   *To speak conscientiously . . .* Morrison, p. 202.

229   *the very midsummer madness of affection. . .* Masson, II, p. 389.

229   *Wilson might be the man. . .* Hogg, p. 18.

229   *these things Wilson can never forgive. . .* Hogg, p. 18.

230   *true hero. . .* 'Confessions', p. 86.

230   *Everyone who noticed the magazine. . .* Morrison, p. 211.

231   *Devil's own drug. . .* David Alec Wilson, *Carlyle till Marriage, 1785–1826*,
        London: Kegan Paul, 1923, p. 250.

231   *more delight than I know how to express. . .* Japp, II, p. 238.

231   *a boast of what. . . Coleridge's diseased egotism. . .* Morrison, p. 211.

232   *Witches and other Night Fears. . . London Magazine*, Oct 1821, p. 387.

232   *Autobiography. . .* One of the earliest appearances of the word 'autobiogra-
        phy' was in 1807 when Southey announced in a review 'an epidemical rage
        for auto-biography'. In the December edition of the *London Magazine*,
        De Quincey described himself as an 'auto-biographer'.

232   *Egotism is the spirit of the age. . . London Museum*, 28 (1822), p. 44.

233   *personality should be avoided. . .* O'Leary, *Regency Editor*, p. 112.

233   *The entire 'Confessions'. . .* Letter to the *London Magazine*, Dec 1821.

234   *the sensation which had made De Quincey a slave to it. . .* Curry (ed.), *New
        Letters of Robert Southey*, II, p. 450.

234   *Did I teach wine-drinking?. . .* Alethea Hayter, *Opium and the Romantic
        Imagination*, Berkeley and Los Angeles: University of California, 1968, p. 107.

234   *De Quincey was not so much breaking a taboo. . .* Mike Jay, *The London
        Review of Books*, Vol. 32, No. 9, May 2010. I am greatly indebted to the
        ideas explored by Mike Jay in this brilliant article.

234   *So too was his response to Wordsworth. . .* The relationship between the
        Confessions and *The Prelude* has been investigated by several De Quincey
        scholars. See in particular Jordan, *De Quincey to Wordsworth*, pp. 358–64;
        V. A. De Luca in both '"The Type of a Mighty Mind", Mutual Influence in
        Wordsworth and De Quincey', Texas Studies in Literature and Language,

13. 2 (Summer, 1971), and *Thomas De Quincey, The Prose of Vision*, Toronto, University of Toronto Press, 1980; D. D. Devlin, *De Quincey, Wordsworth, and the Art of Prose*, London, Macmillan, 1983.

235   *when, for many reasons, the whole will be published.* . . 'Confessions', p. 3.

235   *Meantime, I am again in London. . . nineteen years ago.* . . 'Confessions', p. 41.

236   *Why, pretty well, I thank you, reader.* . . 'Confessions', p. 57.

236   *I was astonished at the depth and reality.* . . Hogg, p. 73.

236   *conventicle appearance.* . . Hogg, p. 76.

236   *before he could have written such a ballad.* . . Hogg, p. 93.

237   *slithered over the sleeping surfaces. . . than at anybody else.* . . Masson, V, p. 246.

238   *Pray, is it true, my dear Laudanum.* . . *Blackwood's Edinburgh Magazine*, Oct 1823, pp. 485–6.

238–9 *certain places & events. . . profanation of a temple.* . . Hogg, pp. 88–9.

239   *Confessions of an English Glutton.* . . *Blackwood's Edinburgh Magazine*, Jan 1823, p. 87.

Chapter 12: Imagination, Impaired and Restored

242   *buying a thing and yet not paying for it.* . . Morrison, p. 263.

242   *infantine feebleness.* . . 'Confessions', p. 71.

242   *aggravated the misery.* . . Eaton, p. 295.

243   *overspread with a dark frenzy* . . . Hayter, *Opium and the Romantic Imagination*, p. 115.

243   *Why am I now in London?* . . . Eaton, p. 292.

243–4 *never entered a great library. . . madness.* . . 'Letter to a young Man whose Education has been Neglected', *London Magazine*, Vol. 7, Mar 1823, pp. 327–9.

244   *murder running through their blood.* . . Masson, XI, p. 347.

245   *Mr. Hazlitt must permit me to smile.* . . 'To the Editor of the *London Magazine*', 4 Nov 1823.

245   *reflected back to the murder a peculiar awfulness* . . . 'On Knocking', pp. 3–4.

246   *The murderers, and the murder, must be insulated. . . passion.* . . 'On Knocking', p. 6.

246   *a pageantry in the clouds.* . . 'On Knocking', p. 7.

246   *a hell within him.* . . 'On Knocking', p. 5.

246   *genius of Mr Williams.* . . 'On Knocking', p. 4.

247   *Jack the Ripper.* . . In 'Homicidal Mania', *Fortnightly Review*, 1888, George H. Savage suggested that the Whitechapel Murders were committed by 'one worthy to join De Quincey's students of murder as a fine art'.

248   *the lineaments of human beings.* . . Eric R. Watson, *The Trial of Thurtell and Hunt*, Edinburgh: William Hodge, 1920, pp. 3, 49.

249   *The gloomy cottage itself became a tourist site.* . . Four years later Sir Walter Scott visited Gill's Hill cottage, finding it, as he recorded in his diary, down 'a labyrinth of intricate lanes, which seemed made on purpose to afford strangers the full benefit of a dark night and a drunk driver. . . The garden has been dismantled, though a few laurels and flowering shrubs, run wild, continue to mark the spot. The fatal pond is now only a green

swamp, but so near the house, that one cannot conceive how it was ever chosen as a place of temporary concealment for the murdered body.'

249 *I have been presented by the Press . . . debauchery. . .* 'An Account of a Late Trial at Hertford', *London Magazine*, Feb 1824, p. 180.

250 *worked himself up into a great actor. . . London Magazine*, Feb 1824, p. 189.

250 *what a Gentleman. . .* see Judith Flanders, *The Invention of Murder: How the Victorians Revelled in Death and Detection*, London: HarperCollins, 2011, p. 40.

251 *the murder is a good one, as you observe. . .* unpublished letter in the British Library, BL MS 37, 215: see A. S. Plumtree, 'The Artist as Murderer, De Quincey's Essay "On Murder Considered As One of the Fine Arts",' in Robert Snyder, ed., *Thomas De Quincey, Bicentenary Studies*, University of Oklahoma Press, 1986.

251 *'Tims on Thurtell!!' . . . I hae laucht so muckle. . .* Blackwood's *Magazine*, Vol. 15, Apr 1824, p. 376.

251 *the sensations. . .* Edgar Allan Poe, 'How to Write a Blackwood Article', *Thirty-Two Stories*, p. 70.

252–3 *We are certainly a blood-thirsty people. . . in all his glory. . .* Blackwood's *Magazine*, Apr 1824, pp. 377–9.

253 *Humbug of the Age. . .* William Maginn, 'Humbugs of the Age: No 1 – The Opium Eater'.

254 *after the fashion of poor Savage the poet. . .* Charles MacFarlane, *Reminiscences of a Literary Life*, New York: Charles Scribners, 1917, p. 83.

254 *studied for himself in the fields. . . singular. . .* Morrison, p. 239.

254 *amongst the most remarkable. . . guilty darkness of this transaction. . .* 'Peter Anthony Fonk', in Morrison (ed.), *On Murder,* pp. 144–54.

254 *To fence with illness . . .* Gordon, *Memoir of John Wilson*, II, p. 80.

255 *Pain and Fuss. . .* Thomas Sadler (ed.), *Diary, Reminiscence and Correspondence of Henry Crabb Robinson*, London: Macmillan, 1869, II, p. 9.

255 *constantly beset by idle fears. . .* Hogg, p. 243.

255 *Oh Miss Wordsworth. . . this service. . .* Jordan, p. 297.

255 *to fly from himself. . .* Hogg, p. 139.

256 *Druggists than to the Shoe Maker. . .* Coburn, p. 310.

256 *pretty uniformly = o. . .* Morrison, p. 248.

257 *What a wonderful city Edinburgh is. . .* Griggs, II, p. 988.

257 *The man is a fool. . .* Miller, p. 128.

257 *Socrates, Plato, Aristotle. . .* Japp, II, pp. 44–5.

258 *a less mysterious outward appearance. . .* Morrison, p. 203.

258 *the double-faced old gentleman. . .* Eaton, p. 309.

259 *I am wedded to you so closely. . .* James Hogg, *The Private Memoirs and Confessions of a Justified Sinner*, edited by John Carey, Oxford: Oxford World's Classics, 1969, p. 229.

259 *O that I had the wings of a dove. . .* Hogg, *Private Memoirs and Confessions*, p. 224.

259 *So often had I been hoaxed. . .* Hogg, *Private Memoirs and Confessions*, p. 245.

260   *Turks, Persians and Chinamen.* . . MacFarlane, *Reminiscences of a Literary Life*, p. 80.

260   *Mrs De Quincey seemed on the whole.* . . . E. de Selincourt (ed.), *The Letters of Dorothy and William Wordsworth, The Later Years, part 1, 1825–1828*, revised by Alan G. Hill, Oxford: Clarendon Press, 1978, p. 485.

260   *tone laconic, or curt.* . . Poe, 'How to Write a Blackwood Article', p. 70.

261   *Pleasant it is, no doubt* . . . De Quincey was remembering Thomas Carew's 'Epitaph on the Lady Mary Villiers': 'For thou perhaps at thy return,/ May'st find thy Darling in an Urn'.

261   *these horrid details* . . . Gordon, *Memoir of John Wilson*, p. 62

261   *created the taste by which he is to be enjoyed.* . . 'On Murder', p. 10.

261   *'Fire! Fire!'.* . . 'On Murder', p. 11.

262   *the great gallery of murder.* . . *the old transcendentalist.* . . 'On Murder', pp. 16–23.

263   *mere plagiarism.* . . 'On Murder', p. 30.

263   *a log on the floor.* . . 'On Murder', p. 27.

264   *the murderer was a poet, the poet was a murderer.* . . see A. S. Plumtree's excellent essay, 'The Artist as Murderer. . .': 'I would propose that De Quincey's conception of the murderer as artist springs from an intuition of the artist as murderer. . .' Also suggestive is Margo Ann Sullivan's *Murder and Art, Thomas De Quincey and the Ratcliffe Highway Murders*, New York: Garland, 1987.

265   *Impenitent as a snake . . . demandin' back their ain atomies.* . . *Blackwood's Magazine*, Mar 1829, p. 389.

265   *'Pray do not be alarmed . . . filthy plagiarist.* . . 'To the Editor of Blackwood's Magazine', in Morrison (ed.), *On Murder*, pp. 156–60.

266   *grew pale as ashes. . . not yet begun to write.* . . C. R. Saunders (ed.), *Collected Letters of Thomas and Jane Welsh Carlyle*, Durham NC: Duke University Press, 1970, IV, pp. 282–3, 300.

267   *some things from my Conversation.* . . Morrison, p. 260.

267   *too florid. . . some peculiar brilliance.* . . Masson, V, pp. 263–8, 278.

268   *I wish you would praise me.* . . Elsie Swann, *Christopher North (John Wilson)*, London: Oliver and Boyd, 1934, p. 197.

268   *Paying only the annual interest* . . . Lindop, p. 292.

268   *the love that we all bear the place* . . . Lindop, p. 308.

269   *Father called on Mr de Quincey.* . . Jordan, p. 300.

Chapter 13: Same Subject (continued)

271   *De Quincey owed money to fifty-one tradespeople.* . . see Kenneth Forward, 'De Quincey's Cessio Bonorum', *PMLA*, liv, No. 2 (Jun 1939), pp. 511–25.

272   *Mr De Qunshy. . . land o' Nod.* . . *Blackwood's Magazine*, Jun 1830.

272   *with a pencil of light.* . . *Blackwood's Magazine*, Jun 1830, pp. 814, 943.

272–3   *Some one of my ancestors . . . interesting creatures. . .* Blackwood's Magazine,
          Jun 1830, p. 943.

273   *the last letter she'll ever write. . .* Lindop, p. 298.

273   *had a father. . .* Lindop, pp. 299–300.

273   *My extremity is complete. . .* Eaton, p. 341.

274   *about the South end of Clerk Street. . .* Morrison, p. 279.

275   *deliver me from an abyss. . .* Lindop, p. 303.

275   *to suit his own eyesight. . .* Virginia Woolf, 'Impassioned Prose', *Times
          Literary Supplement*, 16 Sep 1926.

275   *not the action and situation to the feeling. . .* Brett and Jones (eds), *Lyrical
          Ballads*, p. 293.

276   *most irreclaimable Tories now extant. . .* Saunders (ed.), *Collected Letters of
          Thomas and Jane Welsh Carlyle*, VI, 18 Apr 1833.

276   *bright summer mornings. . .* Eaton, p. 365.

277   *the struggles of departing life. . .* 'Suspiria', p. 102.

278   *an uncared-for dog. . . on the watch in all directions. . .* Morrison, p. 283.

279   *I knew Mrs Hannah More . . . intimate acquaintance. . .* Masson, XIV, pp. 96–7.

279   *pink ribbons. . .* Masson, XIV, pp. 116–17.

280   *I was born in a situation. . .* De Quincey, 'Sketches of Life and Manners,
          from the Autobiography of an English Opium-Eater', *Tait's Edinburgh
          Magazine*, Feb 1834, p. 18.

281   *The reading public of England. . .* J. R. de J. Jackson (ed.), *Coleridge: The
          Critical Heritage*, London: Routledge, 1970, pp. 436–51.

281   *fat flabby incurvated personage. . .* letter to John Carlyle, 1824, quoted in
          Holmes, *Coleridge: Darker Reflections*, pp. 543–4.

282   *a kind of Magus, girt in mystery and enigma. . .* Thomas Carlyle, *The Life of
          John Sterling*, Boston: Philips, Sampson and Co., 1851, pp. 69, 70.

282   *I grieved then that I could not grieve. . .* Charles Lamb, 'On the Death of Coleridge',
          The Works of Charles Lamb, New York: Thomas Y. Crowell, 1882, p. 140.

282   *not in any sense, nor at any time. . .* Lindop, p. 317.

282   *elder brother or doppelgänger. . .* Holmes, *Darker Reflections*, p. 102.

282   *apparition of the Brocken. . .* Payne Collier, *Seven Lectures*, p. 101.

283   *recollection of some family distresses. . .* Morrison, p. 288.

283   *everlasting silence and forgetfulness. . .* H. A. Page, I, p. 305.

283   *I believe that in the course. . .* Eaton, p. 364.

284   *I will assert finally . . . Shakespeare in modern. . .* Recollections, pp. 40–1.

284   *no personal charms. . .* Recollections, p. 53.

284   *no particular civility. . .* Recollections, p. 52.

284   *last person in the world. . .* Recollections, p. 74.

284   *on the highway by himself. . .* Recollections, p. 79.

285   *What is become of all this mighty heap of hope . . .* William Hazlitt, *Spirit of
          the Age, Or Contemporary Portraits*, Oxford: World's Classics, 1904, p. 42.

285   *Worlds of fine thinking. . .* Recollections, p. 76.

285   *speaks of his kindness of heart. . .* H. A. Page, I, p. 301.

285 *an anomaly and a contradiction.* . . MacFarlane, *Reminiscences of a Literary Life*, pp. 81–2.

285 *must be incorrect.* . . Eaton, p. 366.

286 *Rhadamanthine rage* . . . Carlyle, *Reminiscences*, p. 324.

286 *It is not to be doubted.* . . *obnoxious publication.* . . see Daniel Sanjiv Roberts, *Revisionary Gleam: De Quincey, Coleridge and the High Romantic Argument*, Liverpool: Liverpool University Press, 2000, p. 16.

286 *in a disreputable magazine.* . . Japp, II, p. 173.

286 *Any of us.* . . *would be jealous* . . . *Wordsworth's doppelgänger.* . . Masson, XI, p. 461.

287 *echoes of joy* . . . *records of sighs.* . . *Recollections*, p. 299.

287 *I was under a possession.* . . Morrison, p. 291.

287 *Yet in the lowest deep* . . . Masson, XII, p. 158.

287 *Not only has she absorbed.* . . Eaton, p. 365n.

288 *unhinged by sorrow.* . . Japp, II, pp. 219–20.

288 *Delicate health.* . . *than our mother.* . . H. A. Page, I, p. 195.

288 *those who weep in secret.* . . Eaton, p. 363.

288 *trembled with anger.* . . *blindness.* . . Jordan, p. 233.

289 *in a long, long time.* . . Eaton, p. 373.

289 *for his own enjoyment.* . . Eaton, p. 375.

289 *too little discretion.* . . Eaton, p. 373.

290 *no man a shilling.* . . Masson, XII, p. 161.

290 *never ridded myself.* . . Masson, XII, p. 168.

290 *the juggernaut of social life.* . . Masson, XII, p. 160.

290 *suddenly a sound.* . . *who is at the door?.* . . Masson, XII, p. 185.

291 *She is, or she is not, guilty.* . . Masson, XII, p. 204.

291 *Wrath, wrath immeasurable.* . . Masson, XII, p. 208.

291 *My revenge.* . . *was perfect.* . . Masson, XII, p. 233.

291 *misery has a privilege.* . . Masson, XII, p. 189.

291 *as though it were a future thing.* . . Masson, XII, p. 210.

291–2 *that which sometimes.* . . *one deep calling to another.* . . 'The Avenger', in Morrison (ed.), *On Murder*, p. 36.

292 *Mr De Quincey's young, fair-haired* . . . Morrison, p. 299.

292 *north and south banks.* . . Eaton, p. 375.

293 *groanings unutterable.* . . Eaton, p. 375.

293 *the prevailing mystery in which he delighted.* . . Japp, II, p. 192.

293 *when he was the successful man.* . . Eaton, p. 420.

294 *assumed the beau* . . . *Recollections*, p. 167.

294 *And here I may mention* . . . *drowning world.* . . *Recollections*, p. 170.

295 *in expecting too much.* . . *Recollections*, p. 146.

295 *trace, in brief outline* . . . *Recollections*, p. 148.

295–6 *The case of a man who.* . . *availing.* . . *Recollections*, p. 148.

296 *a lover.* . . *in any passionate sense.* . . *Recollections*, p. 185.

296 *how very indelicate it would look* . . . *Recollections*, p. 197.

296 *Whilst foolish people supposed him* . . . *Recollections*, p. 292.

296	*He admits of nothing below*. . . Hazlitt, p. 125.
296	*He condemns all French writers.* . . .Hazlitt, p. 127.
296	*If a greater number of sources* . . . Hazlitt, p. 128.
297	*truth and life of these Lake Sketches*. . . H. A. Page, I, p. 302.
297	*pang of wrath*. . . *Recollections*, p. 369.
297	*This to me! – O ye gods – to me*. . . *Recollections*, p. 320.
298	*with a blind loyalty of homage*. . . *Recollections*, p. 145.
298	*to us who*. . . *were Wordsworth's friends*. . . *Recollections*, p. 185.
298	*all of us loved her*. . . *Recollections*, p. 146.
298	*Farewell, impassioned Dorothy!* . . . *Recollections*, p. 206.
298	*My acquaintance with him*. . . Jordan, p. 347.
299	*extracting money ad libitum*. . . Eaton, p. 386.
299	*I wish to stay a month longer*. . . Eaton, p. 385.
299–300	*I spend months after months*. . . *my shoulders*. . . Eaton, pp. 386–7.
300	*a more absolute wreck of decent prosperity*. . . Eaton, p. 391.
300	*If I give him nothing* . . . *portability*. . . Eaton, p. 392.
300	*Beginning with the small sum* . . . *his executor*. . . Eaton, p. 368n.
300	*Caught and chained*. . . H. A. Page, I, p. 30.
301	*The last body who went into that room*. . . Eaton, p. 394.
301–2	*if once a man indulges himself in murder*. . . 'Second Paper', p. 84.
302	*Even dogs are not what they were, sir*. . . 'Second Paper', p. 85.
302	*great exterminating chef-d'oeuvre* . . . 'Second Paper', p. 86.
303	*utter overthrow of happiness*. . . *Recollections*, p. 323.
303	*by her own fireside*. . . *Recollections*, p. 327.
303	*studious and meditative young boy*. . . *Recollections*, p. 272.
303	*my sole companion*. . . *Recollections*, p. 371.
304	*Men of extraordinary genius*. . . *appear to listen*. . . *Recollections*, pp. 375–6.
304	*denounce them for what they were*. . . *Recollections*, p. 378.
304	*not even read Walter Scott*. . . *Recollections*, p. 383.

Chapter 14: Postscript

307	*Address under cover, if you please*. . . Eaton, p. 404.
307	*It is often shocking*. . . Eaton, p. 405.
308	*half torpid condition under opium*. . . George Gilfillan, *Sketches Literary and Theological, Being selections from an unpublished MS of the late Rev George Gilfillan*, edited by Frank Henderson, Edinburgh: David Douglas, 1881, p. 33.
308	*violent but hopeless attachment*. . . Morrison, p. 323.
308	*This is the End*. . . Eaton, p. 405.
308	*the most absolute harmony*. . . H. A. Page, I, p. 331.
308	*begging about the village for food*. . . MacFarlane, *Reminiscences of a Literary Life*, p. 83.
309	*the misery of her situation*. . . Eaton, p. 408.

309   *Then I partly understood him, now perfectly...* Eaton, p. 416.

309   *vast avenues of gloom...* 'Suspiria', p. 92.

309   *symbolic mirror...* 'Suspiria', p. 164.

309   *flying it pursues...* Eaton, p. 419.

310   *at the root of all this unimaginable hell...* H. A. Page, I, p. 325.

310   *restless legs syndrome...* see M. Miranda, A. M. Williams, D. Garcia-Borreguero, 'Thomas De Quincey and his restless legs symptoms as depicted in *Confessions of an English Opium-Eater*', in *Movement Disorders*, 2010; 25 (13); 2006–9.

310   *as in days of infancy...* Eaton, p. 415.

310   *as one risen from the dead...* Eaton, p. 416.

310   *Note the power of murderers as fine-art professors...* 'New Paper', p. 162.

310   *throws a power about a man...* 'New Paper', p. 163.

311   *living at this moment... own acts and bodies...* 'New Paper', p. 163.

311   *Lifting up his head from the waves...* 'New Paper', p. 163.

311–12 *deader than a door-nail . . . the shadowy and the dark...* Masson, V, pp. 179–211.

312   *Put not your trust. . . homage of the sycophantic...* 'On Wordsworth's Poetry', in Jordan (ed.), *De Quincey as Critic*, p. 400.

313   *forms more complex and oblique... sad into the joyous...* 'On Wordsworth's Poetry', in Jordan (ed.), *De Quincey as Critic*, pp. 404–6.

313   *He has entered upon his seventy-sixth year...* 'On Wordsworth's Poetry', in Jordan (ed.), *De Quincey as Critic*, p. 421.

315   *deluge the room...* Hogg, pp. 146–7.

315   *Of all the tasks I ever had in my life...* Morrison, p. 341.

315   *more splendidly than others* ... 'Suspiria', p. 91.

315   *J. M. Barrie's Neverland...* In a letter to J. M. Barrie on 2 April 1893, written shortly before his death, Robert Louis Stevenson described himself as looking 'Exceedingly lean, dark, rather ruddy-black eyes, crow's-footed, beginning to be grizzled, general appearance of a blasted boy or blighted youth or to borrow Carlyle on De Quincey, "a child that has been in hell".'

315   *intolerable grief* ... 'Suspiria', p. 95.

316   *I was shut out for ever...* 'Suspiria', p. 111.

316   *Again I was in the chamber...* 'Suspiria', p. 143.

316–17 *An adult sympathises with himself... of his sympathy...* 'Suspiria', p. 30.

317   *My heart trembled through from end to end...* Frederic G. Kenyon (ed.), *The Letters of Elizabeth Barrett Browning*, London: Macmillan, 1899, p. 161.

317   *What else than a natural and mighty palimpsest* ... 'Suspiria', p. 150.

318   *the traces of each successive handwriting* ... 'Suspiria', p. 149.

318   *a dilated version of himself...* 'Suspiria', pp. 160–1.

318   *I had never seen your face...* 'Suspiria', pp. 169–70.

319   *epilepsy of planet-struck fury...* Japp, I, p. 8.

319   *Chinese-like reverence...* Japp, I, p. 318.

320   *I stared, almost agape* ... Hogg, p. 119.

320   *garments blackened with writing-ink. . .* David Masson, *De Quincey*, New York: Cambridge University Press, 2011, p. 104.

320   *rapidly becoming tomorrow. . .* Masson, *De Quincey*, p. 106.

320   *reconcile him to leaving. . .* Lindop, p. 378.

321   *No Englishman cares a pin. . .* Japp, II, p. 146.

321   *the originator claimed any part of it. . .* Lindop, p. 367.

321   *Mr. Neocles Jaspis Mousabines. . .* Jordan, p. 333.

321   *the 'Prelude' stands as an opening to nothing. . .* Hogg, p. 153.

322   *terror and terrific beauty. . .* 'Mail-Coach', p. 192.

322   *the horrid inoculation. . . sanctuary of himself. . .* 'Mail-Coach', pp. 209–11.

323   *But the lady!. . . roar of his voice. . .* 'Mail-Coach', p. 235.

323   *desert spaces of the sea. . . persecution of fugues. . .* 'Mail-Coach', pp. 233–6.

324   *with a grave upward glance. . .* Hogg, p. 177.

324   *'Ah!' said the Professor. . . on the table. . .* Japp, II, p. 32.

324   *links in the chain of evidence. . .* Japp, II, p. 21.

324–5   *Crowbars, masks and dark lanterns. . . damned spot. . .* John Paget, 'The Philosophy of Murder', *Tait's Edinburgh Magazine*, 22, 1851, pp. 171–6.

325   *scattered in prodigal profusion. . .* George Gilfillan, *Second Gallery of Literary Portraits*, Edinburgh: James Hogg, 1852, p. 302.

325   *absolutely, insuperably, and for ever impossible. . .* Gilfillan, *Second Gallery*, p. 302.

325   *It is astonishing. . . how much more Boston knows. . .* Masson, VII, pp. 231–2.

326   *chez moi? Or chez la presse?. . .* Japp, II, p. 42.

326   *working through most parts of the night. . .* Japp, II, p. 54.

326   *piled over each other's heads. . .* Gilfillan, *Sketches Literary and Theological*, p. 34.

326   *saying the thing that is not. . .* Masson, I, p. 6.

327   *My unfortunate chattels. . .* Hogg, p. 136.

327   *who ministered to his vanity. . .* Hogg, p. 151.

328   *I often. . . feel an almost irresistible. . .* Hogg, p. 139.

328   *some account of Williams. . . an accomplice?. . .* De Quincey, *Selections Grave and Gay, from Writings Published and Unpublished by Thomas De Quincey*, Edinburgh: James Hogg, 1854, p. vi.

329   *to pursue the successive steps. . . Marr's shop. . .* 'Postscript', p. 107.

329   *stout, fresh-faced young man. . .* 'Postscript', p. 102.

329–30   *Let us leave the murderer alone . . . in her absence. . .* 'Postscript', p. 108.

330   *in an area of London where ferocious tumults . . .* 'Postscript', p. 110.

330   *What was it?. . . different sides. . .* 'Postscript', p. 111.

331   *by way of locking up all . . .* 'Postscript', p. 114.

331   *I was myself at the time nearly three hundred miles . . . for ever on the Thames. . .* 'Postscript', p. 99.

331–2   *the house-door was suddenly shut . . . pull murderer. . .* 'Postscript', pp. 120–6.

332   *murderous malice of the man below. . .* 'Postscript', p. 126.

332   *pass through a prism. . .* Masson, X, p. 226.

332   *the hard fact. . .* Woolf, 'Impassioned Prose', *TLS*, 16 Sep 1926.

333   *we think that the circumstances of that mutiny. . .* James and Critchley, *The Maul and the Peartree*, p. xxi.

334   *one novelty, viz, an account* . . . Japp, II, p. 87.
335   *What would the Baker say?.* . . Hogg, p. 184.
335   *on Tuesday last I saw the death announced.* . . Japp, II, p. 98.
335   *My adversaries are in full chase.* . . Gilfillan, *Sketches Literary and Theological*, p. 34.
335–6 *a door opened . . . no Emily entered at the door.* . . Japp, II, pp. 92–3.
336   *much like other people.* . . Japp, II, p. 192.
336   *Never for one moment have I doubted.* . . Japp, II, p. 119.
336   *I long for the rest of De Quincey.* . . Lindop, p. 377.
336   *Miss Smith has been cruelly treated.* . . Japp, II, p. 132.
336   *at the tail of 666 wagons.* . . Japp, II, p. 142.
336   *a vision of children.* . . Japp, II, p. 132.
337   *like a boy of fourteen.* . . Japp, II, p. 305.

Select Bibliography

Books and articles

Abrams, M. H., *The Milk of Paradise: The Effects of Opium Visions on the Works of De Quincey, Crabbe, Francis Thompson, and Coleridge*, New York: Harper & Row, 1962

Ackroyd, Peter, *Dan Leno and the Limehouse Golem*, London: Minerva, 1995

Appleman, Philip, 'D. H. Lawrence and the Intrusive Knock', *Modern Fiction Studies* 3 (1958)

Bachelard, Gaston, *The Poetics of Space*, translated from the French by Maria Jolas, Beacon Press: Boston, 1994

Bagehot, Walter, 'The First Edinburgh Reviewers', *Literary Studies*, 2 vols, London: Dent, 1911

Barrell, John, *The Infection of Thomas De Quincey: A Psychopathology of Imperialism*, New Haven: Yale University Press, 1991

— 'Sad Stories', *Imagining the King's Death: Figurative Treason, Fantasies of Regicide, 1793–1796*, Oxford: Oxford University Press, 2000

Bate, Jonathan, 'The Literature of Power: Coleridge and De Quincey', *Coleridge's Visionary Languages*, edited by Tim Fulford and Morton D. Paley, Bury St Edmunds: Brewer, 1993

Baxter, Edmund, *De Quincey's Art of Autobiography*, Edinburgh: Edinburgh University Press, 1990

Black, Joel, *The Aesthetics of Murder: A Study in Romantic Literature and Contemporary Culture*, Baltimore: Johns Hopkins University Press, 1991

Booth, Martin, *Opium: A History*, London: Simon and Schuster, 1996

Borges, Jorge Luis, 'The Thousand and One Nights', *The Georgia Review*, vol. 38, No. 3 (Fall 1984)

Bridgwater, Patrick, *De Quincey's Gothic Masquerade*, Amsterdam: New York, 2004

Brooke, Stopford, *Dove Cottage: Wordsworth's Home from 1800–1808*, London: Macmillan, 1894

Burke, Edmund, *Reflections on the Revolution in France*, edited by Conor Cruise O'Brien, Harmondsworth: Penguin, 1984

— *A Philosophical Enquiry into the Origin of our Ideas of the Sublime and Beautiful*, edited by Adam Philips, Oxford: Oxford University Press, 1990

Cafarelli, Annette Wheeler, *Prose in the Age of Poets: Romanticism and Biographical Narrative from Johnson to De Quincey*, Philadelphia: University of Pennsylvania Press, 1990

Carlyle, Thomas, *Reminiscences*, edited by James Anthony Froude, New York: Charles Scribner's Sons, 1881

Caseby, Richard, *The Opium-Eating Editor: Thomas De Quincey and the Westmorland Gazette*, Kendal: Westmorland Gazette, 1985

Cocteau, Jean, *Opium, The Diary of an Addict*, translated by Ernest Augustus Boyd, New York: Longmans Green and Company, 1932

Coleridge, Samuel Taylor, *Christabel, Kubla Khan, The Pains of Sleep*, London: John Murray, 1815

— *Seven Lectures on Shakespeare and Milton*, with an introductory preface by J. Payne Collier, London: Chapman and Hall, 1856

— *Anima Poetae: From the Unpublished Notebooks of Samuel Taylor Coleridge*, edited by Ernest Hartley Coleridge, London: Heinemann, 1895

— *Biographia Literaria*, edited by James Engell and W. Jackson Bate, 2 vols, Princeton: Princeton University Press, 1983

— *The Complete Poems*, edited by William Keach, Harmondsworth: Penguin, 1997

— *The Notebooks of Samuel Taylor Coleridge, 1794–1826*, edited by Kathleen Coburn, 5 vols, Princeton: Princeton University Press, 1957–90, 2002

— *Coleridge's Notebooks: A Selection*, edited by Seamus Perry, Oxford: Oxford University Press, 2002

Cottle, Joseph, *Early Recollections; Chiefly Relating to the Late Samuel Taylor Coleridge*, 2 vols, London: Longman, 1837

— *Reminiscences of Samuel Taylor Coleridge and Robert Southey*, London: Houlston and Stoneman, 1847

Croft, Sir Herbert, *Love and Madness, A Story Too True*, London: G. Kearsly, 1780

Curry, Kenneth (ed.), *New Letters of Robert Southey: 1792–1810*, 2 vols, New York: Columbia University Press, 1965

Curtis, Jared (ed.), *The Fenwick Notes of William Wordsworth*, Bristol: Bristol Classical Press, 1993

Darlington, Beth (ed.), *The Love Letters of William and Dorothy Wordsworth*, London: Chatto and Windus, 1982

Dart, Gregory, 'Chambers of Horror: De Quincey's "Postscript" to "On Murder Considered as One of the Fine Arts"', in *Thomas De Quincey: New Theoretical and Critical Directions*, edited by Robert Morrison and Daniel Sanjiv Roberts, London: Routledge, 2007

De Luca, V. A., *Thomas De Quincey: The Prose of Vision*, Toronto: University of Toronto Press, 1980

De Quincey, Thomas, *The Collected Writings of Thomas De Quincey*, edited by David Masson, 14 vols, Edinburgh: A & C Black, 1889–90

— *Recollections of the Lakes and the Lake Poets*, edited by David Wright, Harmondsworth: Penguin, 1970

— *The Works of Thomas De Quincey*, general editor: Grevel Lindop, 21 vols, London: Pickering and Chatto, 2000–3

— *Confessions of an English Opium-Eater and Other Writings*, edited by Barry Milligan, Harmondsworth: Penguin, 2003

Devlin, D. D., *De Quincey, Wordsworth and the Art of Prose*, London: Macmillan, 1983

Dix, John, *The Life of Thomas Chatterton, including his Unpublished Poems*, London: Hamilton Adams, 1837

Eaton, H. A., *Thomas De Quincey: A Biography*, Oxford: Oxford University Press, 1936

Fairburn, John, *Fairburn's Account of the Dreadful Murder of Mr Marr and Family, at their House in Ratcliffe Highway on Saturday Night, December 7, 1811, including the Whole Investigation before the Coroner's Inquest. . .*

— *Fairburn's Account of the Life, Death and Interment of John Williams, the Supposed Murderer of the Families of Marr and Williamson, and Self-Destroyer*

Findlay, John Ritchie, *Personal Recollections of Thomas De Quincey*, Edinburgh: Black, 1886

Flanders, Judith, *The Invention of Murder: How the Victorians Revelled in Death and Detection*, London: HarperCollins, 2011

Forward, Kenneth, '"Libellous Attack" on De Quincey', *PMLA*, lii (1937)

— 'De Quincey's *Cessio Bonorum*', *PMLA*, liv, No. 2 (Jun, 1939)

Gael, Patricia, '*Lyrical Ballads* in British Periodicals, 1798–1800', *Wordsworth Circle* (Winter 2013)

Gilfillan, George, 'Thomas De Quincey', *A Gallery of Literary Portraits*, Edinburgh: Tait, 1845

— *Second Gallery of Literary Portraits*, Edinburgh: James Hogg, 1852

Gill, Stephen, *William Wordsworth: A Life*, Oxford: Oxford University Press, 1990

Gillies, Robert Pearse, *Memoirs of a Literary Veteran*, 3 vols, London: Bentley, 1851

Goldman, Albert, *The Mine and the Mint: Sources for the Writings of Thomas De Quincey*, Carbondale: Southern Illinois University Press, 1965

Gordon, Mary, '*Christopher North*', *A Memoir of John Wilson*, 2 vols, Edinburgh: Edmonston and Douglas, 1862

Griggs, E. L. (ed.), *Collected Letters of Samuel Taylor Coleridge*, 6 vols, Oxford: Oxford University Press, 1956–7

Grovier, Kelly, 'A Wordsworth Mystery Solved', *Times Literary Supplement*, 16 Feb 2007

Hayter, Alethea, *Opium and the Romantic Imagination*, London: Faber, 1969

— *The Wreck of the Abergavenny: The Wordsworths and Catastrophe*, Basingstoke: Macmillan, 2002

Hazlitt, William, *Spirit of the Age, Or Contemporary Portraits*, Oxford: World's Classics, 1904

Hogg, James, *The Private Memoirs and Confessions of a Justified Sinner*, edited by John Carey, Oxford: World's Classics, 1969

Hogg, James [son] (ed.), *The Uncollected Writings of Thomas De Quincey*, 2 vols, London: Swan Sonnenschein, 1890

Holmes, Richard, *Footsteps: Adventures of a Romantic Biographer*, London: HarperCollins, 1985

— *Coleridge: Early Visions 1772–1804*, London: HarperCollins, 1989

— *Dr Johnson & Mr Savage*, London: Hodder and Stoughton, 1993

— *Coleridge: Darker Reflections*, London: HarperCollins, 1998

— *Sidetracks: Explorations of a Romantic Biographer*, London: HarperCollins, 2000

Hutchinson, Sara, *The Letters of Sara Hutchinson, 1800–1835*, edited by Kathleen Coburn, London: Routledge and Kegan Paul, 1954

Irwin, Robert, *The Arabian Nights: A Companion*, Harmondsworth: Penguin, 1994

James, P. D., and Thomas A. Critchley, *The Maul and the Peartree*, London: Faber, 1986

Japp, A. H., *Thomas De Quincey: His Life and Writings*, 2 vols, New York: Scribner, 1877

— *De Quincey Memorials*, 2 vols, London: Heinemann, 1891

— *The Posthumous Works of Thomas De Quincey*, 2 vols, London: Heinemann, 1891–3

Jennings, Henry H., *Thomas Chatterton, The Boy Poet of Bristol: A Biographical Sketch*, Bristol: St Augustine's Press, 1868

Johnson, Samuel, 'An Account of the Life of Mr Richard Savage', in *Oxford Authors: Samuel Johnson*, edited by Donald Greene, Oxford: New York, 1984

Jones, W., *The Liverpool Guide, Including a Sketch of the Environs*, Liverpool: Crane and Jones, 1801

Jordan, John E., *De Quincey to Wordsworth*, Berkeley: University of California Press, 1963

— (ed.), *De Quincey As Critic*, London: Routledge, 1973

Kelly, Linda, *The Marvellous Boy: Life and Myth of Thomas Chatterton*, London: Weidenfeld and Nicolson, 1971

Kirby's Wonderful and Eccentric Museum, or Magazine of Remarkable Characters including all the Curiosities of Nature and Art, From the Remotest Period to the Present Time, 6 vols, London: R. S. Kirby, London House Yard, St Paul's, 1820

Knight, William (ed.), *Letters of the Wordsworth Family from 1787–1855*, 3 vols, Boston and London: Ginn and Co., 1907

Lamb, Charles, *The Complete Correspondence and Works of Charles Lamb (with an essay on his life and genius by Thomas Purnell)*, 4 vols, London: E. Moxton, 1870

Leask, Nigel, '"Murdering One's Double": Thomas De Quincey and S. T. Coleridge', *British Romantic Writers and the East: Anxiety of Empire*, Cambridge: Cambridge University Press, 1992

Lefebure, Molly, *Samuel Taylor Coleridge: A Bondage of Opium*, London: Quartet, 1974

Lindop, Grevel, *The Opium Eater: A Life of Thomas De Quincey*, Oxford: Oxford University Press, 1981

— 'Innocence and Revenge: The Problem of De Quincey's Fiction', *Thomas De Quincey: Bicentenary Studies*, edited by Robert Lance Snyder, Norman: University of Oklahoma Press, 1985

— 'De Quincey and the Edinburgh and Glasgow University Circles', *Grub Street and the Ivory Tower: Essays on Literary Journalism and Literary Scholarship*, edited by B. Bennett and J. Treglown, Oxford: Oxford University Press, 1998

Linklater, Andro, *Why Spencer Perceval Had to Die: The Assassination of a British Prime Minister*, London: Bloomsbury, 2012

McCalman, Iain, 'Mystagogues of Revolution', *Romantic Metropolis: The Urban Scene of British Culture, 1780–1840*, edited by James Chandler and Kevin Gilmartin, Cambridge: Cambridge University Press, 2005

McCusker, Honor, 'De Quincey and the Landlord', *More Books*, 14.2 (1939)

McDonagh, Josephine, *De Quincey's Disciplines*, Oxford: Oxford University Press, 1994

McFarland, Thomas, 'De Quincey's Journey to the End of Night', *Romantic Cruxes: The English Essayists and the Spirit of the Age*, Oxford: Clarendon Press, 1987

MacFarlane, Charles, *Reminiscences of a Literary Life*, London: Murray, 1917

McNeillie, Andrew (ed.), *The Essays of Virginia Woolf, 1904–1912*, New York: Harcourt Brace Jovanovich, 1986

Maginn, William, 'The Humbugs of the Age, No. 1', *John Bull Magazine and Literary Recorder*, 1 (1824)

Masson, David, *De Quincey*, New York and Cambridge: Cambridge University Press, 2011

Mayo, Robert, 'The Contemporaneity of the *Lyrical Ballads*', *PMLA*, lxix (1954)

Miller, J. Hillis, *The Disappearance of God*, Cambridge, MA: Harvard University Press, 1963

Miller, Karl, *Electric Shepherd: A Likeness of James Hogg*, London: Faber, 2003

Milligan, Barry, *Pleasures and Pains: Opium and the Orient in Nineteenth-Century British Culture*, Charlottesville: University Press of Virginia, 1995.

Moorman, Mary, *William Wordsworth: The Early Years, 1770–1803*, Oxford: John Hopkins University Press, 1957

— *William Wordsworth: The Later Years, 1803–1850*, Oxford: John Hopkins University Press, 1966

Morrison, Robert, 'Blackwood's Berserker: John Wilson and the Language of Extremity', *Romanticism on the Net* 20 (2000)

— 'Poe's De Quincey, Poe's Dupin', *Essays in Criticism*, 51 (2001)

— 'De Quincey on "Mount Pleasant": William Roscoe and *Confessions of an English Opium-Eater*', *Notes and Queries* 52 (2005)

— (ed.), *On Murder*, Oxford: Oxford World's Classics, 2006

— *The English Opium-Eater: A Biography of Thomas De Quincey*, London: Weidenfeld and Nicolson, 2009

Morrison, Robert, and Daniel Sanjiv Roberts, *Thomas De Quincey: New Theoretical and Critical Directions*, London: Routledge, 2008

Nairn, Ian, *Nairn's London*, Harmondsworth: Penguin, 2014

North, Julian, *De Quincey Reviewed: Thomas De Quincey's Critical Reception, 1821–1994*, London: Camden House, 1997

O'Leary, Patrick, *Regency Editor: Life of John Scott*, Aberdeen: Aberdeen University Press, 1983

Paget, John, 'The Philosophy of Murder', *Tait's Edinburgh Magazine*, 22 (1851)

Paine, Thomas, *Rights of Man*, edited by E. Foner, Harmondsworth: Penguin, 1969

Percival, Thomas, *A Father's Instructions: Consisting of Moral Tales, Fables, and Reflections*, Robert Dodsley, 1775

Perry, Curtis, 'Piranesi's Prison: Thomas De Quincey and the Failure of Autobiography', *Studies in English Literature*, 33 (1993)

Place, Francis, *The Autobiography of Francis Place*, edited and with an introduction by Mary Thale, Cambridge: Cambridge University Press, 1972

— 'In the Footsteps of Aladdin: De Quincey's Arabian Nights', *The Wordsworth Circle*, 29 (1998)

Plotz, Judith, 'On Guilt Considered as One of the Fine Arts: De Quincey's Criminal Imagination', *The Wordsworth Circle*, 19 (1988)

Plumtree, A. S., 'The Artist as Murderer: De Quincey's Essay "On Murder Considered as One of the Fine Arts"', *Thomas De Quincey: Bicentenary Studies*, edited by Robert Lance Snyder, Norman: University of Oklahoma Press, 1985

Poe, Edgar Allan, *The Collected Works*, edited by T. O. Mabbott, 3 vols, Cambridge: Harvard University Press, 1968–78

Quincey, Thomas, *A Short Tour in the Midland Counties of England*, London, 1775

Rae-Brown, Colin, 'A Reminiscence of De Quincey', *Universal Review*, 5 (1889)

Rawnsley, Hardwicke Drummond, *Reminiscences of Wordsworth among the Peasantry of Westmoreland*, London: Dillon's University Bookshop, 1968

Roberts, Daniel Sanjiv, 'De Quincey's Discovery of *Lyrical Ballads*: The Politics of Reading', in *Studies in Romanticism*, 36 (Winter 1997)

— *Revisionary Gleam: De Quincey, Coleridge, and the High Romantic Argument*, Liverpool: Liverpool University Press, 2000

Roscoe, Henry, *The Life of William Roscoe*, London: Cadell and Blackwood, 1833

Russett, Margaret, *De Quincey's Romanticism: Canonical Minority and the Forms of Transmission*, Cambridge: Cambridge University Press, 1997

Sackville-West, Edward, *A Flame in Sunlight: The Life and Works of Thomas De Quincey*, London: Cassell, 1936

Sadler, Thomas (ed.), *Diary, Reminiscence and Correspondence of Henry Crabb Robinson,* London: Macmillan, 1869

Sedgwick, Eve Kosofsky, 'Language as Live Burial: Thomas De Quincey', *The Coherence of Gothic Conventions*, New York: Methuen, 1986

Selincourt, Ernest de (ed.), *The Letters of Dorothy and William Wordsworth: The Middle Years, part 1, 1806–1811, part 2, 1812–1820*, revised by Mary Moorman and Alan G Hill, Oxford: Clarendon Press, 1967

— (ed.), *The Letters of Dorothy and William Wordsworth: The Later Years, part 1, 1825–1828*, revised by Alan G. Hill, Oxford: Clarendon Press, 1978

Sisman, Adam, *The Friendship: Wordsworth and Coleridge*, HarperCollins, 2006

Smith, E., *An Estimate of William Wordsworth by his Contemporaries, 1793–1822*, Oxford: Blackwell, 1932

Snyder, Robert Lance (ed.), *Thomas De Quincey: Bicentenary Studies*, Norman: University of Oklahoma Press, 1985

Speck, W. A., *Robert Southey: Entire Man of Letters*, London: Yale University Press, 2006

Stephen, Leslie, *Hours in a Library*, 3 vols, London: Smith, Elder & Co., 1892

Sullivan, Margo Ann, *Murder and Art: Thomas De Quincey and the Ratcliffe Highway Murders*, New York: Garland, 1987

Syers, Robert, *History of Everton: Including Familiar Dissertations on the People, and Descriptive Delineations of the Several & Separate Properties of the Township*, Liverpool, J. and G. Robinson, 1830

Symonds, Barry (ed.), 'De Quincey and his Publishers: The Letters of Thomas De Quincey to His Publishers, and other Letters, 1819–32', PhD thesis, University of Edinburgh, 1994

Tomalin, Claire, *Jane Austen: A Life*, Harmondsworth: Penguin, 1997

Uglow, Jenny, *In These Times: Living in Britain Through Napoleon's Wars, 1793–1815*, London, Faber, 2015

Walpole, Horace, *The Castle of Otranto*, edited by W. S. Lewis, Oxford: World's Classics, 1982

Warton, Thomas, *The History of English Poetry: From the Close of the Eleventh to the Commencement of the Eighteenth Century*, London: J. Dodsley, 1824

Whale, John, *Thomas De Quincey's Reluctant Autobiography*, London: Croom Helm, 1984

— 'In a Stranger's Ear: De Quincey's Polite Magazine Context', in *Thomas De Quincey: Bicentenary Studies*, edited by Robert Lance Snyder, Norman: University of Oklahoma Press, 1985

White, Jerry, *A Great and Monstrous Thing: London in the Eighteenth Century*, London: Bodley Head, 2011

Willcox, Charles Bonnycastle, *The Poetical Works of Thomas Chatterton, with Notices on his Life, History of the Rowley Controversy and Notes Illustrative of the Poems*, Cambridge: W. P. Grant, 1842

Wilson, David Alec, *Carlyle till Marriage: 1785–1826*, London: Kegan Paul, 1923

Wilson, Frances, *The Ballad of Dorothy Wordsworth*, London: Faber, 2008

Wilson, John, 'Extracts from Gosschen's Diary', *Blackwood's Edinburgh Magazine*, vol. 1, no XVII (August 1818)

Wordsworth, Dorothy, *Journals*, edited by Mary Moorman, Oxford: Oxford University Press, 1997

Wordsworth, Jonathan, 'Two Dark Interpreters: Wordsworth and De Quincey', *The Wordsworth Circle*, 17 (1986)

Wordsworth, William, *The Poetical Works of William Wordsworth*, edited by Ernest de Selincourt and Helen Darbishire, 5 vols, Oxford: Oxford University Press, 1940–9

— *The Prelude 1799, 1805, 1850*, edited by Jonathan Wordsworth, M. H. Abrams and Stephen Gill, New York: W. W. Norton, 1979

— *Poems, in Two Volumes, and Other Poems*, edited by Jared Curtis, Ithaca: Cornell University Press, 1983
— *Lyrical Ballads*, edited by R. L. Brett and A. R. Jones, London and New York: Routledge, 2005
Wu, Duncan, *William Hazlitt: The First Modern Man*, Oxford: Oxford University Press, 2008

Newspapers and contemporary magazines

Blackwood's Edinburgh Magazine
The Courier
Edinburgh Review
Hogg's Edinburgh Magazine
London Magazine
Morning Chronicle
Tait's Edinburgh Magazine
The Times
The Westmorland Gazette

Acknowledgements

In true De Quinceyian spirit, I am indebted to those who came before me. Without the scholarship of Grevel Lindop, readers of Thomas De Quincey would still be snowed-in beneath mountains of disordered material. The fine biographies by Grevel Lindop and Robert Morrison, *The Opium-Eater* and *The English Opium Eater*, were my constant guides, as was John Barrell's rich and provocative study, *The Infection of Thomas De Quincey*.

For reading and correcting the manuscript I am grateful to Paul Keegan and A. N. Wilson. Thanks are also due to the staff of the Rare Books Room of the British Library, William St Clair, Ada Wordsworth, my agent, Sarah Chalfant, my editor, Michael Fishwick, my copyeditor, Kate Johnson, and to the irreplaceable Anna Simpson.

Index

and move to Bath, 33, 35–6, 43–4,
59, 66
and move to Chester, 72–4
returns to Bristol, 120, 134
and Richard's return from sea, 169, 333
visits Grasmere, 184–5, 188
Quincey, Elizabeth (sister), 13–22, 24–5,
30–2, 36, 53, 86, 145, 174, 207, 221,
316, 337
Quincey, Henry, 21, 122, 214,
254
Quincey, Jane (died in infancy), 21, 43,
53, 207, 316
Quincey, Jane, 21–2, 122, 148, 162, 167,
174, 254, 321
visits Grasmere, 184–5, 188
Quincey, Mary, 21, 42, 45, 77, 80, 122,
129, 191, 254
visits Grasmere, 184–5, 188
Quincey, Richard ('Pink'), 21, 28, 120,
122, 128–9, 254, 333
returns from sea, 168–71, 333
Quincey, Thomas, 13, 22–4
his book collection, 23–4
death, 24, 43, 53
publishes *A Short Tour in the Midland
Counties of England*, 24
Quincey, William, 21, 33, 74, 85, 93,
135, 159–60, 219, 300, 314, 333
De Quincey's relationship with, 25–8,
43–4
death, 43–4, 50

Racedown, 143
Radcliffe, Ann, 35, 37, 119, 144, 304
Ratcliffe Highway murders, 1–6, 8–10,
191–9, 245–7, 262, 264, 273, 282,
301–2, 337
and murder panic, 6, 196–7, 331
pamphlets on, 200–3, 332
re-imagined in De Quincey's
'Postscript', 328–34
Reform Act, 278
Reynolds, Joshua, 87
Richardson, Captain George, 201
Richter, Jean Paul, 17, 101, 251
Richter, John Frederick, 198

roads, improvement of, 60
Robert of Gloucester, 60
Robinson, Henry Crabb, 5, 152, 200,
214, 218, 231, 237, 267
and Catherine Wordsworth's
death, 205–6
Robinson, Thomas, 74
Romantic movement, beginnings of, 31
Roscoe, William, 71–2, 98, 287
Rosse, Lord, 315
Rousseau, Jean-Jacques, 98, 232
Roxburgh Castle mutiny, 202, 333
Royal College of Surgeons, 250
Royal Institution, 151, 154, 284
Ruscombe, Mrs, 262
Rydal Mount, 213, 215–18, 221, 268,
289
Rydal Water, 141, 145, 213

St George in the East, 2, 6, 199
St Paul, 16, 19
St Paul's Cathedral, 61–2, 75, 81, 83, 85,
179, 203, 221, 311, 336
St Peter, 43
St Thomas Aquinas, 214
Salamanca, Battle of, 191
Samuel, Richard, 40
Saragossa, Battle of, 163
Sartre, Jean-Paul, 341
Savage, Richard, 45, 89–90, 93, 264
Savary, Jean Baptiste, 266
scaffold speeches, 250
Schelling, Friedrich Wilhelm, 214, 312
Schiller, Friedrich, 304
Scotsman, The, 315
Scott, John, 228–30, 233, 236
Scott, Sir Walter, 47, 115, 214, 226, 275,
304
Scott, William Bell, 278
Scottish Enlightenment, 257
Shakespeare, William, 62, 70, 73, 99, 106,
152, 184, 214, 282, 284, 313, 321
Hamlet, 10, 131, 199
Henry IV, Part I, 108
King Lear, 245
Macbeth, 6, 129, 245–7
A Midsummer Night's Dream, 16, 189, 194

INDEX

394

Othello, 129, 199, 250
Romeo and Juliet, 4–5, 194
Shelley, Fanny, 197
Shelley, Mary, 218
Shelley, Percy Bysshe, 51, 197,
    218, 230
Shepherd, William, 71, 98, 287
Sheridan, Elizabeth Linley, 40
Sheridan, Richard Brinsley, 199, 201
Siddons, Mrs, 41
Simpson, John, 213, 268
Simpson, Margaret, *see* De Quincey,
    Margaret
Sinclair, Iain, 342
Slane Castle, 63
slavery, 20, 23, 45
Smith, Adam, 257
Smith, Madeline, 336
Smith, Sydney, 104
Smollett, Tobias, 35, 37
Socrates, 257
Soho, 87–9, 93, 168, 200
Somerset, Duchess of, 75
Sotheby, William, 104
Southey, Robert, 51, 59, 72, 99, 157, 183,
    197, 234, 257, 275, 283, 297, 331
  and Coleridge's marriage, 116–17, 137
  De Quincey meets, 146–7
  and De Quincey's diminutive
      stature, 10
  De Quincey's early enthusiasm
      for, 105–10
  and De Quincey's essays on
      Coleridge, 285–6
  and De Quincey's gossip, 236
  The Fall of Robespierre, 106
  'Ode to Horror', 107–8
  Thalaba the Destroyer, 103–4, 106
Spenser, Edmund, 67, 99
spiders, 22
Spinoza, Baruch, 262
Star, 59
Stark, Miss, 289
Steele (murder victim), 92
Stephen, Leslie, 8, 341
Stevenson, Robert Louis, 250, 258
Stewart, Dugald, 257

Stillwell, Kitty, 194–6, 334
Strachey, Lytton, 342
Strawberry Hill, 41
Stuart, Daniel, 151, 166
sublime, the, 31, 39–40, 53, 63, 105–6,
    263
  London and, 60–2
Suetonius, 283
Swift, Jonathan, 65
Sym, Robert, 227

Tait, William, 278, 285, 287–8, 292, 324
Tait's Edinburgh Magazine, 8, 134–5,
    278–80, 286, 312–13, 324, 326
  and 'Lake Reminiscences', 293–8, 301,
      303
Tasso, 145
Taylor, John, 228–30, 236–7, 243, 254
Tennyson, Alfred, 307
Tennyson, Cecilia, 307
Thackeray, William, 250, 275
thaumatology, 26
theatres, Hannah More and, 40–2
Theroux, Paul, 342
Thomson, James, 99
Thrale, Hester, 40
Thurtell, John, 247–51, 261–3, 302
Ticknor and Fields publishers, 325
Times, The, 192, 194, 197, 200
Tintern Abbey, 57, 72
Tobin, James, 53
Tosh, Mrs, 320
Trafalgar, Battle of, 191
Travels of Sir John Mandeville, The, 62
Turner, John, 194–6, 198, 200, 331–2, 334
Tyrwhitt, Thomas, 49–50

Ullswater, 146, 156
United States Literary Gazette, 231

vagrants, 101–2
Vallon, Annette, 297
Vertue, George, 10
Victoria, Queen, 143
Vittoria, Battle of, 191

Wainewright, Thomas Griffiths, 231, 237,
    264, 341

ALSO AVAILABLE BY FRANCES WILSON

HOW TO SURVIVE THE TITANIC
OR
THE SINKING OF J. BRUCE ISMAY

'A gripping study – part reportage, part biography, part literary criticism – of the more intimate ramifications of a disaster which still haunts the public imagination'
Sunday Telegraph

When the *Titanic* hit the iceberg on 14 April 1912 and a thousand men prepared to die, J. Bruce Ismay jumped into a lifeboat and was rowed away to safety. Had he been an ordinary passenger, little would have been said, but J. Bruce Ismay was the chairman of the White Star Line, the company that had built the *Titanic*. Accused of cowardice and dictating the ship's excessive speed, Ismay became, as one newspaper called him, 'The Most Talked-of Man in the World'. Using never-before-seen letters written by Ismay, Frances Wilson explores his desperate need to tell his story, to make sense of the horror of it all, and to find a way of living with the consciousness of lost honour.

'Beautifully written'
Sunday Times

'Wonderfully rich and multi-layered . . . full of fascinating details . . . a finely written biography of a disgraced human being'
Mail on Sunday

An unusual and creative book . . . in the end, the subject of this fascinating book is not just historical or biographical uncertainty, but psychological and moral ambiguity'
Sarah Churchwell, *Guardian*

ORDER YOUR COPY:
BY PHONE: +44 (0) 1256 302 699
BY EMAIL: DIRECT@MACMILLAN.CO.UK
DELIVERY IS USUALLY 3–5 WORKING DAYS.
FREE POSTAGE AND PACKAGING FOR ORDERS OVER £20.
ONLINE: WWW.BLOOMSBURY.COM/BOOKSHOP
PRICES AND AVAILABILITY SUBJECT TO CHANGE WITHOUT NOTICE.
HTTP://WWW.BLOOMSBURY.COM/AUTHOR/FRANCES-WILSON/

BLOOMSBURY